9.00

POPULATION,
ENVIRONMENT,
AND THE
QUALITY OF LIFE

First edition published 1975
by AMS Press, New York
First paperback edition published 1975
by Halsted Press
a Division of John Wiley & Sons, Inc.,
New York

Library of Congress Cataloguing in Publication Data

Marden, Parker G   comp.
  Population, environment, and the quality of life.

    1. United States—Population—Addresses, essays, lectures. 2. Environmental
policy—United States—Addresses, essays, lectures. I. Hodgson, Dennis, joint comp.
II. Title.
HB3505.M37   301.32'9'73   74-579
ISBN 0-404-10536-X
ISBN: 0-470-56868-2 (pbk)

Manufactured in the United States of America.

POPULATION, ENVIRONMENT, AND THE QUALITY OF LIFE

edited,
with an introduction,
by

Parker G. Marden
and
Dennis Hodgson

A Halsted Press Book

JOHN WILEY & SONS, INC.
New York—Sydney—Toronto

TABLE
OF
CONTENTS

ACKNOWLEDGEMENTS

Acknowledgement is made to the authors and publishers below who have granted permission to reprint material and who reserve all rights in the articles appearing in this anthology.

Coale, "Man and His Environment," *Science*, October 9, 1970, Vol. 170, pp. 132-136. Copyright © 1970 by the American Association for the Advancement of Science.

Commission on Population Growth and the American Future, *Population and the American Future*, Government Printing Office, pp. 42-53, 75-78, and 110-113.

Commoner, "Response," *Bulletin of the Atomic Scientists*, May, 1972, pp. 17-56. Copyright © 1972 by the Educational Foundation for Nuclear Science.

Commoner, Corr, and Stamler, "The Causes of Pollution," copyright © 1971 by the Committee for Environmental Information, Inc. Originally published in *Environment*, April, 1971, Vol. 13, pp. 2-19.

Crowe, "The Tragedy of the Commons Revisited," *Science*, November 28, 1969, Vol. 166, pp. 1103-1107. Copyright © 1969 by the American Association for the Advancement of Science.

Davis, "Overpopulated America," copyright © 1970 by Wayne Davis. Originally published in *The New Republic*, January 10, 1970, pp. 13-15.

Downs, "Up and down with Ecology," *The Public Interest*, No. 28, Summer, 1972, copyright © National Affairs, Inc., 1972.

Ehrlich, "Eco-Catastrophe!" Ramparts, September, 1969, pp. 24-28.

Ehrlich and Holdren, "Critique," Bulletin of the Atomic Scientists, Volume XXVIII,

May, 1972, pp. 16, 18-27. Copyright © 1972 by the Educational Foundation for Nuclear Science.

Ehrlich and Holdren, "Impact of Population Growth," copyright © by the authors 1971 and reprinted by permission of the authors and the editors of *Science* in which it was originally published in the issue of March 26, 1971, Vol. 171, pp. 1212-1217.

Fisher, "Population and Environmental Quality," *Public Policy*, Winter, 1971, Vol. XIX, pp. 19-35.

Hardin, "Population Skeletons in the Environmental Closet," *Bulletin of the Atomic Scientists*, June, 1972, pp. 37-41. Copyright © 1972 by the Educational Foundation for Nuclear Science.

Hardin, "The Tragedy of the Commons," *Science*, December 13, 1968 by the American Association for the Advancement of Science.

Hawley, "Ecology and Population," *Science*, March 23, 1973, Vol. 179, pp. 1196-1201. Copyright © 1973 by the American Association for the Advancement of Science.

Heller, "Coming to Terms with Growth and the Environment," from *Energy, Economic growth and the Environment*, edited by Sam H. Schurr, John Hopkins Press, 1972, pp. 3-29.

Holdren and Ehrlich, "One Dimensional Ecology Revisited," *Bulletin of the Atomic Scientists*, June, 1972, pp. 42-45. Copyright © 1972 by the Educational Foundation for Nuclear Science.

Marx, "American Institutions and Ecological Ideals," *Science*, November 27, 1970, Vol. 170, pp. 945-952. Copyright © 1970 by the American Association for the Advancement of Science.

Nash, "Going Beyond John Locke?" *Milbank Memorial Fund Quarterly*, January, 1971, Vol. XLIX, pp. 7-31.

Ridker, "Resource and Environmental Consequences of Population Growth in the United States," from *Population, Resources, and the Environment*, edited by Ronald G. Ridker, Government Printing Office, 1972, pp. 17-34.

Smith, "Ecological Perspectives," from *Population, Resources and the Environment*, edited by Ronald G. Ridker, Government Printing Office, 1972, pp. 287-300.

Sweezy, "Population, GNP, and the Environment," from *Are Our Descendants Doomed?* edited by Harrison Brown and Edward Hutchings, The Viking Press, 1972, pp. 100-113.

Wattenberg, "The Nonsense Explosion," copyright © 1970 by Ben Wattenberg and reprinted by permission of The Harold Matson Company, Inc. Originally published in *The New Republic*, April 4, 1970.

Williamson, "Population Pollution," *BioScience*, Volume 19, November, 1969, pp. 979-983.

INTRODUCTION

In this collection of readings, we are seeking to explore the possible relationships that exist between population growth and environmental problems in the United States. What contribution has population increase, especially large over the past two decades, made to the deteriorating condition of the environment? What will the future bring for the quality of life as these two variables continue on what many see to be a collision course? Surely, these questions affect all Americans.

In books on current problems, editors usually identify their conerns as "ideas whose time has come." But we may be dealing with an idea whose time has come — and gone. Even as we assembled the readings for this book, a series of rapid changes occurred in the way that the public, at least, assessed environmental problems. The energy crisis, for example, has been discussed more in terms of world politics, governmental machinations, and new life styles than as a consequence of population growth. In addition, the growing knowledge that American fertility has declined to an all-time low in recent years has meant that public interest has waned in population matters other than such personal issues as abortion and contraceptive aid for teenagers.

We are, however prepared to argue that in dealing with the relationship of population and environment, we are concerned with an idea which can be charted along an interesting course. It surfaced as an important problem only to subside under the press of other difficulties, but it will return as an important concern for most Americans in the near future. For reasons that will be considered below, the "rediscovery" of the issue will lead to a more sophisticated analysis of environmental difficulties and the contribution made by population growth. Through this collection of readings, we hope to enrich this analysis.

Let us explain. During the past several years, a number of important attempts have been made to assess either the demographic or environmental condition of the United States, other nations, or the world as "Spaceship Earth." In the United States, for example, the publication in 1972 of *The Limits to Growth* with its dire Malthusian predictions of the future created great controversy in the public and professional literature, including a book-length critique entitled *Prophets of Doom* which challenged its methodology and conclusions. These were only two of many efforts to assess environmental quality or the "carrying capacity" of the nation or the world. Armed with such works for guidance and distressed by littered landscapes and other kinds of pollution, many Americans were moved to become "ecological activists" during the late 1960's and early 1970's.

Population problems have also been discussed by activists who write about their concerns or who act upon them (as well as those who do both). For a brief time, organizations like ZPG (Zero Population Growth, Inc.) were able to mobilize the support of large numbers of Americans alarmed about rapid population growth. Their activities were paralleled by a literature on the consequences of this growth, ranging from shrill prophecies of doom to careful, scholarly assessments exemplified by the National Academy of Sciences' book, *Rapid Population Growth*. Such efforts were capped in 1972 by the publication of *Population and the American Future*, the report of the national Commission on Population Growth and the American Future. Summarizing the work of many during two years, the report assessed the current state and future prospects of population dynamics in the United States and their implications for the quality of life.

There were similar efforts in other nations. In Great Britain, for example, the scientific and academic communities have debated the propositions advanced in *Blueprint for Survival*, published in 1972 in the *Ecologist* and later in book form. Great Britain, too, has a national commission developing recommendations for guiding its future population growth. Similarily, the United Nations conducted a major Conference on the Human Environment in Stockholm in 1972 and has declared 1974 to be the "World Population Year" which will be culminated by a meeting in Bucharest.

Although various opinions have been offered on the impact of population growth on the environment, they have often added more heat than light to the discussion. Even in the major works identified above, the relationship of population and environment has usually been oversimplified. Most writing on the relationship has been done by those with greater professional interest in the environment than in population. Further, the public is quick to become concerned about environmental indignities and can easily accept the simple portrayal of population growth as a villain. Matters of technology and social organization which also influence the relationship are much more difficult to understand. Consequently, those who have sought to sound an ecological alarm have carefully detailed the environmental dimensions of the crisis and provided little specification of its demographic dimensions.

The reason for this imbalance of information on population, however, rests less with those who have articulated their concern with the environment and more with those who have remained silent. Demographers are generally cautious people. Extensive experience with population projections that have proven to be inaccurate as people suddenly changed their patterns of movement or childbearing provides them with good reason for restraint.

In this collection of readings, we attempt to provide a balance of information by exploring the relationship between population growth and the environment while emphasizing its demographic dimensions. We hope to provide assistance to second-generation students of environmental problems which can be approached again with greater understanding. For many, the need for balanced exploration of population and environment is not yet apparent. Current events have temporarily deflected interest from both environmental and demographic problems. With respect to environmental matters, for example, the situation is ironic. In a nation beset by an energy crisis and occasional shortages of food and other commodities, such problems have been considered less as environmental matters than as political concerns. The shortage of oil is seen as the result of international politics, especially concerning the Middle East, and not as a problem of increasing demand outstripping supply, refining capacity, and new technological developments. Similarly, the problems of food supply and soaring prices are seen more as vague consequences of governmental policy, especially mysterious wheat deals with the Soviet Union and domestic price manipulations, and less as the result of a rising demand of the populations of other nations for agricultural commodities. Adding to such problems of perception is the general crisis of confidence that now exists between Americans and their government. Is there a food shortage? How serious is the energy crisis? There is uncertainty about the questions as well as the answers.

Yet the problems are real. There is every indication that Americans will be forced to make significant adjustments in their life style because of shortages in energy and other previously abundant commodities. These shortages will remain even if the Arabs relax their decision on supplying oil to nations friendly to Israel. Shortages will continue even if the agricultural situation is stabilized, and they promise to be with us for a long time.

Simultaneously, there has been what seems to be good news from the population front. The birth rate in the United States has declined to levels that are now below replacement. At present, American women are having fewer children than are required to replace the existing population. This decline has comforted many who have turned their attention to other concerns, but the matter of declining birth rates requires a closer second look for several reasons.

Although fertility may have declined, we are not near the condition of zero population growth, as many people have thought. Population growth has developed a momentum which is very difficult to stop. But past growth has given us so many young couples who are about to have children that even if each couple averages only two children, our population will continue to grow for seventy years. In order to reach zero growth immediately, today's parents would need to have on the average a single child. Such a reproduction rate is highly unlikely.

Birth rates can change very rapidly as the declines of the past several years have shown, but it is just as possible for fertility to increase quickly. In fact, one element in the decline has been the rise in the average age of childbearing. Consequently, in any given year, some proportion of births is postponed to a later time. But, as the Commission on Population Growth and the American Future noted, the effect of this postponement is temporary since the age of childbearing will not rise indefinitely and the birth rate will rise again when it stabilizes. In addition, the other major component of the decline in fertility is also capable of alteration. Today's young people expect to have fewer children than those of several years ago. However, attitudes and aspirations can change and if they do, there are such large numbers of persons in the childbearing years that even small increases in fertility would produce large numbers of children — an echo of the "Baby Boom" during which their parents were born.

Those who currently take comfort in the decline in fertility are deluding themselves. Population continues to grow and there is a definite potential for even greater growth. Certainly, demographic pressure on the environment has not eased and, while one may debate the contribution that population increases makes to environmental distress, the situation will not be relieved by a stabilized population for nearly seventy years, if that soon.

It is inevitable that concern for the environment and population growth will again surface as matters of public attention. This collection of readings can provide those who take a second look at these issues with an opportunity for serious reflection. This new examination can however proceed with a difference, since the events of recent months offer new insights. The identification of political and technological forces conditioning environmental concerns, a growing realization that life styles may need to be altered under different calculations of supply and demand for basic commodities, and increased knowledge of the complexity of population processes can add to our understanding of the relationship between population and the environment. Some of these additional concerns are anticipated in the readings that are assembled here.

The collection begins with a sampler of readings on the population crisis which reflect the confusion that exists over the role of population growth. Although some articles demonstrate how easy it is to point to population growth as a culprit in environmental deterioration, one article even advances the "heretical" view that there is *no* population crisis. The tone of the arguments in the articles, when taken together is very general and often alarmist rather than carefully reasoned. The selections are characteristic of most writings on the topic for popular audiences.

The next section moves our survey to the specific point that the popular articles fail to confront: *how* does population growth contribute to environmental difficulties? This section is organized around a controversy between two viewpoints. One view, offered by Paul Ehrlich and John Holdren, advances the idea that population growth is indeed a major problem for the environment. The other, presented by Barry Commoner and his colleagues, argues that other variables, principally technology, are much more important problems. A direct confrontation occurs between the two perspectives in Ehrlich and Holdren's review of Commoner's book, *The Closing Circle;* in Commoner's response to their criticisms; and finally, in their reply. By considering the two perspectives together, readers can make their own judgments. There should however be no question remaining as to the complexity of the issues and the potential for continued disagreement.

The following three sections provide additional information on these perspectives, including three chapters from the report of the Commission on Population Growth and the American Future. Together, the selections elaborate upon the issues raised in the Commoner-Ehrlich debate.

The concluding section is comprised of four selections that call attention to the context of larger issues within which the population and environment dialogue is embedded. The section opens with another confrontation between Garrett Hardin and Beryl Crowe. Using the analogy of the commons, Hardin argues that the population problem has no technical solution, but requires a fundamental extension in morality instead. Crowe takes issue with Hardin's contention, and in their exchange, problems of organizational forms and basic values are specified. Amos Hawley extends the discussion in a selection that places man in an ecosystem that is more complex than a simple relationship between population and environment — a relationship that has characterized so much of the discussion in this book. Together with a contribution by Keir Nash, Hawley's presentation is a fitting conclusion to this volume, because it organizes various other arguments in a systematic way. Population and environment are but two variables in a larger set of variables that include technology, organization, and human values. Other selections in the collection have raised similar points; some directly, some intuitively, some tentatively. Hawley's article possesses the virtue of a general summary.

We would like to think of this collection of readings as an interesting guide to an important topic. It is not a comprehensive collection, because the literature on population growth and environmental questions is extensive. We hope to assist the reader in moving from one point of discussion to another while guided by specific, but selective details. An introductory balanced guide to the issues of population and the environment, conditioned as they are by other factors, is needed, for both hold important consequences for the American future.

THE
POPULATION CRISIS:
A SAMPLER

INTRODUCTION

In examining the role that population growth plays in the environmental crisis confronting contemporary Americans, an appropriate starting point can be found in the popular literature on the subject. Although articles aimed at non-professional audiences are too frequently more dramatic than reasoned, they are often the only source of information for most persons. The four articles presented here are but a few of the many hundreds that have been published since the volume and pace of population change became matters of grave public concern. Together they do offer reasonable coverage of what we might call a "genre" of selections on population issues.

The first selection, a now-classic article written in 1969 for *Ramparts* by Paul Ehrlich, is representative of many dramatic, indeed frightening statements on the consequences of rapid population growth for the environment. Ehrlich presents a scenerio of life at the end of this decade which will occur if the present rate of population growth continues. It is a grim picture which is perhaps even more spectacular in its re-reading in a nation which, four or five years closer to Ehrlich target date, now faces a serious energy crisis and shortage of many basic items. His predictions may be longer on imagination than accurate prognosis, but current events underscore a basic point that cannot be ignored: population growth, environmental difficulties, political concern, and economic problems are all closely interrelated in a complex way. Changes in any one of these varibles can produce a chain reaction of effects in each of the others.

The selection by Wayne Davis, "Overpopulated America," echoes many of Ehrlich's concerns, but adds specification to a bill of particulars offered against the continuation of population increase in the United States. For those Americans who feel that explosive population growth is a problem of developing nations alone, Davis presents an analysis in terms of "Indian equivalents." Estimating that it takes thirty five Indians to equal the environmental impact of one American, he details a variety of ways in which the United States is overpopulated and the high costs that its citizens represent in terms of destruction of the land, pollution of the atmosphere, and consumption of valued resources.

Quite a different argument is presented by Ben Wattenberg. To him, many of the arguments advanced to show that rapid population growth is a major problem in America are political smokescreens which conceal more important concerns. He provides evidence to show that America need not be viewed as overpopulated and questions the premise that population growth is harmful. Indeed, he argues that *more* people can solve environmental problems more easily than fewer people. Even affluence is less of a problem for Wattenberg than for Ehrlich and Davis as he argues that the wealthy contribute less to population growth than do the poor.

In the final selection, Francis Williamson joins Ehrlich and Davis in predicting the dire consequences that population growth holds for both the environment and such conditions of life as individual freedom and opportunity. With increased numbers, there is a lessened ability to choose among alternatives — a condition of the "good life." He introduces a new dimension into the discussion by considering not only the growing size of the American population, but its increasing concentration in large urban centers. With urban life, Williamson argues, Americans must accept a number of undesirable by-products, including many special environmental hazards that can be life-threatening.

Which arguments are correct? Clearly, it is difficult to reconcile the differences between Wattenberg's optimistic perspective on the consequences of population growth and the gloomy predictions of the other three authors. Further, it is hard to assess either the evidence or the reasoning offered in the various selections. To most of the general public, the arguments seem frightening *and* reasonable — two conditions which reinforce each other. Is it however appropriate to accept them without question? Perhaps the public is misled with oversimplifications and dramatic statements that often characterize popular assessments of difficult problems. Surely the importance of a healthy environment to human life requires that this question be resolved. It is to this task that we now turn.

ECO-CATASTROPHE!

Paul Ehrlich

The end of the ocean came late in the summer of 1979, and it came even more rapidly than the biologists had expected. There had been signs for more than a decade, commencing with the discovery in 1968 that DDT slows down photosynthesis in marine plant life. It was announced in a short paper in the technical journal, Science, but to ecologists it smacked of doomsday. They knew that all life in the sea depends on photosynthesis, the chemical process by which green plants bind the sun's energy and make it available to living things. And they knew that DDT and similar chlorinated hydrocarbons had polluted the entire surface of the earth, including the sea.

But that was only the first of many signs. There had been the final gasp of the whaling industry in 1973, and the end of the Peruvian anchovy fishery in 1975. Indeed, a score of other fisheries had disappeared quietly from over-exploitation and various eco-catastrophes by 1977. The term "eco-castrophe" was coined by a California ecologist in 1969 to describe the most spectacular of man's attacks on the systems which sustain his life. He drew his inspiration from the Santa Barbara offshore oil disaster of that year, and from the news which spread among naturalists that virtually all of the Golden State's seashore bird life was doomed because of chlorinated hydrocarbon interference with its reproduction. Eco-catastrophes in the sea became increasingly common in the early 1970's. Mysterious "blooms" of previously rare micro-organisms began to appear in offshore waters. Red tides — killer outbreaks of a minute single-celled plant — returned to the Florida Gulf coast and were sometimes accompanied by tides of other exotic hues.

It was clear by 1975 that the entire ecology of the ocean was changing. A few types of phytoplankton were becoming resistant to chlorinated hydrocarbons and were gaining the upper hand. Changes in the phytoplankton community led inevitably to changes in the community of zooplankton, the tiny animals which eat the phytoplankton. These changes were passed on up the chains of life in the ocean to the herring, plaice, cod and tuna. As the diversity of life in the ocean diminished, its stability also decreased.

Other changes had taken place by 1975. Most ocean fishes that returned to fresh water to breed, like the salmon, had become extinct, their breeding streams so dammed up and polluted that their powerful homing instinct only resulted in suicide. Many fishes and shellfishes that bred in restricted areas along the coasts followed them as onshore pollution escalated.

By 1977 the annual yield of fish from the sea was down to 30 million metric tons, less than one-half the per capita catch of a decade earlier. This helped malnutrition to escalate sharply in a world where an estimated 50 million people per year were already dying of starvation. The United Nations attempted to get all chlorinated hydrocarbon insecticides banned on a worldwide basis, but the move was defeated by the United States. The opposition was generated primarily by the American petrochemical industry, operating hand in glove with its subsidiary, the United States Department of Agriculture. Together they persuaded the government to oppose the U.N. move — which was not difficult since most Americans believed that Russia and China were more in need of fish products than was the United States. The United Nations also attempted to get fishing nations to adopt strict and enforced catch limits to preserve dwindling stocks. This move was blocked by Russia, who, with the most modern electronic equipment, was in the best position to glean what was left in the sea. It was, curiously, on the very day in 1977 when the Soviet Union announced its refusal that another ominous article appeared in Science. It announced that incident solar radiation had been so reduced by worldwide air pollution that serious effects on the world's vegetation could be expected.

Apparently it was a combination of ecosystem destabilization, sunlight reduction, and a rapid escalation in chlorinated hydrocarbon pollution from massive Thanodrin applications which triggered the ultimate catastrophe. Seventeen huge Soviet-financed Thanodrin plants were operating in underdeveloped countries by 1978. They had been part of a massive Russian "aid-offensive" designed to fill the gap caused by the collapse of America's ballyhooed "Green Revolution."

It became apparent in the early '70s that the "Green Revolution" was more talk than substance. Distribution of high yield "miracle" grain seeds had caused temporary local spurts in agricultural production. Simultaneously, excellent weather had produced record harvests. The combination permitted bureaucrats, expecially in the United States Department of Agriculture and the Agency for International Development (AID), to reverse their previous pessimism and indulge in an outburst of optimistic propaganda about staving off famine. They raved about the approaching transformation of agriculture in the underdeveloped countries (UDCs). The reason for the propaganda reversal was never made clear. Most historians agree that a combination of utter ignorance of ecology, a desire to justify past errors, and pressure from agro-industry (which was eager to sell pesticides, fertilizers, and farm machinery to the UDCs and agencies helping the UDCs) was behind the campaign. Whatever the motivation, the results were clear. Many concerned people, lacking the expertise to see through the Green Revolution drivel, relaxed. The population-food crisis was "solved".

But reality was not long in showing itself. Local famine persisted in Northern India even after good weather brought an end to the ghastly Bihar famine of the mid-'60s. East Pakistan was next, followed by a resurgence of general famine in northern India. Other foci of famine rapidly developed in Indonesia, the Philippines, Malawi, the Congo, Egypt, Colombia, Ecuador, Honduras, the Dominican Republic, and Mexico.

Everywhere hard realities destroyed the illusion of the Green Revolution. Yields dropped as the progressive farmers who had first accepted the new seeds found that their higher yields brought lower prices — effective demand (hunger plus cash) was not sufficient in poor countries to keep prices up. Less progressive farmers, observing this, refused to make the extra effort required to cultivate the "miracle" grains. Transport systems proved inadequate to bring the necessary fertilizer to the fields where the new and extremely fertilizer-sensitive grains were being grown. The same systems were also inadequate to move produce to markets. Fertilizer plants were not built fast enough, and most of the underdeveloped countries could not scrape together funds to purchase supplies, even on concessional terms. Finally, the inevitable happened, and pests began to reduce yields in even the most carefully cultivated fields. Among the first were the famous "miracle rats" which invaded Philippine "miracle rice" fields early in 1969. They were quickly followed by many insects and viruses, thriving on the relatively pest-susceptible new grains, encouraged by the vast and dense plantings, and rapidly acquiring resistance to the chemicals used against them. As chaos spread until even the most obtuse agriculturists and economists realized that the Green Revolution had turned brown, the Russians stepped in.

In retrospect it seems incredible that the Russians, with the American mistakes known to them, could launch an even more incompetent program of aid to the underdeveloped world. Indeed, in the early 1970's there were cynics in the United States who claimed that outdoing the stupidity of American foreign aid would be physically impossible. Those critics were, however, obviously unaware that the Russians had been busily destroying their own environment for many years. The virtual disappearance of sturgeon from Russian rivers caused a great shortage of caviar by 1970. A standard joke among Russian scientists at that time was that they had created an artificial caviar which was indistinguishable from the real thing — except by taste. At any rate the Soviet Union, observing with interest the progressive deterioration of relations between the UDCs and the United States, came up with a solution. It had recently developed what it claimed was the ideal insecticide, a highly lethal chlorinated hydrocarbon complexed with a special agent for penetrating the external skeletal armor of insects. Announcing that the new pesticide, called Thanodrin, would truly produce a Green Revolution, the Soviets entered into negotiations with various UDCs for the construction of massive Thanodrin factories. The USSR would bear all the costs; all it wanted in return were certain trade and military concessions.

It is interesting now, with the perspective of years, to examine in some detail the reasons why the UDCs welcomed the Thanodrin plan with such open arms. Government officials in these countries ignored the protests of their own scientists that Thanodrin would not solve the problems which plagued them. The governments now knew that the basic cause of their problems was overpopulation, and that these problems had been exacerbated by the dullness, daydreaming, and cupidity endemic to all governments. They knew that only population control and limited development aimed primarily at agriculture could have spared them the horrors they now faced. They knew it, but they were not about to admit it. How much easier it was simply to accuse the Americans of failing to give them proper aid; how much simpler to accept the Russian panacea.

And then there was the general worsening of relations between the United States and the UDCs. Many things had contributed to this. The situation in America in the first half of the 1970's deserves our close scrutiny. Being more dependent on imports for raw materials than the Soviet Union, the United States had, in the early 1970's adopted more and more heavy-handed policies in order to secure continuing supplies. Military adventures in Asia and Latin America had further lessened the international credibility of the United States as a great defender of freedom — an image which had begun to deteriorate rapidly during the pointless and fruitless Viet-Nam conflict. At home, acceptance of the carefully manufactured image lessened dramatically, as even the more romantic and chauvinistic citizens began to understand the role of the military and industrial system in what John Kenneth Galbraith had aptly named "The New Industrial State."

At home in the USA the early '70s were traumatic times. Racial violence grew and the habitability of the cities diminished, as nothing substantial was done to ameliorate either racial inequities or urban blight. Welfare rolls grew as automation and general technological progress forced more and more people into the category of "unemployable." Simultaneously a taxpayers' revolt occurred. Although there was not enough money to build the schools, roads, water systems, sewage systems, jails, hospitals, urban transit lines, and all the other amenities needed to support a burgeoning population, Americans refused to tax themselves more heavily. Starting in Youngstown, Ohio in 1969 and followed closely by Richmond, California, community after community was forced to close its schools or curtail educational operations for lack of funds. Water supplies, already marginal in quality and quantity in many places by 1970, deteriorated quickly. Water rationing occurred in 1723 municipalities in the summer of 1974, and hepatitis and epidemic dysentery rates climbed about 500 per cent between 1970-1974.

Air pollution continued to be the most obvious manifestation of environmental deterioration. It was, by 1972, quite literally in the eyes of all Americans. The year 1973 saw not only the New York and Los Angeles smog disasters, but also the publication of the Surgeon General's massive report on air pollution and health. The public had been partially prepared for the worst by the publicity given to the U.N. pollution conference held in 1972. Deaths in the late '60s caused by smog were well known to scientists, but the public had ignored them because they mostly involved the early demise of the old and sick rather than people dropping dead on the freeways. But suddenly our citizens were faced with nearly 200,000 corpses and massive documentation that they could be the next to die from respiratory disease. They were not ready for that scale of disaster. After all, the U.N. conference had not predicted that accumulated air pollution would make the planet uninhabitable until almost 1990. The population was terrorized as TV screens became filled with scenes of horror from the disaster areas. Especially vivid was NBC's coverage of hundreds of unattended people choking out their lives outside of New York's hospitals. Terms like nitrogen oxide, acute bronchitis and cardiac arrest began to have real meaning for most Americans.

The ultimate horror was the announcement that chlorinated hydrocarbons were now a major constituent of air pollution in all American cities. Autopsies of smog disaster victims revealed an average chlorinated hydrocarbon load in fatty tissue equivalent to 26 parts per million of DDT. In October, 1973, the Department of Health, Education and Welfare announced studies which showed unequivocally that increasing death rates from hypertension, cirrhosis of the liver, liver cancer and a series of other diseases had resulted from the chlorinated hydrocarbon load. They estimated that Americans born since 1946 (when DDT usage began) now had a life expectancy of only 49 years, and predicted that if current patterns continued, this expectancy would reach 42 years by 1980, when it might level out. Plunging insurance stocks triggered a stock market panic. The president of Velsicol, Inc. a major pesticide producer, went on television to "publicly eat a teaspoonful of DDT" (it was really powdered milk) and announce that HEW had been infiltrated by Communists. Other giants of the petro-chemical industry, attempting to dispute the indisputable evidence, launched a massive pressure campaign on Congress to force HEW to "get out of agriculture's business." They were aided by the agro-chemical journals, which had decades of experience in misleading the public about the benefits and dangers of pesticides. But by now the public realized that it had been duped. The Nobel Prize for medicine and physiology was given to Drs. J.L. Radomski and W.B. Deichmann, who in the late 1960's had pioneered in the documentation of the long-term lethal effects of chlorinated hydrocarbons. A Presidential Commission with unimpeachable credentials directly accused the agro-chemical complex of "condemning many millions of Americans to an early death." The year 1973 was the year in which Americans finally came to understand the direct threat to their existence posed by environmental deterioration.

And 1973 was also the year in which most people finally comprehended the indirect threat. Even the president of Union Oil Company and several other industrialists publicly stated their concern over the reduction of bird populations which had resulted from pollution by DDT and other chlorinated hydrocarbons. Insect populations boomed because they were resistant to most pesticides and had been freed, by the incompetent use of those pesticides, from most of their natural enemies. Rodents swarmed over crops, multiplying rapidly in the absence of predatory birds. The effect of pests on the wheat crop was especially disasterous in the summer of 1973, since that was also the year of the great drought. Most of us can remember the shock which greeted the announcement by atmospheric physicists that the shift of the jet stream which had caused the drought was probably permanent. It signalled the birth of the Midwestern desert. Man's air-polluting activities had by then caused gross changes in climatic patterns. The news, of course, played hell with commodity and stock markets. Food prices skyrocketed, as savings were poured into hoarded canned goods. Official assurances that food supplies would remain ample fell on deaf ears, and even the government showed signs of nervousness when California migrant field workers went out on strike again in protest against the continued use of pesticides by growers. The strike burgeoned into farm burning and riots. The workers, calling themselves "The Walking Dead," demanded immediate compensation for their shortened lives, and crash research programs to attempt to lengthen them.

It was in the same speech in which President Edward Kennedy, after much delay, finally declared a national emergency and called out the National Guard to harvest California's crops, that the first mention of population control was made. Kennedy pointed out that the United States would no longer be able to offer any food aid to other nations and was likely to suffer food shortages herself. He suggested that, in view of the manifest failure of the Green Revolution, the only hope of the UDCs lay in population control. His statement, you will recall, created an uproar in the underdeveloped countries. Newspaper editorials accused the United States of wishing to prevent small countries from becoming large nations and thus threatening American hegemony. Politicians asserted that President Kennedy was a "creature of the giant drug combine" that wished to shove its pills down every woman's throat.

Among Americans, religious opposition to population control was very slight. Industry in general also backed the idea. Increasing poverty in the UDCs was both destroying markets and threatening supplies of raw materials. The seriousness of the raw material situation had been brought home during the Congressional Hard Resources hearings in 1971. The exposure of the ignorance of the cornucopian economists had been quite a spectacle — a spectacle brought into virtually every American's home in living color. Few would forget the distinguished geologist from the University of California who suggested that economists be legally required to learn at least the most elementary facts of geology. Fewer still would forget that an equally distinguished Harvard economist added that they might be required to learn some economics, too. The overall message was clear: America's resource situation was bad and bound to get worse. The hearings had led to a bill requiring the Departments of State, Interior, and Commerce to set up a joint resource procurement council with the express purpose of "insuring that proper consideration of American resource needs be an integral part of American foreign policy."

Suddenly the United States discovered that it had a national consensus: population control was the only possible sálvation of the underdeveloped world. But that same consensus led to heated debate. How could the UDCs be persuaded to limit their populations, and should not the United States lead the way by limiting its own? Members of the intellectual community wanted America to set an example. They pointed out that the United States was in the midst of a new baby boom: her birth rate, well over 20 per thousand per year, and her growth rate of over one per cent per annum were among the very highest of the developed countries. They detailed the deterioration of the American physical and psychic environments, the growing health threats, the impending food shortages, and the insufficiency of funds for desperately needed public works. They contended that the nation was clearly unable or unwilling to properly care for the people it already had. What possible reason could there be, they queried, for adding any more? Besides, who would listen to requests by the United States for population control when that nation did not control her own profligate reproduction?

Those who opposed population controls for the U.S. were equally vociferous. The military-industrial complex, with its all-too-human mixture of ignorance and avarice, still saw strength and prosperity in numbers. Baby food magazines, already worried by the growing nitrate pollution of their products, saw their market disappearing. Steel manufacturers saw a decrease in aggregate demand and slippage for that holy of holies, the Gross National Product. And military men saw, in the growing population-food-environment crisis, a serious threat to their carefully nurtured Cold War. In the end, of course, economic arguments held sway, and the "inalienable right of every American couple to determine the size of its family," a freedom invented for the occasion in the early '70s, was not compromised.

The population control bill, which was passed by Congress early in 1974, was quite a document, nevertheless. On the domestic front, it authorized an increase from 100 to 150 million dollars in funds for "family planning" activities. This was made possible by a general feeling in the country that the growing army on welfare needed family planning. But the gist of the bill was a series of measures designed to impress the need for population control on the UDCs. All American aid to countries with overpopulation problems was required by law to consist in part of population control assistance. In order to receive any assistance each nation was required not only to accept the population control aid, but also to match it according to a complex formula. "Overpopulation" itself was defined by a formula based on U.N. statistics, and the UDCs were required not only to accept aid, but also to show progress in reducing birth rates. Every five years the status of the aid program for each nation was to be re-evaluated.

The reaction to the announcement of this program dwarfed the response to President Kennedy's speech. A coalition of UDCs attempted to get the U.N. General Assembly to condemn the United States as a "genetic aggressor." Most damaging of all to the American cause was the famous "25 Indians and a dog" speech by Mr. Shankarnarayan, Indian Ambassador to the U.N. Shankarnarayan pointed out that for several decades the United States, with less than six per cent of the people of the world had consumed roughly 50 per cent of the raw materials used every year. He described vividly America's contribution to worldwide environmental deterioration, and he scathingly denounced the miserly record of United States foreign aid as "unworthy of a fourth-rate power, let alone the most powerful nation on earth."

It was the climax of his speech, however, which most historians claim once and for all destroyed the image of the United States. Shankanarayan informed the assembly that the average American family dog was fed more animal protein per week than the average Indian got in a month. "How do you justify taking fish from protein-starved Peruvians and feeding them to your animals?" he asked. "I contend," he concluded, "that the birth of an American baby is a greater disaster for the world than that of 25 Indian babies." When the applause had died away, Mr. Sorensen, the American representative, made a speech which said essentially that "other countries look after their own self-interest, too." When the vote came, the United States was condemned.

This condemnation set the tone of U.S.-UDC relations at the time the Russian Thanodrin proposal was made. The proposal seemed to offer the masses in the UDCs an opportunity to save themselves and humiliate the United States at the same time; and in human affairs, as we all know, biological realities could never interfere with such an opportunity. The scientists were silenced, the politicians said yes, the Thanodrin plants were built, and the results were what any beginning ecology student could have predicted. At first Thanodrin seemed to offer excellent control of many pests. True, there was a rash of human fatalities from improper use of the lethal chemical, but, as Russian technical advisors were prone to note, these were more than compensated for by increased yields. Thanodrin use skyrocketed throughout the underdeveloped world. The Mikoyan design group developed a dependable, cheap agricultural aircraft which the Soviets donated to the effort in large numbers. MIG sprayers became even more common in UDCs than MIG interceptors.

Then the troubles began. Insect strains with cuticles resistant to Thanodrin penetration began to appear. And as streams, rivers, fish culture ponds and onshore waters became rich in Thanodrin, more fisheries began to disappear. Bird populations were decimated. The sequence of events was standard for broadcast use of a synthetic pesticide: great success at first, followed by removal of natural enemies and development of resistance by the pest. Populations of crop-eating insects in areas treated with Thanodrin made steady comebacks and soon became more abundant than ever. Yields plunged, while farmers in their desperation increased the Thanodrin dose and shortened the time between treatments. Death from Thanodrin poisoning became common. The first violent incident occurred in the Canete Valley of Peru, where farmers had suffered a similar chlorinated hydrocarbon disaster in the mid-'50s. A Russian advisor serving as an agricultural pilot was assaulted and killed by a mob of enraged farmers in January, 1978. Trouble spread rapidly during 1978, especially after the word got out that two years earlier Russia herself had banned the use of Thanodrin at home because of its serious effects on ecological systems. Suddenly Russia, and not the United States, was the *bete noir* in the UDCs. "Thanodrin parties" became epidemic, with farmers, in their ignorance, dumping carloads of Thanodrin concentrate into the sea. Russian advisors fled, and four of the Thanodrin plants were leveled to the ground. Destruction of the plants in Rio and Calcutta led to hundreds of thousands of gallons of Thanodrin concentrate being dumped directly into the sea.

Mr. Shankarnarayan again rose to address the U.N., but this time it was Mr. Potemkin, representative of the Soviet Union, who was on the hot seat. Mr. Potemkin heard his nation described as the greatest mass killer of all time as Shankarnarayan predicted at least 30 million deaths from crop failures due to overdependence on Thanodrin. Russia was accused of "chemical aggression," and the General Assembly, after a weak reply by Potemkin, passed a vote of censure.

It was in January, 1979, that huge blooms of a previously unknown variety of diatom were reported off the coast of Peru. The blooms were accompanied by a massive die-off of sea life and of the pathetic remainder of the birds which had once feasted on the anchovies of the area. Almost immediately another huge bloom was reported in the Indian ocean, centering around the Seychelles, and then a third in the South Atlantic off the African coast. Both of these were accompanied by spectacular die-offs of marine animals. Even more ominous were growing reports of fish and bird kills at oceanic points where there were no spectacular blooms. Biologists were soon able to explain the phenomena: the diatom had envolved an enzyme which broke down Thanodrin; that enzyme also produced a breakdown product which interfered with the transmission of nerve impulses, and was therefore lethal to animals. Unfortunately, the biologists could suggest no way of repressing the poisonous diatom bloom in time. By September, 1979, all important animal life in the sea was extinct. Large areas of coastline had to be evacuated, as windrows of dead fish created a monumental stench.

But stench was the least of man's problems. Japan and China were faced with almost instant starvation from a total loss of the seafood on which they were so dependent. Both blamed Russia for their situation and demanded immediate mass shipments of food. Russia had none to send. On October 13, Chinese armies attacked Russia on a broad front. . . .

––––––––

A pretty grim scenario. Unfortunately, we're a long way into it already. Everything mentioned as happening before 1970 has actually occurred; much of the rest is based on projections of trends already appearing. Evidence that pesticides have long-term lethal effects on human beings has started to accumulate, and recently Robert Finch, Secretary of the Department of Health, Education and Welfare expressed his extreme apprehension about the pesticide situation. Simultaneously the petro-chemical industry continues its unconscionable poison-peddling. For instance, Shell Chemical has been carrying on a high-pressure campaign to sell the insecticide Azodrin to farmers as a killer of cotton pests. They continue their program even though they know that Azodrin is not only ineffective, but often *increases* the pest density. They've covered themselves nicely in an advertisement which states, "Even if an overpowering migration (sic) develops, the flexibility of Azodrin lets you regain control fast. Just increase the dosage according to label recommendations." It's a great game — get people to apply the poison and kill the natural enemies of the pests. Then blame the increased pests on "migration" and sell even more pesticide!

Right now fisheries are being wiped out by over-exploitation, made easy by modern electronic equipment. The companies producing the equipment know this. They even boast in advertising that only their equipment will keep fishermen in business until the final kill. Profits must obviously be maximized in the short run. Indeed, Western society is in the process of completing the rape and murder of the planet for economic gain. And, sadly, most of the rest of the world is eager for the opportunity to emulate our behavior. But the underdeveloped peoples will be denied that opportunity — the days of plunder are drawing inexorably to a close.

Most of the people who are going to die in the greatest cataclysm in the history of man have already been born. More than three and a half billion people already populate our moribund globe, and about half of them are hungry. Some 10 to 20 million will starve to death *this year*. In spite of this, the population of the earth will increase by 70 million souls in 1969. For mankind has artificially lowered the death rate of the human population, while in general birth rates have remained high. With the input side of the population system in high gear and the output side slowed down, our fragile planet has filled with people at an incredible rate. It took several million years for the population to reach a total of two billion people in 1930, while a *second two billion will have been added by 1975*. By that time some experts feel that food shortages will have escalated the present level of world hunger and starvation into famines of unbelievable proportions. Other experts, more optimistic, think the ultimate food-population collision will not occur until the decade of the 1980's. Of course more massive famine may be avoided if other events cause a prior rise in the human death rate.

Both worldwide plague and thermonuclear war are made more probable as population growth continues. These, along with famine, make up the trio of potential "death rate solutions" to the population problem — solutions in which the birth rate-death rate imbalance is redressed by a rise in the death rate rather than by a lowering of the birth rate. Make no mistake about it, *the imbalance will be redressed*. The shape of the population growth curve is one familiar to the biologist. It is the outbreak part of an outbreak-crash sequence. A population grows rapidly in the presence of abundant resources, finally runs out of food or some other necessity, and crashes to a low level of extinction. Man is not only running out of food, he is also destroying the life support systems of the Spaceship Earth The situation was recently summarized very succinctly: "It is the top of the ninth inning. Man, always a threat at the plate, has been hitting Nature hard. It is important to remember, however, that NATURE BATS LAST."

OVERPOPULATED AMERICA:
OUR AFFLUENCE RESTS
ON A CRUMBLING FOUNDATION

Wayne H. Davis

I define as most seriously overpopulated that nation whose people by virtue of their numbers and activities are most rapidly decreasing the ability of the land to support human life. With our large population, our affluence and our technological monstrosities the United States wins first place by a substantial margin.

Let's compare the US to India, for example. We have 203 million people, whereas she has 540 million on much less land. But look at the impact of people on the land.

The average Indian eats his daily few cups of rice (or perhaps wheat, whose production on American farms contributed to our one percent per year drain in quality of our active farmland), draws his bucket of water from the communal well and sleeps in a mud hut. In his daily rounds to gather cow dung to burn to cook his rice and warm his feet, his footsteps, along with those of millions of his countrymen, help bring about a slow deterioration of the ability of the land to support people. His contribution to the destruction of the land is minimal.

An American, on the other hand, can be expected to destroy a piece of land on which he builds a home, garage and driveway. He will contribute his share to the 142 million tons of smoke and fumes, seven million junked cars, 20 million tons of paper, 48 billion cans, and 26 billion bottles the overburdened environment must absorb each year. To run his air conditioner we will strip-mine a Kentucky hillside, push the dirt and slate down into the stream, and burn coal in a power generator, whose smokestack contributes to a plume of smoke massive enough to cause cloud seeding and premature precipitation from Gulf winds which should be irrigating the wheat farms of Minnesota.

In his lifetime he will personally pollute three million gallons of water, and industry and agriculture will use ten times this much water in his behalf. To provide these needs the US Army Corps of Engineers will build dams and flood farmland. He will also use 21,000 gallons of leaded gasoline containing boron, drink 28,000 pounds of milk and eat 10,000 pounds of meat. The latter is produced and squandered in a life pattern unknown to Asians. A steer on a Western range eats plants containing minerals necessary for plant life. Some of these are incorporated into the body of the steer which is later shipped for slaughter. After being eaten by man these nutrients are flushed down the toilet into the ocean or buried in the cemetery, the surface of which is cluttered with boulders called tombstones and has been removed from productivity. The result is a continual drain on the productivity of range land. Add to this the erosion of overgrazed lands, and the effects of the falling water table as we mine Pleistocene deposits of groundwater to irrigate to produce food for more people, and we can see why one land is dying far more rapidly than did the great civilizations of the Middle East, which experienced the same cycle. The average Indian citizen, whose fecal material goes back to the land, has but a minute fraction of the destructive effect on the land that the affluent American does.

Thus I want to introduce a new term, which I suggest be used in future discussions of human population and ecology. We should speak of our numbers in "Indian equivalents." An Indian equivalent I define as the average number of Indian citizens required to have the same detrimental effect on the land's ability to support human life as would the average American. This value is difficult to determine, but let's take an extremely conservative working figure of 25. To see how conservative this is, imagine the addition of 1000 citizens to your town and 25,000 to an Indian village. Not only would the Americans destroy much more land for homes, highways and a shopping center, but they would contribute far more to environmental deterioration in hundreds of other ways as well. For example, their demand for steel for new autos might increase the daily pollution equivalent of 130,000 junk autos which *Life* tells us that US Steel Corp. dumps into Lake Michigan. Their demand for textiles would help the cotton industry destroy the life in the Black Warrior River in Alabama with endrin. And they would contribute to the massive industrial pollution of our oceans (we provide one third to one half the world's share) which has caused the precipitous downward trend in our commercial fisheries landings during the past seven years.

The per capita gross national product of the United States is 38 times that of India. Most of our goods and services contribute to the decline in the ability of the environment to support life. Thus it is clear that a figure of 25 for an Indian equivalent is conservative. It has been suggested to me that a more realistic figure would be 500.

In Indian equivalents, therefore, the population of the United States is at least four billion. And the rate of growth is even more alarming. We are growing at one percent per year, a rate which would double our numbers in 70 years. India is growing at 2.5 percent. Using the Indian equivalent of 25, our population growth becomes 10 times as serious as that of India. According to the Reinows in their recent book *Moment in the Sun* just one year's crop of American babies can be expected to use up 25 billion pounds of beef, 200 million pounds of steel and 9.1 billion gallons of gasoline during their collective lifetime. And the demands on water and land for our growing population are expected to be far greater than the supply available in the year 2000. We are destroying our land at a rate of over a million acres a year. We now have only 2.6 agricultural acres per person. By 1975 this will be cut to 2.2, the critical point for the maintenance of what we consider a decent diet, and by the year 2000 we might expect to have 1.2.

You might object that I am playing with statistics in using the Indian equivalent on the rate of growth. I am making the assumption that today's Indian child will live 35 years (the average Indian life span) at today's level of affluence. If he lives an American 70 years, our rate of population growth would be 20 times as serious as India's.

But the assumption of continued affluence at today's level is unfounded. If our numbers continue to rise, our standard of living will fall so sharply that by the year 2000 any surviving Americans might consider today's average Asian to be well off. Our children's effects on their environment will decline as they sink ever lower into poverty.

The United States is in serious economic trouble now. Nothing could be more misleading than today's affluence, which rests precariously on a crumbling foundation. Our productivity, which had been increasing steadily at about 3.2 percent a year since World War II, has been falling during 1969. Our export over import balance has been shrinking steadily from $7.1 billion in 1964 to $0.15 billion in the first half of 1969. Our balance of payments deficit for the second quarter was $3.7 billion, the largest in history. We are now importing iron ore, steel, oil, beef, textiles, cameras, radios and hundreds of other things.

Our economy is based upon the Keynesian concept of a continued growth in population and productivity. It worked in an underpopulated nation with excess resources. It could continue to work only if the earth and its resources were expanding at an annual rate of 4 to 5 percent. Yet neither the number of cars, the economy, the human population, nor anything else can expand indefinitely at an exponential rate in a finite world. We must face this fact *now*. The crisis is here. When Walter Heller says that our economy will expand by 4 percent annually through the latter 1970s he is dreaming. He is in a theoretical world totally unaware of the realities of human ecology. If the economists do not wake up and devise a new system for us now somebody else will have to do it for them.

A civilization is comparable to a living organism. Its longevity is a function of its metabolism. The higher the metabolism (affluence), the shorter the life. Keynesian economics has allowed us an affluent but shortened life span. We have now run our course.

The tragedy facing the United States is even greater and more imminent than that descending upon the hungry nations. The Paddock brothers in their book, *Famine 1975!*, say that India "cannot be saved" no matter how much food we ship her. But India will be here after the United States is gone. Many millions will die in the most colossal famines India has ever known, but the land will survive and she will come back as she always has before. The United States, on the other hand, will be a desolate tangle of concrete and ticky-tacky, of strip-mined moonscape and silt-choked reservoirs. The land and water will be so contaminated with pesticides, herbicides, mercury fungicides, lead, boron, nickel, arsenic and hundreds of other toxic substances, which have been approaching critical levels of concentration in our environment as a result of our numbers and affluence, that it may be unable to sustain human life.

Thus as the curtain gets ready to fall on man's civilization let it come as no surprise that it shall first fall on the United States. And let no one make the mistake of thinking we can save ourselves by "cleaning up the environment." Banning DDT is the equivalent of the physician's treating syphilis by putting a bandaid over the first chancre to appear. In either case you can be sure that more serious and widespread trouble will soon appear unless the disease itself is treated. We cannot survive by planning to treat the symptoms such as air pollution, water pollution, soil erosion, etc.

What can we do to slow the rate of destruction of the United States as a land capable of supporting human life? There are two approaches. First, we must reverse the population growth. We have far more people now than we can continue to support at anything near today's level of affluence. American women average slightly over three children each. According to the *Population Bulletin* if we reduced this number to 2.5 there would still be 330 million people in the nation at the end of the century. And even if we reduced this to 1.5 we would have 57 million more people in the year 2000 than we have now. With our present longevity patterns it would take more than 30 years for the population to peak even when reproducing at this rate which would eventually give us a net decrease in numbers.

Do not make the mistake of thinking that technology will solve our population problem by producing a better contraceptive. Our problem now is that people want too many children. Surveys show the average number of children wanted by the American family is 3.3. There is little difference between the poor and the wealthy, black and white, Catholic and Protestant. Production of children at this rate during the next 30 years would be so catastrophic in effect on our resources and the viability of the nation as to be beyond my ability to contemplate. To prevent this trend we must not only make contraceptives and abortion readily available to everyone, but we must establish a system to put severe economic pressure on those who produce children and reward those who do not. This can be done within our system of taxed welfare.

The other thing we must do is to pare down our Indian equivalents. Individuals in America society vary tremendously in Indian equivalents. If we plot Indian equivalents versus their reciprocal, the percentage of land surviving a generation, we obtain a linear regression. We can then place individuals and occupation types on this graph. At one end would be the starving blacks of Mississippi; they would have the least destructive effect on the land. At the other end of the graph would be the politicians slicing pork for the barrel, the highway contractors, strip-mine operators, real estate developers, and public enemy number one — the US Army Corps of Engineers.

We must halt land destruction. We must abandon the view of land and minerals as private property to be exploited in any way economically feasible for private financial gain. Land and minerals are resources upon which the very survival of the nation depends, and their use must be planned in the best interests of the people.

Rising expectations for the poor is a cruel joke foisted upon them by the Establishment. As our new economy of use-it-once-and-throw-it-away produces more and more products for the affluent, the share of our resources available for the poor declines. Blessed be the starving blacks of Mississippi with their outdoor privies, for they are ecologically sound, and they shall inherit a nation. Although I hope that we will help these unfortunate people attain a decent standard of living by diverting war efforts to fertility control and job training, our most urgent task to assure this nation's survival during the next decade is to stop the affluent destroyers.

THE NONSENSE EXPLOSION:
OVERPOPULATION
AS A CRISIS ISSUE

Ben Wattenberg

As the concern about the environment has swept across the nation, the ghost of the "population explosion" — recently haunting only India and other ugly foreign places — has suddenly been domestically resurrected and we are again hearing how crowded it is in America.

Life magazine, for example, chose to launch the new decade with the headline "Squeezing into the '70s," announcing that, because of the crowds, "the despair of yesterday's soup line has been replaced by today's ordeal of the steak line." Two months later *Life* featured a story about a young New Jersey mathematician who had himself sterilized because he is "deeply worried by this country's wildly expanding population."

Crowded, crowded, crowded, we are told. Slums are crowded, suburbs are crowded, megalopolis is crowded and more and more and more people are eating up, burning up and using up the beauty and wealth of America — turning the land into a polluted, depleted sprawl of scummy water and flickering neon, an ecological catastrophe stretching from the Everglades to the Pacific Northwest. Crisis. Crisis. Crisis.

That so very much of this is preposterous, as we shall see, should come as no real surprise to those who follow the fads of crisis in America. There are no plain and simple problems any more. From poverty to race to crime to Vietnam all we face are crises which threaten to bring down the world upon our heads. And now it is ecology-environment — which is a perfectly good problem to be sure — but with its advent comes dragged in by the heels our old friend the super-crisis of the population explosion, which is not nearly as real or immediate a problem in America, and ends up serving unfortunately as a political smokescreen that can obscure a host of legitimate concerns.

While the rhetoric rattles on about where will we ever put the next hundred million Americans, while the President tells us that the roots of so many of our current problems are to be found in the speed with which the last hundred million Americans came upon us, while the more apocalyptic demographers and biologists (like Dr. Paul Ehrlich) are talking about putting still nonexistent birth control chemicals in the water supply, and about federal licensing of babies — the critical facts in the argument remain generally unstated and the critical premises in the argument remain largely unchallenged. The critical facts are that America is not by any standard a crowded country and that the American birth rate has recently been at an all-time low; the critical premise is that population growth in America is harmful.

In not stating the facts and in not at least challenging the premises, politicans and planners alike seem to be leaving themselves open to both bad planning and bad politics. This happens by concentrating on what the problem is not, rather than on what the problem is. Let's, then, first look at the facts. The current population of the United States is 205 million. That population is distributed over 3,615,123 square miles of land, for a density of about 55 persons per square mile. In terms of density, this makes the United States one of the most sparsely populated nations in the world. As measured by density, Holland is about 18 times as "crowded" (at 975 persons per square mile), England is 10 times as dense (588 persons per square mile), scenic Switzerland seven times as dense (382), tropical Nigeria three times as dense (174) and even neighboring Mexico beats us out with 60 persons per square mile. The U.S., by international standards, is not a very "crowded" country.

But density in some cases can be very misleading in trying to judge "crowdedness." The Soviet Union, for example, is less dense than the U.S. (29 per square mile), but has millions of square miles of uninhabitable land, just as does Brazil and Australia, two other nations also less densely populated than the U.S.

Of course, the US also has large areas of land that are equally uninhabitable: the Rockies, the Western deserts, parts of Alaska and so on.

But while it is of interest to know that America has some land that is uninhabitable, what is of far more importance is that we have in the United States vast unused areas of eminently habitable land, land that in fact was inhabited until very recently. In the last eight years one out of three counties in America actually *lost* population. Four states have lost population: North and South Dakota, West Virginia, and Wyoming; and another two states, Maine and Iowa, gained less than one percent in the eight years. Furthermore, three out of five counties had a net out-migration, that is, more people left the county than came in.

These counties, the net-loss counties and the net-out-migration counties, are the areas in America where the current hoopla about the population sounds a bit hollow. These are the areas, mostly rural and small town, that are trying to attract industry, areas where a smokestack or a traffic jam signifies not pollution but progress, areas that have more open space around them for hunting and fishing than before, and areas where the older people are a little sad because, as they tell you, "the young people don't stay around here anymore."

This human plaint tells us what has been happening demographically in the United States in recent years. It has not been a population explosion, but a population redistribution. And the place people have been redistributing themselves *to* is a place we call "suburb":

American Population by Residence

	Population		Increase
	1950	1968	1950-1968
Residing in Central city	35%	29%	6 million
Residing in Suburb	24%	35%	32 million (!)
Residing in small cities, towns and rural	41%	36%	9 million
	100%	100%	47 million

In less than two decades the proportion of Americans living in suburbs has gone from less than a quarter to more than a third.

But even the total increase in population — rural, city, and suburb — is misleading. The big gains in population occurred ten and fifteen years ago; today growth is much slower. Thus, in calendar year 1956, the U.S. population grew by 3.1 million, while in calendar year 1968 population went up by 2.0 million — and in a nation with a larger population base.

What has happened, simply, is that the baby-boom has ended. When the GIs came home after World War II, they began begetting large quantities of children, and Americans went on begetting, at high rates for about 15 years. The best index of population growth in the U.S. is the fertility rate, that is, the number of babies born per thousand women aged 15-44. In 1940, the fertility rate was 80, just a few points above the 1936 Depression all-time low of 76. Ten years later, in 1950, the baby-boom had begun and the fertility rate had soared to 106, an increase of 32 percent in just ten years. It kept climbing in 1957, it reached 123, up more than 50 percent in two decades.

But since 1957, the rate has gone steadily down: to 119 in 1960, to 98 in 1965, to 85.7 in 1968, not very much higher now than in Depression times. The estimated fertility rate for 1969 was down slightly to 85.5 and there is no reason now to think it will go up, although, as we shall see, it may sink further.

When measured by another yard-stick, the "percent national population growth" (birth plus immigration less deaths), the American population is now growing by about 1.0 percent per year; just a decade ago it was growing by 1.8 percent per year. That may not sound like much of a difference, .8 percent, but in a nation of 200 million people it means 16 million fewer people over a single decade!

With all this, however, comes another important set of facts: our population *is* still growing. At the reduced growth rate there are now about two million people being added to our population each year. This may even go up somewhat in the next few years as the baby-boom babies become young adults and—roughly simultaneously— parents. Moreover, a growing population, even a slowly growing population, grows by larger numbers as it grows. As the two hundred million Americans become two hundred and fifty million Americans there is a proportionately greater number of potential mothers, more babies, and the incremental two million new Americans per year can rise to 2½ or 3 million new Americans even with a relatively low growth rate.

The current, most likely projection of the Census Bureau of the U.S. population in the year 2000 — three decades hence — hovers somewhere in the 280 - 290 million range. That means there will be about 75-85 million more Americans than today, which is many millions more indeed, although not quite the round "hundred million" figure everyone is talking about.

It must be stressed, however, that this is only a projection: it could be high, it could be low. The figure is derived from a series of four alternate projections based on different levels of fertility rates issued by the Census Bureau in 1967. Already the highest two projections — calling for 361 and 336 million — are out of the question. The third projection called for 308 million and that too now seems high, as it called for a fertlity rate of 95 in 1970 — about 10 points higher than the 1969 rate. The lowest of the four projections calls for a fertility rate of 84.6 in 1970 (roughly where we are) and yields a population of 283 million in the year 2000.

But even that is not an immutable figure by any means. Just as the first three of the alternate projections quickly proved themselves false, so it may be that Series D may prove high. After all, the Hoover Depression, in an era with far less effective birth control technology, brought fertility rates down to 76. What might a Nixon Recession do in an era of pills, loops, diaphragms, liberalized abortion?

Already the Census Bureau — quite properly — is preparing to revise its projections for the future. The new set of alternate projections — which will bracket the newer, lower, fertility rates — will unquestionably be lower, with a low-end possibility in the general area of 265 million for the year 2000. That too will only be a projection, based on assumptions which may or may not prove valid. But 'if, such a low fertility rate does indeed occur, population in the U.S. would then begin to level off after the year 2000 as the last of the baby-boom babies have completed their own families. The U.S. might then be in an era of near-stable population along the lines of many Western European nations.

But even that is sixty million more Americans in just three decades — more than the population of Great Britain today.

Those, then, would seem to be the elementary facts. More Americans, although probably not as many as we may have been led to believe. More Americans, but not necessarily inhabiting a statistically crowded country.

With these facts, we can now turn to the premise set forth by the Explosionists i.e.. more Americans are bad.

Are they? My own judgment is — not necessarily.

There are a number of points made by the Explosionists and they can only be briefly examined here.

Because population growth is currently being linked to environmental problems, we can look there first. The Explosionists say people, and the industry needed to support people, cause pollution. Ergo: fewer people—less pollution.

On the surface, a reasonable enough statement; certainly, population is one of the variables in the pollution problem. Yet, there is something else to be said. People not only cause pollution, but once you have a substantial number of people, it is only people that can solve pollution. Further, the case can be made that *more people* can more easily and more quickly solve pollution problems than can fewer people. For example: let us assume that $60 billion per year are necessary for national defense. The cost of defense will not necessarily be higher for a nation of three hundred million than for a nation of two hundred million. Yet the tax revenues to the government would be immensely higher, freeing vast sums of tax money to be used for the very expensive programs that are necessary for air, water, and pollution control. Spreading constant defense costs over a large population base provides proportionately greater amounts for nondefense spending. The same sort of equation can be used for the huge, one-time capital costs of research that must go into any effective, long-range, anti-pollution program. The costs are roughly the same for 200 or 300 million people — but easier to pay by 300 million.

Lake Erie, the Hudson River, The Potomac, are ecological slums today. If the U.S. population did not grow by one person over the current 205 million Americans, these bodies of waters would *still* be ecological slums. These waters, and any others now threatened, will be decent places only if men are willing to devote resources to the job. That is not a function of population growth, but of national will. It can be done if we as a nation, decide that we want it done and are willing to pay for it. It is simple as that and it has relatively little to do with whether the national decision involves 200 or 250 or 300 or 350 million Americans. It should also be remembered that pollution occurs in underpopulated places as well: in Sydney, Australia today, in medieval Europe, in ancient Rome.

Next, the Explosionists view more people as a crisis because of all the demands they will make upon the society. So many new schools, so many more hospitals, more libraries — services and facilities which we are having difficulty providing right now. Similarly with "new towns." If we are to avoid vast and sprawling megalopolitan swaths, we are told, we must build 100 brand-new towns in 30 years. Unfortunately, we've only been able to construct a few in the last couple of decades — so, alas, what possible chance do we have to make the grade in the years to come?

What this argument ignores, of course, is that it is not governments who really create schools, hospitals, libraries, and even new towns. It is *people* who create and build. People pay taxes; the taxes build and staff the schools; the more people, the more need for schools, *and* the more taxes. In an uncanny way it usually works out that every child in America has his own set of parents, and a school to attend. In a nation of a hundred million there were roughly enough schools for the children then present, at two hundred million the same was true and, no doubt, it will hold true at three hundred million. Nor will quality suffer because of numbers; quality suffers if taxpayers aren't willing to pay for quality and it is not harder for 300 million Americans to pay for quality schools for their children than it is for 230 million to buy quality schooling for their offspring.

And those "new towns"? *People* make them too. That's just what's been happening in America in the last few decades. We call them "suburbs," not "new towns," and as the earlier data showed, 32 million Americans opted for this "decentralization" over the past eighteen years, long before it became a fashionable, political fad-word. People did this because people are not damn fools and where they had a chance to trade a rural shack or an urban tenement for a green quarter acre in suburbia, they did so, even though the faddists then were saying that suburbia was not "decentralized" (which is allegedly good), but "conformist" (which is allegedly bad). What smug town-planners like to call urban sprawl, represents uncrowded, gracious living for the former residents of city slums and the quality of such suburban life doesn't necessarily deteriorate if another new suburb rises down the road a mile.

Now, suburbs are not identical to the new town concept. The new towns, in theory, are further away from big cities, they are largely self-contained and they are designed from scratch. But, curiously, as many jobs move from the central cities, suburbs are becoming more and more self-contained; as metropolitan areas get larger, the newer suburbs *are* quite far from central cities; and there are some fascinating new start-from-scratch concepts in planning that are now materializing in suburban areas, particularly in some of the massive all-weather, multi-tiered, multi-malled shopping centers.

All this is not to denigrate new towns or the idea of population decentralization. Far from it. The effort here is only to point out that people often are even faster than their governments in seeking their own best interests. If it is new towns near a babbling brook that Americans feel they want, if the country remains prosperous, some patriot will no doubt step forward and provide same, and even have salesmen in boiler rooms phoning you to sell same. The process is mostly organic, not planned-governmental. It works with 200 or 250 or 300 or 350 million Americans.

There is next the "resources" argument. It comes in two parts. Part one: many of our resources are finite (oil, coal, etc); more people obviously use more resources; the fewer the people, the less the drain on the resources. Part two: we Americans are rich people: rich people use more resources; therefore, we must cut back population particularly fast, and particularily our rich population.

The resources problem is difficult to assess. A demographer now in his sixties seemed to put it in perspective. "Resources are a serious problem" he said. "We've been running out of oil ever since I was a boy."

The fact is, of course, ·sooner or later we *will* run out of oil, perhaps in thirty years or fifty years, or a hundred years or two hundred years. So too will we run out of *all* nonrenewable resources — by definition. We will run out of oil even if population growth stops today and we will run out of oil, somewhat sooner, if population growth continues. Whether oil reserves are depleted in 2020 or 2040 or 2140 does not seem to be of critical importance; in any event a substitute fuel must be found — probably nuclear. If no adequate substitute is developed, then we (all us earthmen) will suffer somewhat regardless of numbers.

Part two, that *rich* people are the real menace both resource-wise and pollution-wise, has recently been particularly stressed by Dr. Jean Mayer who advises the President hunger-wise but would not seem to be fully up to date demography-wise.

For the simple fact is that wealthier people generally have far fewer children than poorer people. With current mortality rates, population stability is maintained if the typical woman has on the average 2.13 children. In a 1964 Census Bureau survey among women who had completed their child-bearing years, it was shown that families with incomes of $10,000 and over had 2.21 children, just a trifle over replacement. This compared with 3.53 children for the poorest women. Since 1964, fertility rates have gone down among young women, and it is possible that when these lower rates are ultimately reflected as "completed fertility" we may see that affluent American women of the future just barely replace their own number, if that.

In short, current population patterns show that affluent people do not cause rapid population growth. And if the entire population were entirely affluent, we certainly would not be talking about a population explosion. Further, if the entire population were affluent and committed to combatting pollution, we wouldn't be talking about a pollution explosion either.

What then is Dr. Mayer's prescription? Is he against affluent people having babies but not poor people, even though the affluent have relatively few anyway? Or perhaps is it that he is just against the idea of letting any more poor people become affluent people, because they too will then consume too many resources and cause more pollution?

There are two important points that run through most of the above. First is that the simple numbers of people are not in themselves of great importance in the United States. There is no "optimum" population as such for the U.S., not within population ranges now forecast in any event. Whether we have 250 million people or 350 million people is less important than what the people — however many of them there are — decide to do about their problems. Second the population problem, at least in the United States, is an extremely long-term proposition, and in a country of this size and wealth, there is more flexibility in solving the potential demographic problems than might be assumed from the current rhetoric-of-crisis.

To be sure, much of the concern about population growth is sane, valid, and important. Certainly the concept of family planning — which for years had been a political stepchild — is now coming into the mainstream, and properly so. That every family in America should at least have the knowledge and the technology to control the size of its family as it sees fit seems beyond question. This knowledge and this technology, previously available largely to middle-class and affluent Americans is now being made available to poorer Americans through growing federal programs. Some of the more militant black leaders have called it "genocide," but that is a rather hollow charge when one realizes a) that the poorest American women now have about 50 percent more children per capita than do middle-class Americans and b) that more-children-than-can-be-properly-provided-for is one of the most classic causes of poverty in America and around the world.

Certainly too, population growth must sooner or later level off. While America could support twice its current population and probably four times its current population — growth can obviously not go on forever and it is wise to understand this fact now rather than a hundred years from now. It is also wise to begin to act upon this knowledge, as indeed we have begun to act upon it. It is, accordingly, difficult to complain about the suggestions for legislation to make conditions easier for women to get and hold decent jobs — the thought being that easier access to employment will slow the birth rate. Our problems in the future probably will be easier to handle with somewhat fewer people than with somewhat greater numbers.

But what is wrong, and dangerous, and foolhardy is to make population a crisis. Doing so will simply allow too many politicians to take their eyes off the ball. When Explosionists say, as they do, that crime, riots, and urban problems are caused by "the population explosion," it is just too easy for politicians to agree and say sure, let's stop having so many babies, instead of saying let's get to work on the real urban problems of this nation. (As a matter of general interest it should be noted that the riot areas, the highcrime areas, the areas of the most acute urban problems *are areas that are typically losing populatio* For example, special censuses in Hough and

Watts showed population loss. Given that kind of data it is hard to accept the Explosionist notion that crowding causes crime.)

When the Explosionists say, as they do, that Yosemite and Yellowstone are crowded and that there is a vanishing wilderness because of too many people — they are wrong again. When visits to national parks have gone up by more than 400 percent in less than two decades, while population growth has gone up by about 30 percent, over the same time, then Yosemite isn't crowded because of population but because of other factors. When you have a nation where a workingman can afford a car, and-or a camper-trailer, when you give him three weeks paid vacation, provide decent roads — there would be something to say for the fact that you have indeed set up the society that Old Liberals, Trade Union Variety, lusted for, and who is to say that is bad? Again, if the population crisis rhetoric is accepted it becomes too easy to say that the way to an uncrowded Yosemite is to have fewer people, and forget about the hard and far more costly problems of creating more recreation areas, which are needed even if our population does not rise.

When the Explosionists say, as they do, that it's because we have so many people that Lake Erie is polluted then once again we are invited to take our eye off the tens-of-*billions*-of-dollars ball of environmental safety and we are simultaneously invited to piddle around with 25-*million* dollar programs for birth control, which are nice, but don't solve anything to do with Lake Erie.

Finally, we must take note of the new thrust by the Explosionists: population control. Note the phrase carefully. This is specifically not "family planning," where the family concerned does the planning. This is *control* of population by the government and this is what the apocalyptics are demanding, because, they say, family planning by itself will not reduce us to a zero growth rate. The more popular "soft" position of government control involves what is called "disincentives," that is, a few minor measures like changing the taxation system, the school system and the moral code to see if that won't work before going onto outright baby licensing.

Accordingly, the demographer Judith Blake Davis of the University of California (Berkeley) complained to a House Committee: "We penalize homosexuals of both sexes, we insist that women must bear unwanted children by depriving them of ready access to abortion, we bind individuals to pay for the education of other people's children, we make people with small families support the schooling of others. . . "

Now, Dr. Davis is not exactly saying that we should go to a private school system or eliminate the tax exemption for children thereby penalizing the poor but not the rich — but that is the implication. In essence, Senator Packwood recently proposed just that: no tax exemptions for any children beyond the second per family, born after 1972.

The strong position on population control ultimately comes around to some form of governmental permission, or licensing, for babies.

Dr. Garrett Hardin, a professor-biologist at the University of California, Santa Barbara, says, "In the long run, voluntarism is insanity. The result will be continued uncontrolled population growth".

Astro-physicist Donald Aiken says. "The government has to step in and tamper with religious and personal convictions — maybe even impose penalties for every child a family has beyond two."

Dr. Melvin Ketchel, professor of physiology at Tufts Medical School writes in *Medical World News:* "Scientists will discover ways of controlling the fertility of an entire population. . . . the compound. . . .could be controlled by adjustments in dosage, (and) a government could regulate the growth of its population without depending upon the voluntary action of individual couples. . . .such an agent might be added to the water supply."

And Dr. Paul Ehrlich of Stanford: "If we don't do something dramatic about population and environment, and do it immediately, there's just no hope that civilization will persist. . . .The world's most serious population-growth problem is right here in the United States among affluent white Americans . . . ."

What it all adds up to is this: why have a longrange managable population problem that can be coped with gradually over generations when, with a little extra souped-up scare rhetoric, we can drum up a full-fledged crisis? We certainly need one: it's been months since we've had a crisis. After all, Vietnam, we were told, was "the greatest crisis in a hundred years." Piker, Here's a crisis that's a beauty: the greatest crisis in two billion years: we're about to breed ourselves right into oblivion.

Finally, look at it all from Mr. Nixon's point of view. It's beautiful. You (Mr. Nixon) take office and the major domestic problems, generally acknowledged, are the race situation and the (so-called) crisis of the cities. They are tough problems. They are controversial problems. They are problems that have given way only gradually, painstakingly, expensively, over the years. Your opponents are in a militant mood. They have been co-opted in Vietnam and you fully expect them to hold your feet on the fire on these tough domestic problems.

Apprehensively, you await the onslaught. And what is the slogan? No, it. . . .can't be — but yes, it is. It's coming into focus. Read it: "Lower Emission Standards"! And in the next rank is another militant sign; and what does it say? It says, "Our Rivers Stink."

Full circle. The opposition sloganeers have gone from the "New Deal" to the "Fair Deal" to the "New- Frontier" to the "Great Society," and now they march to a new banner: "No Shit"!

Beautiful. Of course the environment *is* a real problem, an important problem; we knew that from Senator Muskie. Of course your President will respond to it, particularily since almost everyone is for it, particularly if it takes the heat off elsewhere. But even the environment issue is massively expensive — too expensive to do everything now that ought to be done now.

So wait a minute, you say, your opponents have been good to you so far, let's see how really helpful they'll be. And behold, here come the cavalry.

And what do they say? The problem of pollution is really the problem of too many people. Let the opponents divide among themselves and let the opponents fight among themselves. Let there be a children's allowance, say some of your opponents. Nay, let there not be a children's allowance, it will encourage population growth. Let there be better public schools, say some of your enemies. Nay, let each family pay for their own schooling to discourage population growth. Let us help the poor, say the opponents; nay, let us penalize the poor for having too many children. Let then the Secretary of HEW go forth to the people and say, "Ask not what your country can do for you, ask what you can do for your country — you shall have two children no more. no less, that is your brave social mission in America."

I imagine there have been luckier Presidents, but I can't think of any.

POPULATION POLLUTION

Francis S.L. Williamson

I do not believe that we would still discuss this problem if we did not look hopefully ahead to the technological achievements that may curb—or at least bring to within "tolerable" limits—the tragic, massive, and still-expanding pollution of the air, soil, and water of the earth. This optimism stems from the long overdue consideration of this problem and the implementation of programs dealing with many of its aspects. Environmental pollution, however, is not a point inexorably linked to human population growth (Daddario, 1968): and we must assume that although numbers of people will increase, the technology now available can and will provide some of the solutions necessary for our health and survival. Additionally, many of us have similar hopes for our less fortunate cohabitants of the earth—those lacking a technology or a freedom of choice. These solutions include the provision in adaquate amounts of clean air to breathe, clean water to drink, and clean food to eat. Even if we make the assumption that, as human population growth continues, strict curbs can be simultaneously placed on enviromental abuses, we are still confronted with the unresolved problem of population pollution. This I define as the consequences, mental, and physical, of life in a world vastly more populous and technologically more complex than the one in which we currently find ourselves. In such a world the goals of healthy and happy human beings, free from malnutrition, poverty, disease, and war, seem to me convincingly elusive. The expression of man's full range of genetic potential is perhaps impossible.

Human Population Growth

I believe there is general agreement among *knowledgeable men* that current trends in the growth of human populations are not only unacceptable but will result in disaster. The current rate of growth, 2 percent per year (McElroy, 1969), will result in 150 billion people in 200 years. In terms of the time necessary to double the world's population, it represents only about 35 years. As Ehrlich (1968) points out, this "doubling time" has been reduced successively from one million years to 1000, to 200, to 80, and finally to the present 35 years. If the later rate continues for 900 years, the earth's population will be 60 million people, or about 100 persons for each square yard of the *total* earth surface. Unfortunately, we have no evidence that indicates any lessening of this doubling rate.

Of immediate concern is the world food crisis, a subject dealt with at the Plenary Session of the 19th Annual AIBS Meeting. At this session it was indicated that no efforts are presently being made that would avert global famines by 1985 (McElroy, 1969). Ehrlich (1968) has stated that such famines will be prevalent in tne 1970's. What we are prepared to consider as "widespread global famine" is questionable, but apparently it is not the 3.5 million people or more who will starve this year (Ehrlich, 1968): nor is it the general agreement that one-half of the world's people are presently either malnourished or undernourished. I agree with those who feel that we must increase food production at home and abroad in an intensive effort to avert famine, but obviously the success of such an effort will be pitifully short-lived unless population control is achieved.

While there appears to be general agreement that the growth of human populations must be controlled, both in the long-term sense of allowing for survival and in the immediate sense of averting or alleviating famines, there is little agreement as to how this control is to be achieved.

On 7 January of this year, The Presidential Committee on Population and Family Planning proposed a $120 million increase in the federal appropriation for family planning services to make such services available to all American women who want them. At that time the President stated that no critical issue now facing the world, with the exception of peace, is more important than that of the soaring population. He further stated that world peace will probably never be possible if this latter problem goes unsolved, and he noted that the federal investment in family planning activities had risen from $6 million in fiscal 1964 to $115 million in fiscal 1969. This funding may indicate progress, but certainly not of a magnitude proportional to the enormity and urgency of this situation. A value judgment has been made as to the priority of this problem with that of landing a man on the moon, at least regarding funding and the attraction of intellectual effort.

In my opinion the focus continues to be on family planning, not on population control, and this does little more than achieve a reduction in birth rate of an inadequate nature. I find that I must agree with Kingsley Davis (1967) that "There is no reason to expect that the millions of decisions about family size made by couples in their own interest will automatically control population for the benefit of society". As Davis points out, the family planning campaigns in such "model" countries as Japan and Taiwan have hastened the downward trends in birth rates but have not provided population control. Results of the present approach can only be measured as the difference between the number of children women have been having and the number they want to have. For example, the family planning program in Taiwan, assuming that the contraceptives used are completely effective, would be successful if it resulted in the women having the desired 4.5 children each. This represents a sharp drop from the average 6.5 children previously borne to each woman but results in a rate of natural increase for the country of close to 3 percent. If the social and economic change of Taiwan continues, a further drop in fertility may occur. It may even reach that of the United States, where an average of 3.4 children is currently desired. This would result in Taiwan in a 1.7 percent per year increase, or a doubling of the population in 41 years, and hardly suggests that our country be used as a model or yardstick for other nations.

The plan of Taylor and Berelson (1968) to provide family planning instructions with maternity care may be a logical step in population control, but I fail to see in what way this plan can alter the basic desire of women in the underdeveloped nations to have more than two children. The natural processes of modernization and education have failed to do this in those nations that are developed. With these facts in mind, it is difficult to imagine the acceptance anywhere that any population increase, no matter how trivial, can be tolerated and that the goal must be zero growth.

There is no easy single solution to achieving a zero or near-zero growth rate. Berelson (1969) has recently reviewed the further proposals which have been made to "solve" the population problem. He has appraised them according to scientific, political, administrative, economic, and ethical criteria as well as to their presumed effectiveness. The proposals range from the very nebulous one of augmented research effort to the stringent one of involuntary fertility control. The barriers to acceptance of these criteria, for the truly effective measures, seem insurmountable at the present time. It is my personal view that in the United States a system of tax and welfare benefits and penalties; a liberal voluntary program of abortion and sterlization (government sponsored and financed, if necessary): attempts at the development in women of substitutes for family interests; and greatly intensified educational campaigns are in order. If the United States is to lead the way, and certainly no other nation appears economically prepared to do so, it seems reasonable that we might begin by abolishing those policies that promote population growth. However, I do not believe we will do these things until economic hardship makes them mandatory. Nonetheless, we are nearing the point of either exercising the free choice of methods of population control still available or facing the compulsory ones that otherwise will be necessary for survival.

In the long interim, however, the emphasis of our efforts can be logically focused on the improvement of the quality of the environment and of the people who are to live here. Here, at least temporarily, we can "do things" with some expectation of success.

The Shift to Urban Life

The rapidly rising number of human beings is not resulting in their general distribution over the landscape but rather in the development of enormous urban centers. In 1800 over 90 percent of the population of the United States, albeit only some 5-1/2 million people, lived in a rural environment. By 1900, the population of this country was nearly equally divided between cities and rural areas. In 1950, the urban population was 64 percent; in 1960, 70 percent; and it is presently about 75 percent. The projection for 1980 is 78 percent and for the year 2000 about 85 percent of the expected 300 million people will be urban dwellers. The number of residents in rural areas has not changed over the last 30 years, and is not expected to vary from its present approximately 53 million persons for the next 10 years. There resides in these data. however, the basic fallacy that what we term "rural" is changing also.

Gigantic urban concentrations are developing within the United States, and these have been termed megalopolises. The three best known have been recently termed "Boswash," "Chipitts," and, for lack of an equally ominous name, "Sag." "Boswash" reaches from New England to Washington, D.C. "Chipitts," from Chicago to Cleveland and south to Pittsburgh and, "Sag," a seaside city occupying the coast of California from San Francisco to San Diego. Demographers and urban planners predict the development of hosts of such "super cities." The Task Force on Environmental Health and Related Problems reported to Secretary Gardner in 1967 that virtually no effort is being made to explore ways of preventing this startling growth. A research program must be inaugurated, they reported, aimed at determining and perfecting measures to shift the focus of future population growth away from already crowded urban areas to parts of the country that are *not now* (emphasis mine) burdened by too many people. Unless such an effort is successful, the pollution control efforts of today, and those planned for the future, could be reduced literally to zero by the sheer increase of people and their correspondingly increased demand for goods, services, and facilities. Similarly, Mayr (1963) earlier pointed out that long before man has reached the stage of "standing room only" his principal preoccupation will be with enormous social, economic, and engineering problems. The undesirable by-products of the crowded urban areas are so deleterious that there will be little opportunity left for the cultivation of man's most uniquely human attributes. This could be what is in store for "Chipitts," "Boswash," "Sag," and others.

It seems that there is not only an urgent need for population control but for planned communities and the de-emphasis of the enormous urban concentrations that compound our problems of coping with environmental pollution.

Thus far the data substantiating my remarks are more than adequate. The growth of the world's population is staggering and is attended by increasing urbanization. I still have neglected consideration of man's welfare under the circumstances. The steadily mounting volume of published and unpublished data regarding environmental pollution has focused primarily on the impact of man's activities on his environment and less on the reverse, i.e. the impact of the resultant changes on man himself. Some of these changes are quantifiable, especially those affecting physical well-being. Unfortunately, others affecting such things as mental health and what we refer to vaguely as the "quality of life" are not quantifiable although certainly they are no less real. Obviously, some of these matters cross a number of areas of interest. Consideration of them will be incorporated in the papers of other participants in this book.

I would like to consider first some of the quantifiable effects, prefacing my remarks by reiterating the well-known fact that many environmental hazards are so subtle as to be beyond an individual's perception and control. It is less well known that there are frequently some deleterious effects stemming from the most cleverly contrived technological efforts to improve man's general well-being. If we look briefly at selected data from the United States, there is evidence linking air pollution with major respiratory diseases (Task Force on Environmental Health and Related Problems, 1967). Deaths from bronchiogenic carcinoma range from 15 per 100,000 population in rural areas to 30 or more in urban centers with over one million population. Deaths due to emphysema have risen from 1.5 per 100,000 population in 1950 to about 15 in 1964. The correlation of bigger cities with more air pollution with more related deaths seems well-substantiated. Almost half of the people in the United States, 95 million, drink water that is below present federal standards or of unknown quality. Such diseases as infectious hepatitis appear to be directly related to contaminated drinking water, but very little is known about how the agent of hepatitus gets into the water or how it can be removed (The Task Force on Environmental Health and Related Problems, 1967). The concentration of lead is increasing in the air, water, and food, and the blood levels are sufficiently high in many cases to be associated with sub-acute toxic effects (Dubos, 1965). The accumulation and effects of nonbiodegradable biocides present another serious problem. Documentation is growing that a number of other diseases are associated with environmental pollution, frequently those associated with urbanization.

As alluded to earlier, our best efforts to reduce environmental hazards often have proceeded without adequate knowledge. The development of efficient braking systems for motor vehicles has led to increased exposure of the public to asbestos particles produced by the gradual wearing of brake linings. There is a scientific basis for concern that these particles may promote bronchiogenic carcinoma (Task Force on Environmental Health and Related Problems, 1967). Subsequent to the inoculation of millions of people with a vacine to prevent poliomyelitis was the discovery that some of the stocks of vacine, perhaps as many as 25-35 percent, contained Simian Virus 40 (Sweet and Hilleman, 1960), previously unknown to be resident in the rhesus monkey cells used to culture the virus of poliomyelitis and thus to manufacture the vaccine. The high prevalence of the virus in the cell cultures was compounded by pooling cells from several monkeys. Simian Virus 40 was subsequently shown to be tumorogenic when injected into young hamsters (Eddy, 1962), to possess the capacity of transforming human renal cells in vitro (Shein and Enders, 1962), and to result in the production of neutralizing antibodies in 5.3 percent of cancer patients living in the known limits of distribution of the rhesus monkey (Shah, 1969). Its carcinogenicity in man remains unknown. Poliomyelitis itself is a disease whose spread is enhanced by close human association. Numerous facts support the view that the disease is an enteric infection spread primarily by contaminated excreta (Bodian and Horstmann, 1965).

Without belaboring the matter of pollution and physical well-being excessively, I would like to add that the Food and Drug Administration has estimated that the American people are being exposed to some 500,000 different alien substances, many of them over very long periods of time. Fewer that 10 percent of these have been analyzed in a manner that might provide the basis for determining their effects, and it has been emphasized that we simply cannot assess potential hazards. The Simian Virus 40 example seems to substantiate this opinion. Nonetheless, severe physical manifestations can ultimately result from repeated exposure to small concentrations of environmental pollutants. These pollutants can have cumulative delayed effects such as cancers, emphysema, and reduced life span (Task Force on Environmental Health and Related Problems, 1967). A three-session symposium of the recent meeting of the American Association for the Advancement of Science was devoted to discussions of such unanticipated environmental hazards, including interactions between contaminants and drugs, food and drugs, and among different drugs.

Earlier I stated my view that environmental pollution and population growth are not inexorably linked. Assuming that our technology renders the environmental scene once again "pristine" in the sense of allowing for sufficient ecosystem function, perhaps even to the point of eliminating the potential health hazards just mentioned, what are the consequences to man's mental well-being of continued population growth and social contacts? If for instance, we eliminate the dangerous substances in automobile exhausts and asbestos brake linings, how will we be affected by the increase in vehicles from the present 90 million to the 244 million expected to be present in 30 years? We have no data which allow us to establish levels of tolerance for congestion, noise, odor (perhaps removable) general stress, and accident threats, including those from traffic. Excessive exposure to high noise levels can impair hearing or cause total deafness, but the effects of daily noise and disruptions of all kinds, in terms of average human tolerance, is largely unknown (Task Force on Environmental Health and Related Problems, 1967) Rene Dubos states that: "You can go to any one of the thoughtful architects or urban planners. . .none of them knows what it does to the child to have a certain kind of environment, as against other kinds of environments. The whole process of mental development, as affected by physical development of cities, has never been investigated."

I believe it is germane to this discussion to go back to the pioneer work of Faris and Dunham (1939) on mental disorders in urban areas. A brief summary of the data supplied in that study indicates how the incidence of major psychoses are related to the organization of a city. Mental disorders show a decrease from the center to the periphery of the city — a pattern of distribution shown for other kinds of social and economic phenomena such as poverty, unemployment, juvenile delinquency, crime, suicide, family desertion, infant mortality, and communicable disease. Positive correlations are difficult to draw from these data, but they are certainly suggestive and tempting. Each of the chief types of mental disorders has a characteristic distribution with reference to the differentiated areas found within the large modern city. There is a high degree of association between different types of psychoses as distributed in different urban areas and certain community conditions. It is pointed out that social conditions, while not primary in causation, may be underlying, predisposing, and precipitating factors. Situations involving stress and strain of adjustment may, in the cases of persons constitutionally predisposed, cause mental conflict and breakdown. If social conditions are actually precipitating factors in causing mental illness, then control of conditions making for stress in society will become a chief objective of a preventive program. The study of Faris and Dunham was the first to indicate a relationship between community organization and mental health and to show that urban areas characterized by high rates of social disorganization are also those with high rates of mental disorganization. Finally, it appears that the effect of movement is important to the social and mental adjustment of the person, and precipitating factors in mental breakdown may be found in the difficulties of adjustment to a new situation. Similarly, Dubos (1968) points out that the amount of physical and mental disease during the first phase of the Industrial Revolution had several different causes, one of the most important being the fact that large numbers of people from nonurban areas migrated within a few decades to urban centers. These persons had to make the necessary physiological and emotional adaptations to the new environment.

Our public concern for health, including mental health, has been mainly with frank, overt disease. Since World War II, there has been an increasing understanding of tensions and social stress, enabling workers in mental health to increase their viewpoints and to include these largely psychologically determined disturbances within their area of interest. The solution of such problems requires the skills of many professions and governmental action nationally and internationally (Soddy and Ahrenfeldt, 1965).

Selection in a Changing World

The concentration of urban life is evidenced by the fact that approximately 70 percent of our population is crowding into urban areas which represent 10 percent of the land in the United States. There are presently about 140 million people living on 35 thousand square miles. The evidence reviewed thus far can be reasonably assumed to form the basis for predicting that there will be little or no change in the trend of increasing urbanization. This sequence imposes on man the necessity of ultimately adapting to an environment almost wholly alien to any present today. While our current cities may be no more densely populated than some urban centers have been for centuries, they are infinitely larger and rapidly threaten the existence of all open space. Voluntary population control seems quite unlikely. As long as space and food exist anywhere, it seems reasonable to assume that urbanization will continue until mankind is spread densely over the face of the earth. The luxury of open space appears already threatened and the concept of "getting away from it all" a vanishing one. By 1980, to keep up with today's ratios of people to public space, we will need 49 million acres of national parks, monuments, and recreation areas instead of our present 25 million, and we will require 57 million acres of national forests and 28 million acres of state parks (Task Force or Environmental Health and Related Problems, 1967). It is difficult to speculate what such needs will be in the year 2000, or if at that time it will even be legitimate to consider them as needs.

Dubos (1968) has pointed out that the effects of crowding, safe limits so to speak, cannot be estimated simply from the levels of population density. The populations of Hong Kong and Holland, for example, are among the most crowded on earth, and yet the inhabitants enjoy good physical and mental health. Centuries of crowding have resulted in patterns of human relationships minimizing social conflicts.

The cultural evolution of man from the Neolithic to modern times has taken place without visible biological evolution (Stebbins, 1952). Mayr (1963) points out that Cro-Magnon man differed physically from modern man no more than do the present members of various races one from the other. Crow (1966) views human evolutionary changes as being of such long-term nature as to be considerably less urgent than the problems of increasing population and its relation to natural resources and the quality of life.

Nonetheless, natural selection is important for modern man because it will result in populations of those human beings for whom survival is possible in a uniformly and densely populated world. It is difficult to imagine that time will allow for any considerable shift in man's present genetic makeup, but rather that within the confines of that limitation he must demonstrate the adaptability necessary for continued existence. Such adaptability will necessarily need to be sufficiently flexible to allow for the disappearance of what we now consider basic freedoms and for the increasing regimentation that seems a certain concomitant of future life on earth.

Summary

I would like to summarize by saying that I am optimistic that modern technology can exercise some considerable control over environmental pollution, and that the current ecological crisis in the world makes it seem certain that some progress, perhaps a goodly amount, will be made. I believe that there is less possibility that current trends in the growth of human populations can be changed for a long period of time. Alterations in these trends require changes in the social and cultural fabric of man and society that are linear in nature, while the growth of population numbers is exponential. Family planning is a start, but it must be followed promptly by other programs much more decisive in character. The United States should take the immediate initiative by abolishing all polices promoting population growth and should use its vast economic and intellectual resources to aid in suitable programs elsewhere. Following our earlier and continuing largess in supplying food and medical services abroad, such accompanying programs of aid in population control would seem to constitute a moral responsibility of considerable magnitude.

In the United States efforts must be made to de-emphasize the trend toward huge urban concentrations, to strive for better planned communities, and thus to alleviate simultaneously the problems of pollution and create greater environmental diversification. Predictive technology must be radically increased, and the liberation of substances into the environment curtailed to allow for *at least* a preliminary assessment of effects.

We are presently unable to adequately evaluate those factors influencing mental hygiene in populations and thus to know what the effects of crowding will be on future generations. However, I think it highly unlikely that those people will either think or react as most of us do today. The prospects for continued life as we presently know it seem to me rather remote. Haldane remarked that the society, which enjoys the greatest amount of liberty is the one in which the greatest number of human genotypes can express their peculiar abilities. I am apprehensive as to what these genotypes might be, and in what kind of society they will appear, because the complex environment in which man evolved as the most complex biological species is rapidly disappearing. We must realistically face up to the fact that our biological inheritance, in its currently recognizable form, is not going to persist. I agree that to live is to experience, and that to live well we must maintain ecological diversity, a full range of environmental options so to speak, to insure that a wide range of possibilities exist among men (Ripley, 1968). Nonetheless, a full range of environmental options is different things to different people, and survival in a world restricted in options, of a sort alien to me, brazenly confronts mankind.

References

Berelson, Bernard, 1969. Beyond Family Planning. *Science*, 163: 533-543.

Bodian, David, and Dorothy M. Horstmann. 1965. Polioviruses. In: *Viral and Rickettsial Infections of Man*, 4th ed., Frank L. Horsfall, Jr., and Igor Tamm (eds.). J.P. Lippencott Co., Philadelphia.

Crow, James F. 1966. The Quality of People: Human Evolutionary Changes. *BioScience*, 16: 863-867.

Daddario, Emilio Q. 1968. A Silver Lining in the Cloud of Pollution. *Med. Opinion and Res*, 4: 19-25.

Davis, Kingsley. 1967. Population Policy: Will Current Programs Succeed? Science, 158: 730-739.

Dubos, Rene. 1965. *Man Adapting*. Yale University Press, New Haven.

Dubos, Rene. 1968. The Human Environment in Technological Societies. *Rockefeller Univ. Rev.* July-August.

Eddy, B.E. 1962. Tumors Produced in Hamsters by SV40. *Fed. Proc.*, 21: 930-935.

Ehrlich, Paul R. 1968. *The Population Bomb*. Ballantine Books, Inc., New York.

Faris, Robert E.L., and H. Warren Dunham. 1939. *Mental Disorders in Urban Areas*. University of Chicago Press, Chicago.

Mayr, Ernst. 1963. *Animal Species and Evolution*. Harvard University Press, Cambridge.

McElroy, William D. 1969. Biomedical Aspects of Population Control. *BioScience*, 19: 19-23.

Ripley, S.D. 1968. Statement in Joint House-Senate Colloquium to Discuss a National Policy for the Environment. Hearing before the Committee on Interior and Insular Affairs, United States Senate and the Committee on Science and Astronautics, U.S. House of Representatives, 90th Congress, 2nd Session, 17 July 1968, No. 8, p. 209-215.

Shah, Keerti V. 1969. Investigation of Human Malignant Tumors in India for Simian Virus 40 Etiology. *J. Nat. Cancer Inst.*, 42: 139-145.

Shein, H.M., and J.F. Enders. 1962. Transformation Induced by Simian Virus 40 in Human Renal Cell Cultures. I. Morphology and Growth Characteristics. *Proc. Nat. Acad. Sci.*, 48: 1164-1172.

Soddy, Kenneth, and Robert H. Ahrenfeldt (eds.). 1965. *Mental Health in a Changing World*. Vol. 1 of a report of an international and interprofessional study group convened by the World Federation for Mental Health. J.P. Lippincott Co., Philadelphia.

Stebbins, George L., Jr. 1952. Organic Evolution and Social Evolution. *Idea Exp.*, 11: 3-7.

Sweet, B.H., and M.R. Hilleman. 1960. The Vacuolating Virus, SV40. *Proc. Soc. Exp. Biol. Med.*, 105: 420-427.

Taylor, Howard C., Jr., and Bernard Berelson. 1968. Maternity Care and Family Planning As a World Problem. *Amer. J. Obstet.* Gynecol., 100: 885.

The Task Force on Environmental Health and Related Problems. A Report to the Secretary of Health, Education, and Welfare. 1967. U.S. Govt. Printing Office, Wash., D.C.

THE
RELATIONSHIP
BETWEEN
POPULATION
AND
ENVIRONMENT:
A DEBATE

INTRODUCTION

One of the best ways to identify the issues involved in any controversial topic is to listen to the advocates of conflicting positions debate with each other. Not only does each one advance his arguments in a disciplined way, but his opponent has an opportunity to question and attack them. Especially if the debate takes place before an informed audience, the observer can be reasonably confident about the evidence being assembled and measured, even if the adversaries disagree.

Thus, persons interested in the relationship between population growth and environmental problems are served well by the confrontation between two distinguished biological scientists, Barry Commoner and Paul Ehrlich, who assess the effects of population growth upon the environment in quite different ways. To oversimplify their positions greatly, Ehrlich and his colleague, John Holdren, see population growth as the core of the environmental problem, while Commoner argues that the contribution of population is greatly exaggerated and the real culprits are new patterns of technology.

The debate is written, rather than oral, but it takes place before an informed audience: the American scientific community. The articles selected to represent the two positions are drawn from *Science, Environment* and *Science and Public Affairs* (formerly the *Bulletin of the Atomic Scientists*). All are journals that are well-respected by scientists who, as readers, can be expected to assess the arguments with care. This is not a small point. By moving the debate into an arena where reason is usually more important than emotion, the presentations change in their tone and precision. Compare, for example, Ehrlich's article in the first section of this book, reprinted from *Ramparts*, and the selections that appear here. While the message is no less distressing in a nation where population continues to grow, it is more disciplined and better buttressed by evidence.

The articles are presented in sets. The first two represent a preliminary bout as Ehrlich and Holdren attack the notion that population growth is only a minor contributor to environmental difficulties and cite Commoner and Ansley Coale (in an article that appears in Part III) as persons who advance such "misconceptions." The article goes on to develop five theorems which deserve consideration both as statements of Ehrlich and Holdren's views and their conceptualization of population and environmental issues. Commoner, with Michael Corr and Paul Stamler, offer a different perspective as they explore causes of pollution and attempt to assign quantitative values to three factors: population growth, increase in affluence, and the effects of technology.

But the main event follows. In three selections, Commoner and Ehrlich clash in an unprecedented way. The immediate concern in Commoner's book, *The Closing Circle* (Knopf, 1971). The first article is a review of this book by Ehrlich and Holdren. This is followed by a lengthy, point-by-point response by Commoner to their criticisms which, in turn, is followed by a reply from Ehrlich and Holdren. We have made no attempt to summarize the arguments or pass editorial judgements other than to note that the conflicting views are encapsuled in the titles applied to the exchange in the two journals in which it has been published: "One-Dimensional Ecology" (*Science and Public Affairs*) and "Boardroom *vs.* Bedroom" (*Environment*).

The fact that the exchange has appeared in two places prior to its inclusion in this collection deserves careful attention. The selections here have been reprinted from *Science and Public Affairs*. But they also appear in *Environment*, a journal published the Committee for Environmental Information in which Commoner is a prominent figure. Apparently, the review of *The Closing Circle* was written for *Science and Public Affairs*, but the editor of that publication asked Commoner for his response to Ehrlich and Holdren's review and, through a complicated series of events, both the review and response appeared in *Environment* several weeks prior to its publication in *Science and Public Affairs* — much to the surprise and distress of that journal's editor and Ehrlich and Holdren. (See "Letters to Editor," *Science and Public Affairs*, XXVIII, June, 1972, p. 6). Professional niceties aside, the "pirating" of the manuscript, as alleged by Ehrlich and Holdren, reflects the acrimony between them and Commoner. It has become a matter of some concern and needs to be noted as background to reading the exchange that is reprinted here. The editor of *Science News*, Kendrick Frazier, has put it well:

> A personal dispute between two scientists is in itself of little consequence to the outside world. This one, however, is over important issues, and Ehrlich's and Commoner's steadfast adherence to their opposing points of view at the expense of any more moderate melding of the two seems likely to threaten the cause of a better environment that they and most other responsible persons espouse.

In addition to this quotation in *Science News*, 102 (August 12, 1972), p. 99, the clash between the two men is also the subject of a lengthy news article in *Science* (177, July 21, 1972, pp. 245-247) which merits reading. The selections here provide the reader with an unique opportunity to acquire important insights between population growth and environmental difficulties.

After the struggle between Ehrlich and Commoner, the final article by Garrett Hardin is almost anticlimatic. But Hardin is an important figure in the population/environment debate in his own right and his often-cited article, "Tragedy of the Commons," appears later in this book. Hardin is clearly identified with the position that Ehrlich and Holdren take and his view of the debate might also be contested. But with it, we move to other concerns although echoes of the arguments advanced here will continue. After reading the articles in this section, one cannot help but welcome the relative calm with which the remaining authors approach their task. Yet the ideas from these articles can be placed on the framework for discussion that Commoner, Ehrlich, and the others have erected.

IMPACT
OF POPULATION GROWTH

Paul R. Ehrlich

John P. Holdren

The interlocking crises in population resources, and environment have been the focus of countless papers, dozens of prestigious symposia, and a growing avalanche of books. In this wealth of material, several questionable assertions have been appearing with increasing frequency. Perhaps the most serious of these is the notion that the size and growth rate of the U.S. population are only minor contributors to this country's adverse impact on local and global environments (1, 2). We propose to deal with this and several related misconceptions here, before persistent and unrebuted repetition entrenches them in the public mind — if not the scientific literature. Our discussion centers around five theorems which we believe are demonstrably true and which provide a framework for realistic analysis:

1. Population growth causes a *disproportionate* negative impact on the environment.

2. Problems of population size and growth, resource utilization and depletion, and environmental deterioration must be considered jointly and on a global basis. In this context, population control is obviously not a panacea — it is necessary but not alone sufficient to see us through the crisis.

3. Population density is a poor measure of population pressure, and redistributing population would be a dangerous pseudosolution to the population problem.

4. Environment must be broadly construed to include such things as the physical environment of urban ghettos, the human behavioral environment, and the epidemiological environment.

5. Theoretical solutions to our problems are often not operational and sometimes are not solutions.

We now examine these theorems in some detail.

Population Size and Per Capita Impact

In an agricultural or technological society, each human individual has a negative impact on his environment. He is responsible for some of the simplification (and resulting destabilization) of ecological systems which results from the practice of agriculture (3). He also participates in the utilization of renewable and nonrenewable resources. The total negative impact of such a society on the environment can be expressed in the simplest terms, by the relation

$$I \text{ equals } P \cdot F$$

where P is the population, and F is a function which measures the per capita impact. A great deal of complexity is subsumed in this simple relation, however. For example, F increases with per capita consumption if technology is held constant, but may decrease in some cases if more benign technologies are introduced in the provision of a constant level of consumption. (We shall see in connection with theorem 5 that there are limits to the improvements one should anticipate from such "technological fixes.")

Pitfalls abound in the interpretation of manifest increases in the total impact I. For instance, it is easy to mistake changes in the composition of resource demand or environmental impact for absolute per capita increases, and thus to underestimate the role of the population multiplier. Moreover, it is often assumed that population size and per capita impact are independent variables, when in fact they are not. Consider, for example, the recent article by Coale (1), in which he disparages the role of U.S. population growth in environmental problems by noting that since 1940 "population has increased by 50 percent, but per capita use of electricity has been multiplied several times." This argument contains both the fallacies to which we have just referred.

First, a closer examination of very rapid increases in many kinds of consumption shows that these changes reflect a shift among alternatives within a larger (and much more slowly growing) category. Thus the 760 percent increase in electricity consumption from 1940 to 1969 (4) occurred in large part because the electrical *component* of the energy budget was (and is) increasing much faster than the budget itself. (Electricity comprised 12 percent of the U.S. energy consumption in 1940 versus 22 percent today.) The total energy use, a more important figure than it's electrical component in terms of resources and the environment, increased much less dramatically — 140 percent from 1940 to 1969. Under the simplest assumption (that is, that a given increase in population size accounts for an exactly proportional increase in consumption), this would mean that 38 percent of the increase in energy use during this period is explained by population growth (the actual population increase from 1940 to 1969 was 53 percent). Similar considerations reveal the imprudence of citing, say, aluminum consumption to show that population growth is an "unimportant" factor in resource use. Certainly, aluminum consumption has swelled by over 1400 percent since 1940, but much of the increase has been due to the substitution of aluminum for steel in many applications. Thus a fairer measure is combined consumption of aluminum and steel, which has risen only 117 percent since 1940. Again, under the simplest assumption, population growth accounts for 45 percent of the increase

The "simplest assumption" is not valid, however, and this is the second flaw in Coale's example (and in his thesis). In short, he has failed to recognize that per capita consumption of energy and resources, and the associated per capita impact on the environment are themselves functions of the population size. Our previous equation is more accurately written:

$$I \text{ equals } P \cdot F(P)$$

displaying the fact that impact can increase faster than linearly with population. Of course, whether F (P) is an increasing or decreasing function of P depends in part on whether diminishing returns or economics of scale are dominant in the activities of importance. In populous, industrial nations such as the United States, most economies of scale are already being exploited: we are on the diminishing returns part of most of the important curves.

As one example of diminishing returns, consider the problem of providing nonrenewable resources such as minerals and fossil fuels to a growing population, even at fixed levels of per capita consumption. As the richest supplies of these resources and those nearest to centers of use are consumed, we are obliged to use lower-grade ores, drill deeper, and extend our supply networks. All these activities increase our per capita use of energy and our per capita impact on the environment. In the case of partly renewable resources such as water (which is effectively nonrenewable when groundwater supplies are mined at rates far exceeding natural recharge), per capita costs and environmental impact escalate dramtically when the human population demands more than is locally available. Here the loss of freeflowing rivers and other economic, esthetic, and ecological costs of massive water-movement projects represent increased per capita diseconomies directly stimulated by population growth.

Diminishing returns are also operative in increasing food production to meet the needs of growing populations. Typically, attempts are made both to overproduce on land already farmed and to extend agriculture to marginal land. The former requires disproportionate energy use in obtaining and distributing water, fertilizer, and pesticides. The latter also increases per capita energy use, since the amount of energy invested per unit yield increases as less desirable land is cultivated. Similarly, as the richest fisheries stocks are depleted, the yield per unit effort drops,and more and more energy per capita is required to maintain the supply (5). Once a stock is depleted it may not recover — it may be nonrenewable.

Population size influences per capita impact in ways other than diminishing returns. As one example, consider the oversimplified but instructive situation in which each person in the population has links with every other person — roads, telephone lines, and so forth. These links involve energy and materials in their construction and use. Since the number of links increases much more rapidly than the number of people (6), so does the per capita consumption associated with the links.

Other factors may cause much steeper positive slopes in the per capita impact function, F (P). One such phenomenon is the *threshold effect.* Below a certain level of pollution trees will survive in smog. But, at some point, when a small increment in population produces a small increment in smog, living trees become dead trees. Five hundred people may be able to live around a lake and dump their raw sewage into the lake, and the natural systems of the lake will be able to break down the sewage and keep the lake from undergoing rapid ecological change. Five hundred and five people may overload the system and result in a "polluted" or eutrophic lake. Another phenomenon capable of causing near-discontinuities is the *synergism.* For instance, as cities push out into farmland, air pollution increasingly becomes a mixture of agricultural chemicals with power plant and automobile effluents.Sulfer dioxide from the city paralyzes the cleaning mechansims of the lungs; thus increasing the residence time of potential carcinogens in the agricultural chemicals. The joint effect may be much more than the sum of the individual effects. Investigation of synergistic effects is one of the most neglected areas of environmental evaluation.

Not only is there a connection between population size and per capita damage to the environment, but the cost of maintaining environmental quality at a given level escalates disproportionately as population size increases. This effect occurs in part because costs increase very rapidly as one tries to reduce contaminants per unit volume of effluent to lower and lower levels (diminishing returns again!). Consider municipal sewage, for example. The cost of removing 80 to 90 percent of the biochemical and chemical oxygen demand, 90 percent of the suspended solids, and 60 percent of the resistant organic material by means of secondary treatment is about 8 cents per 1000 gallons (3785 liters) in a large plant (7). But if the volume of sewage is such that its nutrient content creates a serious eutrophication problem (as is the case in the United States today), or if supply considerations dictate the reuse of sewage water for industry, agriculture, or groundwater recharge, advanced treatment is necessary. The cost ranges from two to four times as much as for secondary treatment (17 cents per 1000 gallons for carbon absorption; 34 cents per 1000 gallons for disinfection to yield a potable supply). This dramatic example of diminishing returns in pollution control could be repeated for stack gases, automobile exhausts, and so forth.

Now consider a situation in which the limited capacity of the environment to absorb abuse requires that we hold man's impact in some sector constant as population doubles. This means *per capita effectiveness* of pollution control in this sector must double (that is, effluent per person must be halved). In a typical situation, this would yield doubled per capita costs, or quadrupled total costs (and probably energy consumption) in this sector for a doubling of population. Of course, diminishing returns and threshold effects may be still more serious; we may easily have an eightfold increase in control costs for a doubling of population. Such arguments leave little ground for the assumption, popularized by Barry Commoner (2. 8) and others, that a 1 percent rate of population growth spawns only 1 percent effects.

It is to be emphasized that the possible existence of "economics of scale" does not invalidate these arguments. Such savings, if available at all, would apply in the case of our sewage example to a change in the amount of effluent to be handled at an installation of a given type. For most technologies, the United States is already more than populous enough to achieve such economies and is doing so. They are accounted for in our example by citing figures for the largest treatment plants of each type. Population growth, on the other hand, forces us into quantitative *and* qualitative changes in how we handle each unit volume of effluent — what fraction and what kinds of material we remove. Here economies of scale do not apply at all, and diminishing returns are the rule.

Global Context

We will not deal in detail with the best example of the global nature and interconnections of population resources and environmental problems — namely, the problems involved in feeding a world in which 10 to 20 million people starve to death annually, (9), and in which the population is growing by some 70 million people per year. The ecological problems created by high-yield agriculture are awesome (3, 10) and are bound to have a negative feedback on food production. Indeed, the Food and Agriculture Organization of the United Nations has reported that in 1969 the world suffered its first absolute decline in fisheries yield since 1950. It seems likely that part of this decline is attributable to pollution originating in terrestial agriculture.

A second source of the fisheries decline is, of course, overexploitation of fisheries by the developed countries. This problem, in turn, is illustrative of the situation in regard to many other resources, where similarly rapacious and shortsighted behavior by the developed nations is compromising the aspirations of the bulk of humanity to a decent existence. It is now becoming more widely comprehended that the United States alone accounts for perhaps 30 percent of the nonrenewable resources consumed in the world each year (for example, 37 percent of the energy, 25 percent of the steel, 28 percent of the tin, and 33 percent of the synthetic rubber) (11). This behavior is in large part inconsistent with American rhetoric about "developing" the countries of the Third World. We may be able to afford the technology to mine lower grade deposits when we have squandered the world's rich ores, but the underdeveloped countries, as their needs grow and their means remain meager, will not be able to do so. Some observers argue that the poor countries are today economically dependent on our use of their resources, and indeed that economists in these countries complain that world demand for their raw materials is too low (1). This proves only that their economists are as shortsighted as ours.

It is abundantly clear that the entire context in which we view the world resource pool and the relationships between developed and underdeveloped countries must be changed, if we are to have any hope of achieving a stable and prosperous existence for all human beings. It cannot be stated too forcefully that the developed countries (or, more accurately, the overdeveloped countries) are the principal culprits in the consumption and dispersion of the world's nonrenewable resources (12) as well as in appropriating much more than their share of the world's protein. Because of the consumption, and because of the enormous negative impact on the global environment accompanying it, the population growth in these countries must be regarded as the most serious in the world today.

In relation to theorem 2, we must emphasize that, even if population growth were halted, the present population of the world could easily destroy civilization as we know it. There is a wide choice of weapons—from unstable plant monocultures and agricultural hazes to DDT, mercury, and thermonuclear bombs. If population size were reduced and per capita consumption remained the same (or increased). we would still quickly run out of vital, high-grade resources or generate conflicts over diminishing supplies. Racism, economic exploitation, and war will not be eliminated by population control (of course, they are unlikely to be eliminated without it).

Population Density and Distribution

Theorem 3 deals with a problem related to the inequitable utilization of world resources. One of the commonest errors made by the uninitiated is to assume that population density (people per square mile) is the critical measure of overpopulation or underpopulation. For instance, Wattenberg states that the United States is not very crowded by "international standards" because Holland has 18 times the population density (13). We call this notion "the Netherlands fallacy." The Netherlands actually requires large chunks of the earth's resources and vast areas of land not within its borders to maintain itself. For example, it is the second largest per capita importer of protein in the world, and it imports 63 percent of its cereals, including 100 percent of its corn and rice. It also imports all of its cotton, 77 percent of its wool, and all of its iron ore, antimony, bauxite, chromium, copper, gold, lead, magnesite, manganese, mercury, molybdenum, nickel, silver, tin, tungsten, vanadium, zinc, phosphate rock (fertilizer), potash (fertilizer), asbestos, and diamonds. It produces energy equivalent to some 20 million metric tons of coal and consumes the equivalent of over 47 million metric tons (14).

A certain preoccupation with density as a useful measure of overpopulation is apparent in the article by Coale (1). He points to the existence of urban problems such as smog in Sydney, Australia, "even though the total population of Australia is about 12 million in an area 80 percent as big as the United States," as evidence that environmental problems are unrelated to population size. His argument would be more persuasive if problems of population *distribution* were the only ones with environmental consequences, and if population distribution were unrelated to resource distribution, and population size. Actually, since the carrying capacity of the Australian continent is far below that of the United States, one would *expect* distribution problems — of which Sydney's smog is one symptom — to be encountered at a much lower total population there. Resources, such as water, are in very short supply, and people cluster where resources are available. (Evidently, it cannot be emphasized enough that carrying capacity includes the availability of a wide variety of resources in addition to space itself, and that population pressure is measured relative to the carrying capacity. One would expect water, soils, or the ability of the environment to absorb wastes to be the limiting resource in far more instances than land area.)

In addition, of course, many of the most serious environmental problems are essentially independent of the way in which population is distributed. These include the global problems of weather modification by carbon dioxide and particulate pollution, and the threats to the biosphere posed by man's massive inputs of pesticides, heavy metals, and oil (15). Similarly, the problems of resource depletion and ecosystem simplification by agriculture depend on how many people there are and their patterns of consumption, but not in any major way on how they are distributed.

Naturally, we do not dispute that smog and most other familiar urban ills are serious problems, or that they are related to population distribution. Like many of the difficulties we face, these problems will not be cured simply by stopping population growth; direct and well-conceived assaults on the problems themselves will also be required. Such measures may occasionally include the redistribution of population, but the considerable difficulties and costs of this approach should not be underestimated. People live where they do not because of a perverse intention to add to the problems of their society but for reasons of economic necessity, convenience, and desire for agreeable surroundings. Areas that are uninhabited or sparsely populated today are presumably that way because they are deficient in some of the requisite factors. In many cases, the remedy for such deficiencies — for example, the provision of water and power to the wastelands of central Nevada—would be extraordinarily expensive in dollars, energy, and resources and would probably create environmental havoc. (Will we justify the rape of Canada's rivers to "colonize" more of our western deserts?).

Moving people to more "habitable" areas, such as the central valley of California or, indeed, most suburbs, exacerbates another serious problem — the paving-over of prime farmland. This is already so serious in California that, if current trends continue, about 50 percent of the best acreage in the nation's leading agricultural state will be destroyed by the year 2020 (16). Encouraging that trend hardly seems wise.

Whatever attempts may be made to solve distribution-related problems, they will be undermined if population growth continues, for two reasons. First, population growth and the aggravation of distribution problems are correlated — part of the increase will surely be absorbed in urban areas that can least afford the growth. Indeed, barring the unlikely prompt reversal of present trends, most of it will be absorbed there. Second, population growth puts a disproportionate drain on the very financial resources needed to combat its symptoms. Economist Joseph Spengler has estimated that 4 percent of national income goes to support our 1 percent rate of population growth in the United States (17). The 4 percent figure now amounts to about $30 billion per year. It seems safe to conclude that the faster we grow the less likely it is that we will find the funds either to alter population distribution patterns or to deal more comprehensively and realistically with our problems.

Meaning of Environment

Theorem 4 emphasizes the comprehensiveness of the environment crisis. All too many people think in terms of national parks and trout streams when they say "environment." For this reason many of the suppressed people of our nation consider ecology to be just one more "racist shuck" (18). They are apathetic or even hostile toward efforts to avert further environmental and sociological deterioration, because they have no reason to believe they will share the fruits of success (19). Slums, cockroaches, and rats are ecological problems, too. The correction of ghetto conditions in Detroit is neither more nor less important than saving the Great Lakes — both are imperative.

We must pay careful attention to sources of conflct both within the United States and between nations. Conflict within the United States blocks progress toward solving our problems; conflict among nations can easily "solve" them once and for all. Recent laboratory studies on human beings support the anecdotal evidence that crowding may increase aggressiveness in human males (20). These results underscore long-standing suspicions that population growth, translated through the inevitable uneven distribution into physical crowding, will tend to make the solution of all of our problems more difficult.

As a final example of the need to view "environment" broadly, note that human beings live in an epidemiological environment which deteriorates with crowding and malnutrition — both of which increase with population growth. The hazard posed by the prevalence of these conditions in the world today is compounded by man's unprecedented mobility; potential carriers of diseases of every description move routinely and in substantial numbers from continent to continent in a matter of hours. Nor is there any reason to believe that modern medicine has made widespread plague impossible (21). The Asian influenza epidemic of 1968 killed relatively few people only because the virus happened to be nonfatal to people in otherwise good health, not because of public health measures. Far deadlier virsues, which easily could be scourges without precedent in the population at large, have on more than one occasion been confined to research workers largely by good luck, for example, the Marburgvirus incident of 1967 (22) and the Lassa fever incident of 1970 (21, 23).

Solutions: Theoretical and Practical

Theorem 5 states that theoretical solutions to our problems are often not operational, and sometimes are not solutions. In terms of the problem of feeding the world, for example, technological fixes suffer from limitations in scale, lead time, and cost (24). Thus potentially attractive theoretical approaches — such as desalting seawater for agriculture, new irrigation systems, high-protein diet supplements — prove inadequate in practice. They are too little, too late, and too expensive, or they have sociological costs which hobble their effectiveness (25). Moreover, many aspects of our technological fixes, such as synthetic organic pesticides and inorganic nitrogen fertilizers, have created vast environmental problems which seem certain to erode global producitivity and ecosystem stability (26). This is not to say that important gains have not been made through the application of technology to agriculture in the poor countries, or that further technological advances are not worth seeking. But it must be stressed that even the most enlightened technology cannot relieve the **necessity of grappling forthrightly and promptly with population growth, as Norman Borlaug aptly observed on being notified of his Nobel Prize for the development of the new wheats. (27)).**

Technological attempts to ameliorate the environmental impact of population growth and rising per capita affluence in the developed countries suffer from practical limitations similar to those just mentioned. Not only do such measures tend to be slow, costly, and insufficient in scale, but in addition they most often *shift* our impact rather than remove it. For example, our first generation of smog-control devices increased emissions of oxides of nitrogen while reducing those of hydrocarbons and carbon monoxide. Our unhappiness about eutrophication has led to the replacement of phosphates in detergents with compounds like NTA — nitrilotriacetic acid — which has carcinogenic breakdown products and apparently enhances teratogenic effects of heavy metals (28). And our distaste for lung diseases apparently induced by sulfur dioxide inclines us to accept the hazards of radioactive waste disposal, fuel reprocessing, routine low-level emissions of radiation and an apparently small but finite risk of catastrophic accidents associated with nuclear fission power plants. Similarly, electric automobiles would simply shift part of the environmental burden of personal transportation from the vicinity of highways to the vicinity of power plants.

We are not suggesting here that electric cars, or nuclear power plants, or substitutes for phosphates are inherently bad. We argue rather that they, too, pose environmental costs which must be weighed against those they eliminate. In many cases the choice is not obvious, and in *all* cases there will be some environmental impact. The residual per capita impact after all the best choices have been made, must then be multiplied by the population engaging in the activity. If there are too many people, even the most wisely managed technology will not keep the environment from being overstressed.

In contending that a change in the way we use technology will invalidate these arguments, Commoner (2, 8) claims that our important environmental problems began in the 1940's with the introduction and rapid spread of certain "synthetic" technologies: pesticides and herbicides; inorganic fertilizers, plastics, nuclear energy, and high-compression gasoline engines. In so arguing, he appears to make two unfounded assumptions. The first is that man's pre-1940 environmental impact was innocuous and, without changes for the worse in technology, would have remained innocuous even in a much larger population size. The second assumption is that the advent of the new technologies was independent of the attempt to meet human needs and desires in a growing population. Actually, man's record as a simplifier of ecosystems and plunderer of resources can be traced from his probable role in the extinction of many Pleistocene mammals (29), through the destruction of the soils of Mesopotamia by salination and erosion, to the deforestation of Europe in the Middle Ages and the American dustbowls of the 1930's, to cite only some highlights. Man's contemporary arsenal of synthetic technological bludgeons indisputably magnifies the potential for disaster, but these were evolved in some measure to cope with population pressures, not independently of them. Moreover, it is worth noting that, of the four environmental threats viewed by the prestigious Williamstown study (15) as globally significant, three are associated with pre-1940 technologies which have simply increased in scale (heavy metals, oil in the seas, and carbon dioxide and particulates in the atmosphere, the latter probably due in considerable part to agriculture (30)). Surely, then, we can anticipate that supplying food, fiber, and metals for a population even larger than today's will have a profound (and destabilizing) effect on the global ecosystem under any set of technological assumptions.

Conclusion

John Platt has aptly described man's present predicament as "a storm of crisis problems" (31). Complacency concerning any component of these problems — sociological, technological, economic, ecological — is unjustified and counterproductive. It is time to admit that there are no monolithic solutions to the problems we face. Indeed, population control, the redirection of technology, the transition from open to closed resource cycles, the equitable distribution of opportunity and the ingredients of prosperity must *all* be accomplished if there is to be a future worth having. Failure in any of these areas will surely sabotage the entire enterprise.

In connection with the five theorems elaborated here, we have dealt at length with the notion that population growth in industrial nations such as the United States is a minor factor, safely ignored. Those who so argue often add that, anyway, population control would be the slowest to take effect of all possible attacks on our various problems, since the inertia in attitudes and in the age structure of the population is so considerable. To conclude that this means population control should be assigned low priority strikes us as curious logic. Precisely because population is the most difficult and slowest to yield among the components of environmental deterioration. we must start on it at once. To ignore population today because the problem is a tough one is to commit ourselves to even gloomier prospects 20 years hence, when most of the "easy" means to reduce per capita impact on the environment will have been exhausted. The desperate and repressive measures for population control which might be contemplated then are reason in themselves to proceed with foresight, alacrity, and compassion today.

References and Notes

(1) A. J. Coale. *Science* 170, 132 (1970).

(2) B. Commoner, *Saturday Review* 53, 50 (1970); *Humanist* 30, 10 (1970).

(3) For a general discussion, see P. R. Ehrlich and A. H. Ehrlich, *Population, Resources, Environment* (Freeman, San Francisco, 1970), Chap. 7. More technical treatments of the relationship between complexity and stability may be found in R.H. MacArthur, *Ecology* 36, 533 (1955); D.R. Margalef, *Gen. Syst.* 3, 3671 (1958); E. G. Leigh, Jr., *Proc. Nat. Acad. Sci. U.S.* 53, 777 (1965); and O. T. Loucks, "Evolution of diversity, efficiency, and stability of a community," paper delivered at AAAS meeting, Dallas, Texas, 30 Dec. 1968.

(4) The figures used in this paragraph are all based on data in *Statistical Abstract of the United States 1970* (U. S. Department of Commerce) (Government Printing Office, Washington, D.C., 1970).

(5) A dramatic example of this effect is given in R. Payne's analysis of the whale fisheries (*N.Y. Zool. Soc. Newsl.*, Nov. 1968). The graphs in Payne's paper are

reproduced in Ehrlich and Ehrlich (3).

(6) If N is the number of people, then the number of links is N(N-1)/2, and the number of links per capita is (N-1)/2.

(7) These figures and the others in this paragraph are from *Cleaning Our Environment: The Chemical Basis for Action* (American Chemical Society, Washington, D. C., 1969), pp. 95-162.

(8) In his unpublished testimony before the President's Commission on Population Growth and the American Future (17 Nov. 1970), Commoner acknowledged the operation of diminishing returns, threshold effects, and so on. Since such factors apparently do not account for *all* of the increases in per capita impact on the environment in recent decades, however, Commoner drew the unwarranted conclusion that they are negligible.

(9) R. Dumont and B. Rosier, *The Hungry Future* (Praeger, New York, 1969), pp. 34-35.

(10) L. Brown, *Sci. Amer.* 223, 160 (1970); P. R. Ehrlich, *War on Hunger* 4, 1 (1970).

(11) These figures are based on data from the *United Nations Statistical Yearbook 1969* (United Nations, New York, 1969), with estimates added for the consumption of Mainland China when none were included.

(12) The notion that dispersed resources, because they have not left the planet, are still available to us, and the hope that mineral supplies can be extended indefinitely by the application of vast amounts of energy to common rock have been the subject of lively debate elsewhere. See, for example, the articles by P. Cloud, T. Lovering, A. Weinberg, *Texas Quart.* 11, 103, 127, 90 (Summer, 1968); and *Resources and Man* (National Academy of Sciences) (Freeman, San Francisco, 1969). While the pessimists seem to have had the better of this argument, the entire matter is academic in the context of the rate problem we face in the next 30 years. Over that time period, at least, cost, lead time, and logistics will see to it that industrial economies and dreams of development stand or fall with the availability of high-grade resources.

(13) B. Wattenberg, *New Republic* 162, 18 (4 Apr. and 11 Apr. 1970).

(14) These figures are from (11), from the *FAO Trade Yearbook,* the *FAO Production Yearbook* (United Nations, New York, 1968), and from G. Borgstrom, *Too Many* (Collier-Macmillan, Toronto, Ont., 1969).

(15) *Man's Impact on the Global Environment, Report of the Study of Critical Environmental Problems* (M.I.T. Press, Cambridge, Mass., 1970).

(16) *A Model of Society, Progress Report of the Environmental Systems Group* (Univ. of California Institute of Ecology, Davis, April 1969).

(17) J. J. Spengler, in *Population: The Vital Revolution,* R. Freedman, Ed. (Doubleday, New York, 1964), p. 67.

(18) R. Chrisman, *Scanlan's* 1, 46 (August 1970).

(19) A more extensive discussion of this point is given in an article by P. R. Ehrlich and A. H. Ehrlich, in *Global Ecology: Readings Toward a Rational Strategy for Man,* J. P. Holdren and P. R. Ehrlich, Eds. (Harcourt, Brace, Jovanovich, New York).

(20) J. L. Freedman, A. Levy, J. Price, R. Welte, M. Katz, P. R. Ehrlich, in preparation.

(21) J. Lederberg, *Washington Post* (15 Mar. and 22 Mar. 1970).

(22) C. Smith, D. Simpson, E. Bowen, I. Zlotnik, *Lancet* 1967-II. 1119, 1128 (1967).

(23) Associated Press wire service, 2 Feb. 1970.

(24) P. R. Ehrlich and J. P. Holdren *BioScience* 19, 1065 (1969).

(25) See L.B. Brown (*Seeds of Change,* Praeger, New York, 1970) for a discussion of

unemployment problems exacerbated by the Green Revolution.

(26) G. Woodwell, *Science* 168, 429 (1970).

(27) *New York Times*, 22 Oct. 1970, p. 18; *Newsweek* 76, 50 (2 Nov. 1970).

(28) S. S. Epstein, *Environment* 12, No. 7, 2 (Sept. 1970); *New York Times* service, 17 Nov. 1970.

(29) G. S. Krantz, *Amer. Sci.* 58, 164 (Mar-Apr. 1970).

(30) R. A. Bryson and W. M. Wendland, in *Global Effects of Environmental Pollution*, S.F. Singer, Ed. (Springer-Verlag, New York, 1970).

(31) J. Platt, *Science* 166, 1115 (1969).

THE CAUSES
OF POLLUTION

Barry Commoner,
Michael Corr,
Paul J. Stamler

Until now most of us in the environmental movement have been chiefly concerned with providing the public with information that shows that there *is* an environmental crisis. In the last year or so, as the existence of the environmental crisis has become more widely recognized, it has become increasingly important to ask: How can we best solve the environmental crisis? To answer this question it is no longer sufficient to recognize only that the crisis exists; it becomes necessary, as well, to consider its causes, so that national cures can be designed.

Although environmental deterioration involves changes in natural, rather than man-made, realms — the air, water, and soil — it is clear that these changes are due to human action rather than to some natural cataclysm. The search for causes becomes focused, then, on the question: What actions of human society have given rise to environmental deterioration?

Like every living thing on the earth, human beings are part of an ecosystem — a series of interwoven, cyclical events, in which the life of any single organism becomes linked to the life processes of many others. One well-known property of such cyclical systems is that they readily break down if too heavily stressed. Such a stress may result if, for some reason, the population of any one living organism in the cycle becomes too great to be borne by the system as a whole. For example, suppose that in a wooded region the natural predators which attack deer are killed off. The deer population may then become so large that the animals strip the land of most of the available vegetation, reducing the subsequent growth to the point where it can no longer support the deer population; many deer die. Thus, in such a strictly biological situation, overpopulation is self-defeating. Or, looked at another way, the population is self-controlled, since its excessive growth automatically reduces the ability of the ecosystem to support it. In effect, environmental deterioration brought about by an excess in a population which the environment supports is the means of regulating the size of that population.

However, in the case of human beings, matters are very different; such automatic control is undesirable, and, in any case, usually impossible. Clearly, *if* reduced environmental quality were due to excess population, it might be advantageous to take steps to reduce the population size humanely rather than to expose human society to grave dangers, such as epidemics, that would surely accompany any "natural" reduction in population brought about by the environmental decline. Thus, if environmental deterioration were in fact the ecosystem's expected response to human overpopulation, then in order to cure the environmental crisis it would be necessary to relieve the causative stress — that is to *reduce* actively the population from its present level.

On these grounds it might be argued as well that the stress of a rising human population on the environment is especially intense in a country, such as the United States, which has an advanced technology. For it is modern technology which extends man's effects on the environment far beyond his biological requirements for air, food, and water. It is technology, which produces smog and smoke; synthetic pesticides, herbicides, detergents, and plastics; rising environmental concentrations of metals such as mercury and lead; radiation; heat; accumulating rubbish and junk. It can be argued that insofar as such technologies are intended to meet human needs — for food, clothing. shelter, transportation. and the amenities of life — the more people there are, and the more active they are, the more pollution.

Against this background it is easy to see why some observers have blamed the environmental crisis on overpopulation. Here are two typical statements:

> The pollution problem is a consequence of population. It did not much matter how a lonely American frontiersman disposed of his waste. "Flowing water purifies itself every ten miles," my grandfather used to say, and the myth was near enough to the truth when he was a boy, for there weren't too many people. But as population became denser the natural chemical and biological recycling processes became overloaded, calling for a redefinition of property rights. (1)

> The causal chain of the deterioration (of the environment) is easily followed to its source. Too many cars, too many factories, too much detergent, too much pesticide, multiplying contrails, inadequate sewage treatment plants, too little water, too much carbon dioxide—all can be traced easily to *too many people*.(2)

Some observers, for example M. P. Miller, chief of census population studies at the U.S. Bureau of the Census, believe that in the U.S. environmental deterioration is only partly due to increasing population, and blame most of the effect on "affluence." (3)

Finally, some of us place the strongest emphasis on the effects of the modern technology that so often violates the basic principles of ecology and generates intense stresses on the environment.

Dr. Paul Ehrlich provides the following statement regarding these several related factors: "Population can be said to be the result of multiplying three factors: population size, per capita consumption, and an 'Environmental impact' index that measures in part, how wisely we apply the technology that goes with consumption." (4) As indicated in the previous passage, Dr. Ehrlich appears to consider population size as the predominant factor in this relationship.

Dr. Ehrlich's statement can be paraphrased as an "equation":

population size		per capita consumption		environmental impact per unit of production		level of pollution.
	X		X		=	

This equation is self-evidently true, as it includes all the main factors and relationships which could possibly influence the environment. The product of population size and per capita consumption gives the total goods consumed; since imports, exports, and storage are relatively slight effects, total consumption can be taken to be approximately equal to total production. When the latter figure is multiplied by the environmental impact (i.e., amount of pollution per unit of production) the final result should be equal to the total environmental effect — the level of pollution.

Precisely because it is so inclusive, however, this equation does not advance our understanding of the causes of environmental problems. All human activities affect the environment to some degree. The equation states this formally, but we are still left with the problem of evaluting the extent to which different activities cause environmental problems, and the extent to which these environmental effects increase with population growth, with increasing per capita consumption, or with changing technologies. If we are to take effective action, we will need a more detailed guide than the equation offers. To begin with, we must know the relative importance of the three factors on the left side of the equation.

Two general approaches suggest themselves. One is to find appropriate numerical values for each of the four factors of the equation. Another way is to examine specific pollution problems and determine to what degree they are caused, explicitly, by a rising population, by increased prosperity, or by the increased environmental impact of new technologies. What follows is an effort to provide some preliminary data relevant to both of these approaches.

To begin with, it is necessary to define the scope of the problem, both in space and time. As to space, we shall restrict the discussion solely to the United States. This decision is based on several factors: (a) The necessary data are available — at least to us — only for the United States. (b) The pollution problem is most intense in a highly developed country such as the United States. (c) In any study involving the comparsion of statistical quantities, the more homogeneous the situation, the less likely we are to be misled by averages that combine vastly different situations. In this sense, it might be better to work with a smaller sample of the pollution problem — such as an urban region. Unfortunately, the necessary production statistics are not readily available except on a national scale.

As to time, we have chosen the period 1946-68. There are several reasons for this choice. First, many current environmental problems began with the end of World War II: photochemical smog, radiation from nuclear wastes, pollution from detergents, and synthetic pesticides. Another reason for choosing the post-war period is that many changes in production techniques were introduced during this period. The upper limit of the period is a matter of convenience only; statistical data for the two most recent years are often difficult to obtain.

We shall thus be seeking an answer to the following question for the period 1946-68 in the United States: What changes in the levels of specific polutants, in population size, in environmental impact per unit of production, and in the amounts of goods produced per capita have occurred?

Changes in Pollution and Population Levels

Curiously, the first of these questions is the most difficult to answer. Probably the best available data relate to water pollution. These are summarized in a study by Weinberger. For the United States as a whole, in the period of 1946-68 the total nitrogen and phosphate discharged into surface waters by municipal sewage increased by 260 percent and 500 percent respectively. (5)

Here are some additional data which, although sparse, are suggestive of the sizes of recent changes in pollution levels. As indicated by glacial deposits, airborne lead has increased by about 400 percent since 1946. (6) Daily nitrogen oxide emissions in Los Angeles County have increased about 530 percent.(6) The average algal population in Lake Erie — one response to, and indicator of, pollution due to nutrients such as nitrate and phosphate — increased about 220 percent. (7) The bacterial count in different sectors of New York harbor increased as much as 890 percent. (8) Such data correspond with general experience. For example, the extent of photochemical smog in the U.S. has surely increased at least ten-fold in the 1946-68 period, for in 1946 it was known only in Los Angeles; it has now been reported in every major city in the country, as well as in smaller areas such as Phoenix, Arizona and Las Vegas, Nevada.

Rough as it is, we can take as an estimate of the change in pollution levels in the United States during 1946-68 increases that range from two- to tenfold or so, or from 200 to 1,000 percent.

The increase in U.S. population for the period 1946-68 amounts to about 43 percent. (9) It would appear, then, that the rise in overall U.S. population is insufficient by itself to explain the large increases in overall pollution levels since 1946. This means that in Ehrlich's equation, the increase in population is too small to bring the left side to approximate equality with the right side unless there have been sufficiently large increases in the per capita production and environmental impact factors.

Combined Factors of Population and Production

The equation relates total pollution to three component factors: population size, production per capita, and environmental impact per unit of production. As a second step in evaluating the meaning of this approach, it is useful to determine whether the combined factors of population growth and increased per capita production can account for the changes in pollution levels during the period 1946-68.

A rough measure of overall U.S. production is the Gross National Product (GNP). Changes in GNP and in GNP per capita in 1946-68 are shown in Figure 1. GNP has increased about 126 percent in that time and GNP per capita has increased about 59 percent. (10) As a first approximation, then, it would appear that the overall increase in total production, as measured by GNP, is also insufficient to account for the considerably larger increases in pollution levels. However, since the GNP is, of course, an average composed of the many separate activities in the total production economy (including not only agricultural and industrial production and transportation, but also various services), a true picture of the relationship between production and environmental pollution requires a breakdown of the GNP into, at the least, some of its main components.

Under the auspices of the Committee on Environmental Alterations, of the American Association for the Advancement of Science (AAAS), we have begun to collect some of the relevant data for a joint AAAS-Scientists' Institute for Public Information study of the environmental effects of power production. Most of the required data are available from United States Statistical Abstracts and the Census of Manufacturing regarding year-by-year levels of production in different industrial, agricultural, and transportation activities. In order to facilitate

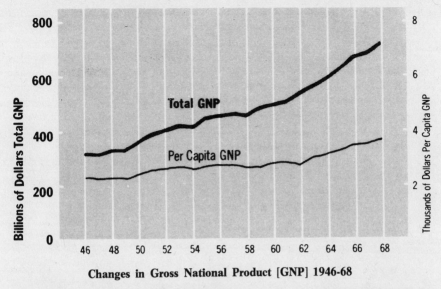

Changes in Gross National Product [GNP] 1946-68

FIGURE 1: The total value of all goods and services produced in the United States (Gross National Product, measured in constant — 1958 — dollars) is shown in the top curve. The Gross National Product divided by the total U.S. population at the time (GNP per capita) is shown in the bottom curve. the increase in per capita GNP can be taken as a rough measure of affluence.

comparisons we have adopted a standard way of plotting such data: curves are drawn for the period 1946-68 for total production, for production per capita, and production per unit GNP. These curves provide a picture of the trends in overall production, in "affluence" or "prosperity" (i.e., consumption or production per capita), and in the relative contribution made by the particular activity to the overall GNP. Some typical curves of this type are shown in Figure 2.

To obtain a preliminary picture of the results of all of the data of this type that are now available to us, we have prepared a tabular summary in Table 1. This table shows, for each of a series of activities, the percentage change in production or consumption per capita over a ten- to twenty-year period. (11)

It should be kept in mind that Table 1, lists *per capita* changes, so that *total* production figures may be derived by multiplying the listed value by 1.43 (to take into account the 43 percent increase in population in 1946-68). The value of zero for fish consumption per capita means that total fish consumption increased about 43 percent.

Several interesting relationships emerge from Table 1. One is that in many cases, the growth in utilization of a particular product is counterbalanced by the reduction in the use of a similar one, the total use of that class of material remaining constant. An example is fiber (or textile) consumption. Total per capita use of fibers of all types increased very slightly (6 percent). However, the major sources of fiber, cotton and wool, declined in per capita consumption by 33 percent and 61 percent respectively. The difference was made up by a very large increase — 1,792 percent — in wholly synthetic (noncellulosic) fibers. Thus, we

TABLE 1

Changes in Production or Consumption Per Capita

Item	Period	% Increase
Nonreturnable beer bottles	1946-69	3,778
Mercury for chlorine and sodium hydroxide products	1946-68	2,150
Noncellulosic synthetic fiber (consumption)	1950-68	1,792
Plastics	1946-68	1,024
Air freight — ton-miles	1950-68	593
Nitrogen fertilizer	1946-68	534
Synthetic organic chemicals	1946-68	495
Chlorine gas	1946-68	410
Aluminum	1946-68	317
Detergents	1952-68	300
Electric power	1946-68	276
Pesticides	1950-68	217
Total horsepower	1950-68	178
Wood pulp	1946-68	152
Motor vehicle registration	1946-68	110
Motor fuel (consumption)	1946-68	100
Cement	1946-68	74
Truck freight — ton-miles	1950-68	74
Total mercury (consumption)	1946-68	70
Cheese (consumption)	1946-68	58
Poultry (consumption)	1946-68	49
Steel	1946-68	39
Total freight — ton-miles	1950-68	28
Total fuel energy (consumption)	1946-68	25
Newspaper advertisements (space)	1950-68	22
Newsprint (consumption)	1950-68	19
Meat (consumption)	1946-68	19
New copper	1946-68	15
Newspaper news (space)	1950-68	10
All fibers (consumption)	1950-68	6
Beer (consumption)	1950-68	4
Fish (consumption)	1946-68	0
Hosiery	1946-68	−1
Returnable pop bottles	1946-69	−4
Calorie (consumption)	1946-68	−4
Protein (consumption)	1946-68	−5
Cellulosic synthetic fiber (consumption)	1950-68	−5
Railroad freight — ton-miles	1950-68	−7
Shoes	1946-68	−15
Egg (consumption)	1946-68	−15
Grain (consumption)	1946-68	−22
Lumber	1946-68	−23
Cotton fiber (consumption)	1950-68	−33
Milk and cream (consumption)	1946-68	−34
Butter (consumption)	1946-68	−47
Railroad horsepower	1950-68	−60
Wool fiber (consumption)	1950-68	−61
Returnable beer bottles	1946-69	−64
Saponifiable fat (for soap products)	1944-64	−71
Work animal horsepower	1950-68	−84

can find in Table 1 a series of pairs in which one item has substituted for another: nonreturnable beer bottles for returnable bottles; plastics for lumber; detergents for soap; truck and air freight for railroad freight; motor vehicles for work animals. Moreover, certain of the other indicated increases in per capita utilization are a result of such substitutions. Thus, mercury use increased partly because chlorine production increased; chlorine production has increased largely because it is heavily used to produce synthetic organic chemicals, which are in turn needed to produce plastics and synthetic fibers. Similarly, one reason for the increase in cement production is the substitution of truck traffic for rail traffic, which necessitates large-scale construction of highways. In the same way, one reason for increased electric power production is the increased production of chemicals, aluminum, and cement, all of which have high demands for power. As we shall see below, most of these changes turn out to be, in environmental terms, unfortunate.

Certain large and basic categories, the necessities of life — food, clothing, and shelter — merit special attention. Data for these categories can be used to determine the degree to which changes in affluence (consumption per capita) or prosperity (production per capita) can account for the large increases in pollution levels for the period 1946-68.

Food production and consumption figures are available from the U.S. Department of Agriculture. Surprisingly, for the period 1910 to 1968, there were very few overall changes in per capita consumption of food materials, especially in the period of interest to us. In 1946-68, total calories consumed dropped from about 3,390 per person per day to about 3,250 per person per day, while protein consumption declined slightly from 104 grams per person per day to about 99 grams per person per day. (12)

It should be remembered that these are *consumption* data, whereas the data of interest in connection with environmental stress are those for *total production* (the difference being represented by storage of farm products and the balance of exports and imports). The difference represents, for instance for the year 1968, no more than about 3 percent of the total value of farm production; (13) the consumption data consequently present a fairly accurate picture of farm production.

The total production figures do in fact reflect the trends evident in per capita consumption. Thus, total grain production, including grain used for meat production, decreased 6 percent in the 1946-68 period. The figures on declining protein intake tell us that increased meat consumption is more than balanced by declines in other types of protein intake, for instance of eggs, milk, and dry beans. Of course, the increased use of beef and other meat (about 19 percent per capita) does represent some increase in affluence. On the other hand, there has been a corresponding decline in another indicator of affluence, the use of fruit. Taking these various changes into account, then, there is no evidence of any significant change in the overall affluence of the average American with respect to food. And, in general, food production in the U.S. has just about kept up with the 43 percent increase in population in that time.

A similiar situation exists with respect to another life necessity — clothing. The following items show either no significant change in per capita production, or a slight decline: shoes, hosiery, shirts, total fibers (i.e. natural plus synthetic), and total fabric production. Again, as in the case of food, the "affluence" or "prosperity" factor in the equation is about 1, so that population increase by itself is not sufficient to explain the large increases in environmental pollution due to production of these items.

PLASTICS

Total Production

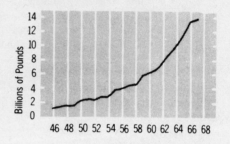

FIGURE 2: Examples of production statistics being collected by the Committee on Environmental Alterations, American Association for the Advancement of Science. Such statistics allow one to relate changes in different parts of the national economy to increased stresses on the environment. It can be seen that production of both steel and plastics is increasing rapidly, and that, in fact, both, are increasing more rapidly than the population (production per capita is rising). Production of steel per unit of the Gross National Product, however, is declining, which reflects the substitution of other metals and plastics for steel in such applications as packaging; plastic's share of the GNP, while still small, is clearly rising.

Total Production

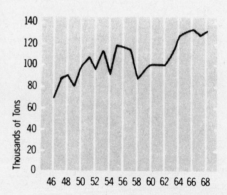

In the area of shelter, we find that housing units occupied in 1946 were 0.27 per capita, and in 1968, 0.30 per capita, an increase of 11 percent, although there was some improvement in the quality of units. (14) Again, this change, even with the concurrent 43 percent increase in population, is simply not enough to match the large increases in pollution levels.

Another set of statistics also allows us to arrive at an estimate of the "affluence" factor. These relate to average personal expenditures for food, clothing, and housing (including purchased food and meals, alcoholic beverages, tobacco, rents and mortgage payments, house repairs, wearing apparel, but excluding furniture, household utilities, and domestic service). Such expenditures, adjusted for inflation, increased, per capita, about 27 percent between 1950 and 1968. (15) Again, this increase when multiplied by the concurrent increase in population is insufficient to produce the large increases in pollution levels. It is important to note that these expenditures comprise a sector which represents about one-third of the total United States economy.

All this is evidence, then, that the increases in 1946-68 in two of the factors in Ehrlich's equation — population size and production (or consumption) per capita — are inadequate to account for the concurrent increases in pollution level. This leaves

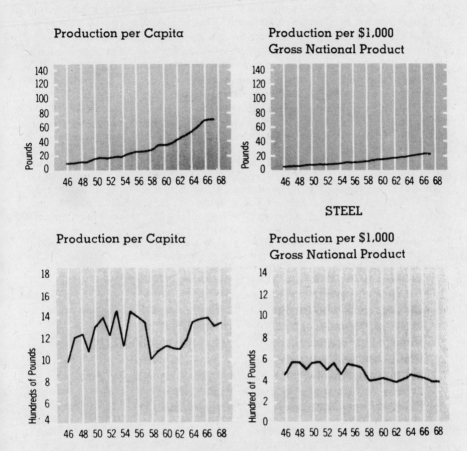

Production per Capita

Production per $1,000
Gross National Product

STEEL

Production per Capita

Production per $1,000
Gross National Product

us with the third factor: the nature of the technologies used to produce the various goods, and the impact of these technologies on the environment. We must look to this factor to find the sources of the large increases in pollution.

Environmental Impact

Reference to Table 1 enables us to single out the activities which have sharply increased in per capita production in the period 1946-68. They fall into the following general classes of production: synthetic organic chemicals and the products made from them, such as detergents, plastics, synthetic fibers, rubber, pesticides and herbicides; wood pulp and paper products; total production of energy, especially electric power; total horsepower of prime movers, especially petroleum-driven vehicles, cement, aluminum; mercury used for chlorine production; petroleum and petroleum products.

Several remarks about this group of activities are relevant to our problem. First is the fact that the increase in per capita production (and also in total production) in this group of activities is rather high — of the order of 100 to 1,000 percent. This fact, together with the data already presented, is a reminder that the changes in the U.S. production system during the period 1946-68 do not represent an across-the-board increase in affluence or prosperity. That is, the 59 percent increase in per capita GNP in that period obscures the fact that in certain important sectors — for example, those related to basic life necessities — there has been rather little change in production per capita, while in certain other areas of production the increases have been very much larger. The second relevant observation about this group of activities is that their magnitude of increased production per capita begins to approach that of the estimates of concurrent changes in pollution level.

These considerations suggest, as a first approximation, that this particular group of production activities may well be responsible for the observed major changes in pollution levels. This identification is, of course, only suggested by the above considerations as an hypothesis, and is by no means proven by them. However, the isolation of this group provides a valuable starting point for a more detailed examination of the nature of the production activities that comprise it, and of their *specific* relationship to environmental degradation. As we shall see in what follows, this more detailed investigation does, in fact, quite strongly support the hypothesis suggested by the more superficial examination.

Nearly all of the production activities that fall into the class exhibiting striking changes in per capita production turn out to be important causes of pollution. Thus wood pulp production and related paper-making activities are responsible for a very considerable part of the pollution of surface waters with organic wastes, sulphite, and, until several years ago, mercury. Vehicles driven by the internal combustion engine are responsible for a major part of total air pollution, especially in urban areas, and are almost solely responsible for photochemical smog. Much of the remaining air pollution is due to electric power generation, another member of this group. Cement production is a notorious producer of dust pollution and a high consumer of electrical energy. The hazardous effects of mercury released into the environment are just now, belatedly, being recognized.

The new technological changes in agriculture, while yielding no major increase in overall per capita food production, have in fact worsened environmental conditions. Food production in the United States in 1968 caused much more environmental pollution than it did in 1947. Consider, for example, the increased use of nitrogen fertilizer, which rose 534 percent per capita between 1946 and 1968. This striking increase in fertilizer use did not increase total food production, but improved the crop yield per acre (while acreage was reduced) and made up for the loss of nitrogen to the soil due to the increasing use of feedlots to raise animals (with resultant loss of manure to the soil). For reasons which have been described elsewhere, (16) this intensive use of nitrogen fertilizer on limited acreage drives nitrogen out of the soil and into surface waters, where it causes serious pollution problems. Thus, while Americans, on the average, eat about as much food per capita as they used to, it is now grown in ways that cause increased pollution. The new technologies, such as feedlots and fertilizer, have a much more serious effect on pollution than either increases in population or in affluence.

One segment of the group of increasing industrial activities in the period 1946-68, that comprising synthetic organic chemicals and their products, raises environmental problems of a particularly subtle, but nevertheless important, kind. In the first place, most of them find a place in the economy as substitute for — some might say, improvements over — older products of a natural, biological origin. Thus synthetic detergents replace soap, which is made from fat — a natural product of animals and plants. Synthetic fibers replace cotton, wool, silk, flax, hemp—all, again, natural products of animals and plants. Synthetic rubber replaces natural rubber. Plastics replace wood and paper products in packaging. In many but not all uses, plastics replace natural products such as wood and paper. Synthetic pesticides and herbicides replace the natural ecological processes which control pests and unwanted weeds. Both the natural products and their modern replacements are organic substances. In effect, we can regard the products of modern synthetic organic chemistry as man-made variations on a basic scheme of molecular structure which in nature is the exclusive province of living things.

Because they are not *identical* with the natural products which they resemble, these synthetic substances do not fit very well into the chemical schemes which comprise natural ecosystems. Some of the new substances, such as plastics. do not fit into natural biochemical systems at all. Thus, while "nature's plastic," cellulose, is readily degraded by soil microorganisms and thus becomes a source of nutrition for soil organisms, synthetic plastics are not degradable, and therefore accumulate as waste. Automatically they become environmental pollutants. Because there is no natural way to convert them into usuable materials, they either accumulate as junk or are disposed of by burning — which, of course, pollutes the air. Nondegradable synthetic detergents, with a branched molecular structure that is incompatible with the requirements of microorganisms which break down natural organic materials, remain in the water and become pollutants. Even degradable synthetic detergents, when broken down, may pollute water with phenol, and add another important water pollutant — phosphate — as well. Thus, these synthetic substitutes for natural products are, inevitably, polutants.

Because of the considerable similarity of the basic biochemical systems in all living things, an active, but synthetic, organic substance such as a pesticide or herbicide is bound to influence not only the insect or weed which it is supposed to control, but also, to some extent — and often in unanticipated ways — a wide range of other organisms that make up the ecosphere. Such substances are, in effect, drugs. When they are introduced in massive amounts into the environment they become a kind of ecological drug which may affect fish, birds, and man, in unwanted, and often harmful, ways.

The point to be emphasized here is that the modern replacements for natural products have become the basis for the new, expansive production activities derived from synthetic organic chemicals, and are, by their very nature, destined to become serious environmental pollutants if they are broadcast into the environment — as, of course, they are.

There is, however, another way in which synthetic organic materials are particularly important as sources of environmental pollution. This relates not to their use but to their production. Let us compare, for example, the implication for environmental pollution of the *production* of, say, a pound of cotton and a pound of a synthetic fiber such as nylon. Both of these materials consist of long molecular chains, or polymers, made by linking together a succession of small units, or monomers. The formation of a polymer from monomers requires energy, part of which is required to form the bond that links the successive monomers. This energy has to be, so to speak, built into the monomer molecules, so that it is available when the inter-monomer link is formed. Energy is required to collect together, through cracking and distillation, an assemblage of the particular monomer required for the synthetic process from a mixture such as petroleum. (That is, the process of obtaining a pure collection of the required monomer demands energy.) And it must be remembered that the energy requirement of a production process leads to important environmental consequences, for the combustion required to release energy from a fuel is always a considerable source of pollution.

If we examine cotton production according to these criteria, we find that it comes off with high marks, for relatively little energy capable of environmental pollution is involved. In the first place the energy required to link up the glucose monomers which make up the cotton polymer (cellulose) is built into these molecules from energy provided free in the form of the sunlight absorbed photosynthetically by the cotton plant. Energy derived from sunlight is transformed, by photosynthesis, into a biochemical form, which is then incorporated into glucose molecules in such a way as to provide the energy needed to link them together. At the same time photosynthetic energy synthesizes glucose from carbon dioxide and water. Moreover, glucose so heavily predominates as a major product of photosynthesis that the energy required to "collect" it in pure form is minimal — and of course is also obtained free, from sunlight. And in all these cases the energy is transferred at low temperatures (the cotton plant, after all, does not burn) so that extraneous chemical reactions such as

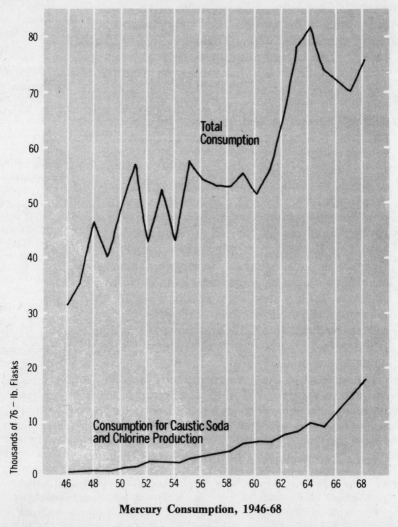

Mercury Consumption, 1946-68

FIGURE 3: Consumption of mercury has increased rapidly, despite occasional erratic fluctuations; the most rapidly growing component of this consumption is in caustic soda and chlorine production, which, although still a small portion of the total, accounts for much of the increase in consumption in recent years.

those which occur in high temperature combustion— and which are the source of air pollutant such as nitrogen oxides and sulfur dioxide — do not occur. In fact, the overall photosynthetic process takes carbon dioxide — an animal waste product, and a product of all combustion — out of the air.

Now compare this with the method for producing a synthetic fiber. The raw material for such production is usually petroleum or natural gass. Both of these represent stored forms of photosynthetic energy, just as does cellulose. However, unlike cellulose, these are nonrenewable resources in that they were produced during the early history of the earth in a never-to-be repeated period of very heavy plant growth. Moreover, in order to obtain the desired monomers from the mixture present in petroleum a series of high-temperature, energy-requiring processes, such as distillation and evaporation, must be used. All this means that the production of synthetic fiber consumes more nonrenewable energy than the production of a natural fiber such as cotton or wool. It also means that the energy-requiring processes involved in synthetic fiber production take place at high temperatures, which inevitably result in air pollution.

Similiar considerations hold for all of the synthetic materials which have replaced natural ones. Thus, the production of synthetic detergents, plastics, and artificial rubber inevitably involves, weight for weight, more environmental pollution than the production of soap, wood, or natural rubber. Of course, the balance sheet is not totally one-sided. For example, at least under present conditions, the production of cotton involves the use of pesticides and herbicides — environmental pollutants that are not needed to produce synthetic fibers. However, we know that the use of pesticides can be considerably reduced in growing a crop such as cotton — and, indeed, must be reduced if the insecticide is not to become useless through the development of insect resistance to the chemicals—by employing modern techniques of biological control. In the same way, it can be argued that wool production involves environmental hazards because sheep can overgraze in pasture and set off erosion. Again, this hazard is not an inevitable accompaniment of sheep-raising, but only evidence of poor ecological management. Similarly, pollution due to combustion could be curtailed and thus reduce the environmental impact of synthetics.

Obviously, much more detailed evaluations of this problem are needed. However, on the basis of these initial considerations it seems evident that the substitution of synthetic organic products for natural ones through the efforts of the modern chemical industry has, until now, considerably intensified environmental pollution.

Two other members of the group of production activities which have shown considerable growth per capita during the period 1946-68, like synthetic organic chemical products, add to pollution problems through their very production. One of these is aluminum, a metal which has increasingly replaced steel (in cans, for example). Aluminum is refined by passing an electric current through the molten ore, and it is therefore no surprise that the total energy required to produce a pound of aluminum (29,860 British thermal units, or BTUs) is about 6.5 times that required to produce a pound of steel (4,615 BTUs). (17) Taking into account that the weight of an aluminum can is less than that of a steel can of equal size, the power requirements are still in the ratio of more than 2 to 1. Of course, a total evaluation of the "pollution price tag" attached to each of these cans requires a full evaluation of the pollutants emitted by steel mills and aluminum refining plants. Nevertheless, with respect to one important part of the environmental cost — air pollution due to power production and fossil fuel consumption, the new product, aluminum, is a far greater environmental polluter than the old one, steel.

This brings us to a distinctive and especially important aspect of the environmentally related changes in production which have taken place in the 1946-68 period — electric power production. Electric power production has been noteworthy for its rapid and accelerating rate of growth. Total power production has increased by 662 percent in the period 1946-68; per capita power production has increased by 436 percent. (18) Electric power production from fossil fuels is a major cause of urban air pollution; produced by nuclear reactors it is a source of radioactive pollution. Regardless of the fuel employed, power production introduces heat into the environment, some of it in the form of waste heat released at the power plant into either cooling waters or the air. Ultimately all electric power, when used, is converted to heat, causing increasingly serious heat pollution problems in cities in the summer. One of the striking features of the present U.S. production system is its accelerating demand for more and more power — with the resultant exacerbation of pollution problems.

Affuence and Increased Production

What is striking in the data discussed above is that so many of the new and expanding production activities are highly power-consumptive and have replaced less power-consumptive activities. This is true of the synthetic chemical industry, of cement, and of the introduction of domestic electrical appliances.

It is useful to return at this point to the question of affluence. To what extent do these increased uses of electrical power, which surely contribute greatly to environmental deterioration, arise from the increased affluence, or well-being, of the American public? Certainly the introduction of an appliance such as a washing machine is, indeed, a valuable contribution to a family's well-being; a family with a washing machine is without question more affluent than a family without one. And, equally clear, this increased affluence adds to the total consumption of electric power and thereby adds to the burden of environmental pollutants. Such new uses of electricity therefore do support the view that affluence leads to pollution.

On the other hand, what is the contribution to public affluence of substituting a power-consumptive aluminum beer can for a less power-demanding steel can? After all, what contributes to human welfare is not the can, but the beer (it is interesting to note in passing that beer consumption per capita has remained essentially unchanged in the 1946-68 period). In this instance the extra power consumption due to the increased use of aluminum cans — and the resulting environmental pollution — cannot be charged to improved affluence. The same is true of the increased use of the nonreturnable bottle, which pollutes the environment during the production process (glass products require considerable fuel combustion) and pollutes it further when it is discarded after use. The extra power involved in producing aluminum beer cans, the extra power and other production costs involved in using nonreturnable bottles instead of reusable ones, contribute both to environmental pollution and the GNP. But they add nothing to the affluence or well-being of the people who use these products.

Thus, in evaluating the meaning of increased productive activity as it relates to the matters at issue here, a sharp distinction needs to be made between those activities which actually contribute to improved well-being and those which do not, or do so minimally (as does the self-opening aluminum beer can). Power production is an important area in which this distinction needs to be made. Thus, the chemical industry and the production of cement and aluminum, taken together, account for 18 percent of the present consumption of power in the United States. (19) For reasons already given, some significant fraction of the power used for these purposes involves the production of a product which replaces a less power-consumptive one. Hence this category of power consumption — and its attendant environmental pollution — ought not to be charged to increased affluence. It seems likely to us that when all the appropriate calculations have been made, a very considerable part of the recent increases in demand for electric power will turn out to involve just such changes in which well-being, or affluence, is not improved, but the environment and the people who live in it suffer.

Transportation is another uniquely interesting area for such considerations. At first glance changes in the transportation scene in the United States in 1950-68 do seem to bear out the notion that pollution is due to increased affluence. In that period of time the total horsepower of automotive vehicles increased by 260 percent, the number of car registrations per capita by 110 percent, the vehicle miles traveled per capita by 100 percent, the motor fuel used per capita for transportation by 90 percent. (20) All this gives the appearance of increased affluence—at the expense of worsened pollution.

However, looked at a little more closely the picture becomes quite different. It turns out that while the use of individual vehicles has increased sharply, the use of railroads has declined — thus replacing a less polluting means of transportation with a more polluting one. One can argue, of course, that it is more affluent to drive one's own car than to ride in a railroad car along with a number of strangers. Accepting the validity of that argument, it is still relevant to point out that it does *not* hold for comparison between freight hauled in a truck or in a railroad train. The fuel expenditure for hauling a ton of freight one mile by truck is 5.6 times as great as for a ton mile hauled by rail. In addition, the energy outlay for cement and steel for a four-lane expressway suitable for carrying heavy truck traffic is 3.5 times as much as that required for a single track line designed to carry express trains. (21) Rights-of-way account for a considerable proportion of the environmental impact of transportation systems. In unobstructed country requiring no cuts or fills, a 400-foot right-of-way is desirable for an express rail line (in both cases, allowing for future expansion to more lanes or two rail lines respectively). (21) Then, too, motor-vehicle-related accidents might be included in environmental considerations; in 1968 there were 55,000 deaths and 4.4 million injuries due to motor vehicle accidents, while there were only about 1,000 railway deaths, almost none of them passenger deaths. Aside from the loss of life and health, motor vehicle accidents are responsible for the expenditure of $12 billion a year on automobile insurance, which is equivalent to 16 percent of total personal consumption expenditures for transportation. (22) In the case of urban travel it is very clear that efficient mass transit would be not only a more desirable means of travel than private cars, but also far less polluting. The lack of mass transit systems in American cities, and the resulting use of an increasing number of private cars is, again, a cause of increased pollution that does not stem from increased affluence.

It seems to us that the foregoing data provide significant evidence that the rapid intensification of pollution in the United States in the period 1946-68 cannot be accounted for solely by concurrent increases either in population or in affluence. What seems to be far more important than these factors in generating intense pollution is the *nature* of the *production* process; that is, its impact on the environment. The new technologies introduced following World War II have by and large provided Americans with about the same degree of influence with respect to basic life necessities (food, clothing, and shelter); with certain increased amenities, such as private automobiles, and with certain real improvements such as household appliances. Most of these changes have involved a much greater stress on the environment than the activities which they have replaced. Thus, the most powerful cause of environmental pollution in the United States appears to be the introduction of such changes in technology, without due regard to their untoward effects on the environment.

Of course, the more people that are supported by *ecologically faulty technologies*— whether old ones such as coal-burning power plants , or new ones, such as those which have replaced natural products with synthetic ones—the more pollution will be produced. But if the new, ecologically faulty technologists had not been introduced, the increase in U.S. population in the last 25 years would have had a much smaller effect on the environment. And, on the other hand, had the production system of the U.S. been based *wholly* on sound ecological practice (for example, sewage disposal systems which return organic matter to the soil; vehicle engines which operate at low pressure and temperature and therefore do not produce smog-triggering nitrogen oxides; reliance on natural products rather than energy-consumptive synthetic substitutes; closed production systems that prevent environmental release of toxic substances, pollution levels would not have risen as much as they have, despite the rise in population size and in certain kinds of affluence.

The Case of Mercury

All of the foregoing discussion is based on overall statistical data rather than on the specific analysis of any particular source of pollution. While such an approach is useful, it is also important to develop data of a more specific kind. This is, of course, a huge task. It calls for a detailed study of the nature of present production technologies and the specific ways in which they affect ecologically important processes. Such studies have hardly been begun; nevertheless it is useful to discuss, at least in a tentative way, a specific example as a means of testing the conclusions derived from the more general statistical evidence.

The use of mercury in the chemical process industries is an informative example. Here its use reflects the increasing value of electrochemical processes, in which electricity is employed to effect chemical reactions, for mercury is unique in combining certain valuable chemical properties (e.g., that it forms an amalgam with metals, such as sodium) with a capacity to conduct electricity. This led, for example, to the introduction in the United States about twenty years ago of a much improved process for producing caustic soda and chlorine. Since both of these substances are very widely used in the manufacture of the numerous synthetic chemical compounds that have been massively produced in the last 30 years, the rapid increase in the use of mercury in an application which permits losses to the environment is one consequence of the increased production of synthetic substances since World War II. Moreover, several major plastics are produced by processes catalyzed by mercury. Plastics production increased about 200 percent in 1958-67; (23) during that time the use of mercury as an industrial catalyst also increased about 200 percent. (24) In that same period the mercury used in chlorine production increased about 210 percent (see Figure 3). (24) These recent changes reflect the trend, beginning with the close of World War II, toward massive technical innovation and intensification of production in the chemical industry (which was discussed in more general terms above). The magnitude of this effect is sharply reflected in the data for the consumption of mercury for electrochemical production of chlorine: an increase of 2,150 percent in the period 1946-68. (24)

These considerations provide an opportunity to test the degree to which population and affluence participate in the generation of environmental pollution by mercury. As already indicated, for the period 1946-68, the U.S. population increased about 43 percent; in the period 1958-68 it increased about 15 percent. In these periods total U.S. consumption of mercury increased 130 percent and 43 percent respectively. (24) A good deal of mercury consumption involves uses in which the mercury is more or less permanently contained (e.g., incorporation of mercury into electrical instruments — although here, too, it becomes important to ask where broken thermometers and burned-out fluorescent and other mercury-containing lamps are disposed of; if they are burned on a dump or in an incinerator, mercury vapor will pollute the air). However, it is perhaps more important to examine uses in those industries, such as chemical processing, which do result in environmental release of mercury. In this connection the following figures are relevant: In 1946-66, use of mercury in the chemical process industries increased about 224 percent; between 1958 and 1968 it increased about 250 percent. (24) These data are sufficient to indicate that the increased industrial activities which are involved in mercury pollution cannot be accounted for by concurrent changes in the U.S. population. Nor can they be accounted for by the contribution of mercury consumption to increased affluence. As indicated earlier, per capita GNP increased about 51 percent in 1946-66. At the same time, the per capita use of mercury in chemical processing increased 250 percent for all chemical processing and 2,100 percent for chlorine production alone. In effect, goods now produced in the United States which are derived from chemical process industries involve a considerably greater use of mercury than previously. Thus, the increased use — and release to the environment — of mercury reflects changes in industrial chemical technology rather than increased population or affluence.

The Primary Cause

These considerations and the ones discussed earlier in connection with agriculture, synthetics, power, and transportation, allow us, we believe, to draw the conclusion that the predominant factor in our industrial society's increased environmental degradation is neither population nor affluence, but the increasing environmental impact per unit of production due to technological changes.

Thus, in seeking public policies to alleviate environmental degradation it must be recognized that a stable population with stable consumption patterns would still face increasing environmental problems if the environmental impact of production continues to increase. The environmental impact per unit of production is increasing now, partially due to a process of displacement in which new, high-impact technologies are becoming predominant. Hence, social choices with regard to productive technology are inescapable in resolving the environmental crisis.

Notes

(1) Hardin, Garrett, *Population, Evolution and Birth Control*, Freeman, 1969, p. 373.

(2) Ehrlich, Paul, *The Population Bomb*, Ballantine, New York, 1966, pp. 66-67.

(3) *New York Times*, February 19, 1971.

(4) Ehrlich, Paul and John Holdren, "The People Problem," *Saturday Review*, July 4, 1970, p. 42.

(5) Weinberger, L.W., et al., "Solving Our Water Problems: Water Renovation and Reuse," reprinted in Hearings before the Subcommittee on Science, Research and Development of the House Committee on Science and Astronautics, *The Adequacy of Technology for Pollution Abatement Vol. II*, U.S. Government Printing Office, Washington, D.C., 1966, p. 756.

(6) Patterson, Clair C., with Joseph D. Salvia, "Lead in the Modern Environment," *Environment*, 10(3): 72, 1968.

(7) Davis, C.C. "Information Bulletin," *Planktol.*, Japan, 12: 53, 1965.

(8) Molof, A.H., E.R. Gidlund and M. Lang, *Proceedings of a National Symposium on Estuarine Pollution*, sponsored by the American Society of Civil Engineers, Stanford University, Stanford, California, 1957, p. 755.

(9) Bureau of the Census, *Statistical Abstract of the United States*, U.S. Government Printing Office, Washington, D.C. 1970, p. 5.

(10) Department of Commerce, *The National Income and Product Accounts* of the United States, 1929-1965, U.S. Government Printing Office, Washington, D.C., 1966, pp. 4-5.

(11) Bureau of the Census, *Statistical Abstract*, U.S. Government Printing Office, Washington, D.C., 1949: pp. 511, 512, 526, 741, 746, 773, 775, 797, 961, 963, 964, 968, 973; 1953: pp. 92, 93, 821; 1955: p. 830; 1969: p. 509; 1970: pp. 83, 84, 498, 505, 506, 507, 535, 544, 548, 590, 628, 637, 658, 661, 666, 712, 713, 717, 718, 719, 722. Bureau of the Census, "Glass Containers," *Current Industrial Reports*, M32G(69)-13, Washington, D.C., 1970. Department of Agriculture, *Agricultural Statistics* 1955, U.S. Government Printing Office, Washington, D.C., 1956, p. 486. Bureau of Mines, *Minerals Yearbook*, U.S. Government Printing Office, Washington, D.C., 1947: p. 772; 1968, Volume 1: p. 695. *Statistical Abstract*, supra note 9, 1970, pp. 535, 548, 554, 555.

(12) *Statistical Abstract*, supra note 11, 1953: pp. 92-93; 1970: pp. 83-84.

(13) Department of Agriculture, Agricultural Research Service, Neg. AR5 5593-69 (10), U.S. Government Printing Office, Washington, D.C. Department of Agriculture, *Commodity Fact Sheet - 1970; Wheat*, U.S. Government Printing Office, Washington, D.C. Department of Agriculture, Economic Research Service, *Supplement for 1969 Feed Statistics*, Supplement for Statistical Bulletin No. 410, U.S. Government Printing Office, Washington, D.C.

(14) *Statistical Abstract*, supra note 11, 1948: p. 811; 1970: p. 685.

(15) *Statistical Abstract*, supra note 11, 1970: pp. 312, 314.

(16) Commoner, Barry, "Nature Unbalanced: How Man Interferes with the Nitrogen Cycle," *Environment*, 10(1): 12, 1968.

(17) Bureau of the Census, *Census of Manufacturing 1963*, U.S. Government Printing Office, Washington, D.C., pp. 33A-44, 33C-41. *Statistical Abstract*, supra note 11, 1966: pp. 737, 810.

(18) *Statistical Abstract*, supra note 11, 1948: p. 493; 1970: p. 507.

(19) *Statistical Abstract*, supra note 9, 1970: p. 507. *Census of Manufacturing 1967*, supra note 17, pp. 28A-41, 28B-24, 28D-23, 28E-16, 28F-18, 28G-21, 32B-19, 33C-32.

(20) *Statistical Abstract*, supra note 9, 1970: pp. 500, 542, 545, 548.

(21) Personal Communications, Missouri State Highway Department, Missouri Pacific Railroad, Forsythe, W., *Smithsonian Physical Tables*, Smithsonian Institution, Washington, D.C., 9th Edition, 1964, pp. 21, 181. Interstate Commerce Commission, Bureau of Accounts, *Transportation Statistics in the United States*, 1968, IC 1.25:968:Part I:Release 2, p. 19. Automobile Manufacturers Association, *Motor Truck Facts: 1969*, p. 52.

(22) *Statistical Abstract*, supra note 11, 1969: p. 552; 1970: p. 314.

(23) *Statistical Abstract*, supra note 11, 1952: p. 801; 1970: p. 703.

(24) *Minerals Yearbook*, supra note 11, 1947: p. 772; 1958, Volume I: p. 756; 1968, Volume I: p. 695.

CRITIQUE

Paul R. Ehrlich,
John P. Holdren

In his recent book, "The Closing Circle," Barry Commoner presents his views of the origins of man's environmental predicament. Commoner has gained great prominence as a spokesman on the environment and has made extensive contributions to debates on issues ranging from the dangers of atomic fallout o the ecological consequences of man's intervention in the nitrogen cycle. His book contains much interesting material on the misuse of technology by industrialized societies, and it is written in a powerful and appealing style. Certainly he summarizes the dilemma beautifully when he states: "We come, then, to a fundamental paradox of man's life on the earth: that human civilization involves a series of cyclically interdependent processes, most of which have a built-in tendency to grow, except one — the natural, irreplaceable, absolutely essential resources represented by the earth's minerals and the ecosphere" (p. 122). Nor will many students of these problems deny that "the lesson of the environmental crisis is . . . If we are to survive, ecological considerations must guide economic ones" (p. 292).

It is especially unfortunate, then, that so prominent and articulate an advocate for the environment should have written a book as inexplicably inconsistent and dangerously misleading as "The Closing Circle" proves to be. The book's principal defects are three. First, Commoner implicity assumes that environmental deterioration consists only of pollution: this oversimplification leads him to discuss the environmental crisis as if it had begun in the 1940s. Second, in his zeal to place the blame for pollution on faulty technology alone, he resorts to biased selection of data, unconventional definitions, numerical sleight of hand and bad ecology: only thus can he explain away the contributions of population growth and increased affluence. Finally his misconceptions concerning certain aspects of demography lead him to draw erroneous conclusions about the "self-regulation" of human populations and viable strategies for population limitation. Because of the importance of these issues — and especially the possibility that uncritical acceptance of Commoner's assertions will lead to public complacency concerning both population and affluence in the United States — we have documented the errors in "The Closing Circle" at some length.

Commoner writes, "So long as human beings held their place in the terrestrial ecosystem — consuming food produced by the soil and oxygen released by plants, returning organic wastes to the soil and carbon dioxide to the plants — they could do no serious ecological harm" (p. 126). Yet only a few lines later he cites erosion, deforestation and destruction of fisheries as serious ecological problems, apparently unaware that he is contradicting himself. Far from starting in the 1940s, as Commoner implies, serious ecological harm has accompanied man's activities ever since the agricultural revolution some 10,000 years ago. In fact, it may date from even earlier; in the period of intensive hunting and food gathering preceding the advent of agriculture, men may have contributed to a dramatic reduction in the number of species of large mammals inhabiting the earth. (1)

Preindustrial Man

Whatever doubt there may be about the impact of human activities prior to farming, man's ecological transformation of the planet since that time has long been recognized. The earth has been badly scarred by the results of ecocatastrophes which predated by centuries the faulty technologies that have attracted Commoner's attention. Perhaps the most frequently cited is the conversion to desert, or desertification, of the lush Tigris and Euphrates Valleys, a process that started more than two millennia before Christ and was completed before Columbus sailed. (2) The destruction of that rich, ancient granary was a direct result of problems with irrigation, a difficult and ecologically risky operation even under the best of conditions. Often irrigation involves a constant battle against silting and salinization (the accumulation of salts in the soil as water evaporates — a problem not present when the water is "distilled" as it is in normal rainfall). The battle was lost in Mesopotamia, and silting and salinization are growing problems today as population growth forces mankind to bring more and more land under irrigation. These difficulties are not confined to underdeveloped countries, as abandonment of large salinized areas in California's rich Imperial Valley clearly shows.

Faulty Practices

Another major aspect of environmental deterioration long recognized by ecologists is the desertification of vast areas of the world through over-grazing and, in some cases, faulty agricultural practices. (3) The Sahara still marches southward at a rate of a mile or more a year, thanks in part to pastoral peoples exceeding the carrying capacity of the range and to inadequate soil husbandry by farmers. Much of Europe, Asia and Africa has been deforested, overgrazed, overfarmed and subject to heavy soil erosion as a result of the activities of preindustrial men. Even in North America the environment has been degraded through the activities of pastoral peoples. Carl Sauer wrote: "The present desolate shifting-sand area that lies between the Hopi villages and the Colorado River was such good pasture land late in the eighteenth century that Father Escalante, returning from his Canyon exploration, rested his travelworn animals there to regain flesh. The effects of Navaho shepherding in little more than a century and mainly in the last sixty years are well documented."(4)

The destruction of the environment by preindustrial man is not limited to relatively arid regions. In tropical forest areas a shifting "slash-and-burn" or "milpa" agriculture is widely practiced. The success of this system is utterly dependent on restricting the size of the clearing and allowing a sufficient recovery period before an area is cut over again and planted. The relationship between population growth and environmental deterioration here is direct; increased population density produces extreme stress in a milpa agricultural system. When fields are made too large or farmed too frequently the soil becomes depleted and is eroded away. Yields per unit area drop, forcing even more frequent and extensive clearing in a vicious cycle. Such a trend is suspected as being at least in part responsible for the collapse of the classic Maya civilization as population densities increased around growing urban centers.(5) A trip to many tropical forest areas in the world today will reveal to the most casual observer the extent of destruction wrought by milpa agriculture and woodcutting in areas where the population density has exceeded the carrying capacity of the land. Furthermore, those who predict the facile transplantation of "modern" agricultural technologies to wet lowland tropics are simply unschooled in tropical ecology. Indeed, the very ecological imperatives that Commoner so often invokes indicate that stabilizing population is a necessary prerequisite for avoiding an irreversible lowering of the human carrying capacity of the tropics.

Commoner's preoccupation with pollution almost to the exclusion of other forms of environmental deterioration leads him to give but scant attention to the general problem of ecosystem simplification. While clearly recognizing that the integrity of the ecosystem of the planet must be preserved, he does not seem aware that the reduction of the diversity of life and thus of the complexity of those systems may pose the most lethal threat of all. It is the complexity of the natural ecosystems that is primarily responsible for their stability. (6) Ecosystems are simplified by the extinction of populations and, more irreversibly, by the extinction of species. The very practice of agriculture on a large scale with its substitution of monocultures (stands of single crops) for natural communities rich in species is a potent force towards the destabilization of the global ecosystem. Because of its dependence on faulty technologies (such as the ritualized application of persistent biocides), modern agriculture has become an even more powerful simplifying force. Although this point supports Commoner's central argument, he largely neglects it.

Crop Monocultures

Of course, man paid the price of the creation of large unstable monocultures long before the first DDT molecule was manufactured. The Irish potato famine is the best known example of an ecocatastrophe entirely traceable to ecosystem simplification (and with no "faulty technology" component a la Commoner). When the potato monoculture in Ireland collapsed under the onslaught of the fungus Phytophthora infestans "in four years, 1,500,000 people had died, over one sixth of the population. A million had emigrated, and millions more were to emigrate over the coming decades until Ireland's population was cut in half. The Irish countryside was never the same again; the old customs and pleasures that had lightened the traditional poverty of the Irish peasant withered away." (7) Clearly, the Irish did serious harm to their environment even though they were living within the rules set down by Commoner (quoted at the beginning of this section).

Curiously, one of the most serious aspects of environmental deterioration is a "faulty technology" that has nothing to do with pollution. The continuance of high-yield agriculture is dependent on man's ability to select strains of plants that not only produce the desired yields but are resistant to the attacks of their enemies. That is, it depends on a genetic technology. There is no such thing as a strain that is permanently resistant to a pest or disease, because the plants and the organisms that attack them make up co-evolving systems. Unless the plant breeder has available to him the requisite genetic variability to use in producing new resistant strains when the biochemical or mechanical defenses of the old strains are breached (as they inevitably are), the whole basis of modern agriculture could be destroyed.

It is ironic that the very success of programs to develop extremely productive crops to feed mankind's burgeoning numbers is now threatening the diversity in the gene pools of some of the most nutritionally important plants. "Miracle" crops are now rapidly replacing large numbers of traditional strains as the high yield varieties are eagerly adopted by farmers. The genetic treasurehouse is being rapidly depleted, and not nearly enough is being done to arrest the process. To the extent that success in plant breeding leads to loss of variability, the genetic technology can be described as "faulty." This leads to the ultimate in ecosystem simplification; not only does greater uniformity increase the vulnerability of crop monocultures to widespread disaster, it also reduces the chances of recovering from disaster.

The foregoing are by no means all of the serious forms of environmental disruption having their origins long before World War II. Another is the injection of dust and smoke into the atmosphere in connection with agricultural burning and the removal of protective plant cover by culitvation or overgrazing. The latter aspects of the problem are especially severe when food producing activities are extended to marginal land, as population pressure makes inevitable. Agricultural hazes are already an important climatic perturbation in parts of Africa and Asia, and man's contribution to the global atmospheric dust burden is rising steadily. (8) (J. Murray Mitchell points out that man's dust contribution is presently small compared to the 120-year average figure for dust of volcanic origin, but is already large compared to the natural "baseline" figure between major eruptions.) Measurable effects on global climate are thought to be possible within 30 years if this long-established trend continues. A major reason for concern here is that global agriculture is dependent on crops highly adapted to present climatic conditions. Because global climate is determined by a balance of many opposing factors, it is possible that a destabilizing imput by man at some leverage point in this rather poorly understood system could cause a sudden change rather than a gradual one — with disastrous consequences for food productivity. Carbon dioxide from the combustion of fossil fuels and heat dissipated when man uses energy of any kind are also potential influences on climate on a large scale.

Another serious form of environmental impact with a long history is the disruption of salt marshes and estuaries that serve as "nurseries" for much of the life in the sea. Salt marshes are continually being lost to landfill operations, and the salinity and temperature of estuaries are affected by irrigation projects upstream. Most of the productivity of the sea occurs on the continental shelves or in areas of upwelling relatively near the shore. (9) The long standing threats to the estuaries and salt marshes sheltering many of the creatures at the base of these food chains, combined with the more recent hazards of industrial and agricultural pollutants and over-fishing, jeopardize one of mankind's principal sources of protein.

Obviously there is no basis whatever on which to conclude, as Commoner does, that man was only an innocuous environmental force prior to 1940. The sorts of human activity being carried on even then were steadily and probably irreversibly eroding the capacity of the planet to support human life. That the world now supports a considerably larger population than it did in 1940 is hardly proof that the environmental impact of this population, or even the 1940 population, could long be sustained. As zoologists know well, animal populations often considerably overshoot the carrying capacity of their environment — a phenomenon invariably followed by a population crash.

Having assumed that man's adverse impact on his environment was negligible before 1940, Commoner then alleges that "pollution levels" increased by an explosive 200 to 2,000 per cent between 1946 and 1968, and that neither population growth nor rising affluence had much to do with it. His argumentation purporting to prove this hypothesis is a house of cards supported by the flimsiest of props: the misleading use of percentages, data and definitions tailored to fit the foregone conclusion, and stubborn refusal to confront the mechanisms by which population growth can cause disproportionate increases in environmental impact.

Consider first the matter of percentages. Commoner admits that the factors contributing to environmental impact are multiplicative rather than additive; he offers (in a footnote to pp. 211-12) the equation,

pollution equals
(population) X
(production/capita) X
(Pollution emission/production).

Here the second factor on the right, production per capita, is in some sense a measure of affluence, and the last factor, pollution per unit of production, is a measure of the relative environmental impact of the technology that provides the affluence. For compactness, let us rewrite this equation.

$$I = P \times A \times T \tag{1}$$

or, in terms of initial values and the subsequent changes over a specified period of time

$$I + \Delta I = (P + \Delta P) \times (A + \Delta A) \times (T + \Delta T). \tag{2}$$

Here I as for impact (a better word than "pollution" for reasons already explained), P is for population, A for affluence, and T for technology. Let us also assume for a moment that the variables P, A, and T are independent, i.e. that a change in P does not cause changes in A or T, and vice versa. We shall find later that this is not true, but it is the simplest assumption and the one most favorable to Commoner's hypothesis.

It is immediately obvious from equation (2) of course, that the actual magnitude of the environmental deterioration engendered by an adverse change in technology depends strongly both on the initial levels of population and affluence and on such changes in these levels as may occur simultaneously with the change in technology. A corollary is that population and affluence would be important factors in environmental degradation even if they were not growing. A change for the worse in the technology of production is more serious environmentally if it occurs in a populous, affluent society than if it occurs in small, poor ones.

In reality, population and affluence in the United States have both grown substantially in the postwar period on which Commoner concentrates. To see how his use of percentages has obscured the importance of the growth of these factors; we rewrite the impact equation to express all quantities as multiples of their initial values:

$$1 + \frac{\Delta I}{I} = (1 + \frac{\Delta P}{P}) \times (1 + \frac{\Delta A}{A}) \times (1 + \frac{\Delta T}{T}). \tag{3}$$

Then $(\Delta I/I)$ times 100 is the percentage increase in environmental impact, $(\Delta P/P)$ times 100 is the percentage change in population, and so on. (Note that an increase of 100 per cent means a doubling of the initial quantity, an increase of 200 per cent a tripling, etc.) Now let us put some typical numbers into the equation and see what happens. Population increased 42 per cent between 1946 and 1968, so $\Delta P/P$ equals .42 and the population factor in equation (3) is 1.42. (10) Let us assume that the affluence factor in this hypothetical example — say, per capita consumption of a commodity whose production entails significant environmental impact — has increased at the same rate as GNP per capita, or 59 per cent between 1946 and 1968, corrected for inflation. Then $\Delta A/A$ equals .59, and the affluence factor in equation (3) becomes 1.59. Suppose, finally, that a change in technology has led to a 33 per cent increase in environmental impact per unit of production, i.e., $\Delta T/T$ equals .33, so the technology factor in equation (3) is 1.33. Then the equation gives

$$1 + \frac{\Delta I}{I} = 1.42 \times 1.59 \times 1.33 = 3.00,$$

or a 200 per cent increase in environmental impact. In this hypothetical example, none of the causative factors is unimportant, and no single one accounts for a large fraction of the increase. It is the multiplicative effect of the three moderate increases occurring simultaneously that yields a dramatic increase in the total.

Yet, of the four relevant figures, Commoner invariably presents only two: the total increase in some index of impact and the increase in population. If he were reporting the example just given, he would cite 200 per cent and 42 per cent as the relevant numbers, leading the casual reader to believe that population was a minor factor. Nor is the deception less when the role of factors other than population is larger. Consider a case where total impact of some kind can be shown to have increased 400 per cent. Are the other factors then ten times as important as population, as Commoner repeatedly asserts? Hardly. The simple algebra of equation (3) shows that an actual increase of 400 per cent would have been only 252 per cent if population had stayed constant. That is, the product of the technology and affluence factors is 3.52:

$$\Delta I/I = 4.00$$
$$1 + \Delta I/I = 5.00 = 1.42 \times 3.52.$$

If, in this hypothetical example, we again assumed that the affluence factor increased in proportion to GNP per capita, we would find that the combination of the population and affluence factors was of equal importance to the technology factor:

$$\overset{P}{1 + \Delta I/I = 5.00 = \underbrace{1.42 \times 1.59}} \times \overset{T}{2.22.}$$

These somewhat tedious arguments have been based on nothing but elementary algebra and arithmetic; we have as yet invoked no cause-and-effect relationships between population size and the nature of the technology needed to support it, nor questioned the validity of the indices Commoner chooses to describe "pollution." Examination of the basic mathematics alone, irrespective of the definitions and analysis behind the numbers Commoner presents, shows that the relationships are not what he claims.

Next to the misleading use of percentages, one of the cornerstones of Commoner's argument is his dismissal of the role of affluence. Like most students of these problems, he is not happy with the strict use of GNP per capita as a measure of affluence. In one sense GNP includes too much (e.g., the costs of war and crime), in another sense too little (e.g., it omits part of the "cost" of our decaying cities, a cost paid not in dollars but in misery by those who must live and work in them). Unfortunately, Commoner's indicators of affluence are, if anything, more superficial than GNP.

First, he confines his attention almost entirely to production of goods, thereby omitting services (many of which surely are part of affluence and almost all of which generate environmental impact through the use of energy). He does mention a dramatic increase in passenger miles of automobile travel per person and on page 176 ascribes it to affluence. With this exception, Commoner apparently would have us believe that affluence in the United States has not risen appreciably since 1946. He supports this view by dividing affluence into "necessities" (food, shelter, clothing) and "amenities" (everything else). He notes that per capita availibility of calories fell 4 per cent between 1946 and 1968; grams of protein per capita fell by a smaller amount; pounds of fiber per person, representing clothing, rose 9 per cent (figures for 1950-68 only); and housing units per capita rose 10 per cent. (For some reason, Commoner used the 1966 rather than the 1968 housing figure, leading him to compute a slightly smaller increase.)

Having thus "proven" that affluence as measured by necessities has not changed much in the postwar period, Commoner deals with amenities mainly by ignoring them. He concedes that "if affluence is measured in terms of certain household amenities, such as television sets, radios, and electric can-openers and corn-poppers, and in leisure items such as snowmobiles and boats, then there have been certain striking increases," but he adds, "again, these items are simply too small a part of the nation's over-all production to account for the observed increase in pollution level" (p. 139). This is precisely the reductionist pitfall that Commoner solemnly deplores several times in his book, but that he cannot himself avoid. No single factor can explain all of the increase of all of the indicators of environmental impact, but the rising per capita availability of amenities plays an important (and multiplicative) role in explaining part of the increase of some of them.

Commoner's general conclusions later in the book are clearly based on a redefinition of affluence that excludes amenities altogether (see, e.g., p. 176). Yet, curiously, he does not mind fattening his list of dramatically increasing kinds of production (p. 143) with items that are obviously affluence-related amenities (air conditioner compressor units, up 2,850 per cent between 1946 and 1968; electric housewares, up 1,040 per cent). Apparently, Commoner thinks he can offer affluence of some kinds as a symptom without admitting affluence of any kind as a cause. He cannot have it both ways.

TABLE 1

AMENITIES AND AFFLUENCE IN THE POSTWAR UNITED STATES

Item	Initial value	Final value	Per cent Increase
1. Automobiles in use p.c.[a]	.208 (1940)	.416 (1968)	100%
2. Telephones in use p.c.	.165 (1940)	.540 (1968)	227
3. Automatic heating units in use p.c.	.042 (1946)	.133 (1960)	217
4. Ranges in use p.c.	.242 (1951)	.305 (1960)	26
5. Water heaters in use p.c.	.122 (1950)	.177 (1960)	45
6. Percentage of households with air conditioners	0.2% (1948)	13.6% (1960)	6,700
7. Refrigerators in use p.c.	.145 (1946)	.277 (1960)	91
8. Clothes dryers p.c.	.0013 (1949)	.053 (1960)	4,000

Source: Items 1 and 2, "Statistical Abstract of the United States, 1970"; all other items, "Resources in America's Future," 1963.

[a] Abbreviation "p.c." stands for "per capita."

Even if one accepts Commoner's narrow view of affluence, however, his conclusions do not follow. The statistics he has used for clothing and housing per capita are utterly inappropriate to an assessment of changing affluence. Specifically, his figures for housing units per capita are taken from the "Statistical Abstract of the United States," which uses the following definition: "A 'household' comprises all persons who occupy a 'housing unit," that is, a house, an apartment or other group of rooms, or a room that constitutes 'separate living quarters.' " Obviously, the most important aspects of affluence in housing — namely, the type of housing people have and its quality — are not reflected in the statistic quoted by Commoner at all. By his measure, a country whose population all resided in one-room flats would be judged as affluent as one where each family lived in an 8-room ranch house — as long as the number of people per "household" were the same in each country. In the postwar United States, growing affluence manifested itself as a steady increase in expenditures per capita on housing (from $149 per person in 1946 to $235 in 1960, corrected for inflation) and in the fraction of the population dwelling in houses as opposed to apartments (most new dwelling units built since the war have been single-family houses, although this trend seems to have ended, or been temporarily interrupted, in the early 1960s) (11). This affluence in housing, in turn, was translated into environmental impact in the form of increased resource consumption (wood, metals, plastics), the overrunning of fertile farmlands by sprawling suburbs, and the increasing use of automobiles attendant upon spreading out the population.

A somewhat different set of defects underlies Commoner's discussion of clothing per capita. He has used the statistics for pounds of fiber produced per capita as a measure of supplies of clothing, in the face of three good reasons not to do so: First, a great deal of fiber is used for nonclothing, purposes such as carpeting, furniture and tire cord. Second, statistics for the production of clothing itself are readily at hand in the same source. Third, the United States is increasingly a net importer of raw textiles and clothing (admitted by Commoner in a footnote), so consumption considerably exceeds production. According to the actual figures, just the production of apparel per capita increased 23.5 per cent between 1950 and 1968, versus the 9 per cent claimed by Commoner. Imports of clothing per capita jumped 2.5-fold between 1960 and 1968 alone.

Evidently, Commoner has appreciably understated the growth of "affluence" in postwar America, even within the confines of his unconventional definition of the term. But if one includes in the accounting the amenities that most Americans surely regard as part of their affluence, the magnitude of Commoner's underestimate grows even larger. In Table 1 we present the figures for a few of these items. The reader may now judge for himself whether Commoner is misleading his public when he writes, "The economy has grown enough to give the United States population about the same amount of basic goods, per capita, as it did in 1946" (p. 177).

The Postwar Growth Items

Commoner's selection of indicators of environmental impact is no more objective than his treatment of affluence. He has simply taken from the industrial statistics for the United States over the past 25 years a "representative" list of items, and ranked them according to percentage increase in production during this period. Table 2 gives the first 18 items on Commoner's list on page 143 of "The Closing Circle." Several questions must be asked concerning this tabulation: Are the top items — those that grew more than 500 per cent — sufficiently representative of the sources of environmental impact to justify Commoner's repeated assertions that "pollution" in the postwar United States grew 10 times as much as population or, indeed, 10 times as much as GNP? What important indicators of environmental impact are missing? Of those on the list, what part of the increases must be attributed to affluence, what part of population, and what part to those changes in technology which were a direct result of rising population and affluence?

The first item on the list, nonreturnable soda bottles, is a good example of the misleading use of numbers. Obviously, a dramatic percentage increase in production of an item does not necessarily mean that present production is enormous in absolute terms: it may only mean that initial production was very small. Nor does a large increase — or even a large absolute level of production — automatically mean that an item is an important index of environmental impact. Nonreturnable soda bottles illustrate both points: while they almost certainly represent a waste of energy, they are neither a major fraction of U.S. glass production nor an ecologically significant pollutant.

The second thing one notices is that several of the items on Commoner's list are closely related to each other; he tabulates separately synthetic organic chemicals, pesticides (the most dangerous of which are a subset of the synthetic organics), chlorine (the principal use of which is the manufacture of synthetic organics), and the mercury used in the production of the chlorine. There is no doubt that these items support, in this instance, Commoner's notion of "the technological flaw" — i.e., that considerable environmental impact has resulted from changes for the worse in technology. The interesting point here is that Commoner has padded his list of dramatic increases with four different aspects of essentially the same flaw. Since few sources of pollution have really increased enough to justify Commoner's general conclusions, he apparently intends to get maximum mileage out of those that have.

TABLE 2
COMMONER'S SELECTION OF POSTWAR "GROWTH" ITEMS*

Item	Percentage Increase Quoted
1. Nonreturnable soda bottles	53,000%
2. Synthetic fibers	5,980
3. Mercury used in chlorine production	3,930
4. Mercury used in mildew-resistant paint	3,120
5. Air conditioner compressor units	2,850
6. Plastics	1,960
7. Fertilizer nitrogen	1,050
8. Electric housewares	1,040
9. Synthetic organic chemicals	950
10. Aluminum	680
11. Chlorine gas	600
12. Electric power	530
13. Pesticides	390
14. Wood pulp	313
15. Truck freight	222
16. Consumer electronics	217
17. Motor fuel consumption	190
18. Cement	150

ᵃ "The Closing Circle," p. 143.

Mercury Consumption

The figures for mercury deserve closer examination. Commoner has cited two particular uses of mercury that have increased dramatically, without noting that total consumption of mercury has changed relatively little. U.S. mercury consumption between 1930 and 1970 was 63,000 metric tons, or an average of 1.575 tons per year; the 1968 figure was 1,827 tons, only 16 per cent above the 40-year average (12). Furthermore, there is good reason to believe that other sources of environmental mercury may be more important than industrial production of the metal. Mercury occurs throughout the earth's crust and is released continuously by outgassing. The global rate for this process, which is accelerated when man disturbs the earth's surface by mining, agriculture and urbanization, has recently been estimated as at least 25,000 metric tons per year. For comparison, world industrial production of mercury in 1968 was 8,800 metric tons, and degassing during the roasting of sulfide ores contributes perhaps an additional 2,000 metric tons of mercury globally per year. The input from burning fossil fuels may be as much as 20,000 metric tons annually. (Some authors have obtained a much smaller figure by using an older value for the mercury content of coal and assuming that 90 per cent of the mercury in the fuel is trapped in bottom ash and does not reach the environment. However, no mercury is reclaimed in connection with the use of fossil fuels, so it seems prudent to assume that all of it reaches the environment by one pathway or another, e.g., leaching from ash piles by rainwater.) It is apparent, then, that the numbers presented by Commoner have little relevance as indicators of the overall level of mercury pollution or its rate of increase since World War II. The major sources have been increasing far more slowly than those he cites, and are rather well explained, it seems, in terms of increases in population and affluence (as measured by total fossil fuel consumption and, possibly, disruption of the land). It is not our intention, of course, to disparage the importance of chlor-alkali plants and paint manufacturing as local sources of mercury — such sources should be controlled wherever possible. However, the evidence simply does not support the use of mercury as an example of pollution increasing many times faster than population or affluence.

What of the other items on Commoner's list? Air-conditioner compressors and electric housewares represent affluence by any definition but Commoner's, so these figures do not support his case. Also, with air conditioners, as with nonrefillable bottles, the percentage increase is so dramatic largely because the initial production was so small. Synthetic fibers, plastics and aluminum also rose from small initial values, and they are now produced in quantities that are significant in absolute terms. (By "synthetic" fibers, Commoner means only the noncellulosic man-made fibers such as nylon. Rayon and acetate, by contrast, are man-made as fibers but they are cellulose based.) Since these commodities are at least plausible indices of environmental impact — the fibers and plastics because they are not easily degraded in nature, the aluminum as a major consumer of electric power — we should examine the relevant data more closely. First all three commodities grew by replacing or supplementing more conventional ones: plastics for wood and steel; aluminum for wood, steel and copper; synthetic fibers for cotton and wool. To this extent, the evidence supports the proposition (with which few would disagree) that technology has often dramatically changed the way man meets established wants and needs, sometimes with serious side-effects. What Commoner has failed to prove, however, is that such changes are not stimulated by the demands of a growing population or by perceived advantages of the new technology over the old, aside from cheapness.

Consider the fibers. The relevant data are presented in Table 3, in a form somewhat more enlightening than Commoner's percentages. It is apparent that providing today's total demand for fiber without the man-made ones would amount to nearly a doubling of the 1945 consumption of both cotton and wool. What would have been the cost of doing it this way in terms of pounds of pesticides and fertilizer applied to cotton fields, the fossil fuels burned in cultivation, planting, harvesting and ginning, the side-effects of irrigation projects, the extra land devoted to monoculture, the overgrazing and subsequent erosion of grassland? Has the environmental cost of meeting the increased demand with synthetics been greater? This is the real issue: not whether the environmental impact of noncellulosic fibers in 1968 is 70 times their impact in 1945, but whether the impact of alternate means to provide the 1968 number of people with the 1968 level of affluence would have been any less. Commoner admits he does not know (see his footnote to page 160), but the uncertainty is forgotten when he draws his conclusions.

A Popular Misconception

Consider aluminum. It is a popular misconception that most aluminum goes into beer cans. Actually, containers of all kinds account for 10 per cent of aluminum consumption, while the building and construction industry uses 23 per cent, the transportation industry uses 20 per cent, and the electrical industry uses 13 per cent. (13) In the building industry, aluminum is replacing wood for siding, window frames, awnings and other applications, not simply because it is cheap, but because it is durable and maintenance free. Many people believe low maintenance is part of affluence. Aluminum is costly in energy, but meeting the demands of a growing population for better housing with wood alone would put an additional demand on forests already being too intensely exploited. (Need we remind Dr. Commoner that "there is no such thing as a free lunch?") In transportation, aluminum replaces iron in automobile engines and steel in aircraft. Aluminum is about 5 times as costly in energy as steel to produce, but lighter cars and aircraft burn less fuel. In the electrical industry, abundant aluminum is replacing scarce copper as a conductor of electricity. This is not coincidence or technological frivolity; it is the classic example of the sort of substitution that is inevitable when a growing, affluent population presses on a finite resource base.

TABLE 3
CONSUMPTION OF FIBERS IN U.S. MILLS, 1945-1968
(MILLIONS OF POUNDS)

| Year | Cotton | Wool | Man-made | |
			Rayon & Acetate	Non-cellulosic
1945	4,516	645	795	50
1955	4,382	414	1,455	448
1968	4,147	330	1,711	3,585

Plastics have replaced wood in some applications, such as furniture, and steel in others. Often they are more durable than wood and need less maintenance (affluence again), and their production requires only about a fourth as much energy per ton as steel (14). Their persistence as a pollutant is a liability. Again, however, Commoner can offer no comparison of the environmental impact of the observed increase in production of plastics since 1946 with the impact of producing from other materials the same goods for the same number of people. It is clear, then, that population growth and rising affluence can stimulate qualitative changes in the technologies of production, and that mere comparsion of percentage increases in the new technologies with those of population and GNP does not clarify the relationship.

Another mechanism by which population and affluence generate environmental impact far out of proportion to their own percentage increases is diminishing returns.

This term refers to a situation in which the additional output resulting from each additional unit of input is becoming less and less. Here "output" refers to a desired good such as food or metal, and "input" refers to what we must supply — say, fertilizer, energy, raw ore or labor — to obtain the output. If diminishing returns prevail, the per capita consumption of inputs needed to provide the fixed per capita level of outputs will increase. Since environmental impact is generated by the inputs as well as by the outputs, per capita impact will also increase.

Consider the problem of providing nonrenewable resources such as minerals and fossil fuels to a growing population, even at fixed levels of per capita consumption. More people mean more demand, and thus more rapid depletion of resources. As the richest supplies of these resources and those nearest to centers of use are consumed, it becomes necessary to use lower-grade ores, drill deeper and extend supply networks. All these activities increase the per capita use of energy, and hence the per capita impact on the environment. In the case of partly renewable resources such as water (which is effectively nonrenewable when groundwater supplies are mined at rates far exceeding natural recharge), per capita costs and environmental impact escalate enormously when the human population demands more than is locally available.

Here the loss of free-flowing rivers and other economic, aesthetic and ecological costs of massive water-movement projects represent increased per capita diseconomies directly stimulated by population growth. These effects would, or course, also eventually overtake a stable population that demands more than the environment can supply on a perpetual basis; growth simply speeds the process and allows less time to deal with the problems created.

Commoner implictly acknowledges the possibility of diminishing returns (p. 133), but declares that this phenomenon cannot explain the increases in environmental impact that have occurred. As we have already noted, no single factor can explain all of the increases, but Commoner's rejection of diminishing returns as a significant contributing factor is based on his evident misunderstanding of the term's economic meaning. Specifically, he restricts attention to productivity, or "value produced per unit of labor used in the process" (p. 134); since this quantity has increased since 1956, he argues, diminishing returns have not been important. Actually, the only justifiable conclusion from this datum is that diminishing returns with respect to labor have not been important. The reason, of course, is that the rampant technology that Commoner deplores has reduced the importance of labor in comparison with other inputs, such as energy, machinery and raw ore. It is with respect to these nonlabor inputs that diminishing returns have occurred. (The phenomenon has become sufficiently dramatic to show up in the very coarse index, energy consumption per dollar of GNP, corrected for inflation, which has been increasing since 1965.) And, of course, it is the nonlabor inputs which generate the sorts of environmental impact with which Commoner concerns himself.

Perhaps the best known example of diminishing returns is the use of nitrogen fertilizer in food production — a situation which Commoner himself describes with admirable clarity on page 85. The essence of the matter is that feeding an extra increment of population from a fixed or dwinding amount of good quality land requires inputs of fertilizer far out of proportion to the increase in yield. That the amount of agricultural land is dwindling is of course partly a consequence of other demands being made on the land by a growing and affluent population — freeways, subdivisions, airports, reservoirs, and so on. It is ironic then, that one of the centerpieces of Commoner's argument — the dramatic postwar increase in the production of nitrogen fertilizer — is so revealing as an illustration of what he has overlooked: namely, that there are striking cause-and-effect connections between the size of a population and the nature of the technology needed to support it.

There are far more aspects of the causal relation among population size, affluence and per capita impact on the environment than we have space to describe here (15). However, those we have mentioned should suffice to show that such connections are important factors in man's rising environmental impact, and that they cannot be defined or wished away.

Having considered the items which are on Commoner's list, we turn to an examination of some that are missing. Probably the most accurate indices of a society's impact on its environment are the production and consumption (production plus imports minus exports) of energy. Commoner discusses electricity, which has grown much more rapidly than energy consumption as a whole (partly by replacing direct uses of fossil fuels in home heating, cooking and industry). He also treats motor fuel consumption, one of the few increases he is willing to attribute partly to affluence. He says almost nothing about energy production or consumption as a whole, however, perhaps because it would damage his case to do so.

Of course, no single statistic now kept by society is designed to measure environmental impact, but the figures on energy at least tend to average out substitutions. Thus they are not subject to the limitations of measures such as aluminum or plastic production, as already discussed. Using energy production or consumption also avoids the pitfall of redundancy into which Commoner has fallen in the case of synthetic organics. Most important, all of man's environmental impacts involve his production and consumption of energy, and virtually all the energy he commands, except that which drives his own body, is accounted for in the statistics. (At least in the United States and other industrial nations where relatively accurate statistics are recorded.)

Our judgment that the energy figures are appropriate indices of environmental impact is confirmed by the prestigious MIT-sponsored Study of Critical Environmental Problems ("Man's Impact on the Global Environment"). Of the five global environmental problems given most attention by the study — oil in the oceans, carbon dioxide and particulate matter in the atmosphere, heavy metals, euthophication and pesticides — the first three are directly related to energy production (the relationship of the heavy metal, mercury, to energy production is discussed above).

U. S. energy production in 1969 was 2.4 times that in 1940. Population increased 53 per cent in this period, and energy production per capita increased 57 per cent (1.53 X 1.57 equals 2.40). Thus, in purely arithmetic terms, population growth and increased production per capita accounted for almost identical shares of the total increase. U.S. energy consumption increased 2.75-fold between 1940 and 1969, corresponding to an 80 per cent increase in consumption per capita (1.53 X 1.80 equals 2.75). Again, even ignoring the interdependence of the factors, the contribution of population growth is hardly unimportant.

Another spectacular omission from Commoner's "representative" list of indices of postwar production is the number of automobiles manufactured. (Discussions of some of the individual impacts of the automobile are scattered through "The Closing Circle," but identifying automobile production as an informative index of resource wastage and environmental degradation does not suit Commoner's purpose.) Between 1940 and 1968 the production of automobiles increased 2.37-fold while population grew 1.52-fold. Per capita production rose 1.56-fold (1.52 X 1.56 equals 2.37). Population growth thus "caused" about half of the increase while affluence (as reflected in the increased number of cars per person) "caused" the rest.

Commuting Syndrome

Commoner argues that "in a sense, the increase in automobile travel during the last 25 years is also a counterecological consequence of a technological change — in the distribution of residences and places of work" (p. 170). We will leave for the reader to decide whether the commuting syndrome is best described as a "technological mistake" or as a complex situation resulting partly from increases in population concentration, which are highly correlated with population growth, and from increased affluence. After all, increased affluence is what permits flight to the suburbs.

Commoner correctly points out that one of the major impacts from the automobile, the production of nitrogen oxides, has increased since 1946 because of a technological mistake. That mistake was raising compression ratios, which increased average emissions of oxides of nitrogen in the exhaust from 500 parts per million to 1,200 parts per million (a 2.4-fold increase) between 1946 and 1968. Commoner notes further that total nitrogen oxide emissions increased 7-fold in the same period. Application of the simple mathematics of impact to these figures shows that the combination of population growth and affluence accounts for a larger portion of the nitrogen oxide problem than does the technological "error":

$$P \times A \text{ equals } 2.9; \quad T \text{ equals } 2.4;$$
$$I \text{ equals } 2.9 \times 2.4 \text{ equals } 7.0.$$

Commoner also neglects to point out an obvious trade-off. The error of raising compression ratios had an effect beyond increasing nitrogen oxides; it reduced the emissions of hydrocarbons, dangerous pollutants implicated in causing cancer. Here, as in many other places in "The Closing Circle," Commoner seems to have forgotten what he calls The Fourth Law of Ecology: there is no such thing as a free lunch. Many of the technological flaws we all deplore will not be easily corrected, for the alternatives, too, are full of defects. Switching from today's automobiles to electric vehicles would simply shift part of the environmental burden of personal transportation from the air over highways to the air over electric power stations. Changing from fossil fuel to nuclear fission electricity generation replaces the problems of strip mining, oil spills and air pollution with an accident hazard of indeterminate magnitude and a burden of radioactive wastes to be stored virtually in perpetuity. Regulating trash burning to minimize air pollution maximizes the burden of solid wastes. The sad fact is that most attempts to eliminate man's impact on his environment only shift and redistribute it. Obviously, some technologies are better than others, and approaches that promise to minimize environmental impact should be vigorously pursued. It is well to admit, however, that barring a repeal of the laws of thermodynamics, no technology can reduce the impact of population and affluence to zero.

On page 237 Commoner points out that the demographic transition is a tendency for population growth to "level off" as a natural social response to prosperity. On page 242, we are told that population growth in the developing nations should be "brought into balance by the same means that have already succeeded elsewhere — improvement of living conditions, urgent efforts to reduce infant mortality, social security measures and the resultant effects on desired family size, together with personal, voluntary contraceptive practice." He then states; "It is this view with which I wish to associate myself."

If it only were that simple. A casual look at the statistics would reveal the most fundamental flaw in Commoner's thesis; even after the completion of the demographic transition the developed countries still have high growth rates. (16) Contrary to Commoner's beliefs, the reduction in birth rates associated with the demographic transition was not adequate to compensate for the even more dramatic fall in death rates that preceded it.

Technically, the demographic transition is the change from a high death rate-high birth rate regime to a low death rate-low birth rate regime—such as has occurred historically in the developed countries, where the transition was essentially over by 1940 (17). Indeed, most of these countries have had low birth and death rates since the 1920s, yet their birth rates are still well above their death rates. For instance, in 1971 Northern Europe had a birth rate of 16 per thousand and a death rate of 11; the birth rate of North America was 18 and the death rate was 9. (Incidentally, that is below the 10 to 12 per thousand Commoner describes as the "minimal death rate" on page 238. In 1971, more than 50 nations had death rates below the Commoner "minimum" and some, such as Singapore and Taiwan, were as low as 5 per thousand.)

To varying degrees, the situation is a result of the age composition of the population as well as of excess fertility. Nonetheless, an examination of net reproductive rates from the 1920s to today in the industrialized nations gives little reason to assume that there is an automatic process of population regulation leading to stationary populations. (Net reproductive rate, NRR, is a measure of whether a population will be growing, stationary or shrinking, when and if the age composition stabilizes and if age specific vital rates remain constant.) Indeed, it seems at least as likely, assuming death rates do not rise, that industrial nations could fluctuate over the long term at growth rates of about 0.5 to 1.0 per cent annually, thus doubling their populations every century or so.

Let's examine, however, what would happen if demographic transitions started immediately in underdeveloped countries (in most cases there is little or no sign of such an event) and followed a pattern similar to that experienced by the developed countries (DCs) in the past. It would be perhaps 80 years before one could expect growth rates in underdeveloped countries (UDCs) to be in the relatively low range now found in developed countries (18). To see even more clearly that such a demographic transition in the UDCs cannot solve the problem in time, it is only necessary to examine a much more optimistic projection. Demographer Nathan Keyfitz has recently calculated the possible results of a population control miracle (which we might call a "super demographic transition") (19). He calculated, in essence, what would happen if family size dropped precipitously in UDCs so that reproduction reached the replacement level around the year 2000. If that should occur, the size of the population of a typical UDC would be 2.5 times its present size when it eventually stopped growing. (Achievement of replacement reproduction, that is, NRR equals 1, does not lead to a stationary population until many decades later if the age distribution is not a stable one. Even in the United States there are so many more young people who will soon be breeding than old people who will soon be dying that achieving and maintaining replacement reproduction would not stabilize our population until well into the next century.) This phenomenon means that, even under wildly optimistic assumptions about population control, the eventual population of India would be some 1.4 billion people; China, perhaps 1.7 billion; Brazil, 240 million; Indonesia, 310 million, and so on. Since most underdeveloped nations are in the tropics, one need only mesh this information with a little knowledge of the ecology of the tropics to see why Commoner's invocation of the demographic transition as a "cure" is a tragic mistake.

Unfortunately, he also perpetuates the myth that population control can be achieved in part by dropping infant mortality rates (page 236, and elsewhere). Laudable as the goal of reducing such rates is on grounds of compassion, it would in many cases result in temporarily rising growth rates, since the projected declines in birth rate will not compensate for the lowered death rates. (This conclusion is supported by recent computer simulation work by Donella Meadows at M.I.T., based on data from Indian villages.) There is virtually no evidence that depressing infant mortality rates anywhere would result in drops in growth rate until at least a generation had passed.

It is of course, not at all clear that UDCs would undergo a classic demographic transition, even if they should be industrialized. The social and economic conditions are so different in those countries today in comparison to those in the now developed countries in the last century that prediction is difficult.

One-Dimensional Approach

Commoner's "optimistic outlook" (page 240) can only be based on his ignoring the rate and magnitude problems outlined above, combined with a misplaced faith in man's ability to industrialize instantly without environmental damage. An examination of statistics on the consumption of energy and material needed to industrialize the underdeveloped countries reveals the difficulties of achieving even partial industrialization of the UDCs without vast damage to the ecosphere. Mankind's only chance for improving the lot of the poor significantly lies in diverting energy and other resources from extravagant affluence in the DCs to necessity-oriented uses in the UDCs.

Although Commoner gives perfunctory acknowledgment to some of the many deficiencies in his argument (mostly in footnotes), he manages to ignore these considerations completely in reaching his conclusions. Thus he writes on page 176 that "the increase of population accounts for from 12 to 20 per cent of the various increases in total pollutant output since 1946," the "affluence factor . . . accounts for 1 to 5 percent, and the technology factor . . . accounts for about 95 per cent" (except in the case of passenger car travel, when Commoner admits the contribution of affluence is larger and that of technology smaller.) The charitable reader may wish to overlook the point that the lesser of these figures add up to 108 per cent of the problem. In no event is an allocation of "blame" remotely like the one Commoner gives justified by the data and arguments presented in his book.

Yet, as several glowing reviews of "The Closing Circle" bear witness, Commoner has produced a tract quite capable of persuading the naive that he has a calm, "scientific" view of the ecological crisis. In fixing the blame for environmental deterioration on faulty technology alone. Commoner's position is uncomplicated, socially comfortable and, hence, seductive. But there is little point in deluding the public on these matters; the truth is that we must grapple simultaneously with overpopulation, excessive affluence and faulty technology. Of course, facing honestly the need for population control and stabilized consumption exposes one to the painful criticism of being both anti-people and anti-poor, but the fact is that these unpopular measures offer mankind's only hope for averting unprecedented misery. It is better to tell the rich that they will have to share to survive, and to tell those who want large families that the price is mortgaging their children's future, than to offer false hopes of an easy way out.

The fallacy in Commoner's one-dimensional approach is perhaps best illustrated by his own, often repeated analogy that pressing for population control "is equivalent to attempting to save a leaking ship by lightening the load and forcing passengers overboard" (page 255 of "The Closing Circle" and, verbally, before several scientific and popular audiences). Needless to say, if a leaking ship were tied to a dock and passengers were still swarming up the gangplank, a competent captain would keep any more from boarding while he manned the pumps and attempted to repair the leak. (20).

Notes

(1) P.S. Martin and T.E. Wright, Jr., eds., "Pleistocene Extenctions: The Search for a Cause" (New Haven: Yale University Press, 1957).

(2) Thorkild Jacobsen and Robert M. Adams, "Science," 128 (1958), 1251-58.

(3) Carl O. Sauer, in "Man's Role in Changing the Face of the Earth," ed. by William L. Thomas (Chicago: The University of Chicago Press, 1956). See also many other papers in this volume, as well as "Arid Lands in Transition," Publication 90 (Washington, D.C.: AAAS, 1970).

(4) Sauer, in "Man's Role in Changing the Face of the Earth."

(5) Jeremy A. Sabloff, in "Patient Earth," ed. by John Harte and Robert Socolow (New York: Holt, Reinhart & Winston, 1971), pp. 16-27.

(6) E.O. Wilson and W.A. Bossert, "A Primer of Population Biology" (Stamford, Conn.: Sinauer Assoc. 1971); and "Diversity and Stability in Ecological Systems," Brookhaven Symposia in Biology No. 22 (BNL 50175, c-56), 1969.

(7) Allen H. Barton, "Communities in Disaster: A Sociological Analysis of Collective Stress Situtations" (New York: Doubleday, 1969), p. 20.

(8) Reid A. Bryson and Wayne M. Wendland, in "Global Effects of Environmental Pollution," ed. by S.F. Singer (New York: Springer Verlag, 1970); and J. Murray Mitchell, in "Global Effects."

(9) John Ryther, "Science," 166 (1969), 72-76.

(10) These figures and all subsequent demographic, economic and industrial statistics not otherwise attributed are from the "Statistical Abstract of the United States, 1970" (Washington, D.C.: U.S. Department of Commerce, 1970).

(11) H. Landsberg, L. Fischman, and J. Fisher, "Resources in America's Future" (Baltimore: Johns Hopkins Press, 1963), p. 549; and Arnold B. Barach, "U.S.A. and Its Economic Future" (New York: MacMillan, 1964), p. 39.

(12) The mercury discussion in this paragraph is based on information from "Man's Impact on the Global Environment" (Cambridge, Mass.: M.I.T. Press, 1970;

Herbert V. Weiss, Minuro Koide, and Edward D. Goldberg, "Science," 174 (1971), 692; and O.I. Joensu, "Science," 171 (1971), 1027.

(13) "Minerals Yearbook, 1968," Vols. I-II (Washington, D.C.: U.S. Department of the Interior, 1969), p. 155.

(14) A.B. Makhijani and A.J. Lichtenberg, An Assessment of Energy and Materials Utilization in the U.S.A. in "Electronics Research Laboratory Memorandum ERL-M310" (Berkeley: University of California, 1971).

(15) See, e.g., P.R. Ehrlich and J.P. Holdren, "Science," 171 (1971), 1212-17.

(16) "1971 World Population Data Sheet" (Washington, D.C.: Population Reference Bureau); or any recent volume of the "U.N. Demographic Yearbook."

(17) Ansley J. Coale, in "Fertility and Family Planning," ed. by S.J. Behrman, Leslie Corso, Jr., and Ronald Freedman (Ann Arbor: University of Michigan Press, 1969).

(18) See, e.g., Donald J. Bogue, "Principles of Demography" (New York: John Wiley, 1969), p. 59.

(19) Nathan Keyfitz, "Demography," 8 (1971), 71-80.

(20) Many technical references to this article have been abbreviated or eliminated in the interest of space. Copies of the more fully documented version are available from the au.hors.

RESPONSE

Barry Commoner

For most readers, the review of "The Closing Circle" by Paul Ehrlich and John Holdren must raise a number of puzzling questions: Is my analysis of the origin of the environmental crisis as grossly wrong as their criticism would suggest? What accounts for the vehemence of what ordinarily might be regarded as an academic dispute over the relative importance of the several factors that influence environmental degradation? What is the relevance of this dispute to the outlook of the concerned citizen — who wants to know how to act to resolve the environmental crisis?

These comments are intended to help answer these questions. However, it is useful, first, to place the Ehrlich and Holdren criticism of my work, and this response to it, in a historical context. I refer here not to history in its large sweep, but to the much more modest arena in which the development of Paul Ehrlich's views, and my own, has occurred over the last few years.

As readers of "The Closing Circle" will know, my concern with the environmental crisis dates from the nuclear issues of the early 1950s. Since then I have made an effort to study the nature of the crisis and, in keeping with my views regarding the scientist's responsibility to society, to share what I have learned with the general public. Until the late 1960s I was largely concerned with identifying instances of environmental degradation, and with analyzing the interactions among them which comprise the environmental crisis. Beginning with the writing of "Science and Survival," which appeared in 1966, I became particularly concerned with the role played by modern technology in the development of the crisis, and soon recognized the importance of a thorough analysis of how all the relevant factors interact to generate environmental degradation. This was intensified when I discovered, during Earth Week 1970, that many of the views about the origins of the environmental crisis held by different Earth Week participants were contradictory and that some lacked scientific support. In particular, I was struck with the sharp contrast between the unalloyed conviction of Ehrlich, Hardin and others that the numerous assaults on the environment "can be traced easily to *too many people*" (Ehrlich, "The Population Bomb," emphasis in the original), and the absence of any firm, especially numerical, supporting data for this conclusion.

In the last few years, together with a number of colleagues, I have tried to assemble and analyze the available data regarding the roles of the several factors — population size, affluence and technology — that might influence the way in which the productive system of the United States affects the environment. In the course of that work it became increasingly evident that changes in productive technology since World War II have played an important role in the development of the environmental crisis. I began to write and speak about some of the examples that we had studied: how the use of more nitrogen fertilizer on less land (the displacement of land by fertilizer) has intensified the environmental impact of agriculture; how the conversion of the prewar car into today's high-powered monsters transformed a means of transportation into a smog generator; how the substitution of detergents for soap has worsened environmental quality. I found that the numerical size of such technological changes (for example a more than tenfold increase in the annual use of inorganic nitrogen fertilizer since 1945) was much larger than the concurrent increase in population (about 42 per cent), and on these grounds suggested that it might be wrong to conclude that the environmental crisis is exclusively, or even chiefly, the result of population growth.

At about this time I had several conversations about these issues with Ehrlich and his followers. In each of these conversations it was conceded by them, in contrast with Ehrlich's initial position (as expressed in "The Population Bomb"), that population growth is not alone responsible for environmental impact, and that technological factors are also significant. I was gratified by this indication that they were prepared to modify their position on the basis of the new data. However, in each of these conversations, I was urged to give up any discussion in public of the relative importance of the several factors that influence environmental impact. Ehrlich and his followers proposed that we should agree that all the factors are important, and not discuss their relative weight in public. It was argued that any public disagreement between Ehrlich and me on this issue would "split the environmental movement" and reduce the chances of effective action toward environmental improvement.

I responded to these suggestions by expressing a position which I have long held: that is, if there is in fact a real and important difference between my views of the origins of the environmental crisis and Ehrlich's, then both of us are obliged to express them openly; otherwise the mechanism by which science generates the truth, open discussion, is thwarted and our obligation, as scientists, to inform the public, evaded. I expressed considerable shock at the proposition that two scientists should agree in private to withhold from the public their views, whether or not conflicting, on so vital a public issue.

Accordingly I continued to study the ways in which the several factors interact and to write and speak about what I had learned of their relative importance in the environmental crisis. I was particularly interested in working out a means of making numerical estimates of the effects of the several factors on environmental degradation in order to provide an objective means of assessing their influence.

Early in 1971, together with my colleagues Michael Corr and Paul Stamler, I wrote an article on this problem for "Environment" (April 1971). We began our considerations with a helpful statement published earlier by Ehrlich and Holdren. We said, "Dr. Paul Ehrlich provides the following statement regarding these several related factors:"

Pollution can be said to be the result of multiplying three factors; population size, per capita consumption, and an "environmental impact" index that measures, in part, how wisely we apply the technology that goes with consumption.

We paraphrased this relationship as follows:

> Population size X per capita consumption X environmental impact per unit of production equals level of pollution.

We then pointed out that:

> If we are to take effective action, we will need a more detailed guide than the equation offers. To begin with, we must know the relative importance of the three factors on the left side of the equation.

Our article then goes on to discuss the relative values of these factors in the United States since 1946 (as revealed in the available statistical tables) and to point out that the technology factor (environmental impact per unit of production) appears to have increased more than the other two factors.

The "Environment" article was followed by the preparation of a detailed paper scheduled for delivery at a symposium of Resources For the Future (RFF) on this same question. I was extremely interested in working out a way of actually using the relationship first proposed by Ehrlich and Holdren, that is, to find a way of entering the actual values for the several factors and thus computing, numerically, their relative importance. Following discussion with my colleagues, we succeeded in working out a mathematically valid way of carrying out this computation, which will be explained later on.

By these means it was possible to collect the necessary data for a series of pollutants (phosphate from cleaners, fertilizer nitrogen and pesticides from agriculture, nitrogen oxides and lead from automobiles, and bottles from beer consumption), and to compute from them the numerical contributions of the three factors. All of these computations were reported in the RFF paper; they all showed that technological changes contributed the major share of the increases in environmental impact since 1946. It was this data which provided the factual basis for my discussion of these issues in "The Closing Circle."

This now brings us to the Ehrlich and Holdren review of "The Closing Circle." I received several copies of this document in the mail, together with a duplicated letter from Ehrlich and Holdren which accompanied it, apparently in order to explain why the review was written. The text of this letter follows:

> The enclosed detailed review of Barry Commoner's "The Closing Circle" is not for publication, but you are welcome to use the information in it in any way you see fit. We have made several personal attempts to persuade Commoner to avoid a debate on which factor in the environmental crisis is "most important." We felt that such a debate would be counterproductive for the goals which we all share. Unhappily, however, he has persisted in carrying out a campaign, both in speeches and the popular media, to dismiss the roles of population growth and affluence, and place the blame entirely on "faulty technology." He has not argued his case in the refereed scientific literature (as for instance, by publishing a reply to our paper The Impact of Population Growth — "Science," 171: 1212-1217, 1971) but instead has presented it in a popular book.
>
> It is clear from the reviews that few laymen are in a position to deal critically

with the arguments in "The Closing Circle." In discussing this problem with colleagues we decided that a comprehensive, well-documented review giving the pertinent data would be useful for circulation among those interested in environmental problems. Thus the enclosed. We intend to publish a version of this manuscript but thought you might have use for a preliminary copy. Comment or additions would be welcome.

Paul R. Ehrlich
John P. Holdren

One obvious error in this letter is the assertion that my analysis of the origins of the environmental crisis has not been published in "the refereed scientific literature." As already noted, the scientific material which forms the basis of my views on the relative importance of the several factors which influence environmental deterioration was first presented in an article which, together with two colleaques, Michael Corr and Paul Stamler, I submitted for publication in "Environment." It was published in the April 1971 issue of that journal following a review of the manuscript by the scientific advisers of "Environment;" indeed my records show that certain changes in the original manuscript were made in response to criticisms elicited in this review. The members of the "Environment" editorial review board are my peers in these matters, and I regard their review of the manuscript quite sufficient to qualify it as a publication in the refereed scientific literature. My analysis of environmental impact has also been published in two journals — "The Monthly Labor Review" (a publication of the U.S. Department of Labor) and "Chemistry in Britain" (a publication of the Royal Institute of Chemistry) — both of which qualify, I believe, as refereed scientific literature. It is perhaps worth noting that Ehrlich first heard a detailed exposition of my analysis at a symposium at the December 1970 meeting of the American Association for the Advancement of Science. I organized the symposium for the purpose of eliciting debate on the subject and Ehrlich participated at my invitation. It might be pertinent to note here, since Ehrlich and Holdren have raised the issue, that Ehrlich's "Population Bomb" was published well before he expressed his views in the refereed scientific literature.

In their letter, Ehrlich and Holdren report — as I have already indicated above — that they had earlier asked me to desist from public discussion of our differing views on the relative importance of the several factors which influence environmental impact, and they voice their regret that I have, nevertheless, "persisted." It would appear from this letter that Ehrlich's present attack on my views is a consequence of my refusal to accept his earlier proposition for joint silence on this issue.

Basic Mathematical Fault

However, if Ehrlich's criticism does not originate in wholly scientific considerations, it is, nevertheless, largely — but not entirely — scientific in content. Hence, I propose to reply to it largely in scientific terms, offering comments outside the context of science only where the criticism in itself departs from that realm.

Central to Ehrlich and Holdren's scientific criticism of "The Closing Circle" is their claim that I have not used proper mathematical methods to analyze the relationships among the several factors which influence environmental impact. Specifically, Ehrlich and Holdren ascribe to me certain procedures (involving mathematical relationships between percentages) which they regard as an invalid means of expressing the relationships among the several factors that might give rise to environmental impact.

They then develop an equation which, in apparent contrast to my treatment, is, in their view, valid.

Obviously if they are correct in this claim, there is little reason for anyone to pay attention to much of what I have written in "The Closing Circle." It becomes essential, then, to compare the validity of my analysis and of that put forward by Ehrlich and Holdren, for either my analysis or their criticism of it must be wrong. In order to permit the reader to choose between these alternatives, I propose (a) to describe the procedures which my colleagues and I used to establish numerical values for the effects of the several environmental factors, as they were presented in the RFF paper and later summarized in "The Closing Circle," and (b) to cast these results into a form which permits a direct mathematical comparison between my analytical procedure and equation (3) of the Ehrlich and Holdren review, which they regard — in contrast with my treatment — as mathematically valid. As will be shown below, it then becomes self-evident whether my analysis, or their criticism of it, is wrong.

As indicated earlier, my colleagues and I developed our approach from an equation proposed earlier by Ehrlich and Holdren. We began with the population factor (P), which is simply the size of the U.S. population in a given year. Then the affluence factor (A) was defined as the amount of goods produced (or consumed) per capita in that same year, and the technology factor (T) as the amount of pollutant emitted per unit of goods produced (or consumed) in that year. The overall amount of pollutant emitted in the year was defined as the environmental impact (I).

Once the several factors are defined in this way, the proper mathematical relationship among them is self-evident from the procedure called "dimensional analysis." (A very simple problem which can be solved by this procedure is the following: What is the proper mathematical relationship between the length of a rectangle (L), its width (W), and its area (A), given that the area is expressed in square feet? Noting that ft X ft equals ft II, it becomes evident that the only relationship which conforms with this requirement is: L X W equals A.) Thus, given the above definitions of the terms I, P, A, and T, it can be seen that the following relationship produces a mathematical identity, in which amount of pollution equals amount of pollutant (i.e., I equals I):

$$\text{Amount of Pollutant (I) equals Population}$$
$$X \; \frac{\text{Production (or consumption)}}{\text{Population}}$$

$$X \; \frac{\text{Amount of Pollutant}}{\text{Production (or consumption)}}$$

Note that both population terms and both production terms cancel out, leaving the relationship: amount of pollutant equals amount of pollutant. Since this relationship is obviously dimensionally correct, the entire equation is also dimensionally correct.

Our primary concern was to explain numerically the increase in the amount of pollutants emitted annually, for what characterizes the environmental crisis is the sharp rise in pollution levels in the years since World War II. Accordingly we needed to compute the increases, over a given span of years, of all four factors: I, P, A, and T. This was done by tabulating, for a variety of pollutants, the actual values of each of these factors for two years: usually 1946, or the earliest year for which the necessary statistics were available, and 1967 or 1968. Then, to show how the factors interacted to produce the increase in pollutants emitted over this period of time, the ratios of the 1946 and 1968 values of the factors were multiplied together. As an example, we present in the table the values for beer bottles for 1950 and 1967. This table illustrates an important feature of such computation, that is, they often involve the use of a figure for pollutant emissions (I) which is not the actual amount of the pollutants entering the environment but the best available indicator of that amount. In this instance, the number of beer bottles directly expresses the environmental impact of beer consumption on solid waste, but it is only indirectly related to the impact due to the air pollutants produced from fuel burned in the production, filling, and distribution of the bottles. However, since Bruce Hannon ("Environment," March 1972) has now computed the latter values, once the number of bottles is known, the effects on air pollution can be computed.

Put into the form of an equation, the operation represented by the underscored line in the above table may be stated as follows:

$$(1 + \frac{\Delta P}{P}) \times (1 + \frac{\Delta A}{A})$$

$$\times (1 + \frac{\Delta T}{T}) = (1 + \frac{\Delta I}{I})$$

where I, P, A, and T represent respectively the 1950 values of impact, population size, goods per capita (affluence factor), and pollutant per unit goods (technology factor) and ΔI, ΔP, ΔA, and ΔT represent the increases between 1950 and 1967 in the corresponding values. Thus, for the example cited above we have:

$$(1 + \frac{45,991}{151,868}) \times (1 + \frac{1.28}{24.99}) \times$$

$$(1 + \frac{1.01}{.25}) = (1 + \frac{38,936}{6,540})$$

or 1.30 × 1.05 × 5.08 = 6.95.

This computation shows that whereas the technology factor has increased about fivefold since 1949, the affluence factor has increased only 1.05-fold (which means that people drink nearly the same amount of beer per capita, annually, as they used to), and the population only 1.30-fold. This leads to the conclusion that the technology factor makes by far the larger contribution to the approximately sevenfold change in beer bottle dissemination that occurred between 1950 and 1967. The table also provides an alternative way of expressing the very same relationships: that the 595 per cent increase in beer bottle dissemination arises from a 30 per cent increase in population, a 5 per cent increase in the affluence factor, and a 40 per cent increase in the technology factor. Note, however, that the operation of multiplication is not carried out on these percentages, but between the ratios, as required by the mathematics of the equation. Similar computations — for the impact of fertilizer and pesticides due to their use in agriculture, of lead and nitrogen oxides due to passenger car operation, and of phosphate due to the use of cleaners — are reported in the RFF paper and summarized in "The Closing Circle." All of them show that, as in the case of beer consumption, the largest contribution to the postwar increase in pollutant emissions is made by the technology factor.

BEER BOTTLES
ENVIRONMENTAL IMPACT INDEX

| | Index Factors | | | Total Index |
	(a)	(b)	(c)	$(a \times b \times c)$[a]
	Population (1000's)	Beer Consumption Population (Gallons/cap)	Beer Bottles Beer Consumption (Bottles/gallon)	Beer Bottles (1000 Gross)
1950	151,868	24.99	.25	6,540
1967	197,859	26.27	1.26	45,476
1967:1950	1.30	1.05	5.08	6.95
% Increase 1950-1967	30	5	408	595

[a] This multiplication applies only to the first three lines, not to the per cent increase 1950 to 1967.

This, then, is the basis for the position developed in "The Closing Circle." Ehrlich and Holdren's most serious criticism of this position is that it depends on a faulty mathematical procedure. In part this criticism is based on their claim that I use an analysis which involves a mathematically inadmissable procedure — the multiplication of percentages. However, as can be seen from the above account (and as shown in detail below), this description is false; nowhere in the procedure are percentages multiplied. Then, in order to validate their overall criticism of my mathematical procedures, Ehrlich and Holdren proceed to develop what they regard to be the proper mathematical procedure: their development culminates in the following statement:

> To examine more closely how Commoner's use of percentages has obstruced the importance of the growth of these factors, we rewrite the impact equation to express all quantities as multiples of their initial values:

$$1 + \frac{\Delta I}{I} = (1 + \frac{\Delta P}{P})$$

$$\times (1 + \frac{\Delta A}{A}) \times 1 + \frac{\Delta T}{T}).$$

Now it will be noted that this equation is precisely the one which my colleagues and I had developed earlier and which had been reported—with several examples of real data (as compared with the universally hypothetical ones put forward by Ehrlich and Holdren) — well before their critique: in April 1971 to the RFF symposium; in a keynote address which I delivered in July 1971 to the Conference of Parliamentary Public Health Specialists of the Parliament of Europe in Stockholm; in a report published in September 1971 by the U.S. Senate Committee on Interior and Insular Affairs ("Selected Readings on Economic Growth in Relation to Population Increase, Natural Resources Availability, Environmental Quality Control, and Energy Needs"); in abbreviated form in the November 1971 issue of "Monthly Labor Review," published by the U.S. Department of Labor. In "The Closing Circle" the material of the RFF paper was summarized without departing in any way from the original mathematical treatment (see below), and in the notes the reader is referred to the RFF paper for details.

Criticism Unfounded

In sum, with regard to this crucial "scientific" criticism of my analysis by Ehrlich and Holdren, the situation is this: With the help of several colleagues, basing our procedure on a simplified relationship among the several pollution-related factors first advanced by Ehrlich and Holdren (and giving credit to them), I refined their equation into a form that expressed changes in time as ratios of the values for two years. (In other words, the values for the later year are expressed as multiples of the corresponding values for the earlier year.) We then accumulated actual data for a number of pollutants, and computed, by means of this equation, the actual numerical relationship among the relevant factors. These computations of the actual data on postwar changes in the United States showed that, among the three relevant factors, technological change had the major effect on environmental impact. These results were reported in several places between April and November 1971 and were incorporated in "The Closing Circle," which was published in October 1971. Some time in December 1971, Ehrlich and Holdren prepared and distributed a review of the book in which they criticized my mathematical treatment of these relationships by contrasting it with a "proper" equation which they claim to have developed. Their equation is identical to the one which I reported earlier, beginning with the RFF paper in April 1971, and which is the basis of treatment developed in "The Closing Circle." Thus, Ehrlich and Holdren propose to correct my supposedly faulty mathematical analysis of the impact factors by offering in its place the very same equation which I had used. Obviously, on their own grounds my analytical method is correct and their criticism of it unfounded. In sum, Ehrlich and Holdren's basic criticism of my analysis of the relative effects of population size, "affluence" and productive technology on environmental impact is not only false, but absurdly so.

Given this background, it should come as no surprise that all of the specific criticisms made by Ehrlich and Holdren of my mathematical analysis of environmental impact turn out to be equally false. These are taken up in what follows.

Ehrlich and Holdren assert, regarding the basic equation:

> Within this framework, an objective discussion of the relative importance of the three factors on the right of equation (1) would attempt to assign numerical values to all of them, rendering the comparison self-evident. Commoner does not do this.

As already established, the first of these sentences repeat my own position on the use of the equation. The second sentence is simply false. What I have done in the RFF paper referred to above is precisely "to assign numerical values" to the three factors. Moreover, the results of this analysis were reported in "The Closing Circle," as follows:

Following a description of the equation, I state (p. 176) that:

> In the United States all three factors have changed since 1946. By comparing these changes with the concurrent increases in total pollutant output it is possible to assign to each of the three factors the fraction of the overall increase in pollutant output for which it is responsible. When this computation is carried out for the economic goods considered above . . . a rather clear picture emerges.

Reference to the notes for this part of the text informs the reader that these computations are to be found in the several papers already referred to. One might expect that, on noting these references, scientifically qualified commentators such as Ehrlich and Holdren would read them in order to determine whether I have or have not carried out the computations as claimed in the passage cited above. As already indicated, there they would find all the required computations set forth in a series of tables, one of which has already been provided as an example above.

At this point Ehrlich and Holdren make an additional and quite crucial statement about my computations. They state:

> Concentrating on the period from 1946 to 1968, he cites percentage increases of 200 per cent or more in various pollutants (claimed to be indications of the impact, I) and he notes that population in this period grew "only" 42 per cent. Thus the reader inexperienced in such calculations is left with the impression that population accounted for only a fifth or less of the increase in pollution (40 per cent / 200 percent equals one-fifth), and that affluence and technology must have accounted for the other four-fifths. But this is not so because the causative factors are multiplicative.

If the foregoing statement is meant to refer to any statement made by me, it is false, for nowhere in "The Closing Circle," or in any other writings have I presented a computation of the form cited above. What follows summarizes all the places in "The Closing Circle" in which the factors are introduced and arithmetic operations are performed.

One, on page 128 data are presented which show that annual emissions of a number of key pollutants have increased by about 200 to 2,000 per cent since 1946. Neither population, affluence, nor technology factors are mentioned here; neither comparisons nor arithmetic operations are made.

Two, on page 133 it is noted that the postwar U.S. population increased about 42 per cent and that this is insufficient, in itself, to account for the much larger concurrent increases in pollution emissions. (This assertion is obviously correct, since annual emissions increased by 200 to 2,000 per cent). No other numbers are mentioned here and no computations are made.

Three, on page 136 it is asserted that "the ratio between the amount of pollution generated in the United States and the size of the population has increased sharply since 1946." (The correctness of this statement is self-evident). The statement continues, "This relationship can be converted to a mathematically equivalent but — as we shall see — highly misleading statement: that there has been a sharp increase in the amount of pollution produced *per person* (emphasis in original). For example if pollution has increased tenfold while population has increased by 43 per cent, then pollution per person has increased about sevenfold (1.43 X 7 equals 10 approximately)." (Note that the term "pollution per capita" is the product of the "affluence" and "technology" terms in the basic equation.) Here for the first time a mathematical relationship between amount of pollution and the product of population X pollution per capita is put forward. Both the prose and the arithmetic are accurate and informative. Note for example that while the increase in population is referred to in per cent (43 per cent), in the arithmetic operation it is converted, as required, to the appropriate ratio or multiple (1.43). Thus, the reader is shown explicitly the proper relationship between the more common percentile expression and the multiple which must be used in the arithmetic operation.

Four, on page 140 the relationship among the three factors is stated as follows:

> While two factors frequently blamed for the environmental crisis, population and affluence, have intensified in that time (i.e., following World War II), these increases are much too small to account for the 200 to 2,000 per cent rise in pollution levels since 1946. The product of the two factors, which represents the total output of goods (total production equals population times production per capita), is also insufficient to account for the intensification of pollution. Total production — as measured by GNP (Gross National Product) — has increased 126 per cent since 1946, while most pollution levels have risen by at least several times that rate.

Again, the statements are accurate and wholly in keeping with the proper arithmetic relationships, as described in the basic equation.

Five, on pages 175 and 176 the necessary multiplicative relationship between all three factors is described as follows:

> It is useful, at this point, to return to a question asked earlier: What are the relative effects of the three factors that might be expected to influence the intensity of environmental pollution — population size, degree of affluence, and the tendency of the productive technology to pollute? A rather simple mathematical relationship connects the amount of pollutant emitted into the environment to these factors: pollutant emitted is equal to the product of the three factors — population times the amount of a given economic good per capita times output of pollutant per unit of the economic good produced.

As indicated earlier (and, in fact, as acknowledged by Ehrlich and Holdren) this is an accurate statement, in prose, of the basic relationship among the three factors.

Six, finally, on pages 211 and 212, an exercise involving the entire equation is proposed; the exercise is described in detail in the notes, where it is evident that the computations are governed by the equations given earlier.

The foregoing is the total presentation of the arithmetic relationships among the several factors as given in "The Closing Circle." Nowhere can one find the relationship put forward by Ehrlich and Holdren as the supposed basis whereby "the reader inexperienced in such calculations is left with the impression that population accounted for only a fifth or less of the increase in pollution (40 per cent / 200 per cent equals one-fifth) and that affluence and technology must have accounted for the other four-fifths." Hence, their statement is false.

The conclusion which Ehrlich and Holdren ascribe to me (i.e., that population increase accounts for one-fifth or less of the increases in pollution level) is accurate. What they have falsely described is the mathematical means by which I reached that conclusion. The method which I used is described in a general way in "The Closing Circle" and in detail in the indicated references. In both places, as already shown above, the computations developed are identical in form to those put forward later by Ehrlich and Holdren as a criticism of my methods.

Following the development of the basic analysis outlined above, Michael Corr and I became interested in finding a way to compare the several computations of different pollutants in order to arrive at possible generalizations about the relative effects of the three separate factors. By expressing the ratios of the impacts for two different years in logarithmic terms, it was possible to evaluate the contribution of the change in any one factor; for example, population (as given by the ratio of the populations in the two years) in terms of the fraction which the logarithm of that ratio represented of the logarithm of the corresponding ratio of the total impacts. Since in multiplication logarithms are added, it becomes possible by this means to compute a relative measure of the contribution of each of the three factors to the total impact. We found that for the several different pollutants, the logarithm of the population ratios was about 15 to 20 per cent of the logarithm of the total impact ratios. These further computations are the basis of the statement in "The Closing Circle" that:

> The increase in population accounts for from 12 to 20 per cent of the various increases in total pollutant output since 1946. The affluence factor (i.e., amount of economic good per capita), accounts for from 1 to 5 per cent of the total increase in pollutant output, except in the case of passenger travel, where the contribution rises to about 40 per cent of the total. . . . The technology factor — that is, the increased output of pollutants per unit production resulting from the introduction of new productive technologies since 1946 — accounts for about 95 per cent of the total output of pollutants, except in the case of passenger travel, where it accounts for about 40 per cent of the total.

Now there are, in fact, two errors in the passage quoted above. One of the figures, "about 95 per cent," is a typographical error; it should read "about 80 to 85 per cent." More important, the passage should have referred to the relationships among logarithms of the increases (as expressed by the ratios) rather than to the increases themselves. Thus, to be precise, the passage should have read: "The logarithm of the increase in population (as given by the ratios of the values for the two years) accounts for from 12 to 20 per cent of the logarithm of the various increases in total pollutant emitted annually since 1946 (again, as given by the ratios)." In other words, the logarithms of the ratios and not the ratios are being compared. While, in mathematical terms this permits the kind of comparison we sought, it is important to note that it does so on a logarithmic rather than on the more common linear scale. While such logarithmic comparisons have the disadvantage of not being readily incorporated into the context of every day thinking, they do permit us to make the sought-for generalizations about the relative rules of the factors involved in environmental impact. The omission of the logarithmic term in the above passage is regrettable, but it in no way changes the actual relationships among the factors; it remains true that the largest effect is due to technology.

I proceed now to detailed comments on the other major points raised in the Ehrlich and Holdren review. I have tried to deal with all of the major criticisms; some of the others are simply too trivial or too patently peevish to warrant space in this already crowded statement.

The basic position taken by Ehrlich and Holdren regarding "The Closing Circle" appears to be that the overall argument of the book consists of "fixing the blame for environmental deterioration on faulty technology alone" and that "uncritical acceptance" of this argument will lead to "public complacency concerning both population and affluence," the other two important factors. They assert — and attempt to demonstrate — that my argument has three defects: it rests on the misuse of data and their mathematical relationships; it ignores environmental problems other than pollution; and it rests on mistakes about "certain aspects of demography."

Numerical Sleight-of-Hand

Ehrlich and Holdren assert that "(Commoner) resorts to biased selection of data, unconventional definitions, numerical sleight of hand, and bad ecology." A good part of this criticism is based on the supposed errors in my mathematical treatment of environmental impact. As already shown above, that criticism is not only false but absurd.

Another major change is that my argument consists of "fixing the blame for environmental deterioration on faulty technology alone." This charge is patently false, for as already shown, a great deal of the effort in "The Closing Circle" (and in the more detailed studies on which it is based) was directed toward estimating the relative effects of all three factors which are involved in environmental impact. Indeed, to my knowledge, the computations presented in the book and in the background papers include the first numerical estimates of the effect of population growth on environmental impact; in no instance have I reported a zero effect, which would be the case if environmental impact were due to "technology alone." Nowhere in "The Closing Circle," or in any other of my writings, can there be found a statement which holds or implies that "faulty technology alone" is to "blame for environmental deterioration."

Ehrlich and Holdren claim that my analysis "resorts to biased selection of data." Presumably a prime instance of this supposed defect is what they call "Commoner's list" of sources of environmental degradation. Here a couple of parenthetical remarks are in order, to begin with.

First, as I shall show below, the list of supposed ecological offenders exist not in my writing but in the imaginations of Ehrlich and Holdren. My list is one of displacements of one means of meeting human needs by another.

Now, let us examine the Ehrlich and Holdren exercise which purports to correct my "omission" of an important source of environmental degradation: "He (Commoner) says almost nothing about energy production or consumption as a whole, however, perhaps because it would damage his case to do so." They attempt to show that in this specific instance the technology factor is not as important a source of environmental impact as I believe. They point out that total U.S. energy production in 1969 was 2.4 times that in 1940; population increased 53 per cent, and energy production per capita increased by 57 per cent in that time. Hence they assert that these two factors contribute about equally to total energy production (since population X production/capita equals production, and 1.53 X 1.57 equals 2.40). On these grounds Ehrlich and Holdren conclude that "the contribution of population growth is hardly unimportant." However, (curiously in contrast with their exhortation elsewhere that all three factors must be related to environmental impact), Ehrlich and Holdren have here omitted to enter the third factor: pollutant/economic good (the technology factor).

It is illuminating to rectify this omission. What we need to know is the amount of pollutant emitted per unit of fuel used in 1940 and 1969. Unfortunately we have this information only for pollutants due to automotive use of energy, but a discussion of this aspect of the fuel problem is sufficient to illustrate where Ehrlich and Holdren have gone astray.

Missing Factor

What is required is to enter the missing technology factor into the equation and, thereby, compute the influence of all three factors on the overall environmental impact of automotive fuel consumption. This is, of course, precisely what I have done in my earlier papers and have reported in "The Closing Circle" (pp 169-170) in the case of passenger cars for two major pollutants, lead and nitrogen oxides. The computations for nitrogen oxides, for example, are as follows for the period 1946-1967. The ratios of the 1967: 1946 values are for population, 1.41; for total fuel consumption, 2.85; for fuel consumption/population, 2.02; for vehicle-miles/population, 2.00; for nitrogen oxide emissions/vehicle mile, 2.58; and for total nitrogen oxide emission (impact), 7.3.

Now, given these data, if we follow the approach of Ehrlich and Holdren, it would be stated that since population increased by a factor of 1.41, fuel consumption per capita by a factor of 2.02 and total fuel consumption by a factor of 2.85, the relevant relationship is: 1.41 X 2.02 equals 2.85. Since the overall impact is only a 2.85-fold increase, and the effect of population growth represents a 1.41-fold increase, it seems valid to conclude, as Ehrlich and Holdren do, that "the contribution of population growth is hardly unimportant."

My approach to these same data is different. First, I define the affluence factor not in terms of fuel consumption, but in terms of the actual good which it yields — in this case vehicle-miles/population. Then, whereas Ehrlich and Holdren deal with only the population and affluence factors, I introduce the third factor, technology, or in this case nitrogen oxides emitted per vehicle mile. Now the whole relationship becomes:

$$1.41 \times 2.00 \times 2.58 \text{ equals } 7.3$$

Note that, according to Ehrlich and Holdren, the contribution of population growth (1.43-fold) is compared to the increase in fuel consumption (2.85-fold), so that the contribution of the population factor does indeed seem relatively important. In contrast, if the missing technology factor is included, and the effect expressed in terms of a real pollutant (nitrogen oxides), the total impact increases 7.3-fold (rather than 2.85-fold), so the importance of the population factor has to be judged against that figure rather than against 2.85. The significance of the population effect relative to the other two factors is thereby diminished.

Thus, in violation of their own admonition — "an objective discussion of the relative importance of the three factors on the right of equation (I) would attempt to assign numerical values to all of them (emphasis mine)" — Ehrlich and Holdren have neglected to consider the third factor, technology. When the third factor is entered, as I have done above, the picture changes drastically, and the relative effect of population growth becomes smaller than Ehrlich and Holdren would have us believe.

This error is repeated in Ehrlich and Holdren's comments on automobile production. Here they consider the environmental impact of the number of cars produced (not used), dividing the effect between population and cars produced per capita. Obviously what is missing here is the technology factor, in this case pollutants emitted per car produced (i.e. environmental pollution due to car manufacturing). Complete data are lacking, but the effect of changes in the amount of electric power used in motor vehicle manufacturing — an important aspect of environmental degradation — gives us at least a partial answer.

In 1937 (the closest year to 1940 for which the necessary data are available to us) about 179 kilowatt-hours of electric power were used to manufacture each motor vehicle; by 1967 that figure was 708 kilowatt-hours per vehicle. Thus, the technology figure (pollution due to power used per vehicle) increased 3.95-fold between 1937 and 1967. During that time, population increased 1.54-fold and affluence, as measured by vehicles produced per capita, increased 1.22-fold. The full equation using the relevant ratios now becomes

$$1.54 \times 1.22 \times 3.95 \text{ equals } 7.43,$$

from which it can be seen that the effect of increased population on total impact is relatively small (i.e., 1.54-fold as compared with 7.43-fold) and that the technology factor has the largest effect (3.95-fold) of the three factors.

However, Ehrlich and Holdren compute the environmental impact of car production from the number of cars produced, and divide this effect between only two factors, population and cars per capita. Hence their relationship is

$$1.54 \times 1.22 \text{ equals } 1.88,$$

and now the effect of population growth (1.54-fold increase) is indeed significant because it is compared with an increase in total impact which is only 1.88-fold. Again we see that when the technology factor is omitted from the computation the population factor can be compared with a relatively small increment in total impact, and to that degree, gains in apparent importance. However, this type of computation, which is used here by Ehrlich and Holdren, violates their earlier emphasis — with which I agree — on the necessity of considering all three factors.

Thus, in this feature of their criticism of "The Closing Circle," Ehrlich and Holdren exhibit a remarkable reversal of position. Whereas earlier they criticize me (falsely, as we have seen) for failing to undertake computations of environmental impact in which values for all three relevant factors are entered, here they do precisely what they accuse me of doing and, as a consequence, exaggerate the role of population growth in environmental impact.

Point Missed

Here Ehrlich and Holdren appear to reflect a serious fault in their understanding of the relationship of the three factors to environmental degradation. One of the ideas that I tried very hard to make clear in the book, because I have found it so essential to an effective understanding of this issue, is that when we attempt to assess the significance of a given level of pollution, it is essential that it be related to the economic good which results from the relevant production process. I have found it particularly important to separate carefully the actual good from its more superficial embodiments. Thus, I point out that when a bottle of beer is purchased the economic good which is received is chiefly the beer and not the container, an insight which tells us that the rising clutter of beer bottles is closely related to the introduction of a new technology, throwaway bottles. This relationship is particularly important to a consideration of the balance between the benefit of a technology and its environmental hazard — a judgment which is the necessary prelude to action on an environmental issue. Thus, if the benefit is defined as beer, then the ratio of benefit-hazard falls as delivery of the same pint of beer is shifted from a returnable bottle to a throwaway one, even though beer consumption per capita remains constant. Unfortunately, Ehrlich and Holdren have missed this point and, as a result, as shown above, are quite thoroughly mistaken in their analysis of the roles of the several factors in environmental degradation.

To take another example, Ehrlich and Holdren have failed to understand that fuel consumption is not in itself an economic good (which is the desired transportation, for example, as measured by passenger miles), but is rather part of one technological factor which contributes to the environmental impact of car-driving. Fuel is the appropriate economic good in a computation regarding the relative effects of population increase, changes in "affluence," and technology only when it is the final product of the process under examination. For example, in the production of gasoline from crude petroleum it would be appropriate to compute the amount of gasoline produced per capita as a measure of affluence and to compute the amount of a pollutant, such as sulfur dioxide, released by the production process per gallon of gasoline as a measure of the technological factor. However, when fuel is used to generate some other economic good, fuel consumption is not the appropriate measure of economic good. Here, fuel consumption is an appropriate measure of the influence of the technological factor on the overall environmental impact in the form: fuel consumed / goods produced.

The failure of Ehrlich and Holdren to understand these relationships — which derive directly from the three-factor equation that they so much admire — largely accounts for their complaints that I have ignored the environmental role of "affluence," as it is often defined — in terms of television sets and fancy cars. What the equation indicates, and what I have tried to express in my writings, is that regardless of the myth created by advertising propaganda and the consequent cultural attitudes, true affluence ought to be measured by the actual consumption of goods that in fact contribute to human welfare.

Ehrlich and Holdren's failure to understand these relationships is reflected in their Table 1, which is designed, apparently, to show that I have neglected to discuss such items of "affluence" as telephones and water heaters in my consideration of the origin of environmental impact. Here they report data on the numbers of these items in use per capita. Now these data reflect not the effect of production of these goods on environmental impact but their use. As already indicated, for the evaluation of the latter it is necessary to consider the environmental impact of the fuel used to operate these items. This is a rather complex problem which at the time of the writing of "The Closing Circle had been insufficiently analyzed, in my opinion, to warrant inclusion in the book. Since then, thanks to a number of current studies of the energy problem we have learned a great deal more about this problem some of which was reported in my recent paper "Power Production and Human Welfare," presented at the annual meeting of the AAAS in Philadelphia in December 1971. It is pertinent to note that the results of this study support the conclusions reached in "The Closing Circle" quite well. For example, in the case of hot-water heaters, if affluence is measured in terms of the actual good (in this case, hot water) it becomes evident that the technology factor (pollution per unit hot water) has increased as electric heaters, which are relatively inefficient in their use of the fuel resource, have displaced the more efficient oil or gas-fired heaters.

On Affluence

It is also pertinent to note that the discussion of affluence in "The Closing Circle" was specifically oriented toward environmental impact, and was in no sense intended to evaluate consumption levels for their own sake. In these terms, importation of items such as clothing is irrelevant to the computation of environmental impact in the United States, since the production took place elsewhere. Of course such imported clothing does involve an environmental impact in the country of origin, but what is at issue in this discussion is the explanation of the rising environmental impact in the United States, and that derives from productive operations within the United States. Similarly, Ehrlich and Holdren's comments about rising per capita expenditures for housing do not necessarily reflect a comparable increase in the contribution of affluence to the environmental impact due to housing. For example, housing costs are dependent on interest rates, which have certainly increased in the postwar years, but the resultant increase in per capita housing cost has nothing to do with environmental impact. Rather we need to know the environmental costs of the construction and maintenance of dwellings; and, again, the technology factor would appear to dominate as steel is displaced by aluminum and as inefficient electric space heating displaces fuel-fired systems.

Apparently, my approach to the problem of affluence has been meaningful to some readers. Thus, in reviewing "The Closing Circle," Sir Eric Ashby comments:

> Pollution is compounded of people, their per capita consumption of goods and services, and the impact on the environment which these goods and service make. The run-of-the-mill Cassandra indicates population and consumption. Commoner maintains that per capita consumption has not risen alarmingly; what has risen alarmingly is the impact of modern, as opposed to traditional, goods and services on the environment. He supports his thesis with some interesting facts. Take beer, for instance. Between 1950 and 1967 the per capita consumption of beer in the United States increased by about 5 per cent. But over the same period the per capita consumption of nonreturnable beer containers increased by 595 per cent. The consumer is no more affluent: it is the beer he wants. ("Spectator," London, Feb. 5, 1972.)

Similarly, Rene Dubos's review of "The Closing Circle" states, regarding criticism of my definition of affluence:

> Indeed, his critics are probably right if affluence is to be measured in terms of two cars in every garage, color television sets, motor boats, snowmobiles, and a multiplicity of convenience foods and garments. However, these criteria are rapidly losing validity. Technological innovation and economic growth are no longer considered to be self-evident goals. Commoner has rendered a great service by providing a factual basis for an inquiry into the options which are available to men at the present stage of scientific technological development in their search for the good life and for a better form of society. ("Environment," January-February 1972.)

Obviously, Ehrlich and Holdren are less receptive to my view of affluence than are

Dubos and Ashby. Ehrlich and Holdren may certainly disagree with me (and with Dubos and Ashby) and may offer a different, more conventional, definition of affluence if they like; but they repeatedly reveal that they have failed to understand my position.

Ehrlich and Holdren also seem to be particularly unable to grasp what I try to say in connection with the relative growth of the production of various goods, as described on page 143. They appear to regard this list as a roster of "indicators of environmental impact" and complain that for a variety of reasons certain of the items on the list are not suitable for this purpose. But the list was not composed for the purpose which Ehrlich and Holdren describe. Rather, as stated explicitly (p. 142), the list was a technique for describing "how the economy has grown." I describe the technique for computing the growth rates and then state "when this list is rearranged in decreasing order of growth rate, a picture of how the United States economy has grown since World War II begins to emerge." I then point out the most interesting feature of the list, that is, "what has changed drastically is the technology of production rather than overall output of the economic good."

Ecological Impact Inventory

Thus, the list deals with the relative rates of growth of different productive technologies, and not with the absolute sizes of the different activities. The list describes the displacement of one technology by another rather than the importance of the environmental impact generated by any given item. Ehrlich and Holdren clearly fail to understand this point. Thus they complain with respect to the high growth rate of non-returnable bottles that the bottles are "neither a major fraction of United States glass production nor an ecologically significant pollutant." Nowhere do I claim that this is the case. Instead I point out from the high rate of growth in throwaway bottles that they have displaced returnable ones which are, after all, ecologically more sound, so that the benefit-hazard ratio involved in the consumption of soda and beer has been reduced.

Again, asserting the false claim that the list is designed as a roster of ecological guilt, Ehrlich and Holdren complain that "Commoner has padded his list of dramatic increases with four different aspects of essentially the same flaw," because I include in the list synthetic organic chemicals, pesticides, chlorine, and mercury used to manufacture chlorine. Here Ehrlich and Holdren have missed a vital aspect of the pollution problem to which many other environmentalists are now giving considerable attention: the great value of input-output analysis in explicating environmental impact. Such an analysis depicts the full extent of the environmental impact associated with the production of a particular good (e.g., pesticides) by showing how the manufacture of necessary raw materials (e.g., chlorine) also generates environmental impacts (e.g., mercury). To most environmentalists these interactions have become a fruitful source of new insights, and it seemed useful to provide a glimpse into them for the readers of "The Closing Circle." It is only in the imaginations of Ehrlich and Holdren that the list is a roster of ecological insults. That I have "padded" it is likewise a view which is peculiarly their own. Ehrlich and Holdren belabor the point that the rate of growth of the use of mercury for chloralkali production has "little relevance" as an indicator "of the overall level of mercury pollution" — still driven by the false notion that this is the purpose of my discussion. This item was included in the list, however, not as a measure of the overall use of mercury, but to illustrate how the displacement of natural substances by synthetic ones intensifies environmental impact, for example, in the manufacture of synthetics chlorine is used which results in the release of mercury to the environment.

What is noteworthy about all of these "defects" in my position is that they are such obvious ones — provided one accepts Ehrlich and Holdren's definition of the purpose of my displacement list. It is, after all, widely known that detergents, most pesticides and materials used to manufacture plastics and synthetic fibers are subsumed under the category "synthetic organic chemicals," so that my supposed "padding" of the list should be evident to almost anyone who, like Ehrlich and Holdren, misconstrued its purpose. It is perhaps worth noting here that among the 100 or so reviews of "The Closing Circle," many of which discuss in some detail the displacement list, there is not a single instance in which the reviewer interprets it as Ehrlich and Holdren do.

The Ehrlich and Holdren review treats us to a display of detailed concern about the elaborate considerations (including longevity and effects on energy use of substitute materials) which need to go into a full analysis of environmental impact. This is, of course, precisely the detailed accounting, an ecological impact inventory, that is called for on page 197 of "The Closing Circle":

> Such pollution price tags are needed for all major products. . . . The foregoing account shows how far we are from the goal and once again reminds us how blind we are about the environmental effects of modern technology.

Ehrlich and Holdren's observations about the environmental hazards associated with an effort to supply present fabric needs from natural sources illustrates this point quite well. We are, indeed, still largely ignorant about the most ecologically sound way to produce the needed fabrics: How cotton might be produced without the ecological insult of pesticides and fertilizers, or how wool could be produced without degrading the soil through over-grazing. What is at issue is that the basic process of producing cotton or wool is biological and, therefore, capable of successful integration into the biosphere, while the synthesis of nylon from petroleum, even with the best possible environmental controls, is nevertheless outside the ecosystem and therefore stresses it. On these matters Ehrlich and Holdren remind us that "Commoner admits he does not know (see his footnote to p. 160), but the uncertainty is forgotten when he draws his conclusions." In the absence of the relevant data, I regard the admission of uncertainty — of ignorance, if need be — as a viture. Not so Ehrlich and Holdren, for they are quite content to conclude, following their recitation of the numerous needed parameters — but of no numbers to match them — that "it is clear, then, that population growth and rising affluence can stimulate qualitative changes in the technologies of production. . ."

Diminishing Returns

Then there is the matter of "diminishing returns," which according to Ehrlich and Holdren are "another mechanism by which population and affluence generate environmental impact far out of proportion to their own percentage increases." They cite the use of nitrogen fertilizer as "the best known example" of this effect, asserting that "the essence of the matter is that feeding an extra increment of population from a fixed or dwindling amount of good quality land requires inputs of fertilizer far out of proportion to the increase in yield." Here Ehrlich and Holdren are promulgating a myth more often heard from "agrobusinessmen" and fertilizer salesmen than from environmentalists — that the intensity (i.e., high yields per acre) of U.S. agriculture is essential to provide food for the growing population, because of "a fixed or dwindling amount of good quality land." The fact is that land has been retired from agriculture in the United States not because it is of "poor quality," but because nonuse of land is economically advantageous: to the farmer because of Land Bank payments and the effects of controlled production on market prices, and to the fertilizer industry (and the farmer as well) because fertilizer is the cheapest way to increase yield per acre and thereby compensates for restricted acreage. Those familiar with actual farm operations know that the retired acreage varies from year to year and is not, on the average, significantly worse than the rest. According to one agricultural expert, the acreage held out of production "is suitable for regular cultivation with no additional investment" (J. C. Headley, Productivity of Agricultural Pesticides in "Symposium on Economic Research on Pesticides for Policy Decision Making." U.S. Department of Agriculture, Washington, D.C. April 27-29, 1970). Moreover, Ehrlich's use of such a concept of land "quality" is surprising in an ecologist. As pointed out in Chapter 12 of "The Closing Circle," this is an economic rather than ecological concept; while on economic grounds land which has a low intrinsic fertility is useless in agriculture (there is no reason to invest in its low return), on ecological grounds such land can certainly be put to productive use so long as the amount of crop extracted is limited to its natural rate of productivity. The reason why the U.S. farmer much perfers to use more fertilizer and less land to obtain a given overall output is quite simple: The economic gain per dollar invested in fertilizer is vastly greater (about fiftyfold or more) than that obtainable from the same investment in land. (See, for example, Headley, Estimating the Productivity of Agricultural Pesticides "Journal of Farm Economics," February 1968, pp. 13-23.) As I took pains to explain in Chapter 5, it is such economic factors, not the demand for food imposed by a growing population, that force the Illinois corn farmer to operate at levels of fertilization that are so high as to result in water pollution. Of course, all of the foregoing rebuttal is hardly needed to establish the weakness of Ehrlich and Holdren's argument that intense fertilization is forced by the need to increase production. Sufficient evidence is the simple fact that in order to maintain farm prices, production is limited by government fiat.

As to Ehrlich and Holdren's effort to involve "diminishing returns" in my discussion of labor productivity (p.15), this is again a case in which they are unable to grant me the right to write my own book. They assert that I have done some kind of violence to the significance of "diminishing returns" by restricting "attention to productivity" and "since this quality has increased since 1956, he (Commoner) argues, diminishing returns have not been important."

A False Description

This is, again, a false description of my position, since I do not, in fact, anywhere in "The Closing Circle," discuss the general problem of "diminishing returns." Although this criticism is therefore irrelevant, it is perhaps worth taking this opportunity to note that Ehrlich and Holdren happen to be wrong about the effects of diminishing returns on environmental impact, or at least on that quite major part due to industry.

Ehrlich and Holdren assert that nonlabor (e.g., energy) aspects of productivity have in fact decreased (i.e., that goods produced per unit energy used have declined as production levels have risen), thereby establishing their notion of the effect of "diminishing returns." As it happens, since publication of "The Closing Circle" the relevant data (not cited by Ehrlich and Holdren) have now been computed (Commoner, "Power Production and Human Welfare," December 1971). They show that for all U.S. industry in 1947, about $5.40 of value was added per million British thermal units (BTUs) of fuel expanded (expressed in 1958 dollars), to industry as a whole; in 1967 about $7.30 of value was added per million BTUs of fuel expended. Clearly, despite the large increase in total production (value added increased by about 228 per cent from 1947 to 1967), the efficiency of use of fuel in industrial production has not declined but has increased. There is no sign of a "diminishing returns" problem here, and no evidence of the exacerbation of resource use which, Ehrlich believes, derives from high levels of production. Or consider the use of water by industry: in 1954 gross water use was about 21 billion gallons, the index of production was 86, and value added amounted to about $130 billion. In 1968 these figures were, respectively, about 36 billion gallons of water; index of production, 160; and $225 billion. Thus the efficiency of water use, measured as production index/water use was 4.1 in 1954 and 4.2 in 1968; the comparable measure, value added-water use, changed from 6.2 in 1954 to 6.3 in 1968. Again, there is no sign of "diminishing returns." Only in one aspect of industrial production — electric power — do we find a decline in efficiency of use: In 1946 U.S. industry produced $0.75 per kilowatt-hour of electricity used; in 1967 it produced $0.45 per kilowatt-hour. However, this is by no means evidence of "diminishing returns," for the drop in efficiency is clearly not associated with high levels of industrial production. Rather the decline in efficiency is due to the progressive displacement, since 1946, of power-thrifty industries (such as wood products) by power consumption industries (such as aluminum production), and by the displacement of labor by power, resulting from increased automation.

In sum, the available evidence regarding U.S. industry, which is after all a major source of environmental deterioration, quite thoroughly invalidates the Ehrlich and Holdren notion that rising population and demand have led to decreased efficiency of resourse use and therefore have exacerbated environmental impact through the mechanism of "diminishing returns."

Non-Pollution Aspects Neglected

Ehrlich and Holdren assert that "Commoner implicitly assumes that environmental deterioration consists only of pollution; this oversimplification leads him to discuss the environmental crisis as if it had begun in the 1940s."

This statement is incorrect, for I state (pp. 126-127):

> Certain human activities — agriculture, forestry, and fishing — directly exploit the productivity of a particular ecosystem. In these cases, a constituent of the ecosystem that has economic value — an agricultural crop, timber, or fish — is withdrawn from the ecosystem. This represents an external drain on the system that must be carefully adjusted to natural and man-made inputs to the ecosystem if collapse is to be avoided. A heavy drain may drive the system out of balance toward collapse. Examples include destructive erosion of agricultural or forest lands following overly intense exploitation or the incipient destruction of the whaling industry due to the extinction of whales.

In addition to the above, a detailed description is provided (pp. 33-39) of how environmental distress may be generated in natural processes by perturbations (for example, the fluctuation of the lynx and rabbit populations) that have nothing to do with pollution.

A Tour de Force

Thus as in the previous matters, Ehrlich and Holdren have misstated my position. In this case, however, their technique of criticism is carried one step further. Having asserted that I equate environmental degradation with pollution, they then proceed to quote the above passage from "The Closing Circle" which belies that assertion, adding: "(he is) apparently unaware that he is contradicting himself." One can almost admire this tour de force: A false statement is made, and then the evidence which shows that it is false is cited as proof of self-contradiction!

There follows a lengthy discussion of various instances of environmental damage resulting from human activities before the 1940s. All this is banging on an open door, for as indicated above, I am aware that overexploitation of agricultural or forest lands can indeed lead to environmental degradation.

In the course of this discussion, however, we are treated to the following: "he (Commoner) does not seem to be aware that the reduction of the diversity of life and then of the complexity of those systems may pose the most lethal threat of all." And Ehrlich and Holdren remind me that "it is the complexity of the natural ecosystems that is primarily responsible for their stability." Yet on page 38 of "The Closing Circle" one finds the following:

> The amount of stress which an ecosystem can absorb before it is driven to collapse is also a result of its various interconnections and their relative speeds of response. The more complex the ecosystem, the more successfully it can resist a stress. For example, in the rabbit-lynx system, if the lynx had an alternative source of food they might survive the sudden depletion of rabbits. In this way, branching — which establishes alternative pathways — increases the resistance of an ecosystem to stress. Most ecosystems are so complex that the cycles are not simple circular paths, but are crisscrossed with branches to form a network or a fabric of interconnections. Like a net, in which each knot is connected to others by several strands, such a fabric can resist collapse better than a simple unbranched circle of threads — which if cut anywhere breaks down as a whole. Environmental pollution is often a sign that ecological links have been cut and that the ecosystem has been artificially simplified and made more vulnerable to stress and to final collapse.

Ehrlich and Holdren then go to great lengths to attempt to establish that "far from starting in the 1940s, as Commoner implies, serious ecological harm has accompanied man's activities ever since the agricultural revolution of some 10,000 years ago." Nowhere in "The Closing Circle," or in any other writings, have I held that "serious ecological harm" has occurred only since 1940. The instances of man-made ecological disasters, such as the Mediterranean desert areas that Ehrlich cites, are, of course, well known, even to me. Why then have I failed to discuss these matters in "The Closing Circle?" Because, by design, it is not a treatise on ecological degradation in general. Rather, as directly stated in the opening chapter of the book, I was concerned with the meaning of "the environmental crisis," which I defined, as it was during Earth Week, as concern with the deteriorating quality of the present environment. And in characterizing the environmental crisis I did, indeed, concentrate on those aspects of deterioration represented by the accumulation of pollutants, rather than on overgrazing and similarly old-fashioned ecological sins, for I believed that these were the more relevant features of the crisis. In this I was not alone. Here is Ehrlich's own characterization of the environmental crisis: "Too many cars, too many factories, too much detergent, too much pesticide, multiplying controls, inadequate sewage treatment plants, too much carbon dioxide. . ." ("The Population Bomb").

Ehrlich and Holdren in their review continue: "Having assumed that man's adverse impact on his environment was negligible before 1940, Commoner than alleges that "pollution levels" increased by an explosive 200 to 2,000 per cent between 1946 and 1968. . ." This statement quite neatly reverses the actual logic of my position. An examination of "The Closing Circle" will show that there is no discussion of the time of origin of the environmental crisis until page 127. There I state:

> Our task, then, is to discover how human activities generate environmental impacts. . . . As a first step we might look at the history of the pollution problem in a highly industrialized country such as the United States . . . a rather striking picture does emerge from the data that are available: *most pollution problems made their first appearance, or became very much worse, in the years following World War II.* (Emphasis in original.)

There then follows a paragraph giving the actual numerical data which support this conclusion (for example that phosphate entering surface waters in the United States from municipal sewage somewhat more than doubled in the 30-year period 1910 to 1940 and increased seven-fold in the succeeding 30 years).

Their Own Invention

Thus, my discussion of the relative environmental impact of human activities before and after World War II did not — as Ehrlich and Holdren state — deal with "man's adverse impact on his environment," but only with "most pollution problems." Moreover, my "assumption" concerning the prewar condition did not precede — as they claim — my statement regarding the postwar rise in pollution levels. Indeed I make no assumption at all, but simply show from actual data that postwar pollution levels have indeed increased by 200 to 2,000 per cent — a factual assertion which Ehrlich and Holdren do not attempt to deny.

Thus Ehrlich and Holdren first complain that I have chosen to discuss the environmental crisis in terms of current pollution problems, rather than including other aspects of man's overall impact on the environment (they neglect to point out that Ehrlich has himself done the same); they then falsify my actual position regarding pollution problems in the United States into precisely the position which they accuse me earlier of avoiding, asserting that I have "assumed that man's adverse impact on the environment was negligible before 1940. . ." What they are criticizing here is their own invention.

Demographic Transition

Ehrlich and Holdren criticize my view that the demographic transition is a reasonable means by which improvements in living conditions can lead, by voluntary control of fertility, toward a balance between death rate and birthrate. They suggest that I am naive to regard the demographic transition as a realistic means of achieving a balanced population by voluntary action rather than by coercion. It should be noted here that the crucial difference between my view of population control and Ehrlich and Holdren's is precisely at this point — that is, the difference between self-made decisions to limit fertility which people reach because they have confidence in their future, and Ehrlich's often-expressed view that "persuasion" and ultimately coercion are needed.

There is a curious contrast between Ehrlich and Holdren's derogation of the demographic transition and the view expressed earlier in Population-Resources-Environment by Paul R. Ehrlich and Anne H. Ehrlich::

> . . . as the industrial revolution progressed, another significant trend appeared. Birthrates in Western countries began to decline . . . this was the start of the so-called "demographic transition" — a falling of birthrates which has characteristically followed industrialization. . . . By the 1930s, decreases in birthrates had in some countries outpaced decreases in death rates. By then the combined death rate of Denmark, Norway and Sweden had decreased to 12 per thousand, but the birthrate had dropped precipitously to 16. Populations in the industrial countries of Europe in the 1930s were in a demographic situation that, if continued, would have led to population declines. True birthrates were still above death rates, but they would not have stayed that way for long . . . However, stimulated by improving economic conditions and World War II, birthrates rose again during the 1930s and 1950s. European growth rates have generally averaged between 0.5 and 1.0 per cent since the War.

This passage clearly presents the demographic transition as a basic, first-order phenomenon that is secondarily affected by fluctuations induced by a variety of social and economic factors. This is, of course, precisely my own position. (Despite Ehrlich and Holdren's derogation of "Commoner's beliefs" on this matter I am quite aware, as most people are, that birthrates in most-developed countries are still somewhat in excess of death rates — a fact which is evident in all my writings, including "The Closing Circle.") As to the secondary fluctuations, it is now evident that there is in the United States a strong trend toward declining birthrates which has been underway for a decade or so and is continuing. Not even Ehrlich has argued, to my knowledge, that this decline is due to "persuasion" — since it began long before the recent public campaigns for "zero population growth." It would appear, then, that current social and economic trends are being translated, voluntarily, into a declining birthrate which is rapidly bringing the United States birthrate to the replacement level — that is, the level at which population will be constant. Of course, it is totally unrealistic to expect a zero growth rate to hold at all times. Given the complexities of the human condition, what can be expected is only a long-term zero growth rate with shorter-term fluctuations above and below that level.

In sum, my view of the nature and significance of the demographic transition is quite in keeping with the available data, and, curiously enough, agrees with the view expressed elsewhere by Ehrlich himself.

The rest of the Ehrlich and Holdren criticism of my position on the population problem is only a recitation of unsupported assumptions about the means whereby underdeveloped countries might achieve population balance, and about my views on this matter. As to the former, they assume that a demographic transition would not "solve the problems in time," because it might take more than a generation, but they offer nothing to support their notion of how long a time we have to bring the world into approximate ecological balance without serious risks of large-scale catastrophe. In fact, elsewhere Ehrlich has indicated that it is already "too late." Thus, in the revised edition of "The Population Bomb," published in 1971, he asserts that "the battle to feed all humanity is over. . .at this late date nothing can prevent a substantial increase in the world death rate." And to make matters perfectly clear he was quoted in an interview as saying: "When you reach a point where you realize further efforts will be futile, you may as well look after yourself and your friends and enjoy what little time you have left. That point for me is 1972." ("Look," April 21, 1970.)

Castastrophe Inevitable?

In a way this statement provides the clearest expression of the gulf which separates Ehrlich's view of the global population problem and my own. He takes the position that ecological catastrophe is inevitable if the peoples of the developing countries — or, for that matter, of the industrialized ones — are left to regulate population growth by their own self-determined actions, following the course taken by the developed countries (as described by the demographic transition). These actions include "improvement of living conditions, urgent efforts to reduce infant mortality, social security measures, and the resultant effects on desired family size, together with personal, voluntary contraceptive practice." ("The Closing Circle"). According to Ehrlich, population growth is governed by the automatic mechanism made famous by Malthus — the inescapable clash between the self-accelerating rate of reproduction of the human population and the slower growth of the resources; especially food, needed to support it. Ehrlich believes, apparently, that human society is today in the grip of an automatic clash between population and resources, and that no self-motivated human effort (either to improve the availability of resources or voluntarily to restrict fertility) can possibly prevent catastrophe.

My view is different. I believe that population control is generated within a given society by a series of complex interactions in which improved well-being and social security motivate people to reduce fertility voluntarily and that, subject to short-term fluctuations, this phenomenon (demographic transition) can achieve long-term population stability. Ehrlich's view stresses the inevitable clash between two biological processes: growth of population and the slower increase of food supply. My view stresses the effects of social action to improve living conditions; such action can affect both personal motivation for reduced fertility and the availability of resources (For example by means of social action to eliminate exploitation of resourses for private profit or to eliminate waste of resources even when it is "cheaper" to waste them).

To put the difference between us more bluntly. This, after all being the year 1972, Ehrlich's advice is to "look after yourself and your friends and enjoy what little time you have left." While I believe that, today and into the future, human society (as distinct from "yourself and your friends") can be organized as a stable, ongoing, humane civilization — by powerful, sustained social action to remove the economic and political barriers that keep people and whole nations in poverty.

Relevance to Political Action

As I pointed out in "The Closing Circle," none of the foregoing positions are scientific estimates; rather, they are political judgments. I find it difficult to believe that the intensity of the conflict on scientific matters which is expressed in Ehrlich's and Holdren's review is accountable by a straightforward disagreement, on their part, with my scientific data and analyses. Surely, if there were nothing more to the conflict than their disagreements with my mathematical techniques and analytical procedures, it would have been fairly simple, as can be seen from the above discussion, to resolve nearly all of them by a reading of my RFF paper, or by a more careful reading of "The Closing Circle." Given the gross misconceptions of my analysis which encumber the Ehrlich and Holdren review, I must conclude that they failed to take this rudimentary step toward resolving the disagreement. Thus I am compelled toward the view that Ehrlich and Holdren are less concerned with resolving the scientific differences between us than they are with the possibility that "uncritical acceptance of Commoner's assertions will lead to public complacency regarding both population and affluence in the United States." Apparently, Ehrlich is so intent upon population control as to be unwilling to tolerate open discussion of data that might weaken the argument for it.

Open Debate

In this connection, the Ehrlich and Holdren covering letter raises an issue which I regard with the utmost seriousness. This relates to the notion which they advance that an honest, open scientific debate can be "counterproductive for the goals which we all share." My goal in environmental matters is to encourage strong, informed public action toward the improvement of environmental quality, by methods which — through appropriate political mechanisms — are the choice of the American people. This requires that the people of the United States become familiar with the basic facts about environmental deterioration, become aware of alternative interpretations of these facts (including the resultant uncertainty which attaches to them), and then undertake the difficult task of weighing this information (and its inadequacies and uncertainties) against their own ethical, social and political beliefs in order to determine what ought to be done. Given this goal, there is no conceivable way that a "debate on which factor in the environmental crisis is 'most important' " can be "counterproductive." Suppose, for the sake of argument, it turns out on examination, that no one factor is "most important"; surely an open debate between two scientists — one of whom is convinced, nevertheless, that some factor is indeed "most important," — can only illuminate the truth and increase public understanding of it.

What is so curious about Ehrlich's position is that, on the record, it is he, not I, who first took a public position as to which factor is "most important" in generating environmental degradation. It was, after all, Ehrlich who in 1968 — well before I undertook to analyze the relative significance of the several factors — in "The Population Bomb" asserted that "the causal chain of the deterioration (of the environment) is easily followed to its source. . .too many people." When, later on, I found from analysis that the technological factor played an important role in environmental deterioration, and said so openly, Ehrlich acknowledged that both factors are important, and indicated that he would be happy if we both agreed to keep to that position without raising any questions about the relative importance of the two factors.

In other words, so long as I refrained from questioning the necessity of population control in a campaign for environmental quality, Ehrlich was prepared to accept my position without debate. He urged silence only when I began to examine precisely this question, in the belief that the public needed to know the relative importance of the several factors in order to decide where an attack on environmental issues is best directed.

Two Alternatives

In my view, the environmental crisis involves very grave and complex social problems that ought to be resolved by public decision and not determined by the force of private agreements among scientists as to which issues are to be openly debated and which are to be hidden from public view. As I have pointed out in "The Closing Circle," these issues confront the American people with two alternative (but not mutually exclusive) paths toward a solution: a reduction in the population sufficient to render tolerable the environmental degradation due to ecologically faulty technology, or social action to correct counter-ecological technologies and to change the economic mechanisms which generate them. Population control (as distinct from voluntary, self-initiated control of fertility), no matter how disguised, involves some measure of political repression, and would burden the poor nations with the social cost of a situation — overpopulation — which is the current outcome of their previous exploitation, as colonies, by the wealthy nations. And as I have also taken pains to point out, the alternative means of resolving the environmental crisis by improvement of productive technology would require sweeping and basic changes in the private enterprise system in a nation such as the United States. Now, I know of no scientific principle which can tell us how much to rely on population control and how much on technological change (and the required economic controls) in order to reduce environmental impact. The choice between these alternative paths is clearly a political one, not a matter of science.

Like everyone else, I have the right as an individual to choose between these political alternatives. My own choice is, I believe, made clear in "The Closing Circle." But more important, I have shared with my readers the data and analysis which have enabled me to make that choice, and I have urged them to make their own. For in a democracy this decision belongs in the hands of every citizen, and ought not to be preempted by one or two scientists, or even a committee of them. Without the information that the scientist can provide, the citizen cannot make his own decision and becomes the ready victim of those who would decide for him. I regard all efforts to deprive the citizen of this right — whether by a government's rule of secrecy or by a scientist's proposition for silence — with equal abhorrence.

There is, of course, an important relationship between such political decisions and the relevant scientific information. Scientific evidence is essential to evaluate the consequences of the alternative decisions. Data are required to answer the questions: What are the relative influences of population size and defective technology on environmental impact? How much would population size, or the ecological impact of present technology need to be changed in order to accomplish a given reduction in environmental impact? What are the economic and social consequences of curtailing population as compared to the alternative of changing technology?

As I have often stated, scientists have a grave responsibility to help find the answers to these questions and to bring them before the public, so that, thus informed, the public can make its own choice between the political alternatives. "The Closing Circle," like most of my writing, is an effort to carry out this obligation. In it I offer to the public the knowledge that I have acquired about the origins of the environmental crisis, about the relative importance of the several factors, and about the economic and social consequences of efforts to control them. On scientific grounds, which — despite Ehrlich's and Holdren's intemperate onslaught — remain valid, I show that environmental degradation is far more responsive to technological improvement than to population control.

Right of the Public

Had I agreed to the urging of Ehrlich and his emissaries to refrain from a discussion of such scientific evidence on the relative importance of population growth and of technology, I might have escaped their critical wrath. But this act would have violated my duty to science and to the public. It would have eroded the only means by which the scientific community can approach the truth — open discussion. It would have eroded the only means, in a democracy, by which the public can exert its political will — to be informed. And need we be ren·nded, in the period of the Pentagon Papers, that when those in power wish to protect their policies from public judgment they cover them with a cloak woven out of private agreements to be silent lest "counter-productive debates" ensue.

In writing "The Closing Circle," I have chosen to speak out about the scientific evidence on the origins of the environmental crisis, the alternative courses of action that might resolve it, and the right of the public, rather than propagandists or scientists, to make that choice. This was my duty to science, to the people whom science must serve, and to the survival of a civilized society.

ONE DIMENSIONAL
ECOLOGY REVISITED:
A REJOINDER

John P. Holdren,
Paul R. Ehrlich

We will not subject readers to a point by point dissection of Professor Commoner's response to our review of "The Closing Circle." Most of the misrepresentations, evasions and errors in his rebuttal will be quite apparent to those who have read the book and review carefully. It is perhaps worth supplying enough examples, however, to convince those still in doubt of two remarkable facts: Commoner has not only paid little attention to what we said in our review, but he also appears to have forgotten a good deal of what he said in his book.

Commoner vigorously denies underestimating the seriousness of the ecological impact of preindustrial man. We trust he will wish to remove from the next printing of "The Closing Circle" the statement, quoted by us in our review and ignored by him in his rebuttal, that "So long as human beings held their place in the terrestrial ecosystems — consuming food produced by the soil and oxygen released by plants, returning organic wastes to the soil and carbon dioxide to the plants—*they could do no serious ecological harm.*" (P. 126, emphasis added.)

Commoner claims, incorrectly, that we have accused him of inadmissably multiplying percentages together. We do accuse him of presenting percentages in such a way as to mislead the reader as to the relative importance of population and affluence. "Yet of the four relevant figures, Commoner invariably presents only two: the total increase in some index of impact and the increase in population." We are unimpressed by Commoner's denial, in which he indignantly notes that nowhere in "The Closing Circle" are the numerical increase in population and the (alleged) numerical increase in pollution mentioned on the same page. Surely the repeated references to both figures, in close proximity (pp. 128, 133, 136, 140, as noted in Commoner's rebuttal), and the repeated assertion that population and affluence have grown much too slowly to account for the observed increase in pollution (pp. 135, 146, 177, etc.) suffice to convey the misleading message. Indeed, Commoner is unable to resist making the same deceptive sort of comparison between the population component alone and the total impact in the rebuttal itself. He claims in connection with his nitrogen oxides example that "the total impact increases 7.3 fold. . .so the importance of the population factor has to be judged against that figure." Actually, as we stated in our review, the population factor should be judged against the factors it multiplies — affluence and technology. Compared against the total, any of the three individual factors seems small.

Commoner claims in his rebuttal that "The Closing Circle" accurately represents the results of his more technical work. He states, "In 'The Closing Circle,' the material of the RFF paper was summarized without departing in any way from the original mathematical treatment. . ." Yet he subsequently admits that two serious errors crept into the paragraph that summarizes his "analysis" of the relative importance of the three factors (Bulletin, May 1972, p. 46). (The main points of this crucial paragraph, from page 176 of "The Closing Circle," were quoted in our review.) The lay reader will have difficulty escaping the impression here that the contributing factors add up to the total impact, and will have no way of knowing that these results were obtained by taking the logarithm of a multiplicative relation. The acknowledged typographical error in the same paragraph happens to further overstate what would have been a substantial exaggeration of the role of technology in any case. The conceptual errors in "The Closing Circle" aside, this typographical carelessness is particularly surprising since it occurs in the course of summarizing one of the main themes of the book — the attempt to assign numerical values to the factors.

Commoner accuses us of never using "real data" in the impact equation, although in fact the use in this equation of data on nitrogen oxides serves as a prominent example in our review. In his rebuttal, Commoner proceeds to run through the nitrogen oxides case once more, as evidence of the way we have left the technology factor out of the accounting: "Then whereas Ehrlich and Holdren deal only with the population and affluence factors, I introduce the third factor, technology, or in this case nitrogen oxides emitted per vehicle mile." One can only conclude that Commoner has not really read our review. We wrote:

> *Commoner correctly points out that one of the major impacts from the automobile, the production of nitrogen oxides has increased since 1946 because of a technological mistake. That mistake was raising compression ratios, which increased average emissions of oxides of nitrogen in the exhaust from 500 parts per million to 1,200 parts per million [a 2.4-fold increase] between 1946 and 1968. Commoner notes further that total nitrogen oxide emissions increased 7-fold in the same period. Application of the simple mathematics of impact to these figures shows that the combination of population growth and affluence accounts for a larger portion of the nitrogen oxide problem than does the technological "error":*

$$P \times A \text{ equals } 2.9; T \text{ equals } 2.4;$$
$$I \text{ equals } 2.9 \times 2.4 \text{ equals } 7.0.$$

Here we used data given by Commoner himself in "The Closing Circle" — data differing only slightly (presumably because of rounding) from those he offers in his rebuttal. In both cases, the result is the same: the technology factor is the largest of the three, but it is less important than the combination of population growth and rising affluence. Although this is probably the strongest example of faulty technology that Commoner has offered, it falls short of supporting his basic hypothesis. It certainly does not justify the numerical assignment of blame given on page 176 (even with the typographical error corrected).

Commoner's defense of some of the mysterious numbers and conclusions appearing in "The Closing Circle" is that the supporting analysis has been published elsewhere. The main source to which Commoner refers his readers is a paper presented at a symposium at Resources for the Future (RFF) in April 1971. The proceedings of this symposium had not been published at the time "The Closing Circle" appeared, and they have still not been published as we write this (April 24, 1972). The April 1971 "Environment" article is in fact, the only document mentioned that could be considered accessible to most readers of "The Closing Circle"; yet it does not describe the details of the "mathematical treatment" that Commoner says leads to his conclusions. No mention is made of logarithms, no mathematical statement of the impact equation is given and a serious arithmetic error (favoring Commoner's hypothesis again) is made as well. Specifically, having been given a table of percentage increases in production per capita in the 1946-1968 time period, "Environment's" readers are instructed that "total production figures may be derived by multiplying the listed value by 1.43 (to take into account the 43 per cent increase in population in 1946-68)." This patently incorrect procedure gives zero increase in total production if there is zero increase in production per capita, no matter how much population increases.

As to whether any of Commoner's publications on this subject have ever been subjected to the critical scrutiny of a qualified scientific referee, we remain in doubt. "Environment" is published by Commoner's close friends and collaborators — he acknowledges the Editor, Consulting Editor, Associate Editor, and Scientific Editor as such on page 325 of "The Closing Circle." The RFF paper was not refereed at all. While it is possible that "The Monthly Labor Review" and "Chemistry in Britain" are refereed journals, one must wonder whether either one has the referees or the readership best able to judge the technical exposition of a new hypothesis on ecological impact. Of course, even if Commoner has indeed published a competent treatment in one forum or another — a hypothesis for which we have as yet seen no evidence — that would scarcely excuse the publication of so misleading a popularization as "The Closing Circle."

Commoner seems to believe that our principal complaint is with his arithmetic. Unfortunately, the flaws in "The Closing Circle" run much deeper than this, as we noted in our review. Most importantly, the evidence Commoner presents fails utterly to support his general conclusion as expressed on page 177 of the book, namely: "The chief reason for the environmental crisis that has engulfed the United States in recent years is the sweeping transformation of productive technology since World War II."

In reality, he has shown only that faulty technology has been more important than either population growth or rising affluence (ignoring cause-and-effect relations between level of consumption and the sorts of technology needed to sustain it) in contributing to the increases in some specific pollutants. (Lead, synthetic pesticides, nitrogen oxides, phosphates and nitrates are probably his strongest examples; but even for some of these technology has not been more important than population and affluence combined.) He has not shown that technology has been even this important for most pollutants; he has not shown that those pollutants in which technology has played a major role are ecologically the most significant ones; he has not even shown that "pollution" as he defines it is the most important facet of the environmental crisis.

The only evidence in "The Closing Circle" even supporting the general assertion (repeated in Commoner's rubuttal) that "postwar pollution levels have indeed increased by 200 to 2,000 per cent" are the scattered examples already referred to (which are insufficient to justify the assertion) and the longer list on page 143, reproduced as Table 2 in our review. We showed there that this latter list, both in what it includes and what it does not, is entirely inappropriate as an index of environmental problems. Commoner now protests in his rebuttal that this list was not intended to be indicative of rising environmental impact, but rather merely illustrated how the economy has grown. This is a preposterous evasion. A principal thrust of the book is the direct connection between environmental problems and the way the economy has grown, and Commoner makes this point explicitly in direct connec ion with the list in question: "In other words, the fact that the economy has grown — that GNP has increased — tells us very little about the possible environmental consequences. For that, we need to know how the economy has grown" (pp. 141-42).

Commoner makes much of "displacements" of one form of technology by another, but often tells only half the story. Thus, in discussing the environmental impact of automobile production in his rebuttal, he tells us how much electricity use per car has increased but not what has happened to total energy use per car. The displacement by electricity of direct uses of fuel may yield more or less environmental deterioration, depending both on the manufacturing process and the way the electricity is generated. Indeed, Commoner is as reluctant in his rebuttal as he was in his book to confront many of the basic issues at all: the potential environmental impact of using old technologies to meet new levels of demand, the usefulness of such affluence indicators as automobiles as measures of impact on resources, the extent to which the United States "exports" its environmental impact by importing pollution-intensive goods.

We have noticed the brief passage on this topic to which Commoner refers in his response. Its brevity and superficiality — and Commoner's failure to integrate this crucial topic into the remainder of what purports to be a comprehensive discussion of threats to the ecosphere ("The Closing Circle" pp. 12-13) — fully justify our description of this treatment as "scant attention." If, as he implies, he is aware that ecosystem simplification may be the most lethal threat of all, one wonders why his discussion of this topic amounts to one paragraph in a 326-page book. Actually, Commoner's assumption that environmental deterioration consists mainly of pollution, criticized at length in our review, is once again evident in his response — witness the continuing fascination with beer bottles.

Does rising total demand stimulate changes in the technology of supply? Have diminishing returns been encountered in important technologies in the United States? Does greater disposable income — a measure of affluence — encourge substitutions that increase perceived well-being at the expense of the environment? (We will persist in using the dictionary definition of affluence: "great plenty, abundance, riches, wealth, opulence"). Commoner apparently recognizes none of these relations.

Thus he contends in his response that strictly economic factors accounted for the changes in agricultural technology since 1940, and that only economic factors now prevent us from returning to low-yield, ecologically sound agriculture. Actually, if the 1969 yield per acre for wheat and corn alone were reduced to the pre-World War II levels, roughly an additional 230 million acres would have to be devoted to these crops to produce the 1969 total harvest. This would mean bringing back into production all the land taken out of cultivation between 1940 and 1964, plus an additional 100 million acres (data from "Resources in America's Future" and "1971 Statistical Abstract of the United States"). Considering raising non-agricultural demands on land during that period, related both to population growth and rising affluence, these figures hardly support Commoner's contention. It should be noted especially, that much of the land that would have to be brought into production in a shift to low-yield agriculture is now serving ecologically important functions—control of erosion and maintenance of diversity, for example. Of course, economic factors are involved, too, as they seem certain to be in the near future. Indeed, these factors are a substantial part of what defines good quality land and "fixes" its amount.

If, as the data suggest, it would be difficult to maintain needed agricultural production in the United States without reliance on the high-yield technologies, then the importance of diminishing returns in fertilizer use is self-evident (see e.g. the curve of yield versus fertilizer input given by Christopher Pratt (Chemical Fertilizers, "Scientific American," June 1965). The statistics Commoner uses in his response to belittle the importance of diminishing returns in other productive activities are too highly aggregated to be illuminating (a criticism that also applies, we concede, to the increase since 1965 in energy use per dollar of GNP, cited in our review). To determine whether diminishing returns with respect to energy and other impact-intensive factors of production is already a general phenomenon in the U.S. economy will require more detailed investigation. That such diminishing returns are significant in specific important industries, however, is easily shown. (see,e.g.,the figures for barrels of oil discovered per foot drilled in "Resources and Man" (Freeman, 1969, p. 181), and the discussion of pollution control in Impact of Population Growth ("Science," vol. 171, 1971).

Redefining Affluence

Finally, concerning affluence and substitutions: Is Commoner prepared to claim that the greater environmental impact attendant on having a home in the suburbs as opposed to an apartment in an urban tenement is not related to affluence? Does he deny that affluence is what permits replacing muscle power with fossil fuels in transportation and household chores? Isn't the man who buys aluminum siding for his home in preference to wood increasing his perceived well-being by reducing the time devoted to maintenance? We do not defend these trends, but neither do we think that science or society is served by redefining affluence to dodge the issue.

How can Commoner try to consider the United States in isolation, after writing, "Everything is connected to everything else"? How can he argue that better technology will permit continued population growth and rising affluence without ecological disruption, after writing, "There is no such thing as a free lunch"? How can he take the simplistic position that there is a single, dominant, independent cause of environmental deterioration, and that it will suffice to attack only this one, after writing (p. 187)". . .unlike the automobile, the ecosystem cannot be subdivided into managable parts, for its properties reside in the whole, in the connections between the parts. A process that insists on dealing only with the separated parts is bound to fail"? Has Commoner forgotten that man and his activities are part of the ecosystem?

Counterproductive Debate

Most of the self-righteous philosophical ramblings in which Commoner indulges himself in his response are irrelevant here, as are his persistent misrepresentations of the writings and "beliefs" of Ehrlich. Since he has so thoroughly misunderstood our concern over a counterproductive debate, however, we will spell it out for him. The debate, in the form Commoner is intent on pursuing it, is counterproductive because it implicitly asks a senseless question: What contributing factors in our environmental problems can be safely ignored while we attack "the most important" factor? In reality, the most elementary considerations indicate that no factor can be ignored. Which one is most important, when this notion can be defined at all, varies from one problem to the next. In many problems, the factors are intimately causally related. Faulty technology should be attacked directly wherever one finds it — a point we have never disputed.

But the complacency Commoner encourages concerning population growth and rising affluence can only guarantee that the many environmental problems not primarily due to faulty technology will continue to worsen. Even for problems more responsive initially to a change in technology than to a brake on population or affluence, continued growth will wipe out the gains (as is amply demonstrated, for example, by the many projections of future air pollution in the Los Angeles Basin). What does one do for an encore, 20 years hence, after the obvious faulty technologies have been repaired? If the environmental crisis is as serious as Commoner claims, what possible justification can there be for ignoring any growing factor that multiplies the total impact? Since no one has argued that society should not try to reform technology with all possible speed, what is productive about this debate?

Loss of Credibility

A public debate on an ill-posed question is counterproductive in other respects, as well. Few members of the public are prepared to spend the time and effort to follow the wealth of arguments that ensue in such a debate. Those who are so prepared are precisely the ones who would be following it anyway if it took place in a widely circulated refereed journal such as "Science." Those who are not can only be confused and disconcerted by the outpouring of conflicting testimony by apparently qualified scientists. In the end, the credibility of the environmental movement is the loser, and so we all lose. Of course, that scientists can disagree is a fact of life that the public must eventually accept. Loss of credibility among part of the public is a price worth paying when meaningful questions affecting the public interest cannot be resolved by any means other than an adversary process. The present case does not meet those requirements.

Finally, a debate so senseless in respect to the question addressed and the public confusion generated thereby is, by definition, counterproductive in terms of the time of the participants. There are too few scientists doing either research or public education on ecological problems to waste the time of any of us on so fruitless an exercise. We persist, reluctantly, in the conviction that the seductive misinformation in "The Closing Circle" would, if unrebutted, do damage exceeding even the painful costs of this debate.

POPULATION SKELETONS
IN THE ENVIRONMENTAL CLOSET

Garret Hardin

First, Barry Commoner wrote a book, "The Closing Circle" (Knopf, 1971). Then Paul R. Ehrlich and John P. Holdren criticized the book; and then Commoner criticized their criticism. The result: a sizable body of controversial literature. How is one to deal with it?

One might go through the antagonists' arguments point by point, carefully comparing and evaluating them. If a lawsuit were involved, with a million dollars at stake, this would be appropriate. But there is no such suit. Consideration for the reader dictates a much simpler approach.

I will try to plunge directly to the heart of the matter, bypassing some of the fascinating interplay of antagonistic rhetoric. I don't want this essay to swell to the length of Adam Sedgwick's scathing review of one of the controversial books of the Victorian age, Robert Chambers' "Vestiges of Creation." Sedgwick's review was 85 pages long. By comparison, Commoner's and Ehrlich and Holdren's contributions are mercifully short — but only by comparison.

The deep question at issue is the importance of the population component in pollution and other forms of environmental disruption (E.D.). In both his book and his critique Commoner goes to great lengths to prove that the population component is minor. Two elements of his argument merit separate treatment: (a) the empirical data and (b) the algebraic procedure.

It is both a weakness and a strength that the data are empirical. On the one hand, they are true, but on the other, one may well ask how general is their significance? Many measures can be determined, but which are the most significant in accounting for E.D.? Beer bottles? Water heaters? Clothes dryers? Automobiles? When one presents some of the percentage increases over a span of years, bias enters in, as is apparent in the Commoner data brought together in Ehrlich and Holdren's Table 2. Nonreturnable soda bottles increased 53,000 per cent in the postwar years for the simple reason that the initial production base used for the calculation was nearly zero. Even the most rabid "econut" would not claim that overall pollution increased by such a large percentage.

How should one weight the items assembled in such a table? What would a complete table look like? (Impossibly long, no doubt.) And how would the E.D. produced by each of the items compare with that produced by each of its many alternative materials or ways of meeting the same demand? (Environmentally minded activists all too easily forget to ask this critical question: they forget the basic rule of ethics and ecology that "We can never do nothing.")

Furthermore, neither the increase in use nor the increase in the resultant pollution over a particular time span can be assumed to be part of a universal law applicable forever into the indefinite future. But it is the future we are primarily concerned about. When first introduced into a wealthy country a desirable product enjoys a population growth that is exponential by a factor many times greater than the exponent for human population growth. Ultimately the market is saturated with the product, thereafter production drops to some constant factor times the human population size.

As for the E.D. caused in the manufacture, use and ultimate disposal of the product, this clearly depends on the state of technology. On the whole, we may assume that technology will improve (particularly if we take care that it does), though at what rate there is no a priori way of knowing. A conservative view would be that E.D. control approaches an asymptotic value, generally an unknown one.

From the past we get only empirical values, and little theory. We have little success in predicting the future of environmental disruption.

As for the algebra of determining what percentage of today's pollution is "caused" by technological growth and change in the recent past, and what percentage should be charged against population growth, this depends on what is to be compared with what. My own reading of the arguments gives the edge to Ehrlich and Holdren, but I will not linger to justify that opinion for there are, I think, more important matters to take up.

Population Asymptote

At a fixed level of population, the amount of environmental disruption is a function of the state and use of technology. For the sake of argument we may grant that the E.D. function could be caused to decrease in time, provided we face this question: Is the asymptote of the E.D. function zero, or something greater than zero? I suspect the latter; true believers in technology may believe in the former.

On the other hand, if we take the level of technology as fixed, then the amount of environmental disruption is a function of population size. Population growth, as Benjamin Franklin, Robert Wallace and T. R. Malthus emphasized is a potentially limitless function — but only in a limitless world. In the real world, the maximum population achievable approaches an asymptote. What asymptote, depends on many factors, including (most importantly) the "amount of environment" allocated to, or taken by, each unit of population. This defines the "level of living." Escape from all asymptotes is not one of man's options; he can merely choose his asymptote.

A low population asymptote permits a high level of living as an option. Those who are ascetically minded need not choose this option; but only if a low population asymptote is adopted and enforced can men be free to enjoy, if they wish, Cadillacs, symphony orchestras, wooded wilderness — and meat with their meals. The highest possible population asymptote permits only one kind of life, namely the ascetic, which is then no longer an option but an inescapable fate.

It should be noted also that the highest possible asymptote can be achieved only by accepting a great deal of environmental disruption. Pollution control always bears a cost, which can be paid for only out of affluence. Even those who care nothing about Cadillacs and symphonies may resent emphysema.

Of course if technology can improve forever without limit, so that the E.D. curve has zero as it asymptote, the above argument is specious. But surely the burden of proof lies on those who assert so remarkable a theorem?

Barry Commoner is not entirely unaware of the relevance of population growth, but he acknowledges it grudgingly. Consider these sentences from page 113 of his book:

> It is easy to demonstrate that the changes in pollution level in the United States since World War II cannot be accounted for simply by the increased population, which in that period rose by only 42 percent. Of course this is but a simplistic response to a simplistic proposal. It is conceivable that even a 40 to 50 per cent increase in population size might be the real cause of a much larger increase in pollution intensity.

The qualifications put Commoner on safe ground no matter what facts later turn up; but the thrust of the rhetoric is another matter. "Simplistic," "conceivable" and "might" — these are surely ways of denigrating the importance of population.

Like the theologian Richard J. Neuhaus, author of "In Defense of People" (Macmillan, 1972), Commoner is very much pro-people in the sense of "the more the merrier." On page 114 Commoner says:

> The earth has experienced not only a "population explosion" but also, and more meaningfully a "civilization explosion." People, and indeed their growth in number, are the source of the vastly elaborated network of events that comprises the civilization of man; the new knowledge of nature generated by science, the power of technology to guide natural forces, the huge increase in material wealth, the rich elaboration of economic, cultural, social, and political processes.

Forever Upward?

There is much truth in this. Looking backward, it is difficult to believe that the same growth in technology (etcetera) could have taken place if the human population had never increased beyond the limit of a single tribe of two thousand people. But what if we look forward? Is it certain that the quality of life graphed against population is a curve that slopes forever upward? Is it not even possible that quality has already passed through a peak and is heading downward? Possible, at least?

I have previously discussed this question in a somewhat different context (S. Fred Singer, ed, "Is There an Optimum Level of Population?" (New York: McGraw-Hill, 1971), p. 263):

> Not even the merits of urbanization requires a large population — only local concentrations of the artists, artisans, philosophers, and scientists who are capable, under peculiar political and social circumstances that are poorly understood, of creating a distinctive "civilization." Athens, in its Golden Age, consisted of only a quarter of a million people, of whom almost half were slaves, and only 40,000 were full citizens. The substitution of machine slaves for human slaves has surely reduced the critical size required for a great center of

culture (given the right attendant circumstances) to considerably less than a quarter of a million.

New York and Athens

Let me pose a related question. The "standard metropolitan statistical area" called New York had a population as of 1970 of 11,529.000 people. That's 46 times the total population of classical Athens, or 288 times the population of Athenians of full citizenship status. In civilization, in urbanity, or in the production of art, new intellectual discoveries, or what have you—is modern New York 288 times as great as classical Athens? Or even 46 times as great? Is it even equal, on a per capita per century basis? No one, to my knowledge, has attempted to quantify an answer to this question. It hardly seems worth the effort. The answer is surely obvious, and lends no support to the conclusion·implied by Commoner that more is always better. Beyond some undetermined, but not large, number the stimulation people give each other becomes more irritating and inhibiting than mind-expanding.

Commoner does not worry about population growth because he believes, with most demographers, that (p. 237): "tendencies for self-regulation are characteristic of human population systems" — a belief that can be comforting if one does not inquire closely into the meaning of the word "tendencies," or the level of living at which ZPG (zero population growth) might be effortlessly achieved. Commoner is confident that the "demographic transition" makes unnecessary any serious consideration of deliberate population control. So we had better look critically at the concept of the demographic transition.

For most of man's existence ZPG prevailed, on the average. (Diseases caused wide fluctuations.) Graphing birth rate and death rate against time for this long period gives two interlaced lines, both fluctuating about a single mean value, which moved upward very slowly. The average rate of growth for hundreds of thousands of years was only 0.001 per cent per year. About 300 years ago, in Europe, the death rate curve began to fall below the birth rate curve. This produced a gap between the two lines which is called the "demographic gap." The greater this gap, the greater the rate of population growth.

Somewhat later the birth rate started to drop, approaching the falling death rate curve. Ultimately, of course, the two curves must once more interweave about a single mean value. At that point, ZPG will be reestablished. If we are lucky, both birth and death rates will be lower than they were among primitive men, and the length of life correspondingly greater. The entire time during which there is a gap between the two curves is called the "demographic transition."

A mystique common among demographers holds that there is something automatic and benevolent about this process, that we need not lift a finger to alter the "natural" course of events. Against this comforting thought several cogent observations can be advanced.

1. The demographic transition has not proceeded to completion in even one country in the world. (Commoner erroneously states on page 118 that the transition "has occurred" already in most of the industrialized nations.) At one time we thought Ireland had safely passed through the transition, with the ambiguous help of the devastating Potato Famine. But we were wrong. Ireland is now off and running again, with a current growth rate of 0.5 per cent. The doubling time for her population is now a mere 140 years; and the demographic gap is widening.

2. There is absouutely no theory to indicate that the demographic gap will close automatically at a level of population consonant with a quality of life that anybody would call good; and much experience and theory supports the contrary expectation.

3. There is no reason to think that the poor countries of the world will duplicate the population history of the rich. The still incomplete transition of the European countries took several centuries. Today's poor countries may have only a few decades to complete their transition, without catastrophe; and they are starting with a demographic gap three times as wide as the one that afflicted Europe.

The superstitious aspects of demographic transition doctrine were beautifully exposed by the sociologist Kingsley Davis in his article, Population, ("Scientific American," September 1963). The tragedy of basing foreign aid on a belief in natural "development" (a metaphor that leans dangerously on embryology) has been amply documented by the economist John M. Culbertson in his "Economic Development: An Ecological Approach" (Knopf, 1971).

Population Control

Commoner is apparently unaware of the shaky foundations of the benevolent demographic transition. In addition I suspect he has a genuine, and understandable, fear of the possible consequences of acknowledging the fictional character of the benevolent transition. If we must eschew this pleasant superstition, and if we are unwilling to settle for the most wretched equilibrium conditions conceivable, then we will have to think about controlling population deliberately.

But who is "we"? Who is controlled? And by what means? It is quite understandable that Commoner (and many others) are so frightened by half-glimpsed answers that they do not seriously investigate the possibilities. "Population control," says Commoner near the end of his article,". . .no matter how disguised, involves some measure of political repression. . . " and is, therefore, in his opinion unthinkable.

Population control (as opposed to personal birth control), by whatever means, must involve either the law or informal (nonstatutory) communal mechanisms that possess the repressive force and universality of statutory law. Recognizing that population control within a sovereign country will be possible only when a large majority of its population can agree on both the aim and the methods, I once stated that such control — if it is ever achieved — will be achieved by "mutual coercion, mutually agreed upon." Commoner, like many others, bridles at this expression, not recognizing that it is, in fact, merely an operational definition of any law in a democracy. A community that rejects all such coercion is, in the strict and literal sense, a lawless community. A village of a hundred souls, insulated from all other peoples, can live happily in a lawless condition. But a nation of 205 million people ain't no village.

It is ironic that biologist Commoner's analysis fails most notably when the logic of the situation is most distinctively biological. On page 214 of his book he says (and the words stressed are his):

If a majority of the United States population voluntarily practiced birth control adequate to population stabilization, there would be no need for coercion. The corollary is that *coercion is necessary only if a majority of the population refuses voluntarily to practice adequate birth control.* This means that the majority would need to be coerced by the minority. That is, indeed, political repression.

The truth is quite otherwise. To begin with, let us agree that mutual coercion in a democracy can successfully be brought about by law only if the majority of the population is in agreement. In fact, our experience with the Prohibition Law taught us that sometimes the acceptance of coercion requires an overwhelming majority.

Commoner maintains that if the majority accepts a program of voluntary population control there is no need for coercion. In a special case, he is right. If deviations from the approved number of children occur solely as a matter of chance, and if there is no causal continuity between the high deviants of one generation and the high deviants of the next then coercion is not necessary. All the community has to do is set the approved number low enough to allow for randomly occurring over-breeding, and successful population control by voluntary means will be achieved.

But this special case is not common, and it is not what creates the situation that can lead to coercive population control. Problems arise when there is a causal continuity between the overbreeders of successive generations, when one group of people, as a matter of policy, decides to outbreed another. When that happens, a purely voluntary system of population control is sure to fail.

Is this a purely theoretical example, of no practical importance now or in the future? It is not. During the 1960s the government of Ceylon actively supported "family planning" in the hope that this voluntary method would bring about population control. At the end of the decade the government withdrew its support from the program. Why?

Because the ruling class, the Sinhalese, had become convinced that a minority group, the politically less powerful Tamils, were not cooperating in the voluntary family limitation program. The Sinhalese, 70 per cent of the population, perceived that if the Tamils (11 per cent) consistently outbred them, the minority group would someday become the majority and might then seize political control.

Note the effect the new policy can be expected to have on population growth. At present, the population of Ceylon is increasing by 2.4 per cent per year. If the new policy of the Sinhalese results in more Sinhalese being born, the overall rate of population increase will increase. On the other hand, even if the call for more Sinhalese babies is ineffective, population still will increase faster as the faster-breeding Tamils come to constitute a ever larger fraction of the total population.

Thus we see that a purely voluntary system of population control can fail even if (contrary to Commoner's supposition) it is only a minority group that refuses to cooperate. Simple mathematical analysis shows that it does not matter how small this minority is, so long as it exists.

Tribalism Defined

We need not go as far as Ceylon to find illuminating examples of the dangers of competition in reproduction. The competitive aspects of reproduction are appreciated also in Northern Ireland and in Belgium. The reader may be able to think of other examples. Dangers arise when ever "tribalism" displaces feelings of loyalty to the larger community. I have defined tribalism in the following way ("Journal of Urban Law," April 1971)::

Any group of people that perceives itself as a distinct group, and which is so perceived by the outside world, may be called a tribe. The group might be a race, as ordinarily defined, but, it need not be, it can just as well be a religious sect, a political group, or an occupational group. The essential characteristic of a tribe is that it should follow a double standard of morality—one kind of behavior for in-group relations, another for out-group.

It is one of the unfortunate and inescapable characterists of tribalism that it eventually evokes counter-tribalism (or, to use a different figure of speech, it "polarizes" society).

When that point has been reached, population control becomes impossible. This may not be the worst of the consequences of tribalism.

The theoretical principle involved in making a shambles of a program of voluntary population control is known as the "competitive exclusion principle." The idea has figured in biological literature, more or less explictly, for more than a century. It was the basis of the microbiologist M. W. Beijerinck's "elective culture method," with which I am sure botanist Barry Commoner is acquainted. I first discussed its human implications in "Nature and Man's Fate." (Rinehart, 1959). The total literature on the human implications is miniscule, and for good reason: no one yet sees an acceptable way around some of its more frightening implications (or what appear to be its implications). Certainly I don't. The subject is, I suspect, under a bit of a taboo. Perhaps it is better so, for the present.

I can sympathize with a biologist who honors the taboo. I am willing to attribute his silence to commendable compassion and caution. Paul and Anne Ehrlich in their "Population Resources Environment" (2d ed; Freeman, 1972), do not so much as hint at either the problem or the principle. Neither do Ehrlich and Holdren in their critical article. I can only suppose that they are observing the taboo. I do not criticize them for that.

On the other hand, I think Barry Commoner can be justly criticized for entering the tabooed area and giving the wrong answer. Look once more at the quotation given above from page 214 of his book. If Dr. Commoner were called in to advise the Ceylonese government in matters of population control, what advice would he give, if he made it consistent with the passage quoted?

It would have to be something like this: "You have nothing to worry about. If the majority of the Ceylonese population voluntarily adopts family planning, guided by the ideal of a small enough family, there is no need for coercion. The noncooperating Tamils constitute only 11 per cent of the Ceylonese population and are hence no threat to a voluntary population control program."

In spite of this adverse comment, I regard "The Closing Circle" as a good book, for the present moment in history. (What more can a successful expositor ask?) Bernard de Fontenelle (1657-1757), the first great popularizer of science, wisely said that "Well established beliefs can be successfully attacked only by degrees." Barry Commoner is also a great popularizer of science, and the science he is explaining — ecology — is, as Paul Sears has said, a subversive one. It is subversive in its implications for human institutions and long established habits of thought. As a practical matter it is not only necessary, it is probably also best, that the full implications of so revolutionary a science as ecology not be fully revealed to the public in an instant. "The Closing Circle," with its overemphasis on the technological factor and its "protesting too much" about population, may well be all that the general public is ready for at this time. Commoner has advanced a few degrees in attacking well-established beliefs, and his powerful voice has been widely heard. For this he deserves praise. That which he has left undone should be regarded by others as an opportunity to continue with the unending work of public education.

OTHER
EVIDENCE
ON
POPULATION
AND THE
ENVIRONMENT

INTRODUCTION

The five selections presented in this section provide additional evidence and new insights into the relationship between population and the environment. All are developed from the perspective of economics, and they seek to relate the variables of "population" and "environment" to such concepts as "economic structure," "technology," "growth," "resources," and "affluence."

One selection deserves special mention because it provides a context within which the reader might consider the ideas of the other articles. Ronald Ridker's contribution, "Resource and Environmental Consequences of Population Growth in the United States: A Summary" is aptly described by its title. It is an interpretative summary of a series of studies prepared by the Resources for the Future, Inc. for its deliberations. It should not surprise anyone to find that Ridker's summary is generally consistent with the Commission's observations about the advantages for the environment if population growth is checked. Ridker, however, treats these topics in a fuller way.

He begins by examining the way in which population growth affects resource needs and the environment through the economy. His concern with the economy is one of two interests he shares with the authors in this section. He then provides a quick inventory of the adequacy of some specific resources and of certain environmental problems. He concludes by looking at some broad institutional and social concerns. Ridker notes that there are non-resource costs in adjusting to growing resource and environmental problems under conditions of continued population growth. He identifies four specific costs: changes in life styles, the postponement of solutions to social problems, the need to seek relief from environmental difficulties through technological solutions for which the side effects are unknown, and the closing off of important options. His consideration of social and institutional costs is the other interest he shares with the five authors represented here. Although their problems and perspectives differ, all raise issues that transcend the narrow protrayal of the relationship of population and environment as, if we can borrow a term, "one-dimensional ecology."

POPULATION AND
ENVIRONMENTAL QUALITY

Anthony C. Fisher

A number of recent studies have emphasized a connection between environmental quality and population size and growth(1). Indeed, deteriorating environmental quality, as measured by such indices as increasing air and water pollution and increasing congestion in various kinds of public facilities, is seen by some as primarily a population problem. Thus Mayer argues: "Our housing problem; our traffic problems; the insufficiency of the number of our hospitals, of community recreation facilities; our pollution problem, are all facets of our population problem." (2) This conclusion seems plausible; more people in a given area presumably results in more crowding of facilities and a greater generation of wastes discharged into environmental media as residuals in the production and consumption processes. It would follow, moreover, that a remedy lies in somehow stabilizing population and indeed at a level much below today's.

I shall argue, on the contrary, that economic theory, supported by some evidence, suggests that this is not the case, i.e., that deteriorating quality is not *primarily* a population problem (3). More specifically, the following propositions may be advanced: 1. the rate of population growth has declined in developed areas, and current low rates of growth may be expected to persist, perhaps to decline still further, and to spread to currently less developed areas; 2. there is nonetheless, a real and quite probably increasing problem of quality deterioration; and 3. the deterioration arises most fundamentally, from a pervasive price distortion, and the remedy lies in policies to correct the distortion which are largely unrelated to population control.

Before proceeding with the demonstration of these propositions, let me define the problem more precisely. The old Malthusian question of population versus food (or even other traditional limiting resources, such as minerals) is not at issue. It is recognized that in large areas of the world, even in some local areas of the U.S., starvation and malnutrition constitute grave threats to human health and survival. Whether this situation is improving or not is a matter of some controversy. It is my impression that, very recently (within, say, the last few years), students of the problem have become increasingly optimistic. The so-called "green revolution" in food production, involving development and wide application of new types of fertilizers, along with other, much more exotic innovations, offers the prospect of removing, perhaps for centuries, food as a limiting factor to population growth (4). More generally, to quote Krutilla, "Those who take an optimistic view would hold that the modern industrial economy is winning its independence from the traditional natural resources sector to a remarkable degree." (5) And these developments refer only to gross production of food, or more generally, energy. If, as discussed below, the rate of population growth continues to decline, and the decline continues to spread, the picture becomes still brighter. In any case, the main concern here is with environmental quality in an affluent society and its relation to population size and growth, and not with the old Malthusian question, which is admittedly still relevant in some areas, and perhaps ultimately relevant in all.

Also not at issue is the relation of migration to environmental problems, except insofar as it affects fertility. Clearly the high concentrations of population resulting in part from large unplanned migration from rural to urban areas have something to do with congestion and pollution problems in these areas. This is not a problem of global or aggregate population growth, but rather of the distribution of population. (6)

Trends in Population Growth

Let us consider the first proposition. The rate of population growth has been declining, and may continue to decline. The facts of past decline are given in Table 1 for the U.S. (figures for other developed areas would show the same broad trends).

Table 1. BIRTH AND DEATH RATES IN THE U.S.
FOR THE SELECTED YEARS, 1820–1968 *

Year	Birth Rate	Death Rate	Natural Growth Rate
1820	55.2	?	3+ (?)
1840	51.8	?	3 (?)
1860	44.3	18.7**	2.56
1880	39.8	19.8**	2.00
1900	32.3	17.2	1.51
1920	27.7	13.0	1.47
1940	19.4	10.8	.86
1960	23.7	9.6	1.41
1968	17.4	9.6	.78

* (Sources: 1820–1950, *Historical Statistics of the United States, Colonial Times to 1957* (Washington, D.C., 1960), pp. 23, 27; 1957–1960, *Natality Statistics Analysis, United States 1963* (Washington, D.C., 1966), p. 2 and *Mortality Trends in the United States, 1954–1963* (Washington, D.C., 1966), p. 3; 1968, *Monthly Vital Statistics Report, Annual Summary for the United States, 1968* (Washington, D.C., 1968), p. 1.

** Death rates for 1860 and 1880 are for Massachusetts only. Massachusetts death rates in the twentieth century have averaged about a point higher than U.S. rates, so that U.S. rates in 1860 and 1880 were probably about a point below those listed.

It can be seen that both birth rates and death rates have been declining throughout this century and, as far as the figures can take us, through most of the nineteenth century as well, with the larger absolute decline in birth rates resulting in a fall in the rate of population growth (neglecting net migration) from probably more than 3 percent per year in 1820 through about 2.5 percent per year in 1860 to less than .8 percent per year in 1968. Before examining the reasons for this long decline and attempting to predict the course of future population growth, let us take a closer look at the figures. The low (below trend) birth rate for 1940 may be explained by a slow emergence from the depression, adding a cyclical component to the secular. During World War II birth rates were up a bit, and just after the war they jumped abruptly (stock adjustment?) to a level above the trend, reaching a peak in 1947. There were small fluctuations in the late 1940s and early and middle 1950s with a peak in 1957. Since 1957, birth rates have been steadily declining in the U.S. through a variety of lesser cyclical fluctuations, resuming apparently the long downtrend. While a more detailed breakdown of vital statistics could facilitate a very short-run prediction of future birth rates, I believe an application of economic theory can carry us further. (7)

Recall that for Malthus, the dynamics of population growth worked exclusively through changes in mortality. A temporary increase in income, due perhaps to a better-than-average harvest one year, would lead to a reduction in infant and other mortality and thence to an increase in population. The increase could only be temporary, however, as diminishing returns to (agricultural) production drove (per capita) income down, eventually to below the subsistence level, where the "positive" checks of famine, pestilence, and war could be relied upon to increase infant and other mortality, reducing population until (per capita) income climbed back to the subsistence level. A permanent increase in population could come only through a permanent increase in income, due perhaps to technological progress. The increase in income would, however, in the absence of fertility control, eventually just support a larger population at the subsistence level.

Malthus did see how technological progress could, for a time, outdistance population growth and raise per capita incomes, but obviously he could not and did not foresee how it could continue to do so indefinitely. Also, he gave scant attention to the possibility of progress in fertility control, more or less dismissing it as "vice," an "unnatural" means of population control. Yet we have seen that falling birth rates have been associated with development in the U.S. and elsewhere. How has this come about, and is it likely to continue?

Cipolla, in his fascinating survey of the economic history of world population, observes that there has been associated with industrialization first a drop in the death rate, and then, after some lag, a drop in the birth rate. (8) He does not, however, inquire into the mechanism of the falling birth rate, and this we must do in order to make predictions about future movements. What we need, then, is a theory of population in which the control works through fertility. Such a theory has been formulated by Becker (9) and elaborated by Mincer, (10) and it can provide an explanation of a number of observations, in particular of the secularly falling birth rate.

In Becker's model, utility-maximizing households determine the number of children they want subject to relative price, income, and technological constraints. Thus as family income rises (if children are not an"inferior good"), the number of children desired increases. On the other hand, as the relative "price" or cost of having and raising children rises, the number of children desired decreases. Also, since the technological constraint is essentially knowledge of contraception, technological progress clearly results in fewer children.

Falling birth rates may then be explained, at least in part, by the dominance of combined technical and relative price effects over an income effect. What has all of this to do with industrialization? Obviously, industrialization has brought rising incomes and, other things equal, they would be expected to lead to higher birth rates.

Industrialization has also fostered the development and spread of contraceptive knowledge which, other things equal, would lead to lower birth rates. More subtly, industrialization and associated urbanization have increased the cost of having and raising children, and this fact, along with the growth in contraceptive knowledge, can explain the falling birth rate. Let us examine some of the reasons for the relative price effect.

It is fairly clear that the value of a child's services in the household, which is one (negative) component of price, typically falls with urbanization. In a rural or farm household a boy can be employed in planting and harvesting and general maintenance, and a girl can help in the processing and preparation of food crops, making clothing, and so on. The banning of child labor, and compulsory education laws, make it difficult to convert value-in-kind in the rural sector to money returns in the urban industrial sector. There seems in addition to have been a shift in preferences for what Becker calls "higher quality" children, children with, for example, increasingly greater amounts invested in their education beyond the legal minimum in formal schooling. For given expenditure, higher quality means lower quantity.

An important positive component of the cost of a child is, as Mincer demonstrates, the mother's opportunity cost. This cost may be roughly approximated by her foregone earnings. Growing opportunities for women in the urban market economy can be expected to lead a woman to the joint decision to participate in the labor force, and to defer or limit numbers of children. It is not that families have refrained from having children because the wife is working; rather, a shift in relative prices, with home work becoming relatively more "expensive" in terms of foregone market income, has resulted in movement out of the home (child-bearing and child-rearing) and into the market. Thus, as birth rates have fallen (see Table 1), the labor force participation rate of married women has risen from 5 percent in 1890 to 40 today.

Related to this movement may be the deferral of marriage and especially family formation (with the reduction in childbearing years leading, perhaps, to a reduction in numbers of children) by young men and women investing in the increasingly greater amounts of education demanded by the modern industrial, or postindustrial, economy.

Further aspects of the relative price effect of economic development on birth rates might be distinguished, but the main tendency seems clear. Broadly, it is for lower birth rates in response to shifting opportunities.

Before assessing the implications of price, income, and technological changes on future fertility patterns (and, given apparently stable mortality, on population growth) in the developed areas, we might make an additional related observation on the situation in the currently less developed areas. There may be a sort of feedback relationship between mortality and fertility, in the sense that current birth rates are a function of (in addition to the price, income, and technological variables considered above) expected death rates. That is to say, as Schultz points out, "The established regime of childhood mortality may influence parents in planning their lifetime reproductive behavior to compensate for what they expect to be the incidence of death among their offspring."(11) Some evidence in support of this hypothesis is cited from a study of Fredericksen of birth and death rates in Ceylon, Mauritius, and British Guiana. (12) If true, it provides a further explanation of falling death rates in earlier years (during the period of falling death rates) in the developed areas, and a further prediction of falling birth rates in future years in the less-developed areas.

As to future birth rates and population growth in the U.S. and other developed areas, one is made wary of prediction by the poor past performance of the demographers. (13) Their predictions are essentially extrapolations of trends, modified somewhat by changing age, race, and other distributions of the population but neglecting consideration of underlying economic determinants. Might we not, employing the tools of economic theory, do better? Of course, some guesswork is still involved. My guess, then, is that the economic development that has characterized the past century will (for some decades, at least) continue, that it will continue to be associated with changes in technology and in relative opportunities, and that these changes will continue to be associated systematically with slowly falling, or at the very least not rapidly rising, birth rates.(14)

Moreover, to the extent that some current social movements are successful, the tendency for birth rates to fall may be strengthened. I am referring to the movement to limit population by changing preferences and relative opportunities, and the movement to "liberate" women. The population movement involves attempts to persuade prospective parents to have fewer children, increasing public and private activity to disseminate knowledge of contraception, and even a proposal (by Senator Packwood) to in effect change the tax incentive structure for the production of children by instituting a declining scale of income tax exemptions for children. Similarly, the focus of "women's liberation" on providing more challenging and remunerative opportunities for women may be expected to lead additional women out of the home and into the market — although the widespread institution of "free" child care centers, another objective of the movement, could work in the opposite direction by reducing child care costs.

Even should population in the U.S. continue for some decades to grow at a rate of about 1 percent per year — the current rate *including* immigration — clearly this *in itself*, would have little effect on the quality of the environment — nor would cessation of growth, *in itself*, be likely to result in any improvement in quality. To understand this point, let us consider briefly some trends in the indices of environmental quality — pollution and congestion — and then attempt an alternative explanation of these phenomena.

Evidence on Deterioration of the Quality of the Environment

Although congestion is a recognized fact of life in most urban areas, some particularly striking figures reflect the growing congestion of natural or wild areas. Thus over a period of just twelve years, from 1947 to 1959, man-days of use in wilderness areas of the U.S. national forests increased from 306,800 to 1,399,000 (15) — an increase of 356 percent, as compared to an increase of just over 20 percent in population over this period. Current density and rates of increase are even greater for the national parks. (16)

With respect to air quality, although considerable evidence has been accumulated over the last few years on levels of pollution and, to a much lesser extent, on the effects of various pollutants, not too much is known about trends. This is, as Freeman observes, because "random factors (such as weather) tend to obscure trends over the relatively short periods of time covered by most available time series on air quality." (17) Obviously, pollution has increased over time in the U.S., if we go back far enough. On the other hand, no trend emerges from an array of figures on major pollutant concentrations in seven major cities in the U.S. over the period 1962-1966. (18) Further, there is even some evidence for a downtrend in the average level of particulates, the most visible of pollutants, in 64 cities over the period 1957-1963. (19)

In Los Angeles, smog was not perceived as a problem during the early years of rapid population growth. It came rather suddenly in the early 1940s associated perhaps with World War II industrialization. And in spite of continued rapid population growth over the last several years, the smog problem has not worsened; indeed, it may have improved slightly. In Pittsburgh, definite improvement over a period of about twenty years has been detected, with no corresponding decrease in population. These (and other) apparently perverse relationships are, as we shall see, to be explained by pollution control policies not related to population.

It should be obvious, even from these somewhat sketchy figures and examples, that there is currently no simple relationship between population and environmental quality in the U.S. By some measures, quality is deteriorating much more rapidly than population is increasing. By others, quality seems to be holding the line, if at costly and dangerously low levels, as population is increasing. There are, however, some qualifications.

The first is that, again, it must be emphasized that we are concerned with aggregate population growth, and not with the (mal) distribution of population stemming from large migrations to urban areas unprepared to handle the resulting congestion.

The second is that, obviously, quality deterioration did not become significant until some lower bound or threshold concentration of population, or perhaps more importantly, economic activity, was reached. But it does not follow, as we shall see, that the only solution, or even the best solution, is now somehow drastically to reduce population and economic activity.

The third is that beyond some upper bound, continued population growth, even at a rate of less than 1 percent per year, is impossible. This has to do with the extreme deterioration of quality associated with an approach to "standing-room-only." But often-expressed inferences of imminent disaster from compound population growth are quite unwarranted. (20) This is because with compound growth most of the increase in absolute numbers come toward the end of a given period, when the (constant) rate of increase is applied to an increasingly larger base. Thus if the population of the U.S. is now 200 million and grows constantly at a rate of 1 percent per year, in 100 years it will have reached a level of approximately 540 million, in another hundred years approximately 1,458 million, and in another hundred years approximately 3,937 million. In the first hundred years, the increase is 340 million, in the second it is 918 million, and in the third 2,479 million. The latter figure would, by the way, give the U.S. (including Alaska) a population density of a little over 1,000 per square mile, or about double the current density in India — uncomfortable, although still some, distance from "standing-room only," I am certainly not advocating, or even predicting, this sort of sustained growth. It seems probable that unless birth rates in the U.S. decline still further within the next hundred years or so, new versions of the old Malthusian checks can be expected to reassert themselves — certainly at some point well before "standing-room-only" can be realized. On the other hand, several more decades of growth at present rates of less than 1 percent or even slightly higher seem feasible, if not optimal.

A much more relevant problem is What, if not increasing population, is the source of the pervasive and quite probably growing deterioration of environmental quality? And what policies are likely to be helpful in improving quality?

Prices and Quality

The phenomena of pollution and congestion cited earlier as examples of environmental decay are often characterized by economists as "external costs," or "externalities." (21) In altering or expanding its operations an economic unit (individual, firm, or even public agency or municipality) may be imposing costs on others, in addition to its costs of operation. Thus a factory discharging quantities of smoke may be increasing costs for nearby farmers, if the smoke has deleterious effects on the growth or health of the farmers' crops or livestock. Similarly, a logging or pulp-making operation polluting a stream may increase the costs of obtaining drinking water or water recreation facilities for downstream users. With respect to congestion, the problem arises because additional users of a facility may, beyond some level of use, impose costs on other users. To take perhaps the most commonly cited example, additional motorists on a highway will increase the travel time, and perhaps also the fuel and maintenance costs, of other motorists.

These examples could be multiplied, but the underlying principle would be the same. It is that external costs in the forms of pollution and congestion are imposed as a consequence of failure to price (or otherwise effectively ration) scarce environmental resources. Thus air, water, and even open land have traditionally been "free goods" for the disposal of gaseous, liquid, and solid wastes. Also traditionally "free" or otherwise unrestricted has been access to (for example)) crowded highways and national parks. But as Ayres and Kneese point out in a stimulating study of the relationship of some economic processes to environmental quality, air and water, and I would add, open land) are, in reality, "common property resources of great and increasing value presenting society with important and difficult allocation problems which exchange in private markets cannot resolve." (22) As Kneese has shown, the problems do not arise at low levels of use, given the capacity of the common property resources to absorb and assimilate wastes. The problems would also not arise if these resources were in private ownership and claims could be exchanged in competitive markets. But these conditions do not hold in a real economy, nor can they be expected to. Thus if a firm (or a householder, or a municipality) had to pay a price for the right to discharge wastes, it may be expected that it would either treat the wastes, seek a new location, or adopt an alternative cheaper production process perhaps involving some recycling; or, failing any of these, simply cut back on production and the associated generation of wastes. Similarly, as a number of writers have shown, (23) the levying of a toll or charge on the use of a public highway or other facility will tend to reduce the level of use, providing potential users with an incentive to seek alternative modes of transport or other substitutes for the tolled facility.

This view of the environmental quality problem carries with it an implicit solution. It is that, in principle, optimal levels (conceivably zero) of various types of pollution and congestion could be achieved by "internalizing externalities," i.e., by pricing relevant environmental resources — and, at a rate equal to the (marginal) social cost of their use. In such an amended pricing system, costs formerly external would be absorbed by those responsible, presumably leading them to modify or curtail activities giving rise to such costs. This is further spelled out by Kneese with special reference to water quality.

The policy of internalizing externalities through a modified incentive structure is widely recognized by economists as likely to be helpful in improving the allocation of resources, (24) and in fact it is embodied in a number of current legislative proposals, from President Nixon's (1970) State of the Union message and a follow-up on environmental quality, to legislation introduced by Senators Nelson and Proxmire and others. (25)

It must be recognized that measurement of losses from air or water pollution or from various types of congestion presents some formidable problems. Further, some aspects of environmental management necessarily involve public investment (e.g., in research and development of sewage facilities, mass transit systems, and so forth). What, then, are the best policy hopes for improving environmental quality?

Obviously, internalizing known externalities where feasible will be optimal. But in the absence of perfect knowledge and perfect pricing mechanisms we need not accept the status quo. Other means of control, having more or less relation to the optimal, have been suggested. Let us examine them briefly. (26)

It has been widely suggested that an effective way to control pollution is simply to set maximum physical emission or discharge levels, with significant penalties attached to their violation. This policy is, however, just a special case of the graded schedule of charges or penalties envisioned in the optimal pricing system. It is essentially a sort of "all-or-nothing" tax on externalities, with a heavy penalty for exceeding allowable limits and no penalty at all for not reaching the limits. In cases where accurate measurement of costs associated with a range of pollution or congestion levels is not technically or economically feasible, it may well be a good policy. Still better, presumably, would be a graded system of charges bearing some relation to costs.

As noted above, a program of public investment in research and development of alternative, less socially costly methods of production and associated treatment of waste materials may be worthwhile. Also, provision of such facilities as highways and large recreation areas has traditionally fallen within the public sector. The case for public investment also rests on the presence of externalities — here, benefits from an investment which cannot be appropriated by private investors. And subsidies to private research and development in, for example, new methods of recycling residuals or otherwise altering a production or consumption process to reduce residuals discharged in harmful form can be viewed as elements of socially optimal pricing to internalize externalities—in this case, putting a *negative* price on *improvement* of environmental quality.

Related to these measures would be subsidies for the treatment of wastes from a given process. Such subsidies are likely to be inefficient, however, for a number of reasons given by Kneese in his criticism of current policies for water pollution control. For these reasons, a tax on pollution giving the polluter an incentive to seek the least (social) cost process (which could turn out to be treatment of wastes from an existing process), or public investment in some form of abatement if the polluter is a public agency, are to be preferred.

A major theme that emerges from many discussions of policies to improve environmental quality, or at least to prevent its futher deterioration, is that a fundamental re-ordering of preferences must be accomplished, involving an acceptance of reduction in rates of growth of personal income, and even in levels of personal income, in exchange for benefits from enthanced quality of the common property resources (air, water, open space, and so forth).(27) While it is quite true that cutting back the level of economic activity would (given the existing structure of relative prices and associated choice of technologies) reduce the pollution and congestion loads placed on the environment, the implicit assumption of fixed prices is misleading. It is hoped that enough has been said to suggest that changing the structure of prices and associated technologies can accomplish the objective in less costly fashion. Some reduction in growth or level of income as traditionally measured, e.g., by GNP, is a price that must be paid for better quality, but the reduction will be minimized by the discriminating pricing policy. Further, it is not clear how an undiscriminating slowdown, much less reversal, of economic activity could be brought about without inducing widespread hardship. For example, perhaps the most important source of reduction in poverty in the last decade (if not before) has been aggregate economic growth. (28) It seems far preferable, then, to channel growth out of harmful paths rather than to stop it completely.

We come, finally, to population policy. In attempting to better environmental quality through reducing population we face much the same problems as in attempting to better quality through reducing aggregate economic activity. For given per capita incomes and relative prices, reducing population may indeed be expected to reduce the loads on environmental resources. But even with population somehow permanently reduced, expanding economic activity will, if otherwise unregulated, increase the loads to undesirable levels. Moreover, it is hard to see how the necessary very substantial reduction could be brought about. Short of disaster, no one is predicting that population can be or will be reduced below current levels, only that its rate of growth can be or will be reduced, perhaps to zero in the near future. Unless, then, we want to return (as we probably cannot) to perhaps pre-industrial levels of population and economic activity with their (for the most part) uncongested environmental common property resources, there is no alternative to dealing directly with our environmental problems.

Thus the reason that population and economic activity have increased over the last several years in Los Angeles without further deterioration of air quality is simply that controls on emissions have been imposed. Conversely, were population stabilized and controls lifted, I would confidently predict rapid further deterioration. And does Mayer, (29) for example, really believe that the flow of 26 billion bottles he cites as discarded annually over the American landscape would, in the absence of incentives for consumers to save and return them, or for producers to supply degradable containers, somehow evaporate, or even be diminished, were population growth somehow reduced immediately from .8 percent per year to zero — or even below — as he advocates?

Again, using our example of growing congestion in outdoor recreation areas: Could not a system of user charges, ideally related to external costs of use, be instituted to reduce congestion (and damage to the areas)? Something like this is already done for some types of use, such as hunting. Very substantial license fees or day-use fees or both limit numbers of hunters and thus, along with individual bag limits, protect the game for sustained hunting and other uses(e.g., research). It is an extension of policies of essentially this sort that is likely to be most effective in protecting the wider environment.

Conclusions

I have tried to demonstrate, and then to relate, several propositions on population and environmental quality. The propositions are 1. that the rate of population growth in the U.S. and other developed economies has been declining, and is likely to continue to decline; 2. that this fact is not very relevant for problems of environmental quality in these areas, which will continue to worsen even in the presence of zero population growth or absolutely reduced population; 3. that the more fundamental source of most quality problems is a distortion of the structure of relative prices, caused in turn by the pervasive presence of technological externalities in production and consumption; and 4. that the most effective policies for improving quality involve essentially correcting the distortion — internalizing externalities in a very broad sense.

Finally, I should like to make it clear that none of the above is intended as opposition to population control, especially in poorer areas. Rather, it is intended to suggest that it is misleading to assert that population control can, *in itself*, be expected to do much for environmental quality.

Notes

(1) See, for example, P. Ehrlich, *The Population Bomb* (New York: Ballantine, 1968).

(2) J. Mayer, "Toward a Non-Malthusian Population Policy," *Columbia Forum* (Summer 1969), 12.

(3) A similar argument is made in B. Wattenberg, "Overpopulation as a Crisis Issue: The Nonsense Explosion," *New Republic* (April 4, 1970).

(4) Mayer, supra note 2, 10-12.

(5) J. V. Krutilla, "Conservation Reconsidered," *American Economic Review,* LVII (September 1967), 778.

(6) This point is made in detail by Wattenberg, supra note 3, 19, who notes that in the last eight years one out of three countries in the United States actually lost population, and three out of five had a net outmigration.

(7) Wattenberg, supra note 3, notes declining fertility rates over the last decade, but does not attempt to analyze the causes.

(8) C. M. Cipolla, *The Economic History of World Population* (Baltimore: Penguin, 1962), pp. 82-91.

(9) G. S. Becker, "Economic Aspects of Fertility," in Universities-National Bureau Committee for Economic Research, *Demographic and Economic Change in Developed Countries* (New York: National Bureau of Economic Research, 1958).

(10) J. Mincer, "Market Prices, Opportunity Costs, and Income Effects," in Carl F. Christ, *et al., Measurement in Economics* (Stanford, Calif.: Stanford University Press, 1963).

(11) T. P. Shultz, "An Economic Model of Family Planning and Fertility," *Journal of Political Economy,* LXXVII (March-April 1969), 160.

(12) H. Fredericksen, "Determinants and Consequences of Mortality and Fertility Trends," in *Public Health Reports,* Vol. LXXXI (Washington, D.C.: U. S. Public Health Service, 1966).

(13) The U. S. Census Bureau has in fact just recently announced major downward revisions in its population projections for the next 30 years, based apparently on the falling birth rates of the last few years. (*Washington Post,* August 13, 1970). The high projections had been based on the relatively high birth rates of the late 1950s and early 1960s.

(14) A caution here is suggested by a purely demographic consideration. The large numbers of births in the early and middle 1950s mean that large numbers of women will be entering the child-bearing ages in the early and middle 1970s. This may result in some deviation from the long trend, perhaps even in increasing birth rates for a few years.

(15) University of California Wildland Research Center, *Wilderness and Recreation: A Report on Resources, Values and Problems* (Outdoor Recreation Resources Review Commission Study Report No. 3; Washington, D.C.: Government Printing Office, 1962), pp. 226-229.

(16) Mayer, supra note 2, 12.

(17) A. M. Freeman, "The Quality of the Natural Environment" (background

paper prepared for the Panel on Social Indicators, Department of Health, Education and Welfare, 1968), p. 30.

(18) *Ibid.*, pp. 27, 28.

(19) *Ibid.*, p. 30.

(20) See, for example, Ehrlich, supra note 1, for perhaps the most prominent expression of this position.

(21) For a rigorous definition and discussion of the concept of externality, see J. Buchanan and W. Stubblebine, "Externality," *Economica,* XXIX (November 1962).

(22) R. U. Ayres and A. V. Kneese, "Production, Consumption, and Externalities," *American Economic Review,* LIX (June 1969), 283.

(23) See, for example, M. Marchand, "A Note on Optimal Tolls in an Imperfect Environment," *Econemetrica,* XXXVI (July-October 1968).

(24) See, for example, K. Boulding, "The Economics of the Coming Spaceship Earth," in Henry Jarrett (ed.), *Environmental Quality in a Growing Economy* (Baltimore: Johns Hopkins Press, 1966). Boulding notes (p. 13) that "many of the immediate problems of pollution. . .arise because of the failure of the price system, and many of them could be solved by corrective taxation. If people had to pay the losses due to the nuisance they create, a good deal more resources would go into the prevention of nuisances." It must, however, be noted that some rather subtle issues concerning the feasibility and optimality of corrective taxation have been raised in the literature. A detailed discussion of these issues is beyond the scope of the present article, but the interested reader might consult, among others, R.H. Coase, "The Problem of Social Cost," *Journal of Law and Economics,* III (October 1960); O.A. Davis and A. Whinston, "On Externalities, Information and the Government-Assisted Invisible Hand," *Economica,* XXXIII (August 1966); F.T. Dolbear, "On the Theory of Optimum Externality," *American Economic Review,* LVII (March 1967); J.M. Buchanan, "External Diseconomies, Corrective Taxes, and Market Structure," *American Economic Review,* LIX (March 1969). Very briefly, I would assert that none of these critiques seriously weakens the case for corrective taxation and public investment to internalize the widely diffused external effects typically associated with pollution and congestion phenomena.

(25) In the State of the Union message, the President says that ". . .the price of goods should be made to include the costs of producing and disposing of them without damage to the environment." In a message to Congress released February 10, 1970, he specifically proposes that "failure to meet established water quality standards. . .be made subject to court-imposed fines of up to $10,000 per day." Along these lines, Senator Proxmire, joined by nine other senators from both parties, has introduced a bill to impose a system of effluent charges, with the revenue collected going into regional water quality management. Senator Nelson has introduced a bill to require manufacturers to pay a fee for selling their goods in containers than cannot be wither recycled or easily degraded, also with revenue going to state and local agencies for construction of solid waste facilities.

(26) For a clear, detailed discussion of the superior features of the proposed marginal social cost pricing scheme, see L.E. Ruff, "The Economic Common Sense of Pollution." *The Public Interest,* No. 19 (Spring 1970).

(27) See, for example, a number of the contributions to G. de Bell (ed.), *The Environmental Handbook* (New York: Ballantine, 1970). This alternative is also discussed by L. Mayer, in an article, "U.S. Population Growth: Would Slower Be Better?" *Fortune* (June 1970). A stimulating statement of the case against a policy of encouraging rapid economic growth is found in E. J. Mishan, *The Cost s of Economic*

Growth (New York: Praeger, 1967). As I understand him, however, Mishan is not so much opposed to increasing personal incomes as he is to some of the undersirable side effects, the external "costs of growth" of the sort we have been discussing. His own policy recommendation is to internalize these external costs through corrective taxation and the price system (pp. 53-57). exactly as proposed above.

(28) Even Anderson, who takes a fairly pessimistic view of future reduction in 1. Anderson, "Trickling Down: The Relationship between Economic Growth and the Extent of Poverty among American Families," *Quarterly Journal of Economics*, LCCVIII (November 1964).

(29) Mayer, supra note 2, 13.

MAN AND
HIS ENVIRONMENT

Ansley J. Coale

The way our economy is organized is an essential cause, if not *the* essential cause, of air and water pollution, and of the ugly and sometimes destructive accumulation of trash. I believe it is also an important element in such dangerous human ecological interventions as changes in the biosphere resulting from the wholesale use of inorganic fertilizers, of the accumulation in various dangerous places such as the fatty tissue of fish and birds and mammals of incredibly stable insecticides. We can properly attribute such adverse effects to a combination of a high level of economic activity and the use of harmful technological practices that are inconsistent with such a high level.

The economist would say that harmful practices have occurred because of a disregard of what he would call *externalities*. An externality is defined as a consequence (good or bad) that does not enter the calculations of gain or loss by the person who undertakes an economic activity. It is typically a cost (or a benefit) of an activity that accrues to someone else. A fence erected in a suburban neighborhood for privacy also affords a measure of privacy to the neighbors — a cost or a benefit depending on how he feels about privacy versus keeping track of what goes on next door. Air pollution created by an industrial plant is a classic case of an externality; the operator of a factory producing noxious smoke imposes costs on everyone downwind, and pays none of these costs himself — they do not affect his balance sheet at all. This, I believe, is the basic economic factor that has a degrading effect on the environment: we have in general permitted economic activities without assessing the operator for their adverse effects. There has been no attempt to evaluate — and to charge for — externalities. As Boulding says, we pay people for the goods they produce, but do not make them pay for the bads.

To put the same point more simply: environmental deterioration has arisen to a large extent because we have treated pure air, pure water, and the disposal of waste as if they were free. They cannot be treated as free in a modern, urban, industrial society.

There are a number of different kinds of policies that would prevent, or at least reduce, the harmful side effects of some of our economic activities, either by preventing or reducing the volume of the harmful activity, or by inducing a change in technique. Other policies might involve curative rather than preventive steps, such as cleaning up trash along the highways, if we cannot prevent people from depositing it there.

Among the possibilities are steps that would make externalities internal. An example that I find appealing, although it is perhaps not widely practical, is to require users of flowing water to take in the water downstream of their operation and discharge it upstream. A more general measure is to require the recycling of air or water used in industrial processes, rather than permitting the free use of fresh water and clean air, combined with the unmonitored discharge of exhaust products.

Public authorities can charge for unfavorable external effects by imposing a tax on operations that are harmful to the environment. The purpose of such taxes is to reduce the volume of adverse effects by inducing a shift in technique or by reducing the volume of production by causing a rise in price. Also, the tax receipts could be used to pay for mitigating the effect. An example of a desirable tax is one imposed to minimize the use of disposable cans and bottles for soft drinks and beer. Not long ago the majority of manufactures produced these commodities in containers that were to be returned. The producer offered a modest price for returning bottles as an inducement. It has proven cheaper to use disposable glass bottles and cans; recently aluminum cans have rapidly increased in popularity, substituting a container that lasts indefinitely for the tin cans that would sooner or later rust away. Everyone is familiar with the resultant clutter on beaches, in parks, and along the highways. If a tax of 10 cents per unit were imposed on each disposable container, it would clearly be cheaper to go back to returnables. If some manufacturers found it advantageous to pay the 10-cent tax, the receipts could be used to pay for cleaning up highways and beaches.

Another approach that would induce people to give up economic activities with harmful effects on others is to make individuals and corporations financially liable for any damage caused by their operations. The resultant litigation would be an unwarranted windfall for lawyers, but financial liability might be a very potent factor in reducing pollution.

There is general agreement that our knowledge of what affects the environment is wholly inadequate. Because of inadequate monitoring and measurement, we do not know what is happening to the atmosphere or the biosphere; we need research to keep track of what is going on as well as to develop the techniques that will produce the goods we want with fewer of the bads we do not want.

An Economist's Review of Resource Exhaustion

One of the questions most frequently raised about the environmental effects of modern life is the rapid and rising rate of extraction of raw materials. Are we running out of resources?

I would first like to note that the distinction between renewable and non-renewable resources is not a clear one. There are, of course, instances of non-renewable resources in the form of concentrated sources of energy, such as the fossil fuels. These are reservoirs of reduced carbon embodying radiant energy from the sun that accumulated over many thousands of years. When these fuels are used, the energy that is released is to a large extent radiated into space, and we have no way of reclaiming it. The geological processes that are constantly renewing the fossil deposits of carbon are so slow compared to the rate at which we are burning the fuels that the designation "nonrenewable" is appropriate.

On the other hand, when we think of our resources of such useful materials as the metallic elements of iron, copper, nickel, lead, and so forth, we should realize that spaceship Earth has the same amount of each element as it had a million years ago, and will have the same amount a million years from now. All we do with these resources is to move them around. The energy we use is lost, but the minerals we find useful are still with us. It does not pay to recycle these minerals (that is to use them repeatedly by reclaiming scrap) because the deposits of minerals in the ground or in the ocean are still such a cheap source. It must be noted that the mining of fresh ore is cheaper than the use of scrap in part because miners are not charged for their "externalities." If harmful by-products of mining could not be discharged into streams, if mine tailings were regulated, and erosion-producing or even unesthetic practices forbidden, minerals would be more expensive and recycling more attractive. In the production of any metallic element, the easier sources are exploited first. As mining gets more difficult, the ore gets more expensive, and recycling becomes more nearly competitive. It seems wholly probable that the technology of recycling will be improved.

The surprising fact is that raw materials are not at the moment very costly, and moreover their cost relative to the cost of finished goods has not been increasing. The gross national product in the United States is more than $4500 per capita and the raw materials component per capita is less than $100. The price of raw materials relative to the price of finished goods is no higher now than at the beginning of the century, and if we were running out of raw materials, they would surely be rising in relative expensiveness. A prominent exception is saw lumber, which is substantially more expensive relative to the cost of finished wooden products than it used to be.

The reason that the future of our resource situation always seems so bleak and the past seems quite comfortable is that we can readily construct a plausible sounding estimate of the future demand for a particular raw material, but cannot form such a plausible picture of the future supply. To estimate the future demand, we need merely note the recent trends in the per capita consumption of whatever it is we are concerned about, utilize whatever plausible projection of population we are prepared to accept, multiply the two together and project an astonishingly high rate of usage 50 years in the future. If this demand does not seem overwhelming, we need only make a projection 100 years in the future. What we cannot so readily foresee is the discovery of new sources and of new techniques of extraction, and, in particular, the substitution of other raw materials or the substitution of other industrial processes which change the demand away from the raw material we are considering. Hence it can always be made to appear that in the future we are going to run out of any given material, but that at present we never have.

It is possible to set plausible limits to the stores of fossil fuels that we are likely to discover, and with the very rapid rise in the use of these fuels they will surely become more expensive in some not too distant time. It should be noted, however, that we will not suddenly "run out" of fossil fuels. Long before the last drop of oil is used, oil will have become much more expensive. If gasoline were $5 or $10 a gallon, we would utilize it much more sparingly, with small economical automobile engines, or perhaps the substitution of some non-petroleum-based fuel altogether. In fact, the principal user of our petroleum deposits may be the petrochemical industries. I have given this special attention to fossil fuels because there is no substitute in prospect for such fuels in small mobile units such as automobiles. On the other hand, the supply of overall energy seems to pose no problem. There seems to be ample fissionable material to supply rising energy needs for many centuries, if breeding reactors are perfected. If fusion proves a practical source, the supply of energy can properly be considered limitless.

Another aspect of the relation of the United States economy to resources that is much publicized today is the fact that we are consuming such a large fraction of the current annual extraction of raw materials in the world. A much quoted figure is that 6 percent of the world's population is using 30 percent of the resources. It is concluded from figures such as these that we are robbing the low-income countries of the world of the basis of their future prosperity — that we are using up not only our resources, but theirs as well. Most economists would find this a very erroneous picture of the effect of our demand for the raw materials extracted in the less developed parts of the world. The spokesmen for the less developed countries themselves constantly complain about the adverse terms of trade that they face on world markets. The principal source of their concern is the low price of raw materials and the high price of finished goods. The most effective forms of assistance that the developed countries (including the United States) give to the less developed countries are the purchases they make from the less developed countries in international trade. A developing country needs receipts from exports in order to finance the purchase of the things they need for economic development. For example, in order to industrialize, a nonindustrialized country must for a long time purchase capital equipment from more advanced countries, and the funds for such purchases come from exports — principally of raw materials. Economists in the developing countries feel that the demand for raw materials is inadequate. Perhaps the most important adverse effect of slowing down the growth of the gross national product in the United States would be that it would diminish the demand for primary products that we would otherwise import from the less developed countries. After all, if a developing country wants to retain its raw materials at home, it can always place an embargo on their export. However, it would be a policy very damaging to economic progress of that very country.

Note that the effect of our high demand for raw materials is a different matter from the desirability of the domestic control of mineral resources within the developing countries. Selling oil on the world market provides immense economic advantages to a developing country. Whether foreign interests should be represented in the extraction of raw materials is another question.

Population Growth in the United States

I shall begin a discussion of population with a brief description of recent, current, and future population trends in the United States. Our population today is a little over 200 million, having increased by slightly more than 50 percent since 1940. I think it is likely to increase by nearly 50 percent again in the 30 years before the end of the century.

This rate of increase cannot continue long. If it endured throughout the next century, the population would reach a billion shortly before the year 2100. Within six or seven more centuries we would reach one person per square foot of land area in the United States, and after about 1500 years our descendants would outweigh the earth if they continued to increase by 50 percent every 30 years. We can even calculate that, at that rate of increase, our descendants would, in a few thousand years, form a sphere of flesh whose radius would, neglecting relativity, expand at the velocity of light.

Every demographer knows that we cannot continue a positive rate of increase indefinitely. The inexorable arithmetic of compound interest leads us to absurd conditions within a calculable period of time. Logically we must, and in fact we will, have a rate of growth very close to zero in the long run. The average rate of increase of mankind from the inception of the species until the present is zero to many decimal places. If we agree that 10,000 years from now we can have no more than one person per square foot, and that the population of the world will at a minimum exceed that of Richmond, Virginia, we can say that the average annual growth of population will be within one per thousand of zero.

The only questions about attaining a zero rate of increase for any population is when and how such a rate is attained. A zero rate of increase implies a balance between the average birth and death rates, so the choice of how to attain a zero rate of increase is a choice between low birth and death rates that are approximately equal. The average growth rate very near to zero during mankind's past history has been attained with high birth and death rates — with an average duration of life that until recently was no more than 30 or 35 years. I have no difficulty in deciding that I would **prefer a zero rate of growth with low rather than high birth and death rates, or with an** average duration of life in excess of 70 years; as has been achieved in all of the more advanced countries of the world, rather than the life that is "nasty, brutish, and short." The remaining question then is *when* should our population growth level off.

A popular answer today is "immediately." In fact a zero rate of increase in the United States starting immediately is not feasible and I believe not desirable. The reason is the age composition of the population that our past history of birth and death rates has left to us. We have an especially young population now because of the postwar baby boom. One consequence is that our death rate is much lower than it would be in a population that had long had low fertility. That is, because our population is young, a high proportion of it is concentrated in ages where the risk of mortality is small. Therefore, if we were to attain a zero growth rate immediately, it would be necessary to cut the birth rate about in half. For the next 15 or 20 years, women would have to bear children at a rate that would produce only a little over one child per completed family. At the end of that time we would have a very peculiar age distribution with a great shortage of young people. The attendant social and economic disruptions represent too large a cost to pay for the advantages that we might derive from reducing growth to zero right away.

In fact, a more reasonable goal would be to reduce fertility as soon as possible to a level where couples produced just enough children to insure that each generation exactly replaced itself. If this goal (early attainment of fertility at a replacement level) were reached immediately, our population would increase 35 to 40 percent before it stabilized. The reason that fertility at the mere replacement level would produce such a large increase in population is again the age distribution we have today. There are many more people today under 20 than 20 to 40, and when the relatively numerous children have moved into the childbearing ages, they will greatly outnumber the persons now at those ages, and when the current population under age 20 moves into the old ages, they will be far more numerous than the people now at the old ages. Thus to move the population to replacement would be to insure approximately that the number of children under 20 will be about the same as it is today, but that the number above that age will be substantially higher. The net effect is the increase of 35 to 40 percent mentioned just above. It is the built-in growth in our age composition that led me to state earlier that I think an increase in the order of 50 percent of the U.S. population is not unlikely.

A sensible choice in reducing our growth rate to zero then is between early or late attainment of fertility at the replacement level. Is there any reason that we should not attempt to attain a fertility at replacement as soon as possible? My own opinion is that an early move in that direction is desirable, but for the sake of completeness, I must point out that there is a non-negligible cost associated with attaining a stationary population — the population that will exist with fertility at replacement after the age distribution left over from the past has worked out its transitory consequences.

A stationary population with the mortality levels that we have already attained has a much older age distribution than any the United States has ever experienced. It has more people over 60 than under 15, and half the population would be over 37 rather than over 27, as is the case today. It would be an age distribution much like that of a health resort.

Moreover, if we view the age pyramid in the conventional way, with the number of males and females being drawn out as in the branches of a Christmas tree (age representing altitude of the tree) the pyramid for the stationary population is virtually vertical until age 50 because of the small number of deaths under the favorable mortality conditions we have attained. In contrast, the age distribution of the United States to date has always tapered more or less sharply with increasing age. The stationary population with its vertical sides would no longer conform in age composition to the shape of the social structure — to the pyramid of privilege and responsibility. In a growing population, the age pyramid does conform, so there is a rough consonance of shape between diminishing numbers at higher ages and the smaller number of high positions relative to low positions. In a stationary population there would no longer be a reasonable expectation of advancement as a person moves through life. I have indicated that sooner or later we must have a stationary population, so that sooner or later we must adjust to such an age composition. I am pointing to this disadvantage to show that there is a choice between moving more gradually to a stationary population at the expense of a larger ultimate population size in order to continue to enjoy for a longer time the more desirable age distribution of a growing population.

Connection between Population and Pollution

The connection between the current growth in our population and the deterioration of our environment of which we have all become aware is largely an indirect one. The problem has arisen because we are permitting the production of bads (pollution, or negative externalities) along with goods. There seems little doubt that the rapid increase in the production of goods has been responsible for the rapid increase in the production of bads, since we have made no effective effort to prevent the latter from accompanying the former. But per capita increase in production has been more important than population growth. It has been calculated that if we were to duplicate the total production of electricity in the United States in 1940 in a population enjoying the 1969 per capita usage of energy, the population could be only 25 million rather than 132 million people there were in 1940. Population has increased by 50 percent, but per capita use of electricity has been multiplied several times. A similar statement can even be made about the crowding of our national parks. The population has increased by about 50 percent in the last 30 years — attendance in national parks has increased by more than 400 percent.

A wealthy industrial urban population of 100 million persons would have most of the pollution problems we do. In fact, Sydney, Australia, has problems of air and water pollution and of traffic jams, even though the total population of Australia is about 12 million in an area 80 percent as big as the United States. Australia is actually more urbanized than the United States, in spite of its relatively small population and large overall area.

If we have the will and intelligence to devise and apply proper policies, we can improve our environment and can do so either with the current population of 200 million, or with the population that we will probably have in another 50 years of 300 million. On the other hand, if we ignore environmental problems and continue to treat pure air and water and the disposal of trash as if they were free, and if we pay no attention to the effects of the techniques that we employ upon the balance of nature, we will be in trouble whether our population grows or not. There is no doubt that slower population growth would make it easier to improve our environment, but not much easier.

Policies That Would Affect the Growth of Population

We must, at some time, achieve a zero rate of population, and the balance should surely be achieved at low birth and death rates rather than at high rates. If, as at present, only about 5 percent of women remain single at the end of the childbearing span, and if 96 percent of women survive to the mean age of childbearing, and if finally the sex ratio at birth remains about 105 males for every 100 females, married couples must have an average of about 2.25 children to replace themselves. What kinds of policies might be designed to assure such a level of fertility or, more generally, to produce the fertility level that is at the moment socially desirable?

I begin with a set of policies that are consistent with general democratic and humanitarian principles, although a minority of the population would oppose them on religious grounds. These are policies that would, through education and the provision of clinical services, try to make it possible for every conception to be the result of a deliberate choice, and for every choice to be an informed one, based on an adequate knowledge of the consequences of bearing different numbers of children at different times. A component of such a set of policies would be the development of more effective means of contraception to reduce the number of accidental pregnancies occurring to couples who are trying to avoid conception. These are policies that call for a substantial government role and I think that an effective government program in these areas is already overdue. I personally believe that education in the consequences of childbearing and in the techniques of avoiding pregnancy, combined with the provision of contraceptive services, should be supplemented by the provision of safe and skillful abortion upon request. It is clear that the public consensus in favor of abortion is not nearly as clear-cut as that in favor of contraception, and I know that the extent and the strength of the moral objection to induced abortion is much greater. Nevertheless, I am persuaded by experience in Japan and eastern Europe that the advantages of abortion provided under good medical auspices to cause the early termination of unwanted pregnancies are very important to the women affected, as is evident in the fact that when medically safe abortion has been made available at low cost, the number of abortions has initially been as great or greater than the number of live births. Later there is a typical tendency for women to resort to contraception rather than repeated abortions.

The reason I favor abortion is that such a high proportion of births that occur today are unwanted, and because a large number of desperate pregnant women (probably more than a half a million annually) resort to clandestine abortions today, with high rates of serious complications. In contrast, early abortion, under skilled medical auspices, is less dangerous than tonsillectomy, and substantially less dangerous than carrying a child to full term.

In recent years the number of births that were unwanted in the United States constituted about 20 percent of the total (an unwanted birth was defined as one in which the woman said that conception occurred either as a result of a failure of contraception or in the absence of contraception but without the intent to become pregnant as soon as possible, when at the time the conception occurred the husband or wife or both did not want another child then or later). The rate at which women are having children today would lead to a completed family size of slightly under three children. If all unwanted births were eliminated, the number of children born per married woman would be about 2.4 or 2.5 on average. This is very little above replacement, and when allowance is made for the likely possibility that women understated the proportion of births that were unwanted, it is probable that the elimination of unwanted births would bring a fertility at or below replacement.

If it is true that the elimination of unwanted pregnancies would reduce fertility very nearly to replacement, it must be conceded that this outcome is fortuitous. It is highly unlikely that over a substantial period of time the free choice by each couple of the number of children they want would lead exactly to the socially desirable level of fertility. The erratic behavior of fertility in America and in other advanced industrialized countries in the last 30 or 40 years is ample evidence that when fertility is voluntarily controlled, the level of fertility is subject to major fluctuations, and I see no logical reason to expect that on average people would voluntarily choose a number of children that would keep the long-run average a little above two per couple. In other words, we must acknowledge the probable necessity of instituting policies that would influence the number of children people want. However, there is no need for haste in formulating such policy, since, as I have indicated, improved contraceptive services combined with a liberal provision of abortion would probably move our fertility at present quite close to replacement, and a gradual increase in population during the next generation would not be a major addition to the problems we already face.

Policies intended to affect people's preferences for children should be designed within the framework of our democratic traditions. They should be designed, for example, to encourage diversity and permit freedom of choice. An average of 2.25 children does not require that 75 percent of couples have two children and 25 percent three, although that would produce the desired average. Another possibility is a nearly even division of family size among zero, one, two, three, four, and five-child families. The ideal policy would affect the decision at the margin and not try to impose a uniform pattern on all. I do not think that people who prefer to have more than the average number of children should be subject to ridicule or abuse.

It is particularly difficult to frame acceptable policies influencing the number of children that people want. While it is still true that so many large families result from unwanted pregnancies, the unwanted child that is the most recent birth in a large family already faces many deprivations. The psychological disadvantages of the unwanted child cause some of our most serious social problems. In addition to these psychological disadvantages, the unwanted child in a large impoverished family faces an inadequate diet, much below average chances for schooling, and generally inferior opportunities. I hardly think it a wise or humane policy to handicap him further by imposing a financial burden on his parents as a result of his birth.

When unwanted births have become negligible in number, we could imagine trying to design a policy in which the couple is asked to pay some part of the "externalities" that an additional birth imposes on society. In the meantime, I suggest as a desirable supplement to better contraception and free access to abortion the extension of more nearly equal opportunities in education and employment for women, so that activities outside of the home become a more powerful competitor to a larger family. We should start now devoting careful attention to formulation of policies in this area — policies that could increase fertility when it fell too low as well as policies to induce people to want fewer children.

Some aspects of the deterioration of our environment appear to be critical and call for prompt action. We need to start now to frame and apply actions that would arrest the careless destruction of the world in which we live. We also need policies to reduce promptly the incidence of unwanted births. In the long run we shall also need ways to influence the number of births people want. To design policies consistent with our most cherished social and political values will not be easy, and it is fortunate that there is no valid reason for hasty action.

POPULATION, GNP, AND THE ENVIRONMENT

Alan R. Sweezy

The average American consumes far more gasoline and electricity, discards more beer cans, Coke bottles, and automobile bodies, and occupies more space than the average Indian, African, or Latin American. The average American today generates more air and water pollution, disposes of more solid waste, and occupies more space than his predecessors did fifty or even twenty years ago. Some people have concluded from this that population growth is not an important cause of environmental problems. The standard of living and the state of technology so predominate, they say, that for all practical purposes one can forget about population growth when dealing with the environmental problems of the future.

Others draw the opposite conclusion. They point out that although today's affluent American may do more damage than today's Indian or yesterday's American, two of today's affluent Americans would do still more damage than one. It's like the old riddle: What makes more noise than a pig stuck under a gate? The answer: two pigs stuck under a gate.

Who is right? Is population important, or isn't it? The answer depends on two things. First, what effect does the size of the population have on the degree of its affluence? If we have twice as many Americans fifty years from now will they be twice as wealthy and do twice as much damage? Second, what is the relative magnitude of the contributions of population growth and of technological progress to environmental deterioration? Does the latter completely dwarf the former?

In exploring these questions it will be useful to distinguish between two different sets of environmental problems; pollution and congestion. Population growth affects pollution primarily through its influence on the size and composition of the gross national product (GNP). It has a direct effect on congestion.

Population and GNP

To understand the size of the GNP, we naturally turn to growth theory. The standard treatment classifies the determinants of growth under three headings: the labor force; the capital stock; and the state of technology and organization or, more broadly, the "residual." The relation between population growth and each of these factors is too complex for a detailed examination here, so I shall mention only a few of the most general influences. In the long run, assuming the maintenance of full employment, the size of the labor force varies directly with the size of the population. The GNP tends to be larger with a larger labor force—though how much larger depends on certain key parameters.

What influence population growth has on technological and organizational progress has been widely debated. For instance, it is argued that with a growing population the number of talented people will also be increasing and this should mean more bright ideas about how to improve organization and technology. Leibenstein's "replacement effect" would mean a more rapid increase in the average level of education and skills when the population is growing than when it is not (1). On the other hand, population growth places an extra burden on the educational system, which in the poorer countries may act as a serious brake on progress. I am inclined to think that population growth, especially rapid growth, reduces the size of the residual in the less developed countries but that it is likely to have little effect one way or the other in the United States.

The amount of capital per worker is likely to grow faster as the rate of population growth slows, assuming that fiscal and monetary policies are used to keep the economy from slipping into a depression. For one thing, smaller families may save a larger proportion of their income, though this is by no means certain. More importantly, the net saving that is done can be used for concentrating capital for the existing labor force rather than spreading capital out for an increasing labor force. How important this will be depends on how sharply returns diminish as the amount of capital per worker increases. I suspect that they diminish rather gently in the less developed countries, especially if the necessary investment in human capital is included, but rather sharply in a highly developed country like the united States.

To pull these various strands together, let me give some numbers based on analyses of past growth in the United States. Using Solow's methods of analysis (2), Nelson (3) finds that the residual accounted for three-fifths of the growth of the potential GNP from 1954 to 1960, i.e., 2.1 per cent of a total 3.5 per cent annual growth rate (assuming b, the exponent of L, is 0.75). If the size of the residual is independent of the rate of growth of the labor force, as I have assumed it to be, this gives a doubling time of the GNP due to technological progress alone of approximately thirty-five years. In his original paper Solow attributed an even larger proportion of growth to the residual, but that was because a large part of the period covered by his statistics was subject to the distorting influence of depression and war. These numbers are in no sense predictions but are designed merely to show what the relative magnitudes might be.

If population remained constant but technical progress and capital accumulation continued at the same rate as in the past, the GNP fifty years from now might be three and half to four times its present size. (This assumes, as above, that the size of the residual is independent of the growth of the labor force but that the amount of capital per worker is not. If capital per worker remained constant, doubling the labor force would also double the GNP.) If in addition the population doubled — which could easily happen — the GNP might be something like one and three-quarters times as large as *that*, or six to seven times its present size. Thus, in a sense both sides are right. Technological progress has been a bigger factor in accounting for past growth of the economy than population growth. But population growth is far from negligible.

A return to the fertility rates of the late 1950s and early 1960s — really rather moderate by world, or its own earlier, standards — would give the United States a population of over 500 million fifty years from now. That is twice as many as it would have if it managed to bring the net reproduction rate down to one in the course of the next decade. Twice the population would mean not a great deal less than twice the GNP, with its associated pollution and other environmental problems.

Direct Effects of Population Growth

Population growth also has direct effects. Pollution depends on the composition, as well as on the size, of the GNP. If people spend more money seeing psychiartists and less money driving cars, there will clearly be less air pollution. If I am right in thinking that slower population growth would mean more rapidly rising per capita income, it is relevant to ask what effect this would have on the composition of the demand for goods and services that make up a GNP and hence on the amount of pollution associated with a GNP. It seems likely that of two equal GNPs the one with higher but fewer incomes would generate less pollution. Unfortunately, this is difficult to prove. Almon estimates the income elasticities of demand for major categories of consumption in *The American Economy to 1975* (4). Rejecting the use of time-series regression as incapable of separating "the effects of variables so closely collinear," he is forced to turn to data on the consumption expenditures of different income groups at the same point in time. The results would be very interesting if we could be reasonably sure they would hold over time rather than only for the period in which the data were collected. His estimate for gasoline, for instance, is 0.7, meaning that the increase in consumption of gasoline is less than proportional to the increase in per capita — actually in this case per family — income. In other words, the air pollution content of a GNP in which per capita income was increasing rapidly but the number of people slowly or not at all, would be significantly smaller than that of a GNP characterized by the opposite combination of factors. It is hard to know, however, how much reliance to put on this finding. For one thing, people's consumption patterns may be influenced by their position in the income scale as well as by the actual amount of their income. Almon himself discards the result he gets from the cross-sectional data for one important category of consumer expenditure — or nonexpenditure — personal saving.

In spite of the theoretical difficulties, I think an examination of all the different types of evidence might throw considerable light on this subject. We are planning to do further research along these lines at Caltech.

Congestion

Pollution depends on the size of the GNP and what might be called its pollution coefficient, which in turn depends on the composition of demand and the state of technology. Population is important only as it affects either of these variables. In the case of congestion, population has a more direct effect. Rising per capita income generates a demand for more space. But beyond a certain point the consequences of an increase in the demand for space will differ radically, depending on whether the source of the demand is higher incomes or more people. For example, if people are so poor that most cannot get to the beach on weekends, those few who are able to get there can enjoy relative peace and quiet. But as the standard of living rises, more and more people will be able to go to the beach, and the amount of space they will have once they get there depends on how many people are there. A further rise in per capita incomes will, at worst, mean that the desire for additional space will be unfulfilled. An increase in the number of people, on the other hand, will mean an actual decrease in the space available to each person or family. In the first case, the problem arises because per capita real income is growing. The second case causes per capita real income to decline. It is the inverse of Alice's problem at the mad tea party; in the case of space, you can never have more, but you can always have less.

But what has this to do with the situation in the United States? Haven't we lots of space, not only for our present population, but for any increase that is likely to occur in the next fifty to a hundred years? In answering this question we must first ask: Enough space for what? The traditional view is that a society needs enough space for its dwellings, its factories, offices, roads and streets, and enough land to grow its food and fiber on. Perhaps it also needs a few parks, race tracks, and sports stadiums. Beyond that, space is superfluous, and there is no reason population should not go on increasing until it is all occupied. (See Coale (5) and Eversley (6). Eversley's views are much more extreme than Coale's since he thinks even Britain could comfortably absorb double or more its present population.)

This narrow view is rapidly changing. We are coming increasingly to admit the validity of other demands for space. These demands, moreover, are for particular kinds of space rather than for space in general: for beach areas in southern California or northern New Jersey, vacation areas in New England or New York State, actual and potential Yosemities and Yellowstones. As people's horizons widen, even more expansive demands are gaining recognition. An increasing number of people think it is important to preserve unspoiled wildlife habitats, natural forests, and wilderness areas. They are reluctant to see encroachment on areas of unusual natural beauty and grandeur.

Several years ago, Murray Gell-Mann was asked what he thought of a scheme for bringing water from Alaska to irrigate land in the Southwest. His reply in a private communication was, "Why ruin two beautiful and distinctive landscapes to make more ordinary farmland when the same thing can be accomplished through birth control." This must have seemed idiosyncratic in the extreme at the time. I am sure it would seem less so now.

Needless to say, we may run out of these special kinds of space long before we run out of space in general. The example of the beach on a warm weekend may have much wider relevance than it would appear at first. The saturation point is particularly low in wilderness or other areas we want to preserve in their natural state. Garrett Hardin gives an accurate and sensitive analysis of the dilemma:

> Wilderness cannot be multiplied; and it can be subdivided only a little. It is not increasing, we have to struggle to keep it from decreasing. But population increases steadily. The ratio of the wilderness available to each living person becomes steadily less — and bear in mind that this is only a statistical abstraction: were we to divide up the wilderness among even a small fraction of the total population there would be no wilderness available to any one. So what should we do? (7)

Rejecting price as a method of rationing, he suggests that access to wilderness areas be limited to those who are willing and able to go in on foot, carrying their provisions with them. (In special cases entry on horseback or by canoe might be permitted.) Some method of rationing is clearly essential to preserve the thing itself, the "wilderness experience" as Hardin calls it. Whether his method will be enough is perhaps open to question. Certainly the more population increases, the more difficult it will be to keep access within the necessary limits.

Redistribution of population is often proposed as a solution to the problem of population growth. I agree that, properly qualified, redistribution is a worthwhile objective—it is worthwhile even without population growth—and that we should be actively thinking about policies to bring it about. We should, however, recognize that it has serious limitations. It will not do much to protect wilderness areas. It must be assessed with regard to the welfare of people who already live in an area. We cannot simply found new cities wherever there is sparsely populated territory. In New England, for example, the Greater Boston area is not only becoming highly congested but is also spreading out in a way that makes it increasingly difficult for most of its inhabitants to reach open country. There is, however, still lots of thinly populated country in New Hampshire and Vermont. The advocates of redistribution suggest that, as population increases, we should stop growth of the Boston area and instead start a second Boston, or several Springfields and Hartfords, in New Hampshire or Vermont.

Would it solve the problem to allow New England to absorb more people without loss of welfare for the present inhabitants? The answer clearly is no. Many of the inhabitants of New Hampshire and Vermont are there because they do not want to live in or near a big city. And many of those who live in Greater Boston find it important to be able to get out into thinly populated country for weekends and vacations. Creating another Boston, or several Springfields, in New Hampshire and Vermont would impoverish life for both these groups of people. (If population continues to grow, redistribution may be a *pis aller*. That is different from saying that redistribution makes it possible to absorb more people without loss of welfare.)

People could, of course, be told where they can and where they cannot live. Or financial and other incentives might be used to try to induce them to live where policy dictates. If the incentives were large enough, they might be effective. But the loss of freedom involved in the use of compulsion and the cost of providing incentives should, at the very least, be compared with the loss of freedom and the cost of compelling or inducing people to have small families — which the advocates of redistribution rarely do. Moreover, although redistribution offers only a temporary and partial solution to the problems of population pressure, limiting family size offers a permanent and complete solution.

As a practical matter I think it would be a mistake to expect much relief from redistribution even in the short run, i.e. the next few decades. After that, continued population growth will clearly swamp any benefits redistribution might bring. (Even Eversley (6), in spite of his great enthusiasm for redistribution as a solution for Britain's population problem, admits that "despite everything successive governments have done to reverse the trend, the concentration into certain residentially attractive areas of the midlands and the southeast is becoming stronger.")

Problems Created by Technology

Many people expect a technological *deus ex machina* to solve our environmental problems for us. They fail to explain, however, why technological development that in the past often had harmful effects on the environment will in the future follow only benign paths. Left to itself technological development will go in whatever directions seem most profitable — either in terms of return on investment or in terms of power and prestige for what Galbraith calls the technostructure (8).

In the past, consumers were free to buy any new gadgets the engineers came up with no matter how much damage they might do to the environment. Producers were free to adopt the cheapest methods without regard to the effect on the environment. The process still goes on. Only recently a new and serious environmental threat, the all-terrain vehicle, or ATV, has been launched on the market. "Through swamp, over ice, up mountains it rides — superblob, the latest in mechanized happiness. Light as a touch on its low pressure tires, the ATV jumps through the air when the going gets rough. Soon, its makers hope, it will jump into backyards across America" (9). However, there are signs a change is in the making. We may be nearing the end of the era of blind, uncontrolled growth. Increasingly people, particularly younger people, are beginning to question the absolute goodness of growth itself.

Producers are the first to feel the pressure, though they will soon have to transmit it to consumers through higher prices or curtailed offerings. This point is worth stressing. People are too much inclined to the comfortable assumption that the costs of halting environmental degradation can be met out of the profits of industry. By and large this is an illusion. The costs will have to be met by all of us in our capacity as consumers and taxpayers, not just by those who own stock in particular industries. The kind of thing that is beginning to happen is nicely illustrated by the following dispatch from Denver, Colorado, to the *New York Times,* December 9, 1969:

> It was once a fairly easy matter to bring a $65 million plant and 725 jobs into a small town. Townspeople celebrated their good luck, rolled out the red carpet and invited the Governor in to cut a ribbon. If the plant filled the air with smoke and the rivers with acrid wastes, few cared.
>
> But times have changed. Growing concern over the environment has taken precedence over economic development in just such a case in New Mexico and Colorado. . .
>
> The issue is air and water pollution. The plant is a kraft paper mill proposed by the Parsons and Whittemore Corp. of New York. . .
>
> Although officers of the company assured state officials that they would install the latest in pollution control equipment, their proposed plant was in effect expelled from New Mexico by public opinion and high anti-pollution standards. Even members of the Albuquerque Chamber of Commerce voted 2 to 1 against having the mill in their area. . .

Many similar episodes have occurred. A group of students and faculty at the University of California in Santa Barbara have successfully protested the construction of a freeway across Goleta Slough on the ground that the Slough is "too valuable an ecological asset to be violated by a ribbon of concrete" (10). The California Environmental Quality Study Council reported in February 1970 that its activities led to the reconsideration of two environmentally hazardous projects: the expansion of a fossil-fueled power plant in Huntington Beach and the construction of two oil refineries in the Coachella Valley (11). BASF, the German chemical producer, under pressure from a diverse group of environmentalists postponed building a new plant at Port Victoria in Beaufort County, South Carolina (12).

A larger-scale battle was fought in Congress in 1970 over a bill to allow increased timber cutting in the national forests. Supporters contended the bill was necessary "to meet the immediate lumber requirements of the nation's housing industry and to assure that future needs will be met through 'intensified forest management'." Opponents maintained that "the bill threatens America's national forests, scuttles historic multiple use practices and undermines prospective parks, wilderness, open space and recreation areas" (13).

The bill was defeated, partly because lumber prices had subsided from their peak the year before, but the industry has announced it is not giving up.

Direct interference with consumers' freedom of choice is not involved in any of these episodes, but hopefully it may soon follow. A vigorous effort was made to stop the supersonic transport, or SST. I hope a similar effort will be made to restrict severely — if not to ban — the less spectacular but perhaps even more obnoxious ATV.

How does population growth fit into this picture? The outcome of the struggle to protect the environment against the consequences of economic growth will depend in large measure on what kind of growth we have: rising per capita income with constant population or constant per capita income with increasing population. The larger the population component in growth is, the more the 'increased output will be for the necessities and long-established comforts of life. The more the increased output takes the form of necessities, the harder it will be to gain consideration for ecological, aesthetic, and recreational values if they stand in the way of expanding production.

For example, it has been relatively easy to ban DDT and related compunds in the developed countries. The standard of living leaves plenty of room to absorb the resulting increase in the cost of food. The less developed countries, on the other hand, protest that they cannot afford to give up DDT. They have at best only a slight margin over subsistence needs. With their rapidly growing populations they desperately need to expand food supplies. Any major obstacle, or any substantial increase in cost, could spell disaster. Confronted with a choice between the starvation of millions and serious damage to the environment, there is little doubt how most people and most governments would decide.

Or take the case of the demand for lumber. As the battle in Congress in 1970 showed, an increasing number of people are becoming concerned about the protection of our national forests. But if population continues to grow, it will be impossible to deny the urgency of the demand for more houses. Policies designed to protect the forests will run into heavy, and no doubt successful, opposition if they entail curtailing the supply of new housing for a growing number of families.

Shortly after the fight in Congress over the timber-cutting bill, the Boise Cascade Corporation ran a full-page advertisement that consisted of a picture of a baby carriage and the legend: "Challenge. Each new arrival dramatizes the urgency of an adequate supply of homes" (14). It is a reminder that if population keeps on growing, the shadow of the baby buggy will loom large over the environmental battles of the future.

To return to the debate between population and affluence, rising affluence is certainly a major source of environmental problems, but population growth is important too. Population growth through its effect on the labor force contributes to the increase in total output. If the increase in output is less than proportional to the increase in population, i.e. if per capita income is higher the smaller the increase in population, two further effects come into play: (a) the composition of demand is likely to be less harmful to the environment with fewer people but higher per capita income, even without conscious efforts at control; and (b) the growth of output will be easier to direct into environmentally harmless channels if it consists of the relative superfluities of a rising standard of living rather than the necessities of a growing population. This last consideration would become even more important if we should reach the point at which we decided that protection of the environment required curbing growth of total output itself.

Finally, population growth has a direct effect on the amount of space available to each person. As affluence increases, people spread out more, and their demand for space increases. But beyond a certain point — which has already been reached with respect to certain kinds of space, even in the United States — the consequences of a further rise in affluence are very different from that of a further increase in the number of people. In the case of rising affluence, what we might call the space standard of living remains constant whereas in the case of rising numbers it falls. The more population grows, the more drastic the fall becomes.

I conclude that we can stop arguing about whether affluence or population is the source of our environmental problems. Both are important. Moreover, there is going to be plenty to do on both fronts if future living conditions are to be tolerable.

References

(1) Harvey Leibenstein. "The Impact of Population Growth on Economic Welfare — Non-Traditional Inputs, and Micro-Economic Elements," *Rapid Population Growth: Consequences and Public Policy Implications*. Baltimore: Johns Hopkins University Press, 1971.

(2) Robert M. Solow. "Technical Change and the Aggregate Production Function," *The Review of Economics and Statistics*, Vol. 39 (August 1957), 312-20.

(3) R. R. Nelson, "Aggregate Production Functions and Medium-Range Growth Projections," *American Economic Review*, Vol. LIV, No. 5 (September 1964), 575-606.

(4) Clopper Almon, Jr. *The American Economy to 1975*. New York: Harper & Row, Publishers, 1966. Pp. 31-47.

(5) Ansley Coale. "Should the United States Start a Campaign for Fewer Births?" Presidential address to the Population Association of America, April, 1968. *Population Index*, Vol. 34, No. 4 (October-December 1968), 457-74.

(6) David Eversley. "Is Britain Being Threatened by Over-Population?" *The Listener*, Vol. LXVIII, Nos. 1999 and 2000 (July 20 and 27, 1967), 78-79, 110-11.

(7) Garrett Hardin. "Effects on Population Growth on Natural Resources and the Environment," *Hearings before a Subcommittee of the Committee on Government Operations*, House of Representatives, Ninety-first Congress, First Session, September 15 and 16, 1969. Washington, D. C.: U. S. Government Printing Office, p. 94.

(8) J. K. Galbraith. *The New Industrial State*. Boston: Houghton Mifflin Company, 1967.

(9) *Business Week*, March 21, 1970, p. 27.

(10) *Los Angeles Times*, December 14, 1969 and April 22, 1970.

(11) Progress Report of the Environmental Quality Study Council, Sacramento, California, February 1970.

(12) *Business Week*, April 11, 1970, p. 29.

(13) *The New York Times*, February 5, 1970.

(14) *Business Week, April 4, 1970.*

RESOURCE AND ENVIRONMENTAL
CONSEQUENCES OF POPULATION GROWTH
IN THE UNITED STATES:
A SUMMARY

Ronald G. Ridker

What are the resource and environmental implications of population growth in the United States during the next 30 to 50 years? How important is population growth relative to other causes of the problems we find? In particular, what difference would a change in population growth make within this time frame?

In an effort to provide answers to these questions within the year allotted for this project, Resources for the Future brought together experts in a variety of fields, provided them with a common set of questions, assumptions and suggested approaches, and set them to work. The result is the set of studies presented in *Population, Resources, and the Environment*. In this opening chapter, we present a brief summary of our principal findings, plus some interpretations and overall conclusions that do not automatically emerge from the diversity of detailed consideration presented in the individual studies.

The central issue emerging from this study is one of choice. While population growth and perhaps economic growth ultimately must come to a halt on this finite planet, there is still considerable room to choose when, where, and how.

If because of personal preferences, we choose to have more rather than less children per family—on the average, say, three rather than two—we commit ourselves to a particular package of problems: more rapid depletion of domestic and international resources, greater pressures on the environment, more independence on continued rapid technological development to solve these problems, fewer social options and perhaps the continued postponement of the resolution of other social problems, including those resulting from past growth. So long as population growth continues, these problems will grow, slowly but irreversibly forcing changes in our current way of life.

If we choose to have fewer children per family, leading to a stable population within the next 50 to 75 years, we purchase time, resources, and additional options: time to overcome our ignorance and to redress the mistakes of past growth, resources to implement solutions, and additional freedom of choice in deciding how we want to live in the future.

Similar consequences could emerge from the choice open to us with respect to alternative rates of economic growth. Indeed, an earlier numerical analysis indicates that a reduction in economic growth would reduce resource consumption and pollution emissions by more than would a comparable reduction in population growth. But growth in the economy can be utilized for different ends than it is put to now. While it adds to problems that need solution, it also adds to capacity to solve problems. It is difficult to find similar offsetting advantages from additional population growth at this stage in United States history.

Such consequences of today's choices will not become evident for some time. But as we project farther and farther out into the future, the two societies they give rise to would become increasingly distinct. Assuming technological options available to both societies would be the same, the one with continuing population growth would be forced to live with far greater risks and fewer options with which to solve problems in a manner compatible with our current way of life.

While a reduction in population growth would be a blessing in these respects, it would hardly be a panacea, at least not within the next half century. During that time period, more direct attacks on problems of resource and environmental depletion will be needed in any case; and as our studies show, they can generally accomplish far more.

Moreover, while we believe the United States can find ways to cope with a continuation of population growth if it has to, we have no similar faith for the less developed two-thirds of the world, unless aided in this task by substantial transfers of resources and appropriate knowhow from richer countries. Struggles amongst the haves and the have-nots will increasingly plague us and make the resolution of our domestic problems more difficult.

But these conclusions are far too encapsulated. To understand them, to see what they mean in specific instances, we must review each of the areas covered by this study, starting with a few comments on general method and approach.

The Approach

In some very long-run, ultimate sense, population growth may well be the single most important factor determining resource adequacy and environmental quality. But this study is limited to the next 30 to 50 years, during which time changes in technology, tastes, institutions, policies, and international relations will all play important roles. Not only may some of these factors be more important in certain contexts, but all of them will significantly influence the nature of the relationship between population variables and resource and environmental variables. Within the confines of this project, it would have been impossible to provide a best single forecast for all these nondemographic variables. Instead, we chose assumptions for them, hopefully useful ones, but assumptions nevertheless. Accordingly, our conclusions should not be viewed as absolute forecasts, but rather as conditional predictions the significance of which depends upon the specific assumptions made about all the other factors that can influence the relationships of principal interest. (1) Sometimes we slip into the terminology of forecasting, but only for convenience in exposition.

Assumptions about these nondemographic variables have been chosen with an eye towards policy relevance. So far as environmental policy is concerned, we have attempted to compare the effects of population growth assuming little or no public interference in the environmental field—more or less the situation that existed in the late 1960's—with a situation in which rather stringent environmental quality standards are imposed. So far as technology is concerned, we have made the conservative assumption that current trends toward more efficient use of labor and resources plus some substitutions of cheaper for more expensive materials continue, but that no dramatic breakthroughs such as cheap electricity from fusion, mining of the seabed, synthesis of high valued materials from common elements, or desalinization occur during the next half century. The possibilities of such breakthroughs are discussed, but they never enter into the quantitative analysis. Consumer preferences are handled in a similar way: Except for a few cases where saturation levels appear to be reached, they are assumed to change with income, demographic factors, and time in much the way they have in the past. The net effect is a continuation of the slow change in the composition of consumption away from durables towards services, but no sudden, significant shift, for example, away from a desire for material goods in general. In addition, international demand for resources is assumed to grow more or less in line with trends since World War II, that is, relatively rapidly compared to earlier portions of this century. Such assumptions are conservative in the sense that they tend to produce pictures of the future with slightly more difficult problems than in fact may occur.

The only explicitly introduced assumption that may violate this criterion pertains to United States military expenditures, which are assumed to level off for a few years and then begin rising again but at a much slower rate than the rate of growth in GNP.

The results of this study are influenced not only by the time horizon and the assumptions made about nondemographic variables, but also by its focus primarily on the United States, a limited set of resources and pollutants, and on two particular population projections, Census Series B, more or less equivalent to a continuation of the three-child norm, and Census Series E, which introduces the two-child norm, and brings population growth to a halt, except for immigration, in about the year 2040. As time and materials permitted, we did attempt to move beyond these initial bounds; but such extensions have been undertaken mainly with an eye to checking out and if necessary qualifying our conclusions, rather than as carefully articulated studies in their own right.

The impact of population growth, as well as that of other variables, can be viewed from two perspectives. First, one can compare how things are today with how they are likely to be in some future year. Second, one can compare two possible situations that may arise in the future. From the first perspective, differences in reasonable population projections appear relatively small. Between now and the year 2000, population will increase by somewhere between 30 percent and 57 percent. From this vantage point, the important question is how to cope with an increase within this general range. On the other hand, if we imagine we are sitting in the year 2000, the difference between the two population estimates — E being 17 percent less than B — is likely to appear much more significant. Whenever possible, we have tried to look at the situation from both perspectives, generally by first asking what the situation would be like in the year 2000 (or 2020) if path B in Figure 1 were to prevail and then asking what difference if would make in that year if the population size were to be smaller, the level that would be reached under the E projection.

The Economy

Population growth affects resource needs and the environment largely through the economy. Our starting point, then, is the development of a picture on a sector by sector basis of what the economy might look like in the next 30 to 50 years. Since we are interested in determining the effects of a change in economic growth rates as well as in population growth rates, four basic scenarios were developed: high population and economic growth (B-High), low population and economic growth (E-Low), and the two intermediate cases (B-Low and E-High). We have already discussed the alternative assumptions used for the population projections. For alternative economic assumptions, we chose to compare a "high" growth case in which man-hour productivity grows at 2.5 percent per year and annual work hours decline by 0.25 percent per year — more or less on trend — with a "low" growth case in which work hours decline by 1.0 percent per year (growth in man-hour productivity remaining the same). The shift towards leisure implied by the growth case is fairly dramatic: While weekly work hours are now close to 40 and would decline over a 30-year period to 37 in the high growth case, they would fall to 29 in the low growth scenario. (2)

Common to all these scenarios is the assumption that changes in productivity, work hours, aggregate savings rates, and the ability of the government to maintain full employment are independent of changes in the population. While there are some arguments to the contrary, within the range of the population estimates and over the time period being considered, we do not believe any other assumption is more defensible. (3) Nevertheless, by comparing the B-High with E-Low or the B-Low with the E-High scenarios, at least limited consideration of some alternative assumptions is possible.

FIGURE 1-1
U.S. POPULATION WITH PROJECTIONS, 1950-2020

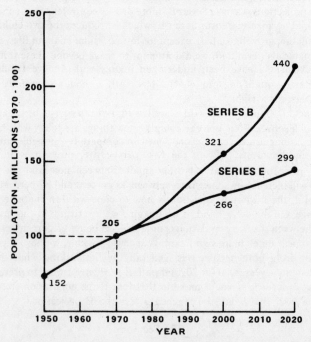

While independent of the above factors, population and associated demographic changes are assumed to affect aggregate demand, consumption patterns, and the size of the labor force. Figures 2 and 3 portray the quantitative effect of these, plus more detailed assumptions on GNP and GNP per capita.

Whether or not these projections actually occur will depend in large part on whether the United States can solve the resource and environmental problems that this growth would entail, an assessment to be made in the course of this study. But assuming for the moment that they can occur, three main conclusions emerge from these materials.

FIGURE 1-2
U.S. GROSS NATIONAL PRODUCT WITH PROJECTIONS,
1950-2020

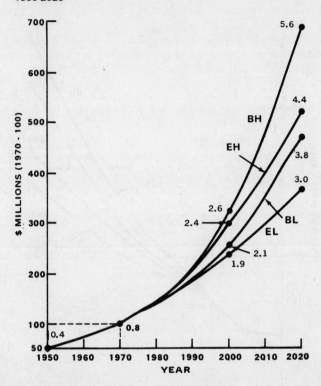

First, under any scenario considered, the American economy, which is alreaady large by world standards, will become gargantuan. Even if there is a substantial shift in preferences towards leisure and a significant slowdown in population growth rates, this economy is likely to be twice its current size in the year 2000 and more than three and one-half times its current size in 2020. With a more rapid growth in population and a less rapid shift in preferences toward leisure (or a more rapid growth in man-hour productivity) the economy would be seven times its current size by the latter date. This would occur not because of any implicit assumption of large annual growth rates — the highest of which is no more than four percent per annum — but merely because these rates are sustained for such a long period. Second, because GNP per capita increases more rapidly under the Series E than under the Series B population projections, total GNP is not lower in proportion to the extent that population is lower; but even so, this difference between total GNP in the two cases grows dramatically over time. In 2000, the difference in projected GNP resulting solely from alternative population assumptions amounts to more than half the total size of GNP today; by 2020, it amounts to more than the total size of today's GNP. And third, sector breakdowns of the economy indicate a gradual shift in output towards services, a shift that proceeds a bit faster under the Series E than under the Series B population assumptions.

FIGURE 1-3
U.S. GROSS NATIONAL PRODUCT PER CAPITA WITH PROJECTIONS, 1950-2020

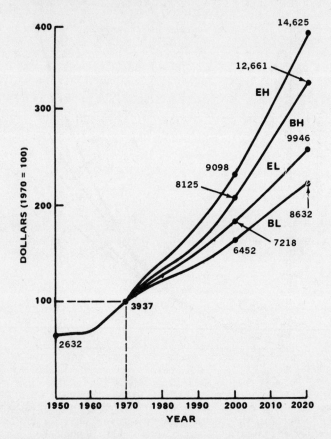

The result is a strong prima facie case in favor of the two-child family on two important welfare grounds. Per capita GNP can be taken as a measure of material welfare, conventionally defined; and since resource use and pollution levels are associated more with total than with per capita output levels, total GNP might be taken as a crude indicator of environmental degradation. In these terms, the E projections, with their higher levels of per capita and lower levels of total GNP — as well as with an environmentally more favorable composition of output — are clearly superior.

Two qualifications must be kept in mind, however. First, parents may prefer larger families than are compatible with the lower population growth rate; if they do, this preference must be balanced against the social benefits of the smaller population. Second, the savings in resources and environmental depletion resulting from a slowdown in population growth rates may not be as great as intuition might lead one to believe based on these projections of total GNP, This could arise as a result of changes in other important factors linking resources and the environment to population and GNP. As we shall see, in several important instances this qualification turns out in fact to be important.

Minerals and Fuels Adequacy

We have studied some 19 minerals plus major sources of energy to determine what United States demand would be under alternative population and economic projections, what difference an increased emphasis on recycling would make, and whether United States plus world reserves are likely to be adequate within the time horizon of this study.

The question of adequacy cannot be answered without a careful definition of the word in mind. Here, adequate means sufficient supplies to meet demand assuming current prices, currently known reserves, and possibilities to substitute one for another material in production. If an item proves to be inadequate in this sense, one must ask about the extent of the price increase necessary to eliminate the gap between demand and supply and the possibilities for adjusting to this increase in order to assess the seriousness of the situation. With this in mind, the following broad generalizations emerge from the analysis.

Minerals

On a worldwide basis and out to the year 2020, there appear to be sufficient reserves of at least nine non-fuel minerals: chromium, iron, nickel, vanadium, magnesium, phosphorous, potassium, cobalt, and nitrogen. Of these, domestic reserves may not be sufficient to meet needs for chromium, vanadium, cobalt, and nickel. Access to foreign supplies is currently quite reliable, but if it became questionable, modest efforts at research and development, recycling, stockpiling, and substitution could overcome this difficulty.

Worldwide reserves as now estimated are inadequate through the year 2020 for 10 of the minerals studied: manganese, molybdenum, tungsten, aluminum, copper, lead, zinc, tin, titanium, and sulfur. However, there are significant differences in the outlook. Modest price increases, for example, in sulfur, would bring in supplies from potential reserves, probably beyond what requirements call for. The same is true for aluminum, for which poorer — and thus initially at least more costly — sources of ore are abundant. At the other end of the scale is tungsten, for which it is difficult to establish a reserve picture that promises adequacy. Here main reliance might have to be placed on gradual phasing out of the metal in applications that can get along, though perhaps at higher cost and reduced efficiency, with substitute materials or substitute processes. In between these extremes lie materials like copper, where a combination of resort to even poorer ores, increased substitution, greater recycling of what is now a very large above-ground stock of copper, and increased exploration seems indicated if requirements as here projected are to be met.

A change in population growth appears to have a smaller impact than a change in economic growth, at least over the range considered in this study. Substitution of the lower for the higher population growth assumption generally results in a reduction of cumulative United States demand by only one to eight percent by the year 2000, and no more than 14 percent by 2020. Most of these modest savings would occur late in the period. In contrast, different assumptions as to economic growth would affect mineral consumption more significantly. Through the year 2000, the low productivity assumption would generally yield savings in cumulative demand of 10 to 14 percent, rising to 18 to 26 percent for demand through the year 2020. These begin to look more interesting. In combination with low population growth, savings would generally rise to 14 and 19 percent through 2000, and 27 to 35 percent through 2020.

An alternative way to compare the impact of population and economic growth on consumption of resources is to ask what the effect would be in a given year, say 2000, of a one-percentage-point reduction in the population size compared to a one-percentage-point reduction in per capita GNP. The conclusion emerging is similar to the above: A one-percent reduction in population would reduce consumption of resources in the year 2000 by 0.2 to 0.7 percent, whereas the equivalent percentage reduction in per capita GNP would reduce consumption in that year 0.6 to 3.5 percent.

The most important reason for this result has to do with the fact that a reduction in population induces some offsetting increase in per capita GNP and hence in demands for resources, whereas a decline in per capita GNP can take place independently of a change in population. While it is unlikely that a change in population would occur without any change in GNP per capita, a trial run of the model in which per capita GNP was held constant when alternative population assumptions were introduced makes the savings from a reduction in population size roughly equal to that of a reduction in GNP per capita.

Increased recycling as a means of stretching reserves was tested for five principal minerals: iron, copper, lead, zinc, and aluminum. Defined as an "active recycling policy," the increased effort directed at recapturing a larger percentage of used material would reduce demand for primary materials significantly for aluminum and zinc, modestly for copper, and barely at all for iron and lead. The differences, which are quite dramatic, result from differences in the extent to which recycling is now taking place: high for iron and lead, moderate for copper, and very low for aluminum and zinc. Savings in terms of reserves would be substantial, especially for zinc and copper (40 and 15 percent respectively of world reserves if projected for 50 years). Extension of "active recycling" to a world scale can be assumed to increase these savings. While these are magnitudes not to be dismissed lightly, costs in terms of additional resources required to achieve such recycling, as well as the additional pollutants arising from the recycling, need careful analysis to ascertain net savings and benefits.

Energy

Historically, energy consumption in the United States has closely paralleled the growth in real GNP. While there are many factors that could alter this relationship — increased needs for energy per unit of output because of recycling and the mining of lower grade ores, and decreased needs because of shifts in composition of output towards services and improvements in efficiency, to mention just a few — it is probably safest to assume that the historical association will continue during our time horizon. Population growth, then, will play the same role in determining energy growth as it does in determining overall growth in GNP.

Increasingly, energy will be used in the form of electricity, although standard projections of the extent to which such a substitution will occur are probably exaggerated. Moreover, more and more electricity in the United States will be produced with nuclear fuel, perhaps as much as half by the year 2000.

World supply projections depend very heavily on the technological changes assumed to occur during the next quarter to half century. Even without assuming any breakthroughs, however, world fossil fuel reserves (including potential as well as proved) appear adequate for at least the next half century. This reckoning appears to be true even leaving out oil reserves in shale and tar sands, and uranium and thorium. Beyond these possibilities, if man learns to harness nuclear fusion — a reasonable possibility within the next 50 to 100 years — the limits of worldwide industrial expansion will be set by factors other than availability of energy.

Relative to other countries, the United States is in good shape, provided we have sufficient lead time to develop domestic alternatives to foreign sources should the need arise. Although proved reserves of gas and oil as a ratio to production have declined somewhat since World War II — more for gas than for oil — estimates of commercially recoverable reserves when added to proved reserves provide adequate coverage for well into the next century. This judgment does not take account of shale oil reserves of the United States and the tar sands of Canada. Coal reserves and nuclear fuels, assuming the development of breeders, are adequate for at least another century. While United States imports as a share of consumption may rise due to the availability of cheaper fuels abroad, given these domestic possibilities, this rise should not necessarily be taken as a sign of increasing long run vulnerability.

Qualifications

All these points suggest that there is no serious reason to believe that projected standards of living cannot be met because of minerals or fuels shortages. Adjustments will be necessary, but none of them are likely to entail a significant loss in material welfare during the next half century. This is not to say that there will be no problems so far as minerals and fuels are concerned. Three in particular need emphasis.

First, environmental concerns could interfere with this prognosis. Virtually every stage of energy use — from mining to transport and conversion — has significant environmental consequences. If public concern over siting of conventional and nuclear electric plants, strip mining, oil spills, and pipelines slows down development of new capacity, a greater price rise will be necessary to close the gap between supply and demand. Even if development is not slowed down in this way, demands for pollution control will have some effect on costs (the extent of which is considered below).

Second, there is a tendency to assume that adjustments will be made smoothly, that prices will correctly reflect scarcity sufficiently far in advance that appropriate remedial action can be taken before the problem becomes severe. But resource markets are not free from monopolistic interferences and governmental interventions; and business decision makers often behave myopically. If too short a time horizon is taken or if markets are dominated by buyers, key prices might remain constant at too low a level until a serious shortage is upon us, only then to rise dramatically as near exhaustion occurred. Alternatively, since major new discoveries and technological changes are difficult to predict, prices may be set too high in some circumstances as well as too low. The only solution may be continuous monitoring to detect growing shortages sufficiently far in advance that appropriate remedial action can be instituted.

Third, far more serious than the threat of overall physical shortages, however, are growing worldwide imbalances. Between 1925 and 1967, energy imports as a fraction of total consumption for Western Europe increased from two percent to 61 percent, and that for Japan from zero to 80 percent. Eastern Europe, which exports over 15 percent of its energy production, now imports five percent. (In contrast, the United States figures are less dramatic, shifting from a three percent net exporter to a seven percent net importer of energy.) Corresponding to these figures are dramatically increased exports from a handful of countries, principally in North Africa, the Middle East, and the Caribbean. Trends for some other minerals are similar. Geographic imbalances are severe today and may well become more severe in the future. While the United States will remain amongst the haves, relatively speaking, these disparities are likely to affect international power balances involving this country in serious ways, whether or not the United States becomes more directly dependent on world supplies.

Pollution

We have divided pollutants into two rough classes. The first class includes major combustion proaucts — carbon monoxide, carbon dioxide, oxides of nitrogen, oxides of sulfur, hydrocarbons, and particulates — and several measures of water pollution — including biological demand for oxygen and suspended and dissolved solids. The primary characteristics of this group are first, that they all have relatively short half-lives — sufficiently short that cumulative effects are not a problem — and second, that sufficient information exists about them to permit linking them to economic sectors or population. In addition, this group contains the more massive and commonly discussed pollutants. The second set of pollutants is a miscellaneous group including those with longer half-lives — radiation, pesticides, and heavy metals — plus a wide variety of ever-changing chemicals emitted by our high technology industries, most of which are emitted in small, though often highly toxic, amounts. For many of these pollutants, future developments depend more heavily on changes in technology than on changes in population and economic growth; in any case, they are very difficult to link to population and economic growth in a simple and quantitative fashion. Accordingly our emphasis here is on the first class of pollutants.

Our principal conclusions regarding this first set are most easily discussed in relation to Figure 4. While this figure relates only to hydrocarbons, the general conclusions are similar for otner pollutants. Bar A for 1970 represents the level of hydrocarbons generated by the production and use of economic goods and services. If no changes in technology associated with the production of this pollutant were to occur, the amount of hydrocarbons generated would be at the levels indicated by one of the other bars labeled A in the year 2000, the difference between them depending on population and economic assumptions.

For 1970, the bar labeled B indicates the amount of hydrocarbons emitted into the atmosphere, the difference between A and B accounted for by treatment. For 2000, B indicates projected emission levels taking into account the changes in technology likely to come along anyway, without public pressures to restrict emission of harmful residuals. In principle, these changes could result in either a higher or a lower level of emission. In fact, however, most of the technological changes we have studied tend on net to reduce residuals. This is because even without pressures to clean up the environment, entrepreneurs have an interest in conserving on raw materials. For example, we anticipate that more and more sawdust and timber trimmings will be used in making paper and pulp rather than being dumped into streams. As a consequence of such technological changes, as well as because the shift towards services makes the year 2000 composition of output slightly less polluting than the 1970 composition, we find the pollutants studied are likely to grow over time less rapidly than the growth in GNP.

The heart of this story involves the bars labeled C. which indicate the levels of emissions that could prevail if an active abatement policy were in force. These estimates are conservative in the sense that no technological breakthroughs (such as the adoption of the Rankine cycle engine which could occur within this time frame) were assumed. (4) As figure 4 indicates — and comparable data for the other pollutants studied confirm — the choice to be made is between no policy change with higher levels of emissions than exist today, and an active abatement policy with lower than current levels of emissions, whatever the rates of population and economic growth within the range investigated. As of 1972, the United States appears to be choosing in favor of the active policy.

How much would an active abatement policy cost? In 1970, annualized costs of pollution abatement were estimated to be $8.45 billion (1967 dollars), about one percent of GNP. Under the active abatement policy, we estimate that these same categories of costs would mount to over $47 billion for the high population-high economic growth-case and $34 billion for the low population-high economic growth case in the year 2000. While these are very large figures, they amount to less than two p⸍rcent of GNP in the year 2000. In terms of growth, these figures signify that we would have to give up less than one-tenth of a percentage point in annual growth of GNP to purchase this active abatement policy.

FIGURE 1-4
HYDROCARBONS GENERATED AND EMITTED UNDER ALTERNATIVE ASSUMPTIONS

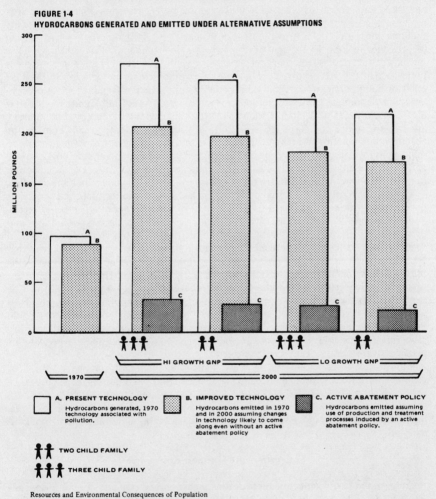

A. PRESENT TECHNOLOGY
Hydrocarbons generated, 1970 technology associated with pollution.

B. IMPROVED TECHNOLOGY
Hydrocarbons emitted in 1970 and in 2000 assuming changes in technology likely to come along even without an active abatement policy

C. ACTIVE ABATEMENT POLICY
Hydrocarbons emitted assuming use of production and treatment processes induced by an active abatement policy.

♟♟ TWO CHILD FAMILY

♟♟♟ THREE CHILD FAMILY

Resources and Environmental Consequences of Population
Growth in the United States: A Summary

At least within the time frame and for the set of pollutants under investigation, then, a direct attack on pollution clearly dominates over a reduction in population or economic growth as a strategy for obtaining a cleaner environment. A brief investigation of other pollution control strategies — for example, a selective reduction in the consumption of commodities which are heavy users of the environment, restrictions on the use of the automobile, and zoning — supports this general conclusion. Considering how little we have done in the past to control pollution, this result should not be all that surprising.

Such direct attacks on pollution will not be easy to implement, and once implemented at whatever levels prove feasible, further reductions in emissions will become very difficult and costly. It is at this point — and especially as we look beyond 2000 when such policies may prove inadequate — that reductions in population and economic growth come into their own as important means of containing pollution.

But even within the next 30 years, special regions of the country will face difficult problems despite improvements in overall emission rates. Data on 47 urbanized areas and three air pollutants were used to illustrate this point, assuming that the land area of these places increases with population in such a way that population density remains constant. In 1970, two cities — Chicago and Philadelphia — had sulfate (SO_2) concentration levels that were above the Environmental Protection Agency's primary standard of 80 micrograms per cubic meter of air. If no change in abatement policy (after 1967-70) occurred, only these two would remain in violation in the year 2000, although many other cities would closely approach the standard. If there were an active abatement policy as defined above, all cities would fall significantly below the standard in 2000. A similar situation exists for particulates except that 36 areas are initially above the standard and some improvement would occur even in the absence of an active abatement policy. For nitrogen oxides, however, where 36 metropolitan areas were above the 100 micrograms per cubic meter standard in 1970, and 41 areas would be above in 2000 with no change in policy, two — Los Angeles and San Diego — would remain above the standard even with an active abatement policy.

The nitrogen oxide situation in Los Angeles, under the assumptions made, is particularly striking. Compared to a 1970 level of 275 micrograms per cubic meter, under any of the four alternative scenarios regarding national population and economic growth rates, the 2000 level will be near 500 with no change in policy and around 150 — still some 50 percent above the standard — with an active policy in that year. This assumes that land area increases in proportion to population. But during the past decade, population density has been increasing. If this trend continues, nitrogen oxide levels in 2000 under the active abatement policy would be around 170; and if land area were to cease expanding, all the increased population being absorbed within the region's current boundaries, the active abatement policy could not hold nitrogen oxide levels below 570. Clearly, in this region of the country, something must give: rates of inmigration, the use of the internal combustion engine especially for personal transport, or the standard itself.

Pollution concentrations are not only distributed unequally amongst urbanized regions. Variations within such regions and even from one hour to the next can be extremely large. Indeed, carbon monoxide levels along downtown streets during rush hours can be more than 10 times those along suburban streets at the same time of day. Such problems will require special treatment whatever national abatement policy is adopted.

Congestion and Outdoor Recreation

Congestion is a difficult concept to define, measure, and project. Clearly, it depends on many more factors than sheer numbers. Geographic distribution of population, transportation facilities, income levels, homogenity of tastes, type of facilities, and the way they are managed all play important roles. Yosemite, for example, is more crowded today than it was 20 years ago not just because the United States population is larger but also because of westward migration, better transportation facilities, especially highways, increased incomes and leisure time, and increased preferences for organized outdoor experiences. In this situation, what can be said about the amount of congestion that the United States will experience in the future under the two population assumptions?

At a general level, perhaps the most important point to make is that with a slower rate of growth, we close off fewer options. If all the land in the United States were divided equally amongst its citizens, each American would have 11 acres at his disposal (nine acres excluding Alaska and Hawaii). Of this amount, approximately two are used to grow crops; six are used (or are available) for pasture and range, forest and recreation; and one-half an acre is occupied, for example, by buildings and roads, or is held out of use by special institutions (the remaining two and one-half acres being a residual, largely unusable category). With the higher population growth rate, each American would have seven acres at his disposal in 2000 and five in 2020. By European standards, the United States would still be considered a land-rich country. But a style of life based on such an abundance of land would be slowly but progressively eliminated, with no possibility of turning back. The same is true with the two-child population with the important difference that the rate of deterioration would be much slower, reaching 7.5 acres per person in 2020, and would all but cease at around 7.1 acres per person in 2040. (See Chapter 8 for a more detailed discussion of future trends in land use).

Beyond such general comments, little can be said about the differential degree of congestion implied by alternative population projections without detailed studies of specific facilities. Within the confines of this project, we have undertaken one such study of a particularly important amenity associated with the American way of life, outdoor recreation. This study uses an econometric model to project participation rates for some 24 different outdoor recreation activities on the basis of information about the supply and location of recreational facilities and the extent to which congestion affects use, as well as important demographic and economic characteristics of the population. Together with other trends, it points to another significant difference between the two population projections.

Between 1970 and 2000, an individual's income and hours of leisure will rise, and recreational facilities will improve, so that he will have more time, money, and opportunities to "recreate" if he wishes. To do so under the high population projection, however, he will have to adopt a different style of life. There will be fewer opportunities for spontaneous communion with raw nature. More and more such contacts will be controlled, regulated, and contrived. On the other hand, his income and the increase in man-made recreational facilities will permit him to substitute organized sports, sightseeing and foreign travel, plus artistic and cultural activities, if he so desires. For a small but important segment of our population, these alternatives are unlikely to provide an adequate compensation; for many others, however, they will.

On the other hand, under the E population in the year 2000, the typical individual will be significantly older and therefore less interested in participating in some kinds of outdoor recreation activities. This fact, plus the smaller population size, will substantially reduce congestion, so that whatever he does participate in is likely to give him more pleasure. Once again, the style of life will change, shifting from more active to more sedentary recreational pursuits; but in this case, it would be voluntary, determined by the needs and preferences of an older population rather than being imposed by the desire to avoid overcrowding.

Water

On a national basis, the United States has more than enough water to meet all of its needs far beyond the year 2020. But to take advantage of it, substantial outlays for treatment facilities and storage will be needed. Such cost will increase at a rate slightly less than that for GNP.

In contrast to our findings with respect to minerals and pollution, population has a dominant role to play in determining these costs. If we substitute the two-child for the three-child population in the year 2000, savings would be 23 percent; by 2020, these savings would mount to 32 percent. In contrast, savings due to a slower growth in income are 11 percent in 2000 and 17 percent in 2020.

But there are great regional disparities in the demand and supply of water. When regions are defined as being deficient in water if, after high levels of treatment are applied, the maximum regulated supply is insufficient to meet requirements for water of given qualities, several regions in the southwest are already in deficit. These deficit regions will slowly spread across the country, faster with the high than with the low population growth rate.

These results are significant not only because deficits are defined in a stringent way, but also because the analytical model used to obtain them does not take account of biological wastes from the non-sewered population, problems of nutrient runoff into groundwater supplies or adequately treat costs of managing slack water areas such as estuaries or of separating storm from sanitary sewers. Moreover, the scope for redistributing water, people, and economic activities between regions is more limited and difficult than might appear at first glance.

On the other hand, there are considerable possibilities for using water more prudently. Most water is used either free of cost or on a flat fee basis that provides no incentive for conservation. Yet in the largest areas of use — for irrigation and cooling — substantial possibilities are present to reduce withdrawals without serious welfare losses. Finding equitable means to increase prices or otherwise ration major users would not be easy, but certainly could be done if the need arises.

Agriculture

The agriculture study is based on the same set of scenarios used for other sectors except that several were added to investigate the impact of a policy which entails a restriction on the use of agricultural chemicals, particularly fertilizers and pesticides, and the possibility of urban sprawl encroaching on high quality agricultural land. In the case where restrictions on chemical inputs are assumed, the use of fertilizer is projected to be half the level it would have been without restrictions and that of pesticides to be 80 percent below levels otherwise projected. These levels were chosen on the basis of the judgment that they are the largest foreseeable reductions that could be made between now and the year 2000 without dramatic increases in costs, but yet sufficient to make significant improvements in environmental quality.

Between now and the year 2000, under the conditions assumed, the United States will have no serious problem in producing sufficient food for its own population even if government-assisted exports continue to be the same proportion of total output as they are today. With the high population and high economic growth rate assumptions, and assuming no restrictions on the use of fertilizer and pesticides, most idle, high quality, cropland would have to be put back into production. But because of its availability, as well as because of expected increases in yields, farm prices relative to other prices would be only marginally higher than they are today. Fertilizer and pesticide use would increase significantly, but for a number of reasons, probably not in proportion to the increase in food output. These reasons have to do with 1. the expected continuation of efforts started in the early 1960's to regulate pesticide applications and find less persistent formulations; 2. increases in the price of fertilizer — which can be expected to induce better timing and placement of application, better distribution over different crops, and use of formulations such as controlled release preparations that improve efficiency and reduce leaching; and 3. the easing of acreage restrictions which in the past two decades have induced excessively rapid rates of increase in fertilizer and pesticide consumption to compensate by increasing yields.

Moreover, urban sprawl is unlikely to have any significant effect on the ability of the United States to meet projected food and fiber requirements. While urban areas are spreading out, rural-to-urban migration is continuing as well, the net effect being a more unequal distribution of people on the land. Such a population implosion, which is expected to continue in the future albeit at a diminishing rate, partly offsets the effect of increases in the population. Of course, local agriculturalists are likely to face increasing challenges in regions where immigration of people and other economic activities is especially rapid; but, once their activities are relocated, total output should not be adversely affected to any appreciable extent.

If, in the interest of environmental quality, restrictions on the use of fertilizer and pesticides were put in force, an additional 50 million acres of land would have to be brought into production. Since most high quality land would already be in use, considerable investment would have to be made to bring these additional acres into production. The result would be something like a 15-percent increase in the farm price of food over what it would otherwise have been in the year 2000. By that time, such a price rise would probably not be very detrimental from a welfare point of view. On the other hand, with the low population growth assumption, restrictions on the use of fertilizer and pesticides could be accomplished without any increase in price. Indeed, if economic growth were to be lower as well, farm prices might fall marginally.

While no formal assessment beyond the year 2000 was made, these differences between the high and the low population growth rates are likely to magnify substantially. By 2020, only the low population growth case might be compatible with a policy of restricting inputs in the interest of environmental quality, since the price increase under the high growth case with restrictions would be considered intolerable, perhaps even as high as 40 to 50 percent. Of course, such a price rise would occur only if we tried to maintain current patterns of consumption; in fact, they would be dampened by shifts away from consumption of animal livestock towards vegetables and synthetic meats which would reduce acreage requirements. Moreover, technological breakthroughs that significantly reduce acreage requirements could also invalidate this assessment. But, in any case, it is clear that much of the fat in our agricultural system would have been trimmed away.

A number of open questions on the environmental consequences of these developments remain. Will any of these different levels of fertilizer use result in nitrate poisoning of groundwater on a significant scale? Without heavy costs, is it possible to shift agriculture from one part of the country to another to the extent implied by this and the water analysis? And how can we stay ahead of the adaptability of pests to our means of control without harming man or other animals in the process? Such questions cannot be answered without substantially more information than is now available. Perhaps in the end a new closed system of agriculture will be necessary. Given these unknowns, an additional advantage of the slower over the more rapid population growth path is that it provides us with more time to find answers to these questions.

Urban Environmental Problems

There is mounting evidence that environmental quality is lower in metropolitan areas that are larger and in regions that are more densely populated. Certainly this is the case with air pollution, noise, traffic congestion, and time spent on journey to work. Other factors are less clear. Sewerage and water treatment costs per capita decline as city size increases to about 100,000; thereafter, engineering data suggest that costs should be more or less constant for conventional facilities, although actual costs appear to rise. Certainly if large cities are forced to use tertiary treatment or separate storm and sanitary sewers—which may be necessary to maintain adequate standards in some cases—per capita costs will be much higher. Similarly, solid waste disposal costs are also either U-shaped or increasing with city size and density over the relevant range. There is evidence that increasing urban scale affects local hydrology and climate; but not all these effects are bad. While raw data indicate a strong correlation between urban scale and crime rates, the effect is greatly attenuated once the effects of race and income are removed.

But it does not necessarily follow from this evidence that a policy of redistributing people and economic activities so as to reduce city size and density would be beneficial as a general proposition. First, there are many tradeoffs for the individual living in the larger city: In general, deflated money incomes for the same jobs are higher; and there are more occupational and social opportunities, and a larger variety of goods and services. To mention one important example, medical services, especially those involving highly trained specialists, are clearly superior in larger urban centers. Given free movement of people between urban areas — a condition which is probably met fairly well despite income and housing discrimination that inhibits movement within urban areas — these tradeoffs are in the nature of compensation payments for poorer environmental quality, payments which everything considered may leave the urban dweller no worse (or better) off than his counterpart in smaller towns. (5) Second, there is some evidence that the large city may be a major generator of national economic growth. Communication and transport costs are lower; greater specialization and division of labor is possible; and growth industries, information industries, and universities tend to locate there. Third, conscious efforts in this and other countries to influence locational decisions, in particular to stop the growth of large cities, have been largely unsuccessful in the past; there is no reason to believe the future will be different on this score.

Finally, the underlying causes of poorer environmental quality in larger urban centers may often not be scale, but factors associated with or exacerbated by scale; urban forms and transportation systems more appropriate to an earlier era; old, unintegrated service facilities; inappropriate pricing of public facilities and common property resources such as roads and waste disposal media; multiple political jurisdictions; and the factors leading to inadequate financing and a predominance of minority groups and poor in many central cities. Many such problems will remain to be solved whatever population distribution policy is adopted. As a consequence, the historical evidence relating environmental quality to urban scale may not be applicable to the building of new cities and the "retrofitting" of older ones.

For these reasons, we are skeptical about the value of proposals to reduce urban size and density across the board. As a general proposition, it is better to work on underlying causes rather than effects, and to attack problems where they exist, permitting people to adjust by moving out or in as they judge best for themselves. Some new town developments are certainly called for, not so much as a way of reducing average urban size and density — hopefully, some of these developments would try out solutions with more rather than less density, and others might usefully occur within existing urban areas — but as an experimental means of gaining information on the best way to solve our real urban problems.

While the studies included in this volume cover a vast range of topics in a fair amount of detail, they obviously do not exhaust the subjects of relevance to the questions posed at the outset of this chapter. Conclusions based solely on what has been covered could provide a misleading overall impression. Before drawing final conclusions, therefore, we wish to emphasize the importance of at least four additional considerations.

Other Environmental Concerns

We must now return to the second set of pollutants mentioned but set aside in the above discussion. These include pollutants with long half-lives and an ever-changing group of potential threats to the environment generated at what seems like an increasing rate by our high technology industries. But what can be said about them? The principal problem here is ignorance.

The case of radioactive wastes from nuclear power plants is instructive. We know there are likely to be more nuclear power plants if rapid population and economic growth occurs; but all dimensions of nuclear management and technology are changing so rapidly that there is no stable launching pad from which to project the amounts of radioactive wastes likely to escape to the environment. Once in the environment, we know they can travel long distances through space and food chains before coming to rest, and we know the kinds of damages they can cause; but we do not know where they will come to rest, the extent of the damages, or when in the future these dangers will occur.

In truth, the situation is similar for all pollutants. It is difficult to link emissions to concentration levels in specific places and, with a few exceptions, close to impossible to make quantitative statements with reasonable confidence about the consequences — the damages — resulting from these concentrations. The crude method we were forced to use to relate emissions to air quality, and in the review of what is known about damage and cost functions for urban pollutants illustrate these points all too well. Nevertheless, often because of longer "half-lives," greater toxicity in smaller doses, rapid changes in types of pollutants, and time lags between emissions and the appearance of damages, the situation is more disturbing for the second group of pollutants. More serious yet, these very characteristics insure that we shall not quickly improve our knowledge in this area.

Apart from adopting a more positive and encouraging posture than now exists towards basic research in many of these areas, perhaps the only way to cope with this ignorance is to proceed cautiously and prudently, playing it safe with nature. Given our affluence and the fact that many pollutants result from attempts to satisfy relatively trivial preferences—for unblemished fruits, labor saving detergents, faster accelerating cars, brightly colored paper products — much could be done within our time frame without significant adverse effects on welfare or growth rates. But a slowdown in population and economic growth would clearly help; and in a longer time frame could possibly be a necessity.

We have also said precious little about global pollutants — rising levels of carbon dioxide and heat in the earth's atmosphere, for example — and the more fundamental concerns of some ecologists about man's threat to the basic life support system of the earth. Here again ignorance dominates. But an up-to-date, careful review of this whole range of problems suggests that while lead times may be long, most such threats are not imminent, at least not the way non-ecologists reckon time. (6)

Our investigation of the resource and pollution problems inherent in attempting to achieve alternative growth rates suggests that all these rates are feasible during the next 30 to 50 years: Problems will arise — more rapidly under the high than under the low growth rate assumptions — but the United States has the physical and technological capability to resolve them without serious losses in material welfare. This country is amazingly rich. If we cannot mine a resource, we can import, design around it, find a substitute, or just reduce our consumption by a small bit. If water deficits threaten a particular part of the country, we can choose between higher charges to reduce its consumption, transfers of population and economic activities to other regions, and longer and larger canals. If pollution emissions cannot be tolerated, we can change production processes, improve treatment, separate polluters and their victims, treat the symptoms, or simply produce less of the commodity causing pollution. Congestion during commuter hours can be handled by restricting the use of private cars, mass transit and, if necessary, staggered work hours. Congestion at recreation sites can be handled by building additional facilities, better management, encouraging substitutes (for example, foreign travel) and, if necessary, staggering vacation periods. Even land shortages for agriculture can be handled, given sufficient lead time, through farming the sea, changes in diet, synthetic foods, and shifts in the direction of hydroponic production. None of these adjustments raises specters of dramatic downfall and collapse.

But physical, technological, and even managerial capabilities of this sort are not enough. Beyond the economic costs of adjusting to growing resource and environmental problems, there are social and institutional prices to pay. Indeed, in a discussion of these difficulties, we come to the real nature of our problem with population growth. Such non-resource costs are of four types.

First, population growth forces upon us a slow but irreversible change in life style. Imbedded in the folklore of what constitutes the American way of life is freedom from public regulation: freedom to hunt, fish, swim, and camp where and when we will; free use of water and access to uncongested, unregulated roadways; freedom to do as we please with what we own; and freedom from permits, licenses, fees, red tape, and bureaucrats. Obviously, we do not live this way now. Maybe we never did. But everything is relative. Americans of 2020 may look back with envy on what from their vantage point appears to be our relatively unfettered way of life, much as some today look back with nostalgia on the Wild West.

Conservation of our water resources, preservation of wilderness areas, protection of animal life threatened by man, restrictions on pollutant emissions, and limitations on fertilizer and pesticide use all require public regulation. Rules must be set and enforced, complaints heard and adjudicated. True enough, the more we can find means of relying on the price system, the easier will be the bureaucratic task. But even if effluent changes and user fees become universal, they would have to be set administratively, emissions and use metered, and fees collected. It appears inevitable that a large portion of our lives will be devoted to filling out forms, arguing with the computer or its representatives, appealing decisions, waiting for our case to be handled, finding ways to evade or move ahead in the queue. In many small ways, everyday life will become more contrived.

Many such changes will have to occur no matter which population projection occurs, merely to correct for the external costs of past growth. But the difference, of small degree at first, would grow with time until, by the year 2020, the two societies may appear qualitatively different.

A second social cost involved is continued population growth is the further postponement of solutions to social problems. While such growth continues, top priority must be given to finding the necessary resources, controlling pollutants, correcting the damages they have done, and building ever larger reservoirs, highways, mass transit systems. A large and perhaps growing fraction of our physical and intellectual capital is directly or indirectly devoted to these tasks, to finding ways to cope with the problems that continuing growth throws up. From past experience, we can predict with a fair degree of confidence that equally impressive efforts will not be devoted to resolving fundamental social problems.

For similar reasons, we are forced to introduce solutions to problems before their side effects are known. It might, for example, be far better environmentally to postpone the introduction of nuclear power plants until the inherently cleaner fusion reactors are developed. When one pesticide or food additive is found to be dangerous to man, it is replaced with another about which we know less. Programs involving the expenditure of billions on water treatment are set in motion without knowing whether the benefits outweigh the costs of other opportunities foregone. Once again, lower population growth will not automatically change this situation, but at least a bit of this urgency, the "crash program" character to much that we do would be eliminated.

Finally, continued population growth closes off options. In the case of the larger population, there is less land per person, less choice, less room for diversity, less room for error. Technology must advance; life styles must change. Many may like this emerging world; but for those who do not there will be fewer alternatives.

To emphasize the point, it is tempting to exaggerate the importance of population as opposed to economic growth in causing these social costs, and to overemphasize the difference that a slowdown in population would make. But, in such an emphasis, perhaps we come closer to the heart of the problem of population growth in this country. For a rich, technologically sophisticated and flexible country like the United States, adequacy of resources and control of pollutants are not seriously in doubt during the next half century; we can conquer these problems if we wish. The real question is whether we will like the society that conquering these problems entails.

International Relations

For the poorer two-thirds of the world, at least, this formulation of the problem is the height of luxury. Not only are social options exceedingly narrow in contrast to those of the United States, but in many of these countries, even concerns about toxic pollutants must be given low priority compared to problems of food and resource adequacy. Short of dramatic technological breakthroughs, rapid declines in birthrates, or massive transfers of resources from richer countries, their relative position, if not their absolute position as well, is likely to deteriorate further during the next 30 to 50 years. The turmoil caused by this poverty and inequality in the distribution of the world's wealth can only grow worse with time. One can be sanguine about America's long-term future only by ignoring this problem.

A reduction in United States consumption of resources will not automatically help these countries. It will do so only if sale of these raw materials is not a particularly important fraction of their exports — but for many it is — and if some means can be found to transfer to them in usable form the resources we release by consuming less. Permitting these resources to remain idle does not help poorer countries.

Because of more rapid population and economic growth rates in the rest of the world, the United States share in world consumption of resources can be expected to fall in coming decades. At the same time, because of rapid increases in domestic consumption, United States dependence on the rest of the world will probably increase. While technological developments could alter this picture, these trends seem highly likely no matter which population and economic growth assumptions come to pass, within the range investigated. Sooner or later, we will also have to face the environmental problems generated by this growth on a worldwide scale.

Realignments of relative power positions and potentially grave issues of clashing national and regional interests will arise from these trends. As such worldwide problems become larger and increasingly interlocked, it becomes more and more an act of self interest and less one of altruism on our part to help in evolving a sensible international economic order capable of dealing with the joint problems of economic development, international trade, resources, and the environment.

Beyond 2020

The most significant aspect of what lies beyond 2020 is the continued divergence in the population projections for the United States. If the high growth rate continues, all the problems discussed above would magnify, increasingly taxing our ingenuity to solve them. Life will continue to become more regulated and contrived. If by 2030-2040 population growth ceased, at least some aspects of this progressive deterioration would all but end; and resources would be released to deal with the others.

Increasingly, therefore, the essential difference between the high and the low projections would become one between necessity and choice. In the first case, dramatic technological breakthroughs must be achieved; in the second, we could get along if they did not. In the first case, life styles must change; in the second, beyond a certain point they need not.

Apart from these few comments, however, we cannot usefully speculate further. Our methods of analysis and imagination are not up to it. It is of course possible to continue projections of demand farther and farther out until our conservative assumptions about technological progress are overwhelmed. But there is no justification for this. Why continue with an assumption that productivity is going to double every 25 to 50 years; why not a slowdown or a technological breakthrough such as fusion that could make a 500 to 1000 fold difference? And why assume that birthrates and demand will continue rising exponentially? Beyond a certain point, there is no basis whatsoever for making any assumptions. Indeed, the year 2020 is probably far beyond this point!

All we can say is that if population growth continues, the long-term future will be dominated by a race between growth in technological knowledge and growth in population. Unless the two rates are positively linked to each other we will always be better off with a smaller population growth rate. But we have no way to know which rate will win, or for how long.

Notes

(1) Of course, all studies of the future are conditional in this sense. But since there has been a tendency to impute absolute forecasting power to some recent long-term projection exercises, it cannot hurt to emphasize this point.

(2) An equivalent low-growth case could also be generated by assuming that growth in man-hour productivity slows down to 1.5 percent per year, the decline in work hours remaining the same, or by assuming some immediate combinations which in fact may be more realistic.

(3) For example, it is sometimes argued that innovation is more rapid with a higher rate of turnover of the labor force, that the need to care for and educate children

induces parents to work harder and save more than they would with fewer children, and that it is easier to maintain full employment when aggregate empirical evidence to support these arguments is weak; some counterarguments can be advanced; and in any case, it is difficult to believe that, within our time frame, whatever negative effects there might be could be so large that they could not easily be offset by appropriate government action. A number of such arguments and related empirical evidence are discussed elsewhere in research reports prepared for the Commission on Population Growth and the American Future. A summary and evaluation of these arguments is included in Ronald G.Ridker, "The American Economy During the Next Half Century" (paper presented to Annual Meeting of the American Association for the Advancement of Science, Symposium on Technology and Growth in a Resource-Limited World, December 1971).

(4) They were obtained by applying emissions standards recommended by the Environmental Protection Agency for introduction in 1973 (for water) and 1975 (for air), and after ascertaining that abatement strategies to meet these standards exist at least on a pilot, if not yet on a commercial use, cost estimates were taken from feasibility studies. On the Rankine cycle engine, see R.U. Ayres and Richard V. McKenna, *Alternatives to the Internal Combustion Engine* (Baltimore: Johns Hopkins Press for Resources for the Future, 1972).

(5) This is not to suggest that this arrangement is optimal in an economic sense. It still fails to appropriately "internalize" th externalities.

(6) Sterling Brubaker, *To Live on Earth* (Baltimore: Johns Hopkins Press, 1972).

ECOLOGICAL
PERSPECTIVES

Frederick J. Smith

This paper is speculative and general, being applied to broad, long-term aspects of human ecology. Interrerlationships between people and their environments change over time, and change greatly over long periods of time. They will certainly continue to change in the future.

Thirty years of human history, however is as short for ecology as it appears to be long for economics. In the United States, it is only three years more than the average time between one generation and the next, and it is less than half the life expectancy. Between now and the year 2000, changes in people and in the environment will be relatively small. Under these circumstances, an ecological crisis would be a surprise, unless it already exists, because incremental change can be met with incremental response.

A better perspective can be gained if a longer period is reviewed. The history of population growth in the United States since 1790 (Table 1) is long enough to span several major periods of development and change. A first period of extension was dominated by the spread of our culture over the landscape. The settling of virgin lands, increases in acreage of cropland, and establishment of additional towns accompanied a more or less exponential growth in population. This began well before independence and continued until late in the nineteenth century.

Growth by extension declined rapidly after 1880, and has been a very minor process since 1910. This first "filling up" of the land ended with the first national programs in conservation.

A second period of growth is dominated by intensification—an increase in population density and in demands per unit area of used land. This process was minor

Thirty years of human history, however, is as short for ecology as it appears to be century. Growth within a system of fixed size is not the same as growth by extension. Ordinarily, growth becomes increasingly difficult as the constraints of the system tighten. Under any one system of operation, growth against these restraints produces a decrease in individual welfare: Returns to the individual per unit of effort declines as more people share the same resources.

The dual problems of growth by intensification and the maintenance of individual welfare can be solved only by change in the system. In 1900, the land of this country supported 76 million people. It is through profound technological, institutional, and social change that this same land today is able to support 205 million people. By contrast, the effects of inadequate change (or, rather, of population growth without adequate compensatory change) are evident in the deterioration of human welfare that plagued China before 1945, and India before 1965.

Intensification in the United States shows two phases. The first, which lasted until about 1940, was based on a continuation of the same kinds of adjustments that had begun on a much smaller scale in the preceding century. The management of renewable resources was pushed toward higher and higher yields as population demands mounted. This led to over-utilization and a loss of environmental "capital," much as in the ancient civilizations of the Middle East. Overgrazing, overcropping, and the plowing of marginal lands produced extensive and erosion and culminated in the era of the dustbowl (1931-1938).

Since 1940, the process of change has been much more profound. Increased yields have been coupled with better inputs, and alternative resources have been developed to supplement living resources. The result has been not only a considerable improvement in individual welfare, but the ability to support an additional 73 million people (Table 1).

Table 1.—Population Growth in the United States over Successive 30-Year Periods

Year	Population (millions)	People added (millions)
1790	4	
1820	10	6
1850	23	13
1880	50	27
1910	92	42
1940	132	40
1970	205	73

Source: U.S. Bureau of the Census.

Although modern technology may have "solved" the problems caused by population growth before 1940, the unprecedented addition of people in the last 30 years has lifted another set of problems to prominence. Among these, urban deterioration and environmental pollution seriously threaten material welfare. These problems are recognized but not solved. Accommodations among life styles, living standards, and population size remain to be worked out.

Under these conditions it is difficult to evaluate expectations of the next 30 years. Increases in population size and in human activity (Table 2) are projected to be nearly another new set of problems, above and beyond those recognized now.

Recent and projected growth in the world population (Table 3) shows this difficulty to be general. Some areas of the world ran out of new land a long time ago, and only trivial additions have occurred since 1950. (1) Thus, all recent and projected growth must be accommodated primarily by intensification. Modern techniques of industrialized production are developed to very different levels in different countries, with the result that problems of over-utilization of renewable resources are paramount in some countries, and problems of industrial pollution are more urgent in others. Continuing population growth makes all of these problems more serious. It is no surprise that ecologists identify population growth as the major ecological problem. (2) Since 1950, the numbers of people added per decade have been more than twice as large as ever before, and the projected increase for the present decade is even greater.

Table 2.—Comparisons of Projections for the Next 30 Years with Additions During the Last 30 Years

Comparison	1940 level	Last 30 years 1940-1970	Next thirty years	
			B-H	E-L
People (millions)	132	+73	+116	+61
Farm output (1967=100)	59	+43	+69	+37
Industrial production (1967 index = 100) .	29	+75	+205	+126
Energy output (10^{15}BTU)	24	+45	+151	+96

Data, when available, from Chapters 2, 5, and 7 of this report; additional 1940 estimates from U.S. Bureau of the Census, *Statistical Abstract of the United States.*

Table 3.—Additions to the World Population in Each Decade Since 1900

Decade	People added (millions)
Ending:	
1910	120
1920	132
1930	208
1940	225
1950	222
1960	488
1970	604
1980 (projected)	848

Source: Workshop on Global Ecological Problems, *Man in the Living Environment* (Madison, Wisc.: The Institute of Ecology, 1971).

Population Growth, Economic Growth, and Individual Welfare

Material welfare has benefited profoundly from the industrial revolution. In their simplest form, these benefits can be estimated in the rising ratio of goods produced per unit of labor input, or man-hour productivity. The use of power driven machinery as a substitute for muscular effort is an unquestioned improvement in life style.

Sometimes, however, the apparent gains from new technology prevent or offset a loss in welfare, rather than offering a real increase. A simple case is the depletion of a nonrenewable resource, for example copper. Technological gains have permitted the use of ores of lower and lower grades without significant changes in the price of the product. These gains have allowed the flow of copper to continue, but have not added a benefit to man that was not there before. Indeed, such changes usually include a larger through-put of energy and/or material, which may have deleterious side effects. In some cases, newer technologies may increase productivity, allowing a decrease in the price of the product, which then gradually reverts to its former level as the average mineral content of ore declines. This is a form of running to stay in place, an important change that allows life to continue unchanged.

A second kind of technological "progress" that offers no increase to individual welfare takes place with population growth by intensification. Since more people in the same space doing the same things would suffer a welfare loss, a certain amount of "progress" must be used to offset that loss. The two processes usually go simultaneously and the relationship is difficult to quantify. The complexities of human systems are such that all kinds of technological change are involved, the same kinds that would improve individual welfare if population growth did not occur. Thus, a better transportation system may shorten commuting time, improving commuter welfare. Increased congestion may erase this gain, translating the increase in individual welfare into the support of more people. Here again, the through-put per capita of materials and energy is generally increased as part of the process.

A third kind is also related to population growth. Some of the most spectacular technological gains in this country are associated with an increased ability to synthesize goods directly from the non-living environment, kinds of goods that used to be available only from living resources. Synthetic fibers in textiles, plastics in furniture and construction, and industrially produced fertilizers are examples of modern supplements to plant and animal products.

The problem here is that the population then outgrows the capacity of living systems to produce the desired volume of products at reasonable costs. Natural supplies are not depleted; they become insufficient. Under these conditions, supplementation by industrial synthesis prevents a welfare loss. This permits the support of more people, but their welfare is little different from that of earlier and smaller populations. Certainly, the basis for preferring a nylon sweater and a plastic chair to a woolen sweater and a wooden chair is small, compared with severe shortages of supply.

A distinction between the industrial revolution and the current chemical revolution can be made. By and large, progress in the use of energy and machinery, to the degree that it has increased man-hour productivity, has allowed improvements in human welfare. Progress in the substitution of synthetic materials for natural products, to the degree that it has little effect on productivity, allows the support of more people. It develops a welfare component only in the sense of avoiding a loss because the population outgrew the capacity of natural sources. Admittedly, the distinction is not clean since these two kinds of processes interact with each other, and exceptions are not difficult to find. Nonetheless, this kind of separation of the gains from technology into additions to individual welfare and support for more people is useful. Social change also accompanies growth by intensification. At the time our nation was established, life styles were adapted firmly to the pioneering spirit, appropriate for exponential population growth and extension across the land. Self-sufficiency, self-employment, and individual free enterprise offered much of the security and opportunity that shaped individual welfare. The concept of minimal government was practiced. Most people worked for themselves or for relatives in a family business, whether it was a farm, a grocery store, or a skilled craft. This mode of life survived well into the 20th century, and the value placed upon it is still strong.

Among the changes that have followed, and which became necessary if losses in welfare were to be prevented, the most universal and continuing processes include increases in job specialization and increased interdependence among individuals, changes that increase the general complexity of living. The pioneering life style is not adapted to these changes. Most workers are now employed outside their families. Free enterprise is much less available to the individual, becoming primarily a corporate activity. Individualism is practiced less, and collectivism is practiced more.

With these changes, the individual is much less able to provide for his security, and opportunity exists primarily to the extent that training and education meet the demands of alternative careers. Provisions for individual security and opportunity have become societal obligations, institutionalized in many programs of social security and in greatly expanded educational systems. These institutions are expensive; to the extent that they substitute for earlier mechanisms, and prevent losses in welfare, they are part of the cost of population growth.

Advances in medicine have increased individual welfare greatly, especially with respect to such attributes as physical health and life expectancy. Increasingly, however, medical gains offer only potential benefits to individuals. The delivery of health services has become increasingly difficult, and often fails to provide all of the benefits that should be available. Sharply rising costs indicate a welfare loss, a failure of the system to cope with problems arising from increased population densities. The radical changes of recent years have not yet solved this problem.

If all of these changes are considered together, it appears that many of the increases per capita in services and industrial output are related to population growth; only a portion results in a higher standard of living. The substitutions forced by population growth are those that have greater capacities, in the sense of being able to support more individuals at the same average level of welfare. The replacement of individual responsibility with social responsibility, and of natural products with synthetic products, are examples in which earlier sources of satisfaction become insufficient, even though human behavior and living resources have not themselves deteriorated.

Expectation that the total resource demand will increase more rapidly than the population, even if individual welfare is held constant, has been noted earlier. (3) The same applies to such aggregate measures as GNP. Some basis for allocating increases in GNP per capita between the cost of population growth and additions to individual welfare would be instructive. Between 1940 and 1970, GNP per capita in the United States increased 2.4 percent per year, while the population increased 1.5 percent per year. Since the most rapidly growing sections of the economy include major substitutions of the kinds discussed above, the portion of the 2.4 percent that was absorbed by population growth cannot be small.

The present ability to produce consumer goods directly from non-living resources has developed primarily in this century, and amounts to a revolution in human ecology. Its significance is as great as that of the industrial revolution, which has been based primarily on the development of non-living resources for energy consumption. The two together will continue to produce high rates of industrial production as part of the process of supporting moderate rates of population growth. Increasing interdependence will continue to force a rapid growth in services. Thus, economic growth and population growth are closely coupled processes.

Man-Made World and Nature

Primitive man, like any other species, was enmeshed completely in his living environment. Much of human progress is the struggle to break some of those bonds, with many setbacks along the way. Early agriculture assured larger and more dependable supplies of living resources, but problems of soil management and water supply became overwhelming to many civilizations. Early towns and cities offered protection from enemies and encouraged the development of new skills, but exposed people mercilessly to pestilence and disease. The breaking of each bond revealed more bonds, more constraints to population growth. Yet, the cumulative achievements of man have been effective. Modern civilization is a large, growing, self-differentiating system.

The man-made world is managed as an open system intermingled with surrounding natural systems. The advantages of the self-maintaining, self-repairing capacities of natural systems for aesthetics, habitat maintenance, resource renewal, and waste removal have been enormous. But problems have arisen from the free exchange of materials between systems. Local overloads of waste have disturbed natural systems, and various pests and diseases have invaded the man-made world to exploit man, his crops, and his animals. When human populations were small, and the material goods used by man were largely of natural origin, these problems of open systems were small compared with the advantages.

With the very large population increase in this century, the built environment has been vastly expanded. The majority of people now live in places where the man-made world dominates nature. Material inputs and outputs have grown to levels well beyond the self-renewing capacities of nature. Thus, the per capita advantages derived from nature have declined.

At the same time, problems of exchange between the man-made world and nature have increased. The pollution of nature is more general. Problems of waste overload are aggravated by larger inclusions of toxic materials. Totally new compounds become new forces in natural systems, and nondegradable materials accumulate. Whereas pollution formerly led to local losses of amenities and local health hazards, it now adds to these effects a regional and possibly global deterioration of nature.

Problems of pests and diseases have also increased. The list of crop pests now runs to several thousand species, and more are continually appearing. As agricultural industry intensifies, differing more and more from natural systems, more species find in agriculture an escape from the complex bounds of their natural habitats.

The man-made environment deteriorates. Buildings, roads, and most other structures decay or corrode. Lawns, parks, and farmlands revert spontaneously toward the natural condition. No inherent process of recycling removes dirt and debris. Without human intervention, natural systems would gradually invade and replace the man-made world. The per capita burden of effort needed to maintain and repair the man-made world has become very large. It has for many years exceeded actual effort in many urban areas.

Thus, as people become free from natural bonds, and also become more numerous, they acquire greater problems of environmental maintenance. These now extend throughout the man-made and natural worlds. One view of the environmental crisis is that man has taken on more problems than he can manage.(4) Although the magnitude and severity of present problems are difficult to assess, it is certain that further population growth will add to the burden.

With all of its faults, the man-made world is essential to the maintenance of human welfare, and increasingly so as the population grows. Highly industrialized, socialized societies offer material wealth a diversity of occupation, and an excitement of interaction that are accepted eagerly wherever they become available. Continued development of the man-made world is definitely part of the future.

Natural systems are also essential to human welfare, providing man with many benefits. (5) They maintain the habitability of the planet, especially with respect to the composition of the atmosphere. They produce most of the fish yields that now average, globally, about 40 pounds of fish per year. (6) They provide biological control for most of the potential pests of forests and grasslands. They modify regional climate; the air-conditioning accomplished by vegetation is several orders of magnitude above human efforts. They prevent flash floods and erosion, create a more continuous flow of water in rivers, and produce the highest quality of water for domestic use.

Natural systems offer aesthetic benefits. As a source of beauty, fascination, relaxation, and recreation, nature is unexcelled. Nature has inspired many of the best creations in poetry, music, and art. The value placed upon contact with nature increases as more and more of human life is surrounded by the man-made world. The continued ability of natural systems to provide these various benefits is intended to be part of the future.

Continuing development of man-made systems and continuing function of natural systems have become more difficult to achieve. As the former changes qualitatively and quantitatively, differing more and more from nature, exchanges between them become more disrupting. The time will arrive when the man-made world can no longer be managed as an open system. Enclosing portions will be a simpler solutions. Some aspects of agriculture may already be at this point; isolating them in vast greenhouses may offer better solutions to pest control and pollution abatement. The doomed city is another example of a closed system that may soon be needed.

A mixed pattern of closed systems for intensely industrialized activities and open systems for more relaxed activities may permit large populations to enjoy the best of both worlds, just as small populations are able to do without using closed systems. The larger the population, the fewer the activities that can safely be allowed "outdoors."

If changes of these kinds are not accomplished, population growth will lead to the progressive deterioration and elimination of nature. This has long been happening on a local scale. As pavement spreads in cities, the trees beome weakened, diseased, ugly, and are finally removed. New trees fail to survive, and soon the area is treeless — better looking without broken, dead limbs. Ponds and streams attract development, which eventually fouls the water. But many suburban ponds have been filled, and many streams covered over to become sewers. Natural systems rapidly lose attractiveness as they deteriorate, often becoming noisome sources of pests. The final stage of elimination is often not mourned.

So far, severe environmental deterioration has been local, and disturbance of the vast ecological systems that dominate the planet has been slight. (7) Should large-scale deterioration become severe, however, the entire planet will take on the unwanted characteristics of the man-made world: It will deteriorate in all of its aspects unless prevented by human effort. This would be an inevitable result if the population succeeded in growing large enough.

At population levels far short of such global saturation, nature can remain vigorous and useful if changes such as the development of closed systems are made. The effect is not an improvement to human welfare, but the prevention of a loss due to population crowding. The advantages will not even prevent a loss in welfare if they are used instead to support more people — unless more changes are made, such as restricting more activities to closed systems. This cycle of growth and change can be continued for a long time.

In earlier studies, perspectives were developed in which population growth influences the style of living, and continues to do so no matter how many adjustments have been made to accommodate earlier population growth. To the degree that change is endless, it is difficult to imagine a "maximum population size" unless it is conditional upon a defined life style. It is simpler, and perhaps more useful, to identify the sequence of constraints to human activity that is forced by population growth, beginning at population levels lower than the present (history) and continuing into levels that are considerably higher (projection). Such a task is well beyond the capacities of an individual, but would be feasible for a working group of appropriate specialists.

Speculations that a portion of per capita economic growth is required to support population growth, and that only the remainder can contribute to a net increase in individual welfare, lead to further interpretations of the model output. It is still assumed that per capita gains in GNP, disposable income, and other aggregates are useful measures of potential contributions to human welfare, but it has not previously been assumed that population growth with a constant per capita GNP diminishes individual welfare. The portion of per capita gains absorbed by population growth is unknown. It must have been very small in the 19th century, when population growth was accompanied by extension, rising more rapidly with the shift toward growth by intensification. Concepts of environmental resistance, and the equivalent concept of diminishing returns, suggest that a larger and larger and larger allocation is needed as population growth continues.

Let us suppose, as an arbitrary decision, that the present population level is one that requires a rate of increase in GNP per capita that is two-thirds the population growth rate, if losses in welfare are to be prevented. Table 4 shows the resulting estimates of potential gains to individual welfare under the four projections of the study. The difference between the Series B and E projections becomes large, so much so that the welfare component of B-H (high rates of population and per capita economic growth) and of E-L (low rates of population and per capita economic growth) are alike.

Since this relationship may be significant, a major study to define it more clearly and quantitatively would greatly improve our perceptions of the relations between population growth and economic growth.

Modern Agriculture

Since 1940, agriculture has become a rapidly evolving system. The industrial production of fertilizers and synthetic pesticides, the mechanization of husbandry, and new achievements in breeding (such as the development of hybrid varieties) have been combined in an integrated technology whose potential for agriculture production is well ahead of demand. The historical effect is profound. Between 1920 and 1940, crop output per acre changed very little. Since 1940, it has increased with an average annual growth rate of 1.9 percent.(8) The yields of meat and other livestock products per unit of livestock (including poultry) have also increased.

With these changes the production process has become more like that in other industries, in which output is dependent primarily on input, and less like a system in which output depends strongly upon self-renewing resources. Before this century, very little went into the land (except sunlight, carbon dioxide, and water) that did not previously come from that land (namely, seed, manure, mulch, horsepower, and human labor). Today, much less of the input (seed, fertilizer, pesticides, mechanized power, etc.) comes from a previous harvest. To a considerable degree, the biological processes of production are cogs in an industrial machine, managed for much higher rates of production than were possible when they were managed as renewable resources.

Table 4.—Allocation of Rates of Increase in GNP Per Capita to the Prevention of Losses in Welfare Due to Population Growth, and to Net Increases in Individual Welfare. (Allocation assumes arbitrarily that the former is equal to two-thirds the population growth rate.)

Annual percentage growth rate	B-H	E-H	B-L	E-L
Gross National Product	3.9%	3.7%	3.1%	2.9%
Population	1.5	0.9	1.5	0.9
GNP/Capita	2.4	2.8	1.6	2.0
Offset losses from population growth	1.0	0.6	1.0	0.6
Net potential gains to individual welfare	1.4	2.2	0.6	1.4

Source: Chapter 2
Population, Resourses, and the Environment.

Greater yields can be achieved with further increases in the various inputs, and feeding the population of the United States through the year 2000 is not a critical issue under any of the projections. Several problems that exist now, or that may arise in the near future, can be alleviated with changes in management practice and in the mix of inputs.

There remain, however, some issues of major concern in relation to the long-term development of industrialized agriculture. It is still managed as an open system, it occupies very large acreages, and it is increasingly different from the interspersed and surrounding natural systems. Two areas emerge in which problems may become very difficult to control: pollution and pest control.

The use of fertilizers has increased very rapidly. Agricultural inputs of primary nutrients (N, P_2O_5, K_2O) in the United States rose from four million tons in 1950 to seven in 1960 and 14 in 1970.(9) The use of nitrogen fertilizers increased from one to more than six million tons within this period. Thus, in most places the history of heavy use is not only relative short, but one of continuing rapid increase. The side effects of intense fertilization are poorly known. For a variety of physical and biological reasons, nitrogen fertilizers pose the greatest pollution threat.(10)

In some areas, but not others, pollution of waterways has been observed. The direct loss of nitrates by leaching from the soil to surface water or groundwater can be monitored; but in fact, the number of such efforts over a series of years at the same sites has been small. A variety of such programs are now in progress.

The longer-term effects of high fertilizer levels on the microflora of the soil, soil organic matter, and the future ability of soil to hold fertilizers, are also poorly known. In Britain, which has one of the most intensive farming systems in the world, evidence is appearing that increased production no longer follows increased inputs; and, for some products, the yields have begun to decline. Soil structure appears to be deteriorating. (11) Some of the most desirable characteristics of soil (ability to hold water and to bind ions, loosely enough to prevent loss and yet allow roots to take them up) are biological products of decomposition, a process likely to be affected by chemical fertilizers.

For these reasons, judgment on the side-effects of present levels of fertilizer use is impossible. Soil deterioration and regional water contamination are possibilities, and their probabilities will increase with increased levels of fertilizer use.

Pest control has a greater probability of becoming a serious problem. The first pesticides used in large amounts were general poisons, compounds of lead, arsenic, copper, etc. These were harmful to people and other life as well as to the pest, and had to be used carefully. They were followed after World War II by a rapidly growing list of synthetic organic compounds, much more powerful and specific in their action, in the sense that they are more toxic to the target and less toxic to many other organisms that their predecessors. A third generation of pesticides based on the target's biochemical idiosyncracies, and still more specific in action than their predecessors, is now being developed.

The use of more specific pesticides, however, has brought with it a new problem: pest resistance. By hindsight, it is easy to predict. Since all organisms operate with much the same biochemical machinery, resistance should develop more easily to a chemical that is much less toxic to other organisms, than to a chemical that is strongly toxic to everything. Only 10 cases of pesticide resistance were recognized before 1940. There were 60 in 1958 and over 200 in 1967.(12) These arise from genetic change (evolution) in the pest populations. It is impossible to achieve a 100 percent kill, and among the survivors are those happening to have more resistance. The use of pesticides selectively breeds strains of pests that are resistant, if the genetic potential for resistance is present.

The usual response to resistance is to change pesticides. The use of DDT in this country is declining primarily because an increasing number of target species have become immune. Thousands of pesticides are available for use, but choosing another one has a complication. Many pesticides are chemically similar, so much so that resistance to one commonly confers resistance (sometimes less, sometimes more) to others.(13)

Among the modern insecticides, four chemical families can be recognized: 1. DDT and its relatives, 2. dieldrin and its relatives, 3. organophosphorus compounds, and

4. carbamates.(14) Cross-resistance is common within members of each family, much less common between families. Multiple resistance has also appeared; and, in the laboratory, a strain of boll weevils has become immune to all four chemical groups. (15)

The effect of this is that new families of pesticides will be needed periodically as the utility of the old ones fails. Here a squeeze is developing: New pesticides harmful to a broad spectrum of organisms will not be approved for use, and those with a narrow target are not likely to be useful for very long (a short useful life of third generation pesticides can be predicted). The problem becomes critical when choices have to be made between pesticides that are not safe and pesticides that are not adequate.

The general problem of pesticide pollution will not be reviewed here. Environmental consequences of using persistent pesticides are familiar to all. To these effects, resistant pests add another. Loaded up with the pesticide in which they are resistant, they can become a lethal food for their natural enemies.(16)

The movement of potential pests into agricultural systems, and the movement of nutrients and pesticides out, are problems that result from the open boundaries between agricultural and natural systems. A quantum jump in agricultural technology would be to close these boundaries.(17) Nutrients would no longer be able to leak out and pollute natural waters. Pests would no longer be able to wander in and out. High doses of strong pesticides could be used inside to achieve complete control (100 percent kill), preventing the development of resistance. The ecological balance of natural systems, including biological control of potential pest species, would be unimpaired.

Other benefits could be realized. Most, perhaps 80 percent of the phosphate fertilizers presently being used is lost in place, bound in insoluble salts of iron and aluminum. (18) Unless more is added each growing season, the levels of available phosphate decline rapidly to maximal "natural" levels, well below those needed for present levels of production. Since phosphate ores are limited, and phosphate is essential to life, this ecological waste of a resource will not be appreciated by future generations. If sand or water were used instead of soil, the problem of phosphate binding could be reduced greatly. Erosional loss would be eliminated.

Water requirements would be reduced. Not only does wind exclusion reduce evaporation, but water that is transpired (through the plants) or evaporated could be condensed and recycled. Closed systems could be located in more arid regions where more sunshine is found, freeing the more humid regions for other uses. If enclosed systems were heated, several crops a year could be grown in temperate regions.

Altogether, benefits from the development of closed agricultural systems would be very great. Large acreages of greenhouse agriculture already exist, especially to produce vegetables in the southwest where water conservation is critical. Many of the technological components of hydroponic agriculture have been developed, but large-scale implementation appears to be well in the future because of currently very high cost. Other variants may also be useful, such as isolating the below-ground area to prevent water loss and nutrient leaching, or recycling the stream outflow, where these are the only serious problems.

In addition to support for research on the improvement of present-day agriculture, a well-supported long-term program to develop closed-system agriculture would be a profoundly significant investment in the future.

For the last 15 years, forest production has increased slowly (Table 5), both in the United States and in the world. Within the United States, the volume of manufacture of lumber has changed little since 1953, when the production of pulp has more than doubled.(19) Net imports for the period 1963-68 changed little.(20)

Any large increase in the demand for forest products will force major changes in forest practice. Fischman and Landsberg have noted this problem; they recommended a number of measures that could be taken to match demand with supply.

Table 5.—Annual Percentage Increases in Yield from Agriculture, Forestry, and Fisheries, Compared with Population Growth. (Data for the period 1953-1968.)

	Population	Agriculture	Forestry	Fisheries
United States . . .	1.5%	1.7%	1.3%	−0.6%
World	1.8	2.7	1.6	6.0

Source: United Nations, *Statistical Yearbook,* 1969.

To an ecologist, a major issue concerns whether forestry adopts the intensive practices of agriculture, complete with fertilizers and pesticides. Intensive forestry already exists on relatively small acreages, and a sharp increase in demand would tend to increase this trend. Large acreages of forests will be managed more like agriculture. Forests contain hundreds of thousands of potential pest insect species whose gradual release from biological control would create problems considerably greater than those in agriculture.(21) Most forest management is directed toward sustained yields from a renewable resource, with minimal inputs. These are the forests that require the least amount of pesticide, best conserve the soil, and produce the highest quality of water.

A burst of "catch-up" construction in this century could be accommodated with a sufficient amount of product substitution. More plywood and particle boards would use more of the tree; plastics, aluminum, and other materials can be substituted, and more forest products can be recycled. If population growth follows the Series E projection, most of the forests could continue to be managed as renewable resources. If population growth follows the Series B projection, either we will substitute plastics and metals on a larger scale than the model contemplates, or demands for forest products will eventually exceed the capacity of this form of management.

The industrialization of forestry is presently encouraged, when it should be deterred. The existence of forests as agents of climatic modification, creators of aesthetic pleasures, and producers of clean water is more valuable to society than the value of its product.(22) These roles are best served if forests are managed as renewable resources, from which the yield is not inconsiderable.

Fisheries

The harvest of fish has declined slowly in the United States (Table 5), but increased rapidly for the world as a whole. Although United States production is down, net imports are up.(23) The United States is the largest importer of fish meal, and also imports a variety of other fish products. Total consumption, expressed as the original fresh weight of the fish, is about 70 lbs. per person per year. This is 75 percent higher than the world average. The larger part is used as a feed supplement (substituting for more than two million acres of soybeans); direct human consumption accounts for less than a third of the total.

World catches have increased from 29 million tons in 1953 to 70 million tons in 1968.(24) Much of the increase is due to the development of new fisheries (growth by extension). Increases in catch from the developed fisheries have been accomplished with large increases in gear and equipment (growth by intensification).(25) From an analysis of potential fisheries that remain to be developed, and those that are already maximally harvested, world catches of as high as 110 million tons may be possible on a sustained yield basis.(26) This is a large and significant source of protein in world nutrition.

The critical problem with marine fisheries is their protection. Most fisheries are near land, and the life cycles of a majority of the commercial species are linked with the costal zone, especially the estuaries. Nutrient enrichment, a problem in many freshwaters, is not known to be detrimental to marine production. At present levels, it probably stimulates production. Toxic wastes, however, have excluded many species from many areas. Dredging and filling have destroyed many environments. Food-chain accumulations of materials harmful to man have made some stocks inedible.(27)

Commerce, industry, and recreation make heavy demands upon the coastline and adjacent rivers. Conflicts between incompatible developments of the coast are as frequent as conflicts between development and protection of the marine environment. If present trends continue, marine shipping will double twice more before the end of the century.(28) Survival of the fisheries is already judged to be critical;(29) so, unless major policy changes in costal development are implemented soon, the difference between the Series B and E projections of population growth may be academic.

Overfishing is a second threat. Catch-per-unit-effort is declining in many of the developed fisheries, and high yields are maintained by greater uses of capital and power.(30) Several fish stocks have declined greatly, probably through a combination of fishing pressure and natural events. When fish recruitment fails from natural causes, continued intense fishing prevents recovery; the next period of unfavorable conditions produces a further decline. The demand for protein is already so great that many nations compete in each of the major fisheries, making their management for sustained yield virtually impossible to implement.

Fish farming (managed production in enclosed areas) produces about three million tons of fish annually. This can be increased by the year 2000 to 30 million tons without large increases in acreage.(31) Unless more protein is produced from fish farming, or from crops such as soybeans, overfishing seems inevitable. Obviously, the problem is greater if the population grows rapidly than if it grows slowly; but, it remains insurmountable if adequate protein is planned for the present world population. Loss of the marine fisheries would be equivalent to losing about half of the world meat production.(32)

Amenities

Limitations of water supplies and crowding in recreation areas describe tradeoffs between population size and amenity aspects of environmental quality. Perhaps the most serious effect is that lower-income groups will lose the most.

Projected increased costs of water resulting from population growth will reduce many uses of water: less use for lawns, gardens, swimming pools, air conditioners, fountains, etc. The combined effects of individual and municipal responses to rising water costs will be to surround inner-city people with fewer amenities that consume water. The full value of these amenities should not be underestimated. The lavish display of pools and fountains in desert cities moderates the hot dry air as well as providing visual delights. Evaporative air conditioners in the southwest add moisture to dry air, their substitutes will add heat to hot air. Urban vegetation plays a considerable role in evaporative cooling;(33) the summer coolness of trees and grass uses a lot of water. Urban trees offer sunshade and windbrake, and lawns are efficient, self-cleaning dust-traps. Vegetation that is not watered plentifully is less vigorous and more susceptible to disease. It is not only less pleasing to the eye, but less able to ameliorate the climate. Finally, dry dusty neighborhoods compare poorly with green neighborhoods at any economic level of life.

Amenity benefits from outdoor recreation areas decline as areas of high quality become more expensive, and inexpensive areas become more congested. Increasing distance to satisfying areas adds to these losses. The amenity loss from overuse is just as severe in a city park where grass, if it is to survive, must be barred from use, as it is in a national park where the natural vegetation and wildlife, if they are to survive, must be fenced against trespass. Letting the grass die, and the natural systems deteriorate, are also amenity losses.

In both of these problems, amenity losses will be greater among the lower-income groups. These will be added to other components of environmental quality that are distributed unequally. The distribution of people, pollution, and urban decay assures that urban amenity losses are concentrated among the poor. Any component of individual welfare that has an economic value will be distributed this way (it is the definition of rich versus poor), and this fact is not the focus of discussion. Rather, it is the relative magnitude of free and purchased benefits that is the issue.

Assume that income has risen at all levels of income, at similar percentage growth rates for all levels, over the last 20 years. The distribution of welfare in the population may not appear to have changed much. But income, and purchased benefits, adds to free benefits. If these have been declining, the spread of welfare in the population has been increasing. Since free benefits have been declining, it is entirely possible that the individual welfare of lower-income groups has been declining while the average of the whole population has been increasing. This study suggests that the spread will continue to increase, more rapidly under the Series B than under the Series E projection. The successive losses of free benefits can be balanced only by a correspondingly more equable distribution of income. The relationship involved between population growth and individual welfare is similar to those discussed in section two of this paper.

As stated earlier the principal conclusions of this study are that we can find solutions to the problems generated by future population growth if we have to, but that we will not like many of the social and institutional consequences of these solutions. As an ecologist, I would go somewhat further. Before we find solutions to problems of future population growth, we must find solutions to the problems of past population growth; we will not like many of the social and institutional consequences of these solutions either.

Notes

(1) Study of Critical Environmental Problems (SCEP), *Man's Impact on the Global Environment* (Cambridge, Mass.: MIT Press, 1970).

(2) Workshop on Global Ecological Problems, *Man in the Living Environment* (Madison, Wisc.: The Institute of Ecology, 1971).

(3) *Ibid.* and SCEP, supra note 1.

(4) SCEP, supra note 1.

(5) *Ibid.*

(6) Workshop on Global Ecological Problems, supra note 2.

(7) SCEP, supra note 1.

(8) U.S. Department of Agriculture, *Changes in Farm Production and Efficiency*, Statistical Bulletin 233, 1964 and 1970.

(9) U.S. Department of Agriculture, *Consumption of Commerical Fertilizers, Primary Plant Nutrients, and Micronutrients*, Statistical Bulletin 472, 1971; and Statistical Reporting Service, Crop Reporting Board, Commercial Fertilizers, Consumption in the United States, 1970 and 1971.

(10) American Chemical Society, *Cleaning Our Environment: The Chemical Basis for Action* (Washington, 1969).

(11) "A Blueprint for Survival," *The Ecologist*, 1972, Vol. 2, No. 1, pp. 1-42.

(12) G.R. Conway, "Better Methods of Pest Control," in *Environment, Resources, Pollution, and Society*, W.W. Murdoch, ed. (Stanford, Conn.: Sinauer Assoc., Inc., 1971).

(13) *Ibid.*

(14) *Ibid.*

(15) Workshop on Global Ecological Problems, supra note 2.

(16) G.R. Conway, supra note 12.

(17) Workshop on Global Ecological Problems, supra note 2.

(18) *Ibid.*

(19) United Nations, *Statistical Yearbook*, 1969.

(20) Food and Agriculture Organization (FAO), *Trade Yearbook*, 1969.

(21) Workshop on Global Ecological Problems, supra note 2.

(22) F.E. Smith, "Ecological Demand and Environmental Response," *Journal of Forestry*, December 1970, Vol. 68.

(23) FAO, supra note 20.

(24) United Nations, supra note 19.

(25) Workshop on Global Ecological Problems, supra note 2.

(26) *Ibid.*

(27) *Ibid.*

(28) United Nations, supra note 19.

(29) Workshop on Global Ecological Problems, supra note 2.

(30) *Ibid.*

(31) *Ibid.*

(32) *Ibid.*, and United Nations, supra note 19.

(33) *Symposium on the Role of Trees in the South's Urban Environment* (Athens, Georgia: University of Georgia Center of Continuing Education, 1971).

ADDITIONAL PERSPECTIVES ON THE ENVIRONMENT

INTRODUCTION

In examining a topic as specific as the relationship between population growth and environmental problems, a real danger exists of ignoring other concerns that may influence that relationship. A large number of factors are subsumed under the concept "environment," and a choice must be made between breadth and depth. Given the lack of systematic concern for the specific issue in question, the decision has been made to favor depth.

Within this section, however, we would like to call attention to several ideas that enrich the demographic dimensions of the environmental crisis. For example, what is the state of current concern for environmental issues? In answering this question, Anthony Downs positions such concern within an "issue-attention cycle." He contends that public interest in any particular issue does not remain high for very long. Rather, important issues pass through a series of stages; leaping to prominence, remaining there briefly, and then subsiding. Concern for the environment is presently at that point in the "issue-attention cycle" where intensity of interest must decline. But environmental problems are unique ones in their causes, their visibility, the "villains" associated with them, the possibility for their resolution through technology, their status in the marketplace, and their very ambiguity. These qualities of uniqueness, as well as Downs' other observations, are worthy of adding to an inventory of ideas about environmental problems.

Walter Heller provides a perspective on the general issue of growth as he tries to resolve the differences in opinion between economists and "ecologists." He argues that the economist sees the continuation of growth as "a price of social survival" and as a condition for progress, while the ecologist sees it as a threat to biological survival. In the course of developing his argument, Heller attempts to mediate between these different perspectives, thereby adding sophistication to the present discussion. His article is helpful in evaluating the arguments presented in the previous section.

In the third article, Leo Marx looks at American literature for its presentation of the nature of social institutions and environmental ideals. Through his "literary-ecological perspective," Marx shows how deeply rooted in American social institutions the present problems with the environment are. He argues that "the devastation of the environment is at bottom a result of the kind of society we have built and the kind of people we are." His argument has special consequences for the possibility of change, be it through anti-pollution laws, new forms of technology, or alterations in social institutions. Marx's article foreshadows a later discussion about the place of social structure and values in the relationship of population and environment.

These selections provide some important ideas for consideration and serve as a reminder about the need for humility in measuring what might be learned about environmental concerns. Although one issue has been examined in reasonable depth, mastery of environmental concerns is a task for a career, not a single volume.

UP AND DOWN
WITH ECOLOGY—
THE "ISSUE-ATTENTION CYCLE"

Anthony Downs

American public attention rarely remains sharply focused upon any one domestic issue for very long — even if it involves a continuing problem of crucial importance to society. Instead, a systematic "issue-attention cycle" seems strongly to influence public attitudes and behavior concerning most key domestic problems. Each of these problems suddenly leaps into prominence, remains there for a short time, and then — though still largely unresolved — gradually fades from the center of public attention. A study of the way this cycle operates provides insights into how long public attention is likely to remain sufficiently focused upon any given issue to generate enough political pressure to cause effective change.

The shaping of American attitudes toward improving the quality of our environment provides both an example and a potential test of this "issue-attention cycle." In the past few years, there has been a remarkably widespread upsurge of interest in the quality of our environment. This change in public attitudes has been much faster than any changes in the environment itself. What has caused this shift in public attention? Why did this issue suddenly assume so high a priority among our domestic concerns? And how long will the American public sustain high-intensity interest in ecological matters? I believe that answers to these questions can be derived from analyzing the "issue-attention cycle."

The Dynamics of the "Issue-Attention Cycle"

Public perception of most "crises" in American domestic life does not reflect changes in real conditions as much as it reflects the operation of a systematic cycle of heightening public interest and then increasing boredom with major issues. This "issue-attention cycle" is rooted both in the nature of certain domestic problems and in the way major communications media interact with the public. The cycle itself has five stages, which may vary in duration depending upon the particular issue involved, but which almost always occur in the following sequence:

1. The pre-problem stage. This prevails when some highly undesirable social con-

dition exists but has not yet captured much public attention, even though some experts or interest groups may already be alarmed by it. Usually, objective conditions regarding the problem are far worse during the pre-problem stage than they are by the time the public becomes interested in it. For example, this was true of racism, poverty, and malnutrition in the United States.

2. Alarmed discovery and euphoric enthusiasm. As a result of some dramatic series of events (like the ghetto riots in 1965 to 1967), or for other reasons, the public suddenly becomes both aware of and alarmed about the evils of a particular problem. This alarmed discovery is invariably accompanied by euphoric enthusiasm about society's ability to "solve this problem" or "do something effective" within a relatively short time. The combination of alarm and confidence results in part from the strong public pressure in America for political leaders to claim that every problem can be "solved." This outlook is rooted in the great American tradition of optimistically viewing most obstacles to social progress as external to the structure of society itself. The implication is that every obstacle can be eliminated and every problem solved without any fundamental reordering of society itself, if only we devote sufficient effort to it. In older and perhaps wiser cultures, there is an underlying sense of irony or even pessimism which springs from a widespread and often confirmed belief that many problems cannot be "solved" at all in any complete sense. Only recently has this more pessimistic view begun to develop in our culture.

3. Realizing the cost of significant progress. The third stage consists of a gradually spreading realization that the cost of "solving" the problem is very high indeed. Really doing so would not only take a great deal of money but would also require major sacrifices by large groups in the population. The public thus begins to realize that part of the problem results from arrangements that are providing significant benefits to someone — often to millions. For example, traffic congestion and a great deal of smog are caused by increasing automobile usage. Yet this also enhances the mobility of millions of Americans who continue to purchase more vehicles to obtain these advantages.

In certain cases, technological progress can eliminate some of the undesirable results of a problem without causing any major restructuring of society or any loss of present benefits by others (except for higher money costs). In the optimistic American tradition, such a technological solution is initially assumed to be possible in the case of nearly every problem. Our most pressing social problems, however, usually involve either deliberate or unconscious exploitation of one group in society by another, or the prevention of one group from enjoying something that others want to keep for themselves. For example, most upper-middle-class whites value geographic separation from poor people and blacks. Hence any equality of access to the advantages of suburban living for the poor and for blacks cannot be achieved without some sacrifice by middle-class whites of the "benefits" of separation. The increasing recognition that there is this type of relationship between the problem and its "solution" constitutes a key part of the third stage.

4. Gradual decline of intense public interest. The previous stage becomes almost imperceptibly transformed into the fourth stage: a gradual decline in the intensity of public interest in the problem. As more and more people realize how difficult, and how costly to themselves, a solution to the problem would be, three reactions set in. Some people just get discouraged. Others feel positively threatened by thinking about the problem; so they suppress such thoughts. Still others become bored by the issue. Most people experience some combination of these feelings. Consequently, public desire to keep attention focused on the issue wanes. And by this time, some other issue

is usually entering Stage Two; so it exerts a more novel and thus more powerful claim upon public attention.

5. The post-problem stage. In the final stage, an issue that has been replaced at the center of public concern moves into a prolonged limbo — a twilight realm of lesser attention or spasmodic recurrences of interest. However, the issue now has a different relation to public attention than that which prevailed in the "pre-problem" stage. For one thing, during the time that interest was sharply focused on this problem, new institutions, programs, and policies may have been created to help solve it. These entities almost always persist and often have some impact even after public attention has shifted elsewhere. For example, during the early stages of the "War on Poverty," the Office of Economic Opportunity (OEO) was established, and it initiated many new programs. Although poverty has now faded as a central public issue, OEO still exists. Moreover, many of its programs have experienced significant success, even though funded at a far lower level than would be necessary to reduce poverty decisively.

Any major problem that one was elevated to national prominence may sporadically recapture public interest; or important aspects of it may become attached to some other problem that subsequently dominates center stage. Therefore, problems that have gone through the cycle almost always receive a higher average level of attention, public effort, and general concern than those still in the pre-discovery stage.

Which Problems Are Likely to Go Through the Cycle?

Not all major social problems go through the "issue-attention cycle." Those which do generally possess to some degree these specific characteristics. First, the majority of persons in society are not suffering from the problem nearly as much as some minority (a numerical minority, not necessarily an ethnic one). This is true of many pressing social problems in America today — poverty, racism, poor public transportation, low-quality education, crime, drug addiction, and unemployment, among others. The number of persons suffering from each of these ills is very large absolutely — in the millions. But the numbers are small relatively — usually less than 15 per cent of the entire population. Therefore, most people do not suffer directly enough from such problems to keep their attention riveted on them.

Second, the sufferings caused by the problem are generated by social arrangements that provide significant benefits to a majority or a powerful minority of the population. For example, Americans who own cars — plus the powerful automobile and highway lobbies — receive short-run benefits from the prohibition of using motor-fuel tax revenues for financing public transportation systems, even though such systems are desperately needed by the urban poor.

Third, the problem has no intrinsically exciting qualities — or no longer has them. When big-city racial riots were being shown nightly on the nation's television screens, public attention naturally focused upon their causes and consequences. But when they ceased (or at least the media stopped reporting them so intensively), public interest in the problems related to them declined sharply. Similarly, as long as the National Aeronautics and Space Administration (NASA) was able to stage a series of ever more thrilling space shots, culminating in the worldwide television spectacular of Americans walking on the moon, it generated sufficient public support to sustain high-level Congressional appropriations. But NASA had nothing half so dramatic for an encore, and repetition of the same feat proved less and less exciting (though a near disaster on the third try did revive audience interest). So NASA's Congressional appropriations plummeted.

A problem must be dramatic and exciting to maintain public interest because news is "consumed" by much of the American public (and by publics everywhere) largely as a form of entertainment. As such, it competes with other types of entertainment for a share of each person's time. Every day, there is a fierce struggle for space in the highly limited universe of newsprint and television viewing time. Each issue vies not only with all other social problems and public events, but also with a multitude of "non-news" items that are often far more pleasant to contemplate. Those include sporting news, weather reports, crossword puzzles, fashion accounts, comics, and daily horoscopes. In fact, the amount of television time and newspaper space devoted to sports coverage, as compared to international events, is a striking commentary on the relative value that the public places on knowing about these two subjects.

When all three of the above conditions exist concerning a given problem that has somehow captured public attention, the odds are great that it will soon move through the entire "issue-attention cycle" — and therefore will gradually fade from the center of the stage. The first condition means that most people will not be continually reminded of the problem by their own suffering from it. The second condition means that solving the problem requires sustained attention and effort, plus fundamental changes in social institutions or behavior. This in turn means that significant attempts to solve it are threatening to important groups in society. The third condition means that the media's sustained focus on this problem soon bores a majority of the public. As soon as the media realize that their emphasis on this problem is threatening many people and boring even more, they will shift their focus to some "new" problem. This is particularly likely in America because nearly all the media are run for profit, and they make the most money by appealing to the largest possible audiences. Thus, as Marshall McLuhan has pointed out, it is largely the audience itself — the American public — that "manages the news" by maintaining or losing interest in a given subject. As long as this pattern persists, we will continue to be confronted by a stream of "crises" involving particular social problems. Each will rise into public view, capture center stage for a while, and then gradually fade away as it is replaced by more fashionable issues moving into their "crisis" phases.

The Rise of Environmental Concern

Public interest in the quality of the environment now appears to be about midway through the "issue-attention cycle." Gradually, more and more people are beginning to realize the immensity of the social and financial costs of cleaning up our air and water and of preserving and restoring open spaces. Hence much of the enthusiasm about prompt, dramatic improvement in the environment is fading. There is still a great deal of public interest, however, so it cannot be said that the "post-problem stage" has been reached. In fact, as will be discussed later, the environmental issue may well retain more attention than social problems that affect smaller proportions of the population. Before evaluating the prospects of long-term interest in the environment, though, it is helpful to analyze how environmental concern passed through the earlier stages in the "issue-attention cycle."

The most obvious reason for the initial rise in concern about the environment is the recent deterioration of certain easily perceived environmental conditions. A whole catalogue of symptoms can be arrayed, including ubiquitous urban smog, greater proliferation of solid waste, oceanic oil spills, greater pollution of water supplies by

DDT and other poisons, the threatened disappearance of many wildlife species, and the overcrowding of a variety of facilities from commuter expressways to National Parks. Millions of citizens observing these worsening conditions became convinced that someone ought to "do something" about them. But "doing something" to reduce environmental deterioration is not easy. For many of our environmental problems have been caused by developments which are highly valued by most Americans.

The very abundance of our production and consumption of material goods is responsible for an immense amount of environmental pollution. For example, electric power generation, if based on fossil fuels, creates smoke and air pollution or, if based on nuclear fuels, causes rising water temperatures. Yet a key foundation for rising living standards in the United States during this century has been the doubling of electric power consumption every 10 years. So more pollution is the price we have paid for the tremendous advantages of being able to use more and more electricity. Similarily, much of the litter blighting even our remotest landscapes stems from the convenience of using "throw-away packages." Thus, to regard environmental pollution as a purely external negative factor would be to ignore its direct linkage with material advantages most citizens enjoy.

Another otherwise favorable development that has led to rising environmental pollution is what I would call the democratization of privilege. Many more Americans are now able to participate in certain activities that were formerly available only to a small, wealthy minority. Some members of that minority are incensed by the consequences of having their formerly esoteric advantages spread to "the common man." The most frequent irritant caused by the democratization of privilege is congestion. Rising highway congestion, for example, is denounced almost everywhere. Yet its main cause is the rapid spread of automobile ownership and usage. In 1950, about 59 per cent of all families had at least one automobile, and seven per cent owned two or more. By 1968, the proportion of families owning at least one automobile had climbed to 79 per cent, and 26 per cent had two or more cars. In the 10 years from 1960 to 1970, the total number of registered automotive vehicles rose by 35 million (or 47 per cent), as compared to a rise in human population of 23 million (or only 13 per cent). Moreover, it has been estimated that motor vehicles cause approximately 60 per cent of all air pollution. So the tremendous increase in smog does not result primarily from larger population, but rather from the democratization of automobile ownership.

The democratization of privilege also causes crowding in National Parks, rising suburban housing density, the expansion of new subdivisions into formerly picturesque farms and orchards, and the transformation of once tranquil resort areas like Waikiki Beach into forests of high-rise buildings. It is now difficult for the wealthy to flee from busy urban areas to places of quiet seclusion, because so many more people can afford to go with them. The elite's environmental deterioration is often the common man's improved standard of living.

Our Soaring Aspirations

A somewhat different factor which has contributed to greater concern with environmental quality is a marked increase in our aspirations and standards concerning what our environment ought to be like. In my opinion, rising dissatisfaction with the "system" in the United States does not result primarily from poorer performance by that system. Rather, it stems mainly from a rapid escalation of our aspirations as to what the system's performance ought to be. Nowhere is this phenomenon more striking than in regard to the quality of the environment. One hundred years ago, white Americans were eliminating whole Indian tribes without a qualm. Today, many serious-minded citizens seek to make important issues out of the potential disappearance of the whooping crane, the timber wolf, and other exotic creatures. Meanwhile, thousands of Indians in Brazil are still being murdered each year — but American conservationists are not focusing on that human massacre. Similarly, some aesthetes decry "galloping sprawl" in metropolitan fringe areas, while they ignore acres of rat-infested housing a few miles away. Hence the escalation of our environmental aspirations is more selective than might at first appear.

Yet regarding many forms of pollution, we are now rightly upset over practices and conditions that have largely been ignored for decades. An example is our alarm about the dumping of industrial wastes and sewage into rivers and lakes. This increase in our environmental aspirations is part of a general cultural phenomenon stimulated both by our success in raising living standards and by the recent emphases of the communications media. Another cause of the rapid rise in interest in environmental pollution is the "explosion" of alarmist rhetoric on this subject. According to some well-publicized experts, all life on earth is threatened by an "environmental crisis." Some claim human life will end within three decades or less if we do not do something drastic about current behavior patterns.

Are things really that bad? Frankly, I am not enough of an ecological expert to know. But I am skeptical concerning all highly alarmist views because so many previous prophets of doom and disaster have been so wrong concerning many other so-called "crises" in our society.

There are two reasonable definitions of "crisis." One kind of crisis consists of a rapidly deteriorating situation moving towards a single disastrous event at some future moment. The second kind consists of a more gradually deteriorating situation that will eventually pass some subtle "point of no return." At present, I do not believe either of these definitions applies to most American domestic problems. Although many social critics hate to admit it, the American "system" actually serves the majority of citizens rather well in terms of most indicators of well-being. Concerning such things as real income, personal mobility, variety and choice of consumption patterns, longevity, health, leisure time, and quality of housing, most Americans are better off today than they have ever been and extraordinarily better off than most of mankind. What is not improving is the gap between society's performance and what most people — or at least highly vocal minorities — believe society ought to be doing to solve these problems. Our aspirations and standards have risen far faster than the beneficial outputs of our social system. Therefore, although most Americans, including most of the poor, are receiving more now, they are enjoying it less.

This conclusion should not be confused with the complacency of some superpatriots. It would be unrealistic to deny certain important negative trends in American life. Some conditions are indeed getting worse for nearly everyone. Examples are air quality and freedom from thievery. Moreover, congestion and environmental deterioration might forever destroy certain valuable national amenities if they are not checked. Finally, there has probably been a general rise in personal and social anxiety in recent years. I believe this is due to increased tensions caused by our rapid rate of technical and social change, plus the increase in worldwide communication through the media. These developments rightly cause serious and genuine concern among millions of Americans.

Concern about the environment has passed through the first two stages of the "issue-attention cycle" and is by now well into the third. In fact, we have already begun to move toward the fourth stage, in which the intensity of public interest in environmental improvement must inexorably decline. And this raises an interesting question: Will the issue of environmental quality then move on into the "post-problem" stage of the cycle?

My answer to this question is: Yes, but not soon, because certain characteristics of this issue will protect it from the rapid decline in public interest typical of many other recent issues. First of all, many kinds of environmental pollution are much more visible and more clearly threatening than most other social problems. This is particularly true of air pollution. The greater the apparent threat from visible forms of pollution and the more vividly this can be dramatized the more public support environmental improvement will receive and the longer it will sustain public interest. Ironically, the cause of ecologists would therefore benefit from an environmental disaster like a "killer smog" that would choke thousands to death in a few days. Actually, this is nothing new; every cause from early Christianity to the Black Panthers has benefited from martyrs. Yet even the most powerful symbols lose their impact if they are constantly repeated. The piteous sight of an oil-soaked seagull or a dead soldier pales after it has been viewed even a dozen times. Moreover, some of the worst environmental threats come from forms of pollution that are invisible. Thus, our propensity to focus attention on what is most visible may cause us to clean up the pollution we can easily perceive while ignoring even more dangerous but hidden threats.

Pollution is also likely to be kept in the public eye because it is an issue that threatens almost everyone, not just a small percentage of the population. Since it is not politically divisive, politicians can safely pursue it without fearing adverse repercussions. Attacking environmental pollution is therefore much safer than attacking racism or poverty. For an attack upon the latter antagonizes important blocs of voters who benefit from the sufferings of others or at least are not threatened enough by such suffering to favor spending substantial amounts of their money to reduce it.

A third strength of the environmental issue is that much of the "blame" for pollution can be attributed to a small group of "villains" whose wealth and power make them excellent scapegoats. Environmental defenders can therefore "courageously" attack these scapegoats without antagonizing most citizens. Moreover, at least in regard to air pollution, that small group actually has enough power greatly to reduce pollution if it really tries. If leaders of the nation's top auto-producing, power-generating, and fuel-supplying firms would change their behavior significantly, a drastic decline in air pollution could be achieved very quickly. This has been demonstrated at many locations already.

Gathering support for attacking any problem is always easier if its ills can be blamed on a small number of "public enemies" — as is shown by the success of Ralph Nader. This tactic is especially effective if the "enemies" exhibit extreme wealth and power, eccentric dress and manners, obscene language, or some other uncommon traits. Then society can aim its outrage at a small, alien group without having to face up to the need to alter its own behavior. It is easier to find such scapegoats for almost all forms of pollution than for other major problems like poverty, poor housing, or racism. Solutions to those problems would require millions of Americans to change their own behavior patterns, to accept higher taxes, or both.

The possibility that technological solutions can be devised for most pollution problems may also lengthen the public prominence of this issue. To the extent that pollution can be reduced through technological change, most people's basic attitudes, expectations, and behavior patterns will not have to be altered. The traumatic difficulties of achieving major institutional change could thus be escaped through the "magic" of purely technical improvements in automobile engines, water purification devices, fuel composition, and sewage treatment facilities.

Financing the Fight against Pollution

Another aspect of anti-pollution efforts that will strengthen their political support is that most of the costs can be passed on to the public through higher product prices rather than higher taxes. Therefore, politicians can demand enforcement of costly environmental quality standards without paying the high political price of raising the required funds through taxes. True, water pollution is caused mainly by the actions of public bodies, especially municipal sewer systems, and effective remedies for this form of pollution require higher taxes or at least higher prices for public services. But the major costs of reducing most kinds of pollution can be added to product prices and thereby quietly shifted to the ultimate consumers of the outputs concerned. This is a politically painless way to pay for attacking a major social problem. In contrast, effectively combatting most social problems requires large-scale income redistribution attainable only through both higher taxes and higher transfer payments or subsidies. Examples of such politically costly problems are poverty, slum housing, low-quality health care for the poor, and inadequate public transportation.

Many ecologists oppose paying for a cleaner environment through higher product prices. They would rather force the polluting firms to bear the required costs through lower profits. In a few oligopolistic industires, like petroleum and automobile production, this might work. But in the long run, not much of the total cost could be paid this way without driving capital out of the industries concerned and thereby eventually forcing product prices upwards. Furthermore, it is just that those who use any given product should pay the full cost of making it — including the cost of avoiding excessive pollution in its production. Such payment is best made through higher product prices. In my opinion, it would be unwise in most cases to try to pay these costs by means of government subsidies in order to avoid shifting the load onto consumers. We need to conserve our politically limited taxing capabilities to attack those problems that cannot be dealt with in any other way.

Still another reason why the cleaner-environment issue may last a long time is that it could generate a large private industry with strong vested interests in continued spending against pollution. Already dozens of firms with "eco-" or "environ-" in their names have sprung up to exploit supposedly burgeoning anti-pollution markets. In time, we might even generate an "environmental-industrial complex" about which some future President could vainly warn us in his retirement speech! Any issue gains longevity if its sources of political support and the programs related to it can be institutionalized in large bureaucracies. Such organizations have a powerful desire to keep public attention focused on the problems that support them. However, it is doubtful that the anti-pollution industry will ever come close to the defense industry in size and power. Effective anti-pollution activities cannot be carried out separately from society as a whole because they require changes in behavior by millions of people. In contrast, weapons are produced by an industry that imposes no behavioral changes (other than higher taxes) on the average citizen.

Finally, environmental issues may remain at center stage longer than most domestic issues because of their very ambiguity. "Improving the environment" is a tremendously broad and all-encompassing objective. Almost everyone can plausibly claim that his or her particular cause is another way to upgrade the quality of our life.

This ambiguity will make it easier to form a majority-sized coalition favoring a variety of social changes associated with improving the environment. The inability to form such a coalition regarding problems that adversely affect only minority-sized groups usually hastens the exit of such problems from the center of public attention.

All of the factors set forth above indicate that circumstances are unusually favorable for launching and sustaining major efforts to improve the quality of our environment. Yet we should not underestimate the American public's capacity to become bored — especially with something that does not immediately threaten them, or promise huge benefits for a majority, or strongly appeal to their sense of injustice. In the present mood of the nation, I believe most citizens do not want to confront the need for major social changes or any issues except those that seem directly to threaten them — such as crime and other urban violence. And even in regard to crime, the public does not yet wish to support really effective changes in our basic system of justice. The present Administration has apparently concluded that a relatively "low-profile" government — one that does not try to lead the public into accepting truly significant institutional changes — will most please the majority of Americans at this point. Regardless of the accuracy of this view, if it remains dominant within the federal government, then no major environmental programs are likely to receive long-sustained public attention or support.

Some proponents of improving the environment are relying on the support of students and other young people to keep this issue at the center of public attention. Such support, however, is not adequate as a long-term foundation. Young people form a highly unstable base for the support of any policy because they have such short-lived "staying power." For one thing, they do not long enjoy the large amount of free time they possess while in college. Also, as new individuals enter the category of "young people" and older ones leave it, different issues are stressed and accumulated skills in marshaling opinion are dissipated. Moreover, the radicalism of the young has been immensely exaggerated by the media's tendency to focus attention upon those with extremist views. In their attitudes toward political issues, most young people are not very different from their parents.

There is good reason, then, to believe that the bundle of issues called "improving the environment" will also suffer the gradual loss of public attention characteristic of the later stages of the "issue-attention cycle." However, it will be eclipsed at a much slower rate than other recent domestic issues. So it may be possible to accomplish some significant improvements in environmental quality — if those seeking them work fast.

COMING TO TERMS
WITH GROWTH AND
THE ENVIRONMENT

Walter W. Heller

A conference of ecologists and environmentalists, economists and technologists — convened to illuminate the complex interplay of energy, economic growth, and the environment — should open, not with a declaration of war or of conflicting faiths, but with a declaration of humility. Conceptually, to be sure, we know quite a lot about this interplay — about the *processes* of resource use and disposal that overload and degrade our natural environment; about the chilling *possibility* that untrammeled growth and uncontrolled technology would eventually destroy the ecosystem that sustains us; about the *methods*, both economic and technological, by which man can arrest or reverse the march to environmental ruin; and about the *directions of changes* in priorities and institutions needed to put these methods to work.

But empirically, we really know very little. In trying to determine the causal relationship, assess the trade-offs, and strike a reasoned cost-benefit balance between economic growth and environmental integrity, we constantly run into the unknown or unknowable (or even the unthinkable), into the unmeasured or unmeasurable (or even the infinite). Not surprisingly, then, much of what we "know," much of the evidence, is fragmentary and inconclusive. More disconcertingly, the findings are often contradictory. A case in point: qualified and concerned analysis of the energy-growth-environment linkage have arrived at radically different assessments of future shock to the environment — almost a "no-big-deal" versus a "crime-against-humanity" split on the projected impact of energy growth on the environment by the year 2000.

Humility should lead us, then, to acknowledge and define our collective ignorance, as well as our sparse knowledge, with two purposes in mind: 1. Identifying our joint research needs and priorities and 2. Shaping our responses to clear and present environmental dangers in light of that ignorance, i.e., pursuing courses of action that permit flexible and automatic adjustment to new information, new techniques, new values, and new resource parameters.(1)

But humility in the context of this forum calls for more. It demands a sensitivity in one discipline to the concepts, concerns, and convictions in another. Lest anyone fear, however, that I am about to submerge controversy in a sea of humility, let me reassure you. Let me set the framework for my further discussion in terms of the apparent differences in perception between ecologists and economists that have to be narrowed or reconciled if we are to make a productive joint attack on the growth-energy-environment problem. At many points, as you will see, I humbly beg to differ.

First, in starkest terms, the ecologist lays down an environmental imperative that requires an end to economic growth — or sharp curtailment of it — as the price of biological survival.(2) The economist counters with a socioeconomic imperative that requires the continuation of growth as the price of social survival. Some ecologists see the arresting of growth as a necessary, though not sufficient, condition for saving the ecosystem. The economist sees growth as a necessary, though not sufficient, condition for social progress and stability. To focus differences even more sharply, the economist tends to regard the *structure* rather than the *fact* of growth as the root of environmental evil and indeed views growth itself as one of the prerequisites to success in restoring the environment.

Second, the ecologist counters that the Great God Growth has feet of clay. In his view, if we counted the full costs of water, air, land, visual, and noise pollution — i.e., the drawing down of our environmental capital — the advance of measured gross national product (GNP) in the past quarter-century might well turn out to be an illusion. In responding, the economist is at pains to make clear that he is anything but Mecca-nistic about GNP. He is under no illusion that GNP is an index of social welfare (or, for that matter, that it is even feasible to construct a single index of welfare, or that greater material welfare is a guarantee of greater happiness). But he does believe that a careful reading of economic and social data yields persuasive evidence that real GNP per capita *has* advanced even after adjusting for increases in population, prices, and pollution; and that a rise in social welfare has accompanied the rise in output of goods and services.

Third, in a very real sense, the most vexing difference between ecologists and economists may not be in their conflicting interpretations of the evidence but in their divergent modes of thinking. At the risk of exaggerating a bit for emphasis, I perceive the dedicated environmentalist as thinking in terms of exponential rates of deterioration, thresholds, flash points, and of absolute limits to be dealt with by absolute bans. (And I confess to a bit of absolutism myself when it comes to roads in the North Cascades, oil exploration in Puget Sound, and 70,000 tons a day of taconite tailings dumped into Lake Superior.)

In basic approach, the economist could hardly agree less. He thinks in terms of marginalism, trade-offs, and a careful cost-benefit calculus — not marginalism in the sense of minor adjustments but in the sense of balancing costs and benefits at the margin. As he sees it, the right solution in striking a balance between nature and man, between environment and growth, and between technology and ecology, would be the one that pushes depollution to, but not beyond, the point where the costs — the forgone satisfactions of a greater supply of additional goods and services — just equal the benefits — the gained satisfaction of clear air, water, landscape, and sound waves. What the economist regards as rational is to seek, not total or *maximum* cleansing of the environment — prohibitions tend to be prohibitively expensive — but an *optimum* arising out of a careful matching of the "bads" that we overcome and the "goods" that we forgo in the process.

Fourth, when economists and ecologists turn to the search for solutions, they find a considerable area of agreement. They would agree, for example, that where the trade-off is between today's "goods" and tomorrow's "bads," government has to step in to enforce a rational calculus. Indeed, many environmental problems can be handled only by government prohibitions and regulations (mercury and DDT come to mind) and by public expenditures for collective sewage disposal, land reclamation, and environmental clean-up. They can also join in identifying the essentially costless changes that serve growth and the environment simultaneously, thus requiring no trade-offs. One thinks, for example, of technological advances that have substituted coal and oil for wood as energy sources (the per capita consumption of timber in the United States was no higher in 1968 than thirty years earlier) and have enabled us to reduce both costs and diesel engine pollution by moving oil and coal by pipeline rather than rail. And one looks forward to the day when thermal byproducts of energy production can be converted from pollutants to a productive source of space heating and cooling for industrial, commercial, and apartment buildings.

But where hard choices will have to be made, the economist wants to put as much of the load on the price system as it can efficiently carry. His main device would be to put price tags — for example, in the form of effluent fees or pollution permits or refundable materials fees — on the now largely free use of air, water, and land areas as dumping grounds for industrial and commercial wastes. The environmentalist's instinct is to recoil against this "license to pollute." By the same reasoning, perhaps, he feels way down deep that to let mineral resources and fossil fuels be managed through the pricing system constitutes a "license to exploit" the biosphere, a license that should be revoked or subjected to tighter regulation. But the economist wants to spread the net of the pricing mechanism widely to capitalize on its automaticity in digesting information and responding to it, its ability to integrate a vast range of decisions, its stimulus to natural resource conservation, and its lowering of demands on the government bureaucracy. His goal, of course, is not to collect fees or taxes but to build enough economic incentives into the market system to bring pollution to bay.

The Role of Economic Growth

Turning to the first of these four issues, one should keep in mind that the growth-versus-environment contest is in one sense a mismatch: economic growth is a means, an instrumental goal, while environmental quality is an end in itself, an important component of the quality of existence. In assessing the instrumental goal of growth, we need to inquire: 1. Whether it is growth itself, or its particular forms, that lead to environmental trouble (and if the latter, how production and technology can be redirected into environmentally more tolerable channels), 2. What social costs the nation would incur in giving up growth, and 3. Whether the war on pollution could, as a practical matter, be pressed and won without growth.

Can Growth Be Stopped?

To discuss the benefits of growth in the context of environmental quality implies, first, that a realistic option exists — one that is conceptually and institutionally possible — of stopping growth or slowing it to a crawl and, second, that there is a trade-off, an inverse relation, between the rate of economic growth and the quality of the natural environment.

Whether no-growth is a conceivable alternative depends first on the nature of the growth process and the sources of growth.(3) Growth of the U.S. economy in the basic sense of growth of output per capita is anchored in 1. increases in the stock of human capital through investments in education, training, and experience; 2. increases in the stock of nonhuman capital through investment in equipment, machinery, and plant; and 3. improvements in the state of U.S. scientific and managerial technology through investments in research and development, better management and organization, and more efficient production techniques. The deepest wellspring — the "major permissive source," as Simon Kuznets puts it — of modern economic growth is the advance of technology in its broadest economic sense, that is, the advance of knowledge.

Considering man's unquenchable thirst for understanding through better education and his enduring quest for increased knowledge and easier ways of doing things — through research and development, large-scale experimentation, and small-scale tinkering — one can only conclude that growth in output per man-hour cannot be stopped. Conceivably, total output could be held in check by highly restrictive taxes and tight monetary policy or by direct controls. Since output per man-hour would continue to rise, stopping total growth would require a rapid decline in the average workweek — one calculation puts it at twenty-six hours by 1980 — and a corresponding increase in leisure and non-market activity. (My secretary asks, "What's so bad about *that?*") This appraisal recognizes also that the labor force would continue to grow. Even with a zero population growth policy, it would take several decades to stabilize the population.(4)

The point of a no-growth policy would be to check and reverse the erosion of the environment. But there is nothing inherent in a no-growth economy that would change our polluting ways. So one has to posit active and costly steps to restore and protect the environment. This would require an absolute reduction in material living standards, as conventionally measured, in exchange for a more livable natural environment.

Just to sketch this picture is to raise serious questions of its social, political, and economic feasibility. Short of a believable threat of human extinction, it is hard to imagine that the public would accept the tight controls, lowered material living standards, and large income transfers required to create and manage a stationary state. Whether the necessary shifts could be accomplished without vast unemployment and economic dislocation is another question. The shift to a no-growth state of being might even throw the fragile ecology of our economic system so out of kilter as to threaten its breakdown. Having said this, let me quickly add that if the human race were to discover that it would be committing suicide unless it reduced its standard of living (at least for its affluent people), I dare say it would develop ways of managing the economic system to accommodate this necessity. Short of dire threats, however, economic growth seems destined to continue. To cope with growing contamination of the environment, the United States is thus driven to a redirection of growth and technology and to a reordering of priorities in the uses of growth.

But this still does not resolve the question of whether national policy makers should continue to stimulate growth or should seek consciously to retard it. That depends not just on the benefits of growth, which I will discuss in a moment, but on its environmental costs, on the growth-ecology trade-off. To the question of how much growth may have to be given up to protect the natural environment and maintain a habitable planet, both ecologists and economists offer a wide range of answers.

Among those who focus on global environmental problems, the spectrum runs from those who are persuaded that global pollution puts life on this planet in jeopardy to those who conclude that no one knows enough to answer the question. So far as I know, the category of ecologists (or economists, for that matter) who hold a "no-problem" view of this matter is an empty box. In its significant but selective survey, the group for the Study of Critical Environmental Problems (SCEP) offered some reassurance on the climatic effects of growth in output and fossil fuel energy but called for prompt counteraction to the ravages of toxic pesticides and heavy metals and excessive nutrient run-offs.(5)

Among economists there are those who accept the "spaceship earth" concept of finite limits to the assimilative capacity of the environment and who believe that growth will test those limits within relevant time horizons and must therefore be retarded. But a majority of the economics profession lean toward the findings of a recent econometric probe of this problem by William Nordhaus and James Tobin.

With respect to appropriable resources like minerals and fossil fuels, which the market already treats as economic goods, the Nordhaus-Tobin estimates show "little reason to worry about the exhaustion of resources." As in the past, rising prices of fossil fuels are expected to provide strong incentives for conserving supplies and developing substitute materials and processes. For nonappropriable resources, for "public goods" like air and water, they see the problem of abuse as much more serious. But the environmental disturbance and misdirection of resources that result from treating public natural resources as if they were free goods could, they believe, be corrected by charging for them. "The misdirection is due to a defect in the pricing system--a serious but by no means irreparable defect and one which would in any case be present in a stationary economy." With respect to global ecological collapse, they appropriately conclude that "there is probably very little that economists can say."(6)

The issue is far from resolved. But the evidence to date supports the view that it is less the *fact* of growth than the *manner* of growth and the *uses* made of growth that lie at the bottom of U.S. environmental troubles. And elusive as a consensus on the basic growth-environment trade-offs may be, it appears that a concensus on the urgency of changing the forms and uses of growth is already materializing. As a consequence, the nation already is being confronted with hard choices and the need for painful institutional changes. I submit that both are hard choices and the painful changes required to restore the environment will come much easier in an atmosphere of growth than of stagnation.

Turning to the benefits side of the picture, we are well advised, first of all, to take growth out of the one-dimensional context of the natural environment. In a broader context, the environmental claims against the bounties of growth must include shares not only for cleansing the physical environment of air, water, and food pollution and of urban congestion and sprawl, but also for: 1. Cleansing the social environment of the cancers of poverty, ignorance, malnutrition, and disease, 2. Cleansing the human environment of the degradation and blight of the urban ghetto and the rural slum, and 3. Cleansing our personal environment of the fear of crime and violence.

Even with the aid of a rise of 55 percent in GNP and 34 percent in real per capita personal income from 1959 to 1969, we have found in the United States that our inroads on these problems have not kept pace with our rising expectations and aspirations. Imagine the tensions between rich and poor, between black and white, between blue-collar and white-collar workers, between old and young, if we had been forced to finance even the minimal demands of the disadvantaged out of a no-growth national income instead of a one-third increase in that income.

A specific example may be instructive. Between 1959 and 1969 the number of persons below the poverty line fell from 39 million to 24 million, from 22.4 percent to 12.2 percent of a rising population. The improvement came from a 3 percent increase in productivity per year, a drop in unemployment from 6 percent to 4 percent, shifts of the poor from lower to higher income occupations and regions, and an extraordinary growth in governmental cash transfers, from over 2 billion in 1960 to over $50 billion in 1970. Every one of these factors was in some way the direct outgrowth of, or was associated with or facilitated by per capita economic growth.(7) Given their huge stake in growth as a source of the wherewithal and much of the will to improve their lot, the poor could be pardoned for saying, "Damn the externalities, full speed ahead."

Looking ahead, the Council of Economic Advisors projected a rise in real GNP (in 1969 dollars) of roughly $325 billion, or 35 percent, from 1970 to 1976. In the face of claims on these increases that are already staked out or clearly in the making — claims that leave only a small net "fiscal dividend" by 1976 — it will be hard enough to finance the wars on poverty, discrimination, and pollution even with vigorous economic growth.(8) Consider the problem in a no-growth setting: to wrench resources away from one use to transplant them in another, to wrest incomes from one group for transfer to another, to redeploy federal revenues from current to new channels (even assuming that we could pry loose a substantial part of the $70 billion devoted annually to military expenditures) — and to do all this on a sufficient scale to meet the urgent social problems that face us — might well involve us in unbearable social and political tensions.(9) In this context, one rightly views growth as a necessary condition for social advance, for improving the quality of the *total* environment.

Apart from the tangible bounties that growth can bestow, we should keep in mind some of its intangible dividends. Change, innovation, and risk thrive in an atmosphere of growth. It fosters a social mobility and opens up options that no stationary state can provide. This is not to deny that a no-growth economy, with its large rations of leisure, would appeal to those in the upcoming generation who lay less store by the work ethic and material goods than their forebears. But if they associate this with tranquility — in the face of the intensified struggle for shares of a fixed income on the part of their more numerous and more competitive contemporaries — I believe they are mistaken.

Let me return now to the context of the natural environment, to the growing consensus that we have to stop and reverse the ugly and destructive waste disposal practices of our modern society. To accomplish this, the taxpayer must foot huge bills to overcome past neglect as well as to finance future collective waste treatment and preserve open space and wilderness. Producers and consumers will have to bear the brunt of outright bans on ecologically dangerous materials and to pay rent for the use of the environment's waste assimilation services that they have been enjoying largely free of charge.

A modest estimate of the demands on the federal budget for an adequate environmental program would raise the present outlay of $5 billion a year to about $15 billion, an increase of some $50 billion over the next five years. Without growth, and given the limits to the congressional will to tax, how could we hope to raise the required revenues?

Or take the case of agricultural and industrial pollution. Imagine the resistance of producers to the internalizing of external costs in a society without expansion and the profit opportunities that go with it. How could consumers be induced to accept the necessary price increases in a world of fixed incomes? Again, if the only alternative, if the ultimate cost, were biological self-destruction, the answers would be different. But in the absence of that fate, or because of its extreme remoteness, growth enters as a vital social lubricant and is the best bet for getting people to give up private "goods" to overcome public "bads."

GNP and Social Welfare

To some of what I just said, the ecologist may reply, "Not so fast, not so fast — when you count all the costs, especially when you subtract the costs of chewing up the environment, you'll find that what you call growth in output and income since World War II is really a case of living off our environmental capital." Or he may say, "The composition of production has changed in such a way that we are no better off than twenty-five years ago." True, he may say these things, but the evidence does not bear him out. But if he adds, "GNP is a mighty sorry index of welfare, you'll have to show me something better than that in rebuttal," the economist says, "Right on!"

Granting that rising GNP is a poor index of human betterment is not to deny that one is generally associated with the other. It should require no lengthy demonstration to show that, while a significant part of GNP is illusory in a welfare sense,(10) wide differences and large advances in per capita GNP are associated with significant differences and advances in well-being. In a careful appraisal of the growth-welfare correlation, Robert Lampman found that a 26 percent gain in real GNP per capita from 1947 to 1962 brought with it a 26 percent gain in per capita private consumption, a distinct improvement in income security, and a significant reduction in poverty. He concluded: "All things considered, the pattern of growth in the United States in the post-war years yielded benefits to individuals far in excess of the costs it required of them. To that extent, our material progress has had humane content.(11)

A question that has more recently intrigued students of GNP is whether it is possible within the framework of a national accounts system to develop a better approximation of welfare. (Noneconomists may be pleased to hear that four observers who have written on this problem in the past four months have come up with four different positions on the subject.)

Economists labor under no illusion that GNP is a satisfactory measure of welfare or that it can be turned into one. They would agree with J. Petit-Senn that "not what we have, but what we enjoy, constitutes our abundance." What makes people think that GNP has become the economist's Holy Grail is the indispensable role it plays in measuring the economy's output potential and its performance in using that potential. It is highly useful and constantly used by economists as a guide to fiscal and monetary policy for management of aggregate demand, and as a measure of the availability of output to meet changing national priorities.

For these purposes, the emphasis of the national accounts must be primarily on market, and secondarily on governmental, demand and output since these are central to national stabilization policies and priority-setting.(12) And for these purposes, the national income and product accounts — with a bit of tinkering here and there — are generally respected and defended by economists.

But when the scene of battle moves to measurement of *social* performance, there is a sharp division of opinion over the possibility and advisability of modifying the GNP — or more properly, the net national product (NNP) — accounts to make them more useful in gauging social performance. Arthur Okun flatly rejected any such thought in his communication to the Office of Business Economics. "I urge that you not try to 'fix it'—to convert GNP into a purported measure of social welfare . . . Resist at all costs, because . . . nobody can do that job." Edward Denison writing in a somewhat similar vein, noted that to convert NNP into a welfare measure would require such unattainable measures as an index of real, rather than money, costs incurred in production; a measure of changes in needs that U.S. output must satisfy; measures of the quality of both the human and the physical environment; and a measure of the "goodness" of the size-distribution of income.(13)

Denison also weighed the possibility of getting a better measure of net gains from production by subtracting from the value of greater output the value of the environmental damage caused by producing it. But he concluded that the impossibility of measuring the "goodness" of the environment and the portion of its deterioration traceable to production rules out such an attempt; and that to deduct, as a proxy for that deterioration, outlays made to improve the environment is totally undesirable, since it would mean that the more resources we diverted from other uses to improve the environment, the more we would reduce measured NNP.

But F. Thomas Juster and the Nordhaus-Tobin team take quite a different tack. Juster proposed a comprehensive alternative framework for the national accounts, with emphasis on "extension and refinement of the existing accounts to make them more useful for the analysis of trends in social and economic welfare, while at the same time insuring that a market subsector is retained to facilitate cyclical analysis."(14)

Going beyond the Juster proposals, Nordhaus and Tobin have Boldly undertaken to appraise the rough quantitative significance of some of the deficiencies of GNP and, more particularly, of NNP as measures of economic welfare. The flavor of their pioneering probe is suggested by some of the adjustments they make in the NNP numbers (all in 1958 prices): 1. According to their estimates, putting dollar tags on the value of leisure and do-it-yourself work adds a huge $925 billion to the recorded NNP of $560 billion in 1965 (as against an add-on, for example, of $627 billion to the NNP of $292 billion in 1947). 2. They also add in almost $80 billion to represent the stream of services of private and public capital goods (against $37 billion in 1947), and 3. Their subtractions from NNP include $95 billion in 1965 (and $32 billion in 1947) representing "regrettables" like police services and national defense, that is, intermediate expenditures that are really costs, not enjoyments, of an advanced industrial society; $91 billion of capital consumption allowances in 1965 (versus $51 billion in 1946) and $101 billion for the capital-widening requirements of growth in 1965 (and a negative $5 billion in 1947); and an allowance of $31 billion in 1965 (as against $11 billion in 1947) for "disamenities" or "negative externalities" representing deterioration of the environment.

Having made these heroic adjustments, they concluded:

> There is no evidence to support the claim that welfare has grown less rapidly than NNP. Rather, NNP seems to underestimate the gain in welfare, chiefly because of its omission of leisure from consumption. Subject to the limitations of the estimates, we conclude that the economic welfare of the average American has been growing at a rate that doubles every 30 years.(15)

All observers agree that no amount of adjustment of the national accounts can capture the myriad values and subtleties that are required to measure social welfare. Indeed, no single index of social welfare can be calculated, because we have nothing like the pricing system to solve the impossible problem of attaching weights to the various components, be they pollution, crime, health, discrimination, or whatever. But to conclude that no *single* index can be constructed is not to undermine or discourage the efforts to develop a set of social indicators, not anchored in the GNP accounts, that will permit us to make better judgments on advances as well as failures in social performance.

Divergent Modes of Thought

Part of the difficulty in achieving, a meeting of the minds between economists and ecologists is that the economist tends to seek optimality by selecting the right procedures--for example, forcing the producer to bear the cost and the consumer to pay the price for waste-disposal access to the environment, thereby creating incentives to abate pollution — rather than prescribing the right outcome, namely, ending or drastically curtailing pollution. He is dedicated to that outcome but prefers to have the market system, rather than a government regulator, do as much of the work for him as possible. Whether a meeting of minds will evolve remains to be seen. Moderates in both camps are moving toward a middleground, but given existing attitudes, I doubt that full accommodation will be easy.

For his part, the ecologist will have to overcome his natural impatience with concepts of fine balancing of costs and benefits, an impatience that probably grows out of his feelings that cost-benefit analyses lack ethical content and moral inputs and that the more or less infinite benefits of environmental preservation make refined cost calculations more or less irrelevant. And he rightly stresses the nonlinearity of the cost curves of waste disposal as output rises: no-cost or low-cost in the early stages when discharges stay well within the absorptive capacity of the environment, then rising fairly sharply when accumulation and concentration begin to exceed that capacity, and exponentially when they saturate it.

For his part, the economist will have to break out of the web of marginal cost-benefit balance in cases where the relevant costs and benefits can't be captured in that web. (16) Irreparable damage—whether to human health by arsenic and lead poisoning, or to bald eagles by DDT, or to the Alaskan tundra by hot oil, or to the beauty of a canyon by a hydroelectric dam—cannot be handled by the fine tuning of marginalism. Nor is this approach applicable where the benefits are short-run and calculable while costs are long-run and incalculable. So the economist should beware of forcing onto the pricing mechanism jobs that it will almost surely do badly. But he rightly insists that, despite these limitations, the cost-benefit principle is applicable to a very broad range of pollution problems where measurements or reasonable approximations *are* possible.

The question of nonlinearity is a tougher one, in application if not in concept. Few would dispute that there is an initial zone where discharges are not pollutants, because they are well within the regenerative ability of land and water ecosystems that eliminate waste by cycling it through plants and animals and decomposers. Nor is it difficult to agree that, at the opposite end, costs can rise exponentially and ecocycles can be destroyed by overloading waters with nutrients, the atmosphere with noxious gases and particulate matter, and so on.

It is in the middle zone that things get sticky. An economist tends to believe that the zone of gradual and roughly linear rise in environmental damage is broad and that it widens—that the cost curve moves to the right—especially when the impetus of full-cost pricing moves science and technology to devise and put in place new techniques of waste disposal and recycling. Where the zone of tolerance or reasonable cost is very limited, as in the case of mercury, marginalism obviously won't do. The total or near-total ban is the only remedy. Whether mercury is a proxy for just a handful of cases or the forerunner of an exponential rise in contamination of the earth, land surface, air mass, and waterways, will determine in good part our relative reliance on total-ban versus marginal-adjustment approaches to environmental action.

The economist is inclined to doubt that such cases will multiply rapidly. Past demonstrations of the capacity of our economy, our technology, and our institutions to adapt and adjust to changing circumstances and shocks are impressive. We are still in the early stages of identifying, quantifying, and reacting to the multiple threats to our environment. It may be that we are too quick in accepting the concept of finite limits and closing physical frontiers implicit in the concept of spaceship earth (dramatized by Kenneth Boulding).(17) At least two previous episodes in U.S. history come to mind to suggest that we may yet escape (or push into the remote future) the ultimate biophysical limits, may yet be able to turn the ecological dials back from the "self-destruct" position without stopping growth in output, energy, technology, and living standards.

The first was the closing of America's geographical frontiers, which allegedly robbed the country of much of its mobility and dynamism. But other frontiers — scientific, technological, economic — soon opened up new vistas and opportunities, new frontiers that far surpassed any physical frontiers.

The second episode is much more recent. We do not need to stretch our memories very far to recall the great furor some twenty or twenty-five years ago about "running out of resources," especially energy, mineral, and other natural resources. We were being told by presidential commissions that we were about to exhaust our supplies of mineral resources and the productive potential of our agricultural land. But as we now know, intensive scientific research and technological development — responding partly to the alarms that were sounded but mostly to the signals sent out by the pricing system — resulted in the upgrading of old resources, the discovery of new ones, the development of substitutes, and the application of more efficient ways of utilizing available resources and adjusting to changes in relative availabilities.

Today, the problem is less one of limited resource availability and more one of growing threats to environmental quality and the metabolism of the biosphere. Concentrations of toxic and nondegradable wastes pose a mounting problem. But at this relatively early stage of our environmental experience and awareness, it seems premature to conclude that mounting problems are insurmountable. As our new knowledge and concern are translated into changes in our institutional arrangements and cost-price structure, strong incentives will be generated to redirect production and technology into less destructive channels.

Letting imagination soar a bit, one can conceive of scientific and technological discoveries enabling us to exploit solar energy, at least for purposes of photosynthesis, and perhaps even to build a proxy for the sun in the form of fusion power sometime in the next half century or so. Such developments might well provide the key to unlock the doors that the ecologist tells us are closing all around us. One gallon of water would give us the energy we now get from seven barrels of crude oil. Electricity would be penny cheap but no longer pound foolish. The recycling of wastes would be routine. The reconstituting of natural resources would come into the realm of the possible. I do not assert that this will happen, only that it may.

Coming back to our own era and moving from the global to the local impact of our environmental debauchery, one can also base some hope on the benign examples of what determination plus the application of fairly modest resources can do in reclaiming resources that once seemed beyond redemption. Striking examples are provided by the reclaiming of San Diego Bay, Lake Washington in Seattle, and the Thames near London (where dolphins again frolic). These examples are hardly decisive, but they offer a significant demonstration, in microcosm, that the process of ecological destruction can be halted and reversed once the volume of pollutants is reduced below the level of natural regeneration or dispersal. One should add that no rounded judgment is possible without taking into account whether pollution was curbed by recycling and changing waste into harmless forms or simply by redirecting the flows and discharging wastes into some other harmful form. The economist who lives by cost-benefit analysis must occasionally die by it.

Implicit in the foregoing discussion is that much of the difference between economists and ecologists on the speed and certainty of our descent into environmental hell rests in their divergent views on the role of technology. The ecologist sees pollution-intensive technology at the core of a mindless pursuit of economic growth. The economist points to the frequency of an inverse relationship between technological advance and pollution, as in materials-conserving and waste-recycling technology. And by institutional changes — such as creating property rights in, and charging for the use of, our collectively owned air, water, and landscape — he believes that technology will become ever more mindful of the environment.

What is important to note here is that the dichotomy runs much deeper than a disagreement on facts. For even if we accept Barry Commoner's verdict that the technology accompanying U.S. growth is the Frankenstein that is destroying our environment, there remains the critical operational question: Is this technology autonomous and out of control, an inevitable concomitant of growth? (18) Or does progress in science and technology respond to social and economic forces? If so, can it be bent to our will?

An affirmative answer to the last two questions is gaining support in recent investigations. The direction of technical changes in the private sector as well as the emphasis of research in the public sector are shown to respond to differences in the relative prices of resource endowments and other factors of production.(19) For decades the pattern of technical change has been biased in the direction of excessive production of residuals by zero-pricing or underpricing the use of the environment into which they are dumped. It follows that assessing the appropriate charges for waste-disposal (and putting the right prices on resource amenities) will not only improve the pattern of production to the benefit of the environment but will also stimulate pollution-abating technology. Indeed, as relative prices are changed to reflect real economic and social costs, the longer-run impact on the direction of technological effort may be considerably more important than the short-run resource allocation effects.(20)

As the biases on the cost and pricing system that make pollution profitable are diminished or eliminated, we may well find more technical complementarities than our limited experience leads us to think. Making pollution abatement mandatory by regulation or making continued pollution painfully costly by waste disposal charges will create a sharp spur to pollution-abatement technology. The relevant technology will no longer be treated on a corrective, bandaid, and after-thought basis, an approach that is likely to be inefficient and costly. Instead, it will be done on a preventive, built-in, and advanced-planning basis. Heartening examples of making virtue out of necessity in the form of profitable recycling already abound. And as economic growth leads to the replacement of old processes, equipment, and plants with new ones, it will hasten the change to cleaner and healthier methods of production.

This brings me back to an earlier theme. In the past, the market mechanism (with some assistance from government inducements, incentives, and research and development investments) altered the technical coefficients for traditional natural resources like coal, iron, and oil in response to the signals sent out by the pricing mechanism. Those resources were conserved, while the ones that were largely left out of the pricing mechanism suffered. If prices are put on them now by internalizing the external costs of air, water, quiet, and landscape, it seems reasonable to assume that the market mechanism will cause new shifts in resource use and technology leading us to conserve *these* resources and let Spaceship Earth cruise on a good deal longer.

Although ecologists and economists are not likely to agree on precisely how far the battle against pollution should be pushed -- on how many social and material goods should be given up to overcome environmental "bads" -- one perceives some early signs of convergence on the policy approaches and instruments that should be used in that battle. When Barry Commoner traces much of our trouble to the fact that "pollution pays" (or at least that pollution-intensive technology pays) and seven environmental organizations from the Coalition to Tax Pollution, economists and environmentalists are beginning to get on the same policy wave-length.(21)

A greater measure of agreement on the direction of environmental policy action need not and indeed does not imply agreement on ultimate goals, i.e., what level of pollution is tolerable. First, the ecologist is more conscious of, and gives more credence and weight to, pollution's hazards to health, life, and ecosystems. Second, the working environmentalist places a very high value on the aesthetics and amenities of the environment — he is willing to pay a higher price and a higher percentage of his income for a high-quality environment than is the population as a whole.

However strongly the economist may be committed personally to the environmental cause, he tends, first, to put relatively more weight on dangers arising from the social environment. He puts more emphasis on the trade-offs between environmental and social progress, perhaps regarding environmental deterioration as more reversible than social deterioration. Second, as an economist, he feels more bound by society's, than by his own, value judgment as to the desirable level of environmental quality, i.e., the permissible level of pollution.

A third kind of difference in objectives or focus arises out of the conflicting roles of economic growth as both a generator of pollution and a source of weapons to fight it. The ecologist tends to concentrate on the scarcity of physical and natural resources in the earth's skin and its limited supply of fossil fuels, metals, clear air, and water. The economist focuses on the scarcity of total resources, of the total supply of goods and services available in consumable form. Not surprisingly, then, the ecologist sees growth and the technology underlying it mainly as a part of the *problem*. The economist, viewing the huge costs and difficulties of redirecting resources to rescue the environment, regards the bounties of growth as a vital part of the *solution*.

I cannot attempt here anything like a thorough appraisal of the various components of a program to overcome pollution. But neither can I resist making some selected observations on the approaches the nation needs to take. For if we are indeed to make economic growth our environmental servant, not our master, we have to translate general principals and values into operational specifics without delay.

There is little disagreement among students of the environmental problem, of whatever discipline, that government has a vital direct role to play in providing public sewage disposal facilities; cleaning up the no-man's land of past pollution whose costs can no longer be internalized; preserving park, forest, and wilderness space; relieving congestion; developing pollution monitoring devices; and financing research in the techniques of pollution abatement and environmental protection.

Research in specific anti-pollution techniques and, more broadly, in pollution-averting technology is a particularly appropriate object of public sector support. Such research tends to be very costly. Since its benefits are largely external — much of the gain spills over to the benefit of other productive units and to future generations — private units are often unwilling or unable to incur its costs. In the energy field, the development of controlled thermonuclear fusion and of new methods to exploit solar energy fit into this category. Only government has the resources and the perspective to determine whether and how we can harness such energy sources.

In programming its own resource-using expenditures, government should also set an example by plugging in the implicit environmental costs. Military and space efforts, for example, are voracious consumers of energy and materials. This heavy draught on our physical environment should be given full weight in the cost-benefit calculations. We would find, I believe, that redirecting technical efforts and resources away from military and related space enterprises would have a high environmental payoff.

One should also underscore the need for sophisticated monitoring devices, both to measure waste and heat discharges and to measure the damage they do. Emissions of noxious gases, particulate matter, heat, and other effluents must be measured as a basis for administering either regulations or effluent charges. Yet the *amount* of any given discharge into the air, for example, tells us little about its actual *cost*. Even if we can measure the total load of gas and smog carried by the ambient air in a region, this does not tell us what costs are inflicted on things and people. To the extent possible, then, costs of corrosion of metal surfaces, deteriorated property values, damage to painted surfaces, impairment of health, and so on must be measured.

Even then, we have only begun to measure the costs of pollution and the benefits we will enjoy from curtailing it. What about cleaning and air conditioning bills, smarting eyes, loss of wildlife and recreational space, not to mention the subtle inroads on ecocycles? Even if we could measure these, we can at best only approximate, perhaps by polling techniques, the subjective values attached to clean water and air and quiet surroundings.

Balanced against the benefits must be an appraisal of the costs of installing anti-pollution machinery and processes or altering production techniques to overcome pollution. On these, we are getting more quantitative data and experience every day as we intensify anti-pollution efforts. In devising specific programs to restore the environment, we must be keenly aware of the need for improved cost and benefit information, and the importance of designing programs that take realistic account of our limited knowledge of actual costs and benefits.

As already mentioned, direct regulation and prohibition are instruments for environmental protection that must be used where intolerable dangers to health and life are involved or where irreversible and infinite damage to the environment is threatened. Also, a combination of regulations and user charges (22) may be the best way to go about certain pollution control problems, especially during a transitional period. For example, an absolute limit on emissions might be established by regulation to prevent really dangerous abuses of air or water at the same time that a uniform tax per unit of discharge is imposed as the main anti-pollution instrument. By and large, however, economists strongly prefer taxes and user charges to direct regulation on at least four grounds.

First, the regulatory power is often slow and cumbersome. By the time regulations are designed and applied, and then enforced through prolonged and costly court proceedings, much of the battle is lost.

Second, under the unrelenting pressure of producing units to internalize benefits and externalize costs, regulators bend more readily than tax collectors. Since the large and powerful can exercise far greater pressure than the small and weak, the impersonal and objective approach implicit in a tax per unit of discharge provides a fairer competitive environment. And for both large and small producers, it is a far healthier incentive atmosphere when energies are devoted, not to out-maneuvering the regulators, but to reducing pollution taxes by reducing pollution.

Third, fees or taxes accomplish any desired level of pollution abatement more cheaply than regulation. Reduce sulfur oxide pollution by a ban on emissions in excess of a certain amount, and all emitters have to conform to the regulation, even though the cost per unit of reduction will be far higher for some producers than for others. But put a tax on the emissions — a proportional or progressive penalty on discharge of sulfur oxide — and the factories that use processes conducive to low-cost cutbacks of pollution will reduce emissions more than those for whom it is a high-cost undertaking. Any prescribed quality of ambient air can be achieved at a lower cost through the proportional charge approach than through an arbitrary limit. And the incentive to depollute does not stop at some arbitrary cutoff point — the more pollution is cut, the lower the tax.

Fourth, by decentralizing some of the decision making and leaving discretion in the hands of the individual polluter to decide how far to go and what methods to use in minimizing his payments to the government, the tax or charge approach does not require as much centralized information. Also, the process of collecting the tax or charge will itself yield additional information -- and the level of the tax or charge can be fairly readily adjusted in the light of the new information. In a field beset by large factual gaps and uncertainties, this economizing of information is no small advantage.

The tax or charge is also far superior to the subsidy approach, which has two damning flaws. First, in its usual form — fast tax write-offs or direct subsidies for installation of pollution control equipment — it is a very costly way to stop pollution. In effect, it prescribes a particular way of doing the job. i.e., through waste treatment facilities, when there might be considerably cheaper ways of doing it, e.g., modifying production techniques, substituting less toxic for more toxic materials, recycling wastes, relocating production, and so on. Moreover, since the alternative is free use of the air and water for waste disposal, the subsidy may have to cover the full cost of abatement before the producer will accept it. The second flaw is found in the very nature of the subsidy. The subsidy does not internalize the costs, but simply shifts them from one segment of the public — the users of foul air and water — to another segment, the general taxpayer.

What kind of a system of taxes or user charges would be most effective? Fortunately, this question is engaging the energies and ingenuity of many economists today. Effluent charges, taxes, auctioning of pollution rights, materials-use fees — these are a few of the entries. The effluent fee, charge, or tax would simply charge so-and-so-much per unit of pollutant. The Coalition to Tax Pollution, for example, would tax sulfur emissions at 20 cents a pound by 1975, arriving at this level via four annual 5-cent steps. (23)

Another approach is to determine the permissible level of air or water pollution, issue certificates to pollute in this amount, and auction them off to the highest bidders. Competitive bidding for the certificates would raise the cost of pollution so high as to create a strong incentive to depollute.(24)

An intriguing proposal to impose a comprehensive materials-use fee has recently been made by Edwin Mills. He would charge a materials-use fee to the original producer or importer of specified materials removed from the environment. The level of the fee would be set high enough to cover the social cost of the most harmful way in which the material would normally be discharged into the environment. To the degree that the actual waste disposal was less harmful than the maximum, the fee would be refunded. Mill's proposal, though hardly operational in its present form, has the advantage of focusing on the total problem of materials disposal and making a comprehensive correction for the divergence between social costs and private costs.(25)

As a guide to thinking, the Mills proposal is particularly helpful because it underscores the fact that not just the level of output but the form of our technology and the nature of our disposal processes are important in determining the environmental impact of economic growth. True, as Allen Kneese notes, the physical law of the conservation of mass means that we don't really consume things in any ultimate sense. We simply change them from usables to residuals.(26) But even a growing mass of residuals can leave less and less pollution in its wake if we succeed in changing the form, the degree of recycling, the location, and the durability of those residuals in a constructive way. Under present institutional arrangements, the price system is rigged against constructive disposal. Once we redress the balance, it will be financially advantageous to minimize the burden of residuals on the environment.(27)

Before leaving the subject of charges and taxes, I should record several caveats and reminders. Even after we have devised workable techniques of internalizing the external costs of pollution, we still have to resolve a very difficult problem of choice. It is one in which the obvious and reasonably measurable costs of overcoming pollution are set against benefits that are in large part intangible and unmeasurable. Ths social cost of upgrading the quality of air or water is, if not yet known, at least knowable. The social benefit of an additional unit of water or air quality is in large part in the realm of values and hence unknowable. That does not, however, make the choice in any sense unique. Like many other social choices, it has to be made through the political process. Science can develop solutions and inform the political process, but it cannot dictate the answers.

Further, in setting up any system of charges, we should not overlook the potential for large-scale economies through collective methods of industrial waste disposal and recycling. We already do it in the treatment of municipal sewage. Perhaps there are opportunities for gathering liquid effluents, and possibly even smoke emissions, into central depollution and recycling facilities that would cost materially less per unit of output than handling them on a plant-by-plant basis. (The use of a Rhine tributary in this way is one case in point.) If it is kept in mind that the objective is to get the full costs of environmental use into the prices that consumers pay — and at the same time to cut those costs — rather than to force costs on individual producers, the net cost of pollution control may be reduced substantially.

The potential of other forms of institutional change should also be explored. For example, in seeking to minimize the intrusion on the environment associated with the production of energy, we should look not just at cleaner sources but at more efficient uses. Electricity is one of the most rapidly increasing uses of energy, yet we dump about two-thirds of the heat into the environment, using only one-third in constructive application. If we can develop complementarities through the joint production of steam and electricity for space heating and water heating and air conditioning, we could reduce both the energy costs and the related capital costs. The problem is institutional. The way the relevant industries are regulated and the products are priced joint production is not interesting. Moreover, we have the wrong urban design for the purpose. As it happens, what we need for efficient heat and energy use is also optimal for transportation and communication. Whether we would tolerate the drastic changes in zoning ordinances and the degree of central planning that would be required to achieve the potential complementarities and economies is very doubtful. But we should not ignore the possibilities.(28)

It should also be recognized that anything short of a comprehensive system of materials-use fees will require taxes not just on discharges from productive processes but also on the purchases of products whose use inflicts injury on the environment. The case of herbicides and pesticides is most directly in point. Levying taxes on the sale of these products will bring their use more in line with total social costs. And it will produce revenue to help government cleanse the water of eutrophying residuals.

Finally, as we work to terminate the subsidies that are implicit in our failure to charge for fouling the environment with liquid, solid, gaseous, and thermal wastes, we should also work to end the huge explicit subsidies in existing government programs that have the same effects, namely, to overstimulate high-pollution processes and technology, overproduce many products, and over-exploit natural resources. Agricultural subsidy programs that idle good land, with consequent chemical "overkill" to force more output from the remaining land, are one obvious example. Some aspects of transport regulation fall under a similar shadow.

But the most flagrant example is provided by our tax system. To continue stimulating the overexploitation of oil, coal, timber, and every mineral from iron to vermiculite and spodumene by big tax subsidies in the form of excessive depletion allowances, capital gains shelters, and special deductions becomes very more anomalous. Here is another case where the believers in the market-pricing system ought to live by it. The public is subsidizing these industries at least twice — once by rich tax bounties and once by cost-free or below-cost discharge of waste and heat.

Far from stimulating conservation and rational use of fossil fuels, both the form and the price impact of the tax preferences work the wrong way. In the case of oil, neither the percentage depletion allowances nor the deductions for intangible drilling, and development costs offer any incentive to more efficient and thorough exploitation of oil in the ground, no premium for fuller-recovery of the potential oil in the well. And since much of the subsidy is reflected in higher prices of oil lands and lower prices of oil products, economic incentives for full use of the available technology to achieve higher recovery ratios are once again reduced. Adding to the diseconomies are refinery discharges of effluents into the air and water, tanker flushings and spillages, offshore oil well fires and spills, all of which inflict costs on the general public and do not now find their way into the costs of production. The net result is to underprice and overproduce petroleum products and the energy derived from them. It should be noted that oil import quotas work, uneconomically, in the opposite direction, as do the tight oil allowables set by state regulatory commissions.)

Coal is another case in point. Its capital gains and percentage depletion preferences, while less flagrant than in the case of oil and gas, cut the price of mining coal below its social costs and hence speed up the rate of exploitation. The entire polluting sequence — from the strip mining that scores the land to the smoke and heat emissions involved in production — is magnified. With coal coming into generating plants at too low a cost, public utility commissions set the price of electricity below actual cost (private and˚social combined). Too much electricity is produced and sold. As a result, physical capital and other productive resources are pulled away from their optimal uses in other, less pollution-intensive industries. The net effect of tax subsidies interacting with failure to charge for the use of air and water is both a less efficient use of the nation's resources and a greater pressure on the environment.(29)

In the environmental context. the temptation is to make the tax preferences conditional on proof of nondespoiling extraction and nonpolluting utilization of coal. But this would load onto the tax system and Internal Revenue Service agents a burden of policing environmental crimes that they should not have to bear. In this case, the simplest solution (conceptually, though not politically) is also the most effective: end the specific tax subsidies as well as the general spillover cost subsidies that mining and drilling now enjoy.

As we increasingly inject the costs of waste disposal into the prices of our products, GNP may not suffer greatly in quantity, but it will change in quality, containing more environmental safeguards and amenities and less material output. Given the high income-elasticity of demand for environmental services, the intuitive reaction of most readers of this paper will be inwardly to smile with satisfaction.

But how will the poor and the black ghetto dweller view the matter? What do environmental attractions, aesthetics, and amenities mean to them? Perhaps they mean somewhat cleaner air and waste, but more pertinently they mean higher prices of the goods that will now bear the costs of producing those three A's and little help with what Congressman Charles Rangel from Harlem says: "ecology" means to his constituents: "Who's gonna collect the damned garbage!"

So before we at this forum take much solace in the improved mix of the national output as we see it, we had better be sure that the ghetto dweller is cut in on the environmental dividends as *he* sees them, and that as the prices of goods and services are raised because industry's free ride on public air and water and land is ended, the nation simultaneously, compensates the poor through more effective measures to redistribute income and opportunity.

Conclusion

In the complex and often baffling field of environmental control, no one surely not the economist has all the answers. But good economics is the handmaiden, not the enemy, of the good environment. What the economist believes he can contribute is a better understanding of how economic growth, cost-benefit analysis, and the market-pricing system can be made to work for us rather than against us in the battle to protect our natural environment and improve the quality of existence.

Those who defend economic growth rest their case essentially on the following points: 1. For all the misallocations and mistakes, environmental and otherwise, that have been made in the process of growth, it is still demonstrably true that growth in per capita GNP has been associated with rising levels of human well-being. 2. Much if not most of the environmental damage associated with growth is a function of the *way* we grow — of the nature of our technology and the forms of production. By prohibiting ecologically deadly or dangerous activities and forcing producers to absorb the cost of using air, water, and land areas for waste disposal, growth, technology, and production can be redirected into environmentally more tolerable channels. 3. To provide social and financial lubrication for this painful process as well as to repair the ravages of past neglect of the environment requires the resources, revenues, and rising incomes that growth can put at our disposal. 4. Side by side with the problem of restoring our physical environment is the even greater problem of overcoming the ills of our human and social environment. Those ills seem to be cumulating even faster and to be even more stubbornly, resistant to reversal than our environmental ills. How we could hope to cope with them and avoid unbearable sociopolitical tensions within the context of a stationary state is not apparent.

Coupled with a conviction that economic growth can more than atone for its sins is a belief that its environmental vices can be diminished and its virtues magnified by greater use of the pricing system, by putting appropriate price tags on use of the public environment for private gain. The economist readily recognizes that environmental quality is a highly subjective good on which it will be difficult to put those price tags. He also readily acknowledges that where damage to health, life, or the biosphere — either now or in the future — are severe or even infinite, the pricing system has neither the speed nor the capacity to deal with the problem.

But even recognizing such limits, the economist rightly asserts that across a large part of the pollution spectrum the pricing system *is* applicable. By charging producers — and ultimately consumers — for the full cost of waste disposal, their self-interest will be put to work in slowing or even reversing the march toward a degraded or exhausted environment.

To make economic growth not only compatible with, but a servant of, a high-quality environment won't be easy. Even after ecologists identify the source of the trouble, engineers identify solutions and develop monitoring devices, and economists identify appropriate taxing and pricing schemes, there remain crucial tests of public will and political skill. To get producers and consumers to pay the full cost of using the environment for waste disposal and to get the public to accept the reordered priorities and pay the higher taxes that will be needed to redirect growth and clean up past environmental mistakes will require great acts of both will and skill.

Notes

(1) After writing this, I encountered something in much the same vein in the introductory comments in the October 1970 *Bulletin of the Atomic Scientists* concerning the summary of the Massachusetts Institute of Technology Study of Critical Environmental Problems (SCEP); "One of the striking aspects of SCEP is its humility. It does not attempt to ring the doomsday bell. Rather, it stands as a sober, reflective, and careful statement of what man knows about the effects of these pollutants (carbon dioxide, sulfur dioxide, oxides of nitrogen, chlorinated hydrocarbons, other hydrocarbons, heavy metals, and oil) on the environment and what he has yet to learn. . . .It goes on to suggest what man can do about the problems he does understand and how he can acquire essential information about those he doesn't." The SCEP approach commends itself to this forum.

(2) I use the term "ecologist" here, not in the technical sense of a natural-systems biologist, but as a proxy for "noneconomist environmentalists."

(3) For an authoritative and detailed examination of this subject, see Edward F. Denison, *The Sources of Economic Growth in the United States and the Alternatives before Us* (Committee for Economic Development, 1962), and Denison's *Why Growth Rates Differ* (Brookings Institution, 1967).

(4) In *Economic Report of the President,* February 1970, p. 110, the Council of Economic Advisers reported that because of the high proportion of young people in the population, cutting the fertility rate to a level consistent with zero population growth would not stabilize the U.S. population until 2037 (at 276 million). Recent studies and new fertility data strongly suggest that, barring a reversal of present trends, the United States is already well on its way toward the desired slowdown or even stabilization of population growth. In a recent analysis, Glen G. Cain concluded that "the widely-discussed issue of the threat of the U.S. population bomb is. . . .a non-issue." ("Issues in the Economics of a Population Policy for the United States," a discussion paper of the Institute for Research on Poverty, the University of Wisconsin, 1971.) In the context of the RFF forum, it should also be noted that other new studies warn us that a slowdown or cessation of population growth won't solve as much of the environmental problem as we might hope. Ansley J. Coale, for example, stated, "There is no doubt that slower population growth would make it easier to improve our environment, but not much easier." ("Man and His Environment," *Science,* vol. 170, no 3954, October 9, 1970). Herman B. Miller, Chief of the Population Division of the Bureau of the Census, is more specific: "Two-thirds of the rise in expenditure for goods and services would take place even if our population stopped growing tomorrow but continued to increase its income and spend its money in the same old way." (*New York Times,* February 19, 1971.)

(5) The SCEP group concluded, for example, that "the probability of direct climate change in this century resulting from CO_2 is small, "though its long-term consequences might be large. With respect to particulate matter, SCEP found that "the area of greatest uncertainty in connection with the effects of particles on the heat balance of the atmosphere is our current lack of knowledge of their optical properties in scattering or absorbing radiation from the sun or the earth." On thermal pollution: "Although by the year 2000 global thermal power output may be as much as six times the present level, we do not expect it to affect global climate," but they noted that the problem of "heat islands" may become severe. They concluded that atmospheric oxygen is practically constant, having stood very close to 20,946 percent since 1910, and that "calculations show that depletion of oxygen by burning all the recoverable fossil fuels in the world would reduce it only to 20.800 percent." They recommended drastic curtailment of the use of DDT and mercury as well as the control of nutrient discharges, together with early development of technology to reclaim and recycle nutrients in areas of high concentration. (*Man's Impact on the Global Environment: Assessment and Recommendations for Action,* Report of the Study of Critical Environmental Problems sponsored by the Massachusetts Institute of Technology MIT Press, 1970, pp. 12, 13, 19, 75, 136, 138, 149).

(6) William Nordhaus and James Tobin, "Is Growth Obsolete?" (paper presented at the National Bureau of Economic Research Colloquium on Economic Growth, San Francisco, December 10, 1970, to be published by the NBER in the proceedings, 1972).

(7) Testimony of Robert J. Lampman in *Economic Opportunity Amendments of 1971.* Hearings before the Subcommittee on Employment, Manpower, and Poverty of the Senate Committee on Labor and Public Welfare, 92 Cong. 1 sess. (March 23, 1971).

(8) For the underlying numbers on GNP increases and the claims against them, see the *Economic Report of the President.* February 1971, p. 95. See also chap. 7 of Charles L. Schultze· and others, *Setting National Priorities: The 1972 Budget*

(Brookings Institution, 1971). Schultze and his colleagues projected a rise in real GNP (1970 dollars) of $353 billion. In current dollars (i.e., allowing for inflation), they foresee a rise from $977 billion in 1970 to $1,585 billion in 1976, a rise of $608 billion. Even with the resulting automatic growth of federal revenues from a full-employment-equivalent level of some $230 billion in fiscal 1972 to $312 billion in fiscal 1976, the "built-in" growth of federal expenditures would leave only a $17 billion net "fiscal dividend" in 1976 to utilize for new programs or expansion of existing programs (pp. 321-33).

(9) For example, in Robert S. Benson and Harold Wolman, eds., *Counterbudget: A Blueprint for Changing National Priorities, 1971-1976* (Praeger, 1971), the National Urban Coalition coverted the easy rhetoric of "reordering priorities" into a chart of specific needs. Putting most of its emphasis on "human development programs," the coalition called for a $52 billion rise in federal expenditures on health care in the next five years, $29 billion for income support, $11 billion for education, and $16 billion for aid to state and local governments. Even with its judgment that $24 billion could be cut from military spending over the next five years, this adds up to increased federal spending of nearly $100 billion — apart from the outlays on the battle against pollution!

(10) In the Godkin Lectures, five years ago, I put this point as follows: "If, as *byproducts* in our quest for growth, we destroy the purity of our air and water, generate ugliness and social disorder, displace workers and their skills, gobble up our natural resources, and chew up the amenities in and around our cities, the repair of that damage should have first call on the proceeds of growth. If the damage is essentially a private cost forced on society, as in the case of industrial effluents and smoke discharge, it should be forced back on those private units. But much of the problem and the cost can be met only by government. (If we could isolate that part of it which is a direct cost or byproduct of growth. . . .we should probably make a subtraction each year from our total output, an adjustment of our GNP figures, to take account of it.)" Walter Heller, *New Dimensions of Political Economy* (Harvard University Press, 1966), p. 111.

(11) Robert J. Lampman, "Recent U.S. Economic Growth and the Gain in Human Welfare," in Walter W. Heller, ed., *Perspectives on Economic Growth* (Random House, 1968), pp. 143-62.

(12) To be precise, net national product is the appropriate measure for gauging the quantity of output available to meet our needs — provided, of course, that the depreciation that represents the differences between GNP and NNP is calculated in a rational and consistent way.

(13) See the comments contributed by Arthur M. Okun to the 50th Anniversary Edition of the Department of Commerce *Survey of Current Business*, January 1972, preprinted in *Brookings Bulletin*, vol. 8, no. 3, Summer 1971; and Edward F. Denison, "Welfare Measurement and the GNP," *Survey of Current Business*, January 1971.

(14) His ambitious proposals are developed and explained in detail in "On the Measurement of Economic and Social Performance," *51st Annual Report of the National Bureau of Economic Research* (New York: September 1971), pp. 43-52. See also F. Thomas Juster, "A Framework for the Measurement of Economic and Social Performance"; Wassily Leontief, "National Income, Economic Structure, and Environmental Externalities"; and Orris C. Herfindahl and Allen V. Kneese, "Measuring Social and Economic Change" (papers delivered at the National Bureau of Economic Research Conference on Measurement of Economic and Social Performance, Princeton University, November 4-6, 1971, mimeo.).

(15) Nordhaus and Tobin, "Is Growth Obsolete?"

(16) The combination of high-intensity feed-grain farming with a high concentration of feedlots for livestock near urban centers may be a case in point. The

feed-grain farmer -- using chemical fertlizers, pesticides, and herbicides that increase both feed-grain yields and the nutrient runoff that ruins surrounding waters -- has been able to bring feed-grain prices down to a level that makes the concentrated feedlots profitable. They, in turn, discharge staggering quantities of animal wastes into urban sewage systems or onto the surrounding land and water. If some way is found of forcing the cost of this discharge back onto these "animal factories," the marginalist's reaction may be to invest in expensive equipment to recycle the wastes back to the land as substitutes for the present chemical fertilizers. But it is quite possible that the high-technology approach that is likely to result from marginal cost-marginal benefit thinking will be the more costly one. The optimal solution may be to decentralize, to go back to the more primitive recycling process of putting the cattle back on grazing land where they can turn forage into waste available as substitutes for chemical fertilizers. (On the other hand, if some agricultural economists are right in their belief that the animal factories are "economic" only because they do not have to absorb the costs of waste disposal, even the marginal approach may do the trick.)

(17) Kenneth Boulding, "The Economics of the Coming Spaceship Earth," in Henry Jarrett, ed., *Environmental Quality in a Growing Economy* (Johns Hopkins Press for Resources for the Future, 1966).

(18) One economist who answers in the affirmative is D. J. Mishan, who says: "As a collective enterprise, science has no more social conscience than the problem-solving computers it employs. Indeed, like some ponderous multi-purpose robot that is powered by its own insatiable curiosity, science lurches onward. . . ." (*Technology and Growth: The Price We Pay*, Praeger, 1970, p. 129).

(19) See, for example, Jacob Schmookler, *Invention and Economic Growth* (Harvard University Press, 1966), a searching study of inventive activity in which Schmookler concluded that the greater part of technical change in the United States has been a response to technical problems or opportunities perceived in economic terms.

(20) I am indebted to my colleague, Vernon W. Ruttan, for this line of thought. He develops and documents his thesis at length in "Technology and the Environment," the Presidential Address delivered before the American Agricultural Economics Association, August 16, 1971, to be published in a forthcoming issue of the *American Journal of Agricultural Economics*.

(21) In July 1971, the Coalition to Tax Pollution was formed by Environmental Action, Inc., The Federation of American Scientists, Friends of the Earth, Metropolitan Washington Coalition for Clean Air, the Sierra Club, The Wilderness Society, and Zero Population Growth. Their first target is the enactment of an effective tax on sulfur oxide emissions.

(22) Robert M. Solow has been particularly instructive on the subject of regulations and subsidies versus taxes in "The Economists' Approach to Pollution," his vice-presidential address to Section K of the American Association for the Advancement of Science, at the annual meeting in Chicago, December 1970. An adaptation of the address was published in *Science*, August 6, 1971.

(23) In its release on the subject (Washington, D.C., July 22, 1971) the Coalition said: "We believe that pollution taxes are a much-needed tactic to combat pollution. It will be necessary to make the economic self-interest of polluters consistent with the goal of a clean environment if we are to achieve this objective. Pollution taxes, unique among pollution control strategies, accomplish this."

(24) See J. H. Dales, *Pollution, Property, and Prices* (University of Toronto Press, 1968); and the discussion in *Economic Report of the President, February, 1971*, pp. 114-22.

(25) Edwin S. Mills, "User Fees and the Quality of the Environment," an essay to be published in a volume honoring Richard A. Musgrave, which will be edited by

Warren Smith, Department of Economics, University of Michigan.

(26) Allen V. Kneese, "Environmental Pollution: Economics and Policy," in American Economic Association, *Papers and Proceedings* (May 1971).

(27) For illuminating discussions of the role of the pricing system and means of putting it to work in preserving the environment, see the papers by Solow, Ruttan, and Mills already cited, as well as the article by Larry E. Ruff, "The Economic Common Sense of Pollution," *The Public Interest*, Spring 1970, pp. 69-85; R.U. Ayres and A.V. Kneese, "Production, Consumption and Externalities," *American Economic Review*, June 1969, pp. 282-97; and Hendrik S. Houthakker, "The Economy and the Environment" remarks before the Cleveland Business Economists Club, April 19, 1971, available as a mimeographed release by the Council of Economic Advisers, Washington, D.C.).

(28) My colleague, Ralph Hofmeister, provided the foregoing example.

(29) In the context of the earlier discussion of GNP impacts, one might note the resulting effect on the national accounts. Owing to resource transfers, the net effect on measured GNP has probably been limited. But GNP is overstated because the social costs of waste disposal and disamenities are not counted and subtracted, nor is the cost treated as a depreciation of our environmental capital.

AMERICAN INSTITUTIONS
AND
ECOLOGICAL IDEALS

Leo Marx

Anyone familiar with the work of the classic American writers (I am thinking of men like Cooper, Emerson, Thoreau, Melville, Whitman, and Mark Twain) is likely to have developed an interest in what we recently have learned to call ecology. One of the first things we associate with each of the writers just named is a distinctive, vividly particularized setting (or landscape) inseparable from the writer's conception of man. Partly because of the special geographic and political circumstances of American experience, and partly because they were influenced by the romantic vision of man's relations with nature, all of the writers mentioned possessed a heightened sense of place. Yet words like *place, landscape,* or *setting* scarcely can do justice to the significance these writers imparted to external nature in their work. They took for granted a thorough and delicate interpretation of consciousness and environment. In fact it now seems evident that these gifted writers had begun, more than a century ago, to measure the quality of American life against something like an ecological ideal.

The ideal I have in mind, quite simply, is the maintenance of a healthy life-enhancing interaction between man and the environment. This is a layman's language for the proposition that every organism, in order to avoid extinction or expulsion from its ecosystem, must conform to certain minimal requirements of that system. What makes the concept of the ecosystem difficult to grasp, admittedly, is the fact that the boundaries between systems are always somewhat indistinct, and our technology is making them less distinct all the time. Since an ecosystem includes not only all living organisms (plants and animals) but also the inorganic (physical and chemical) components of the environment, it has become extremely difficult, in the thermonuclear age, to verify even the relatively limited autonomy of local or regional systems. If a decision taken in Moscow or Washington can effect a catastrophic change in the chemical composition of the entire biosphere, then the idea of a San Francisco, or Bay Area, or California, or even North American ecosystem loses much of its clarity and force. Similar difficulties arise when we contemplate the global rate of human population growth. All this is only to say that, on ecological grounds, the care for world government is beyond argument. Meanwhile, we have no choice but to use the nation-states as political instruments for coping with the rapid deterioration of the physical world we inhabit.

The chief question before us, then, is this: What are the prospects, given the character of America's dominant institutions, for the fulfillment of this ecological ideal? But first, what is the significance of the current "environmental crusade"? Why should we be skeptical about its efficacy? How shall we account for the curious response of the scientific community? To answer these questions I will attempt to characterize certain of our key institutions from an ecological perspective. I want to suggest the striking convergence of the scientific and the literary criticism of our national life-style. In conclusion I will suggest a few responses to the ecological crisis indicated by that scientific-literary critique.

Limits of Conservationist Thought

In this country, until recently, ecological thinking has been obscured by the more popular, if limited, conservationist viewpoint. Because our government seldom accorded protection of the environment a high priority, much of the responsibility for keeping that end in view fell upon a few voluntary organizations known as the "conservation movement." From the beginning the movement attracted people with enough time and money to enjoy the outdoor life: sportsmen, naturalists (both amateur and professional), and of course property owners anxious to protect the sanctity of their rural or wilderness retreats. As a result, the conservationist cause came to be identified with the special interests of a few private citizens. It seldom, if ever, has been made to seem pertinent to the welfare of the poor, the nonwhite population, or, that matter, the great majority of urban Americans. The environment that mattered most to conservationists was the environment beyond the city limits. Witness the names of such leading organizations as the Sierra Club, the National Wildlife Federation, the Audubon Society, and the Izaac Walton League. In the view of many conservationists nature is a world that exists apart from, and for the benefit of, mankind.

The ecological perspective is quite different. Its philosophic root is the secular idea that man (including his works — the secondary, or man-made, environment) is wholly and ineluctably embedded in the tissue of natural process. The interconnections are delicate, infinitely complex , never to be severed. If this organic (or holistic) view of nature has not been popular, it is partly because it calls into question many presuppositions of our culture. Even today an excessive interest in this idea of nature carries, as it did in Emerson's and in Jefferson's time, a strong hint of irregularity and possible subversion. (Nowadays it is associated with the antibourgeois defense of the environment expounded by the long-haired "cop-outs" of the youth movement.) Partly in order to counteract these dangerously idealistic notions, American conservationists often have made a point of seeming hardheaded, which is to say, "realistic" or practical. When their aims have been incorporated in national political programs, notably during the administrations of the two Roosevelts, the emphasis has been upon the efficient use of resources under the supervision of well-trained technicians (1). Whatever the achievements of such programs, as implemented by the admirable if narrowly defined work of such agencies as the National Park Service, the U.S. Forest Service, or the Soil Conservation Service, they did not raise the kinds of questions about our overall capacity for survival that are brought into view by ecology. In this sense, conservationist thought is pragmatic and meliorist in tenor, whereas ecology is, in the purest meaning of the word, radical.

The relative popularity of the conservation movement helps to explain why troubled scientists, many of whom foresaw the scope and gravity of the environmental crisis a long while ago, have had such a difficult time arousing their countrymen. As early as 1864 George Perkins Marsh, sometimes said to be the father of American ecology, warned that the earth was "fast becoming an unfit home for its noblest inhabitant," and that unless men changed their ways it would be reduced "to such a condition of impoverished productiveness, of shattered surface, of climatic excess, as to threaten the depravation, barbarism, and perhaps even extinction of the species" (2). No one was listening to Marsh in 1864, and some 80 years later, according to a distinguished naturalist who tried to convey a similar warning, most Americans still were not listening. "It is amazing," wrote Fairfield Osborn in 1948 (3, p. 194), "how far one has to travel to find a person, even among the widely informed, who is aware of the processes of mounting destruction that we are inflicting upon our life sources."

The Environment Crusade, circa 1969

But that was 1948, and, as we all know, the situation now is wholly changed. Toward the end of the 1960's there was a sudden upsurge of public interest in the subject. The devastation of the environment and the threat of overpopulation became too obvious to be ignored. A sense of anxiety, close to panic seized many people, including politicans and leaders of the communications industry. The mass media began to spread the alarm. Television gave prime coverage to a series of relatively minor yet visually sensational ecological disasters. Once again, as in the coverage of the Vietnam War, the close-up power of the medium was demonstrated. The sight of lovely beaches covered with crude oil, hundreds of dead and dying birds trapped in the viscous stuff, had an incalculable effect upon a mass audience. After years of indifference, the press suddenly decided that the jeremiads of naturalists might be important news, and a whole new vocabulary (*environment, ecology, balance of nature, population explosion,* and so on) entered common speech. Meanwhile, the language of reputable scientists was escalating to a pitch of excitement comparable with that of the most fervent young radicals. Barry Commoner, for example, gave a widely reported speech describing the deadly pollution of California water reserves as a result of the excessive use of nitrates as fertilizer. This method of increasing agricultural productivity, he said, is so disruptive of the chemical balance of soil and water that within a generation it could poison irreparably the water supply of the whole area. The *New York Times* ran the story under the headline: "Ecologist Sees U.S. on Suicidal Course" (4). But it was the demographers and population biologists, worried about behavior even less susceptible to regulatory action, who used the most portentous rhetoric. "We must realize that unless we are extremely lucky," Paul Ehrlich told an audience in the summer of 1969, "everybody will disappear in a cloud of blue steam in 20 years" (5).

To a layman who assumes that responsible scientists choose their words with care, this kind of talk is bewildering. How seriously should he take it? He realizes, of course, that he has no way, on his own, to evaluate the factual or scientific basis for these fearful predictions. But the scientific community, to which he naturally turns, is not much help. While most scientists calmly go about their business, activists like Commoner and Ehrlich dominate the headlines. (One could cite the almost equally gloomy forecasts of Harrison Brown, George Wald, René Dubos, and a dozen other distinguished scholars.) When Anthony Lewis asked a "leading European biologist" the same question — how seriously should one take this idea of the imminent extinction of the race?—the scholar smiled, Lewis reports, and said, "I suppose we have between 35 and 100 years before the end of life on earth" (6). No — what is bewildering is the disparity between words and action, between the all-too-credible prophecy of disaster and the response — or rather the nonresponse — of the organized scientific community. From a layman's viewpoint, the professional scientific organizations would seem to have an obligation here — where nothing less than human survival is in question — either to endorse or to correct the pronouncements of their distinguished colleagues. If a large number of scientists do indeed endorse the judgment of the more vociferous ecologists, then the inescapable question is: What are they doing about it? Why do they hesitate to use the concerted prestige and force of their profession to effect radical changes in national policy and behavior? How is it that most scientists, in the face of this awful knowledge, if indeed it is knowledge, are able to carry on business more or less as usual? One might have expected them to raise their voices, activate their professional organizations, petition the Congress, send delegations to the President, and speak out to the people and the government. Why, in short, are they not mounting a campaign of education and political action?

Why Are Most Scientists Undisturbed?

The most plausible answer seems to be that many scientists, like many of their fellow citizens, are ready to believe that such a campaign already has begun. And if, indeed, one accepts the version of political reality disseminated by the communications industry, they are correct: the campaign *has* begun. By the summer of 1969 it had become evident that the media were preparing to give the ecological crisis the kind of saturation treatment accorded the civil rights movement in the early 1960's and the anti-Vietnam War protest after that. (Observers made this comparison from the beginning.) Much of the tone and substance of the campaign was set by the advertising business. Thus, a leading teen-age magazine, *Seventeen*, took a full-page ad in the *New York Times* to announce, beneath a picture of a handsome collegiate couple strolling meditatively through autumn leaves, "The environment crusade emphasizes the fervent concerns of the young with our nation's 'quality of life.' Their voices impel us to act now on the mushrooming problems of conservation and ecology" (7). A more skeptical voice might impel us to think about the Madison Avenue strategists who had recognized a direct new path into the lucrative youth market. The "crusade," as they envisaged it, was to be a bland, well-mannered, clean-up campaign, conducted in the spirit of an adolescent love affair and nicely timed to deflect student attention from the disruptive political issues of the 1960's. A national survey of college students confirmed this hope. "Environment May Eclipse Vietnam as College Issue," the makers of the survey reported, and one young man's comment seemed to sum up their findings: "A lot of people are becoming disenchanted with the anti-war movement," he said. "People who are frustrated and disillusioned are starting to turn to ecology" (8). On New Year's Day 1970, the President of the United States joined the crusade. Adapting the doomsday rhetoric of the environmentalists to his own purposes, he announced that "the nineteen-seventies absolutely must be the years when America pays its debt to the past by reclaiming the purity of its air, its waters and our living environment. It is literally now or never" (9).

Under the circumstances, it is understandable that most scientists, like most other people (except for the disaffected minority of college students), have been largely unresponsive to the alarmist rhetoric of the more panicky environmentalists. The campaign to save the environment no longer seems to need their help. Not only have the media been awakened, and with them a large segment of the population, but the President himself, along with many government officials, has been enlisted in the cause. On 10 February 1970, President Nixon sent a special message to the Congress outlining a comprehensive 37-point program of action against pollution. Is it any wonder that the mood at recent meetings of conservationists has become almost cheerful — as if the movement, at long last, really had begun to move? After all, the grim forecasts of the ecologists necessarily have been couched in conditional language, thus: *If* California farmers continue their excessive use of nitrates, *then* the water supply will be irreparably poisoned. But now that the facts have been revealed, and with so much government activity in prospect, may we not assume that disaster will be averted? There is no need, therefore, to take the alarmists seriously—which is only to say that most scientists still have confidence in the capacity of our political leaders, and of our institutions, to cope with the crisis.

But is that confidence warranted by the current "crusade"? Many observers have noted that the President's message was strong in visionary language and weak in substance. He recommended no significant increase in funds needed to implement the program. Coming from a politician with a well-known respect for strategies based on advertising and public relations, this high-sounding talk should make us wary. Is it designed to protect the environment or to assuage anxiety or to distract the antiwar movement or to provide the cohesive force necessary for national unity behind the Republican administration? How can we distinguish the illusion of activity fostered by the media — and the President — from auguries of genuine action? On this score, the frequently invoked parallel of the civil rights and the antiwar movements should give us pause. For, while each succeeded in focusing attention upon a dangerous situation, it is doubtful whether either got us very far along toward the elimination of the danger. At first each movement won spectacular victories, but now, in retrospect, they too look more like ideological than substantive gains. In many ways the situation of blacks in America is more desperate in 1970 than it was in 1960. Similarly, the war in Southeast Asia, far from having been stopped by the peace movement, now threatens to encompass other countries and to continue indefinitely. This is not to imply that the strenuous efforts to end the war or to eradicate racism have been bootless. Some day the whole picture may well look quite different; we may look back on the 1960's as the time when a generation was prepared for a vital transformation of American society.

Nevertheless, scientists would do well to contemplate the example of these recent protest movements. They would be compelled to recognize, for one thing, that, while public awareness may be indispensable for effecting changes in national policy, it hardly guarantees results. In retrospect, indeed, the whole tenor of the civil rights and antiwar campaigns now seems much too optimistic. Neither program took sufficient account of the deeply entrenched, institutionalized character of the collective behavior it aimed to change. If leaders of the campaign to save the environment were to make the same kind of error, it would not be surprising. A certain innocent trust in the efficacy of words, propaganda, and rational persuasion always has characterized the conservation movement in this country. Besides, there is a popular notion that ecological problems are in essence technological, not political, and therefore easier to solve than the problems of racism, war, or imperialism. To indicate why this view is a mistaken one, why in fact it would be folly to discount the urgency of the environmental crisis on these grounds, I now want to consider the fitness of certain dominant American institutions for the fulfillment of the ecological ideal.

Seen from an ecological perspective, a salient characteristic of American society is its astonishing dynamism. Ever since the first European settlements were established on the Atlantic seaboard, our history has been one of virtually uninterrupted expansion. How many decades, if any, have there been since 1607 when this society failed to expand its population, territory, and economic power? When foreigners speak of Americanization they invariably have in mind this dynamic, expansionary, unrestrained behavior. "No sooner do you set foot upon American ground," wrote de Tocqueville, "than you are stunned by a kind of tumult; a confused clamor is heard on every side, and a thousand simultaneous voices demand the satisfaction of their social wants. Everything is in motion around you. . ."(10). To be sure, a majority of these clamorous people were of European origin, and their most effective instrument for the transformation of the wilderness — their science and technology — was a product of Western culture. But the unspoiled terrain of North America gave European dynamism a peculiar effervescence. The seemingly unlimited natural resources and the relative absence of cultural or institutional restraints made possible what surely has been the fastest-developing, most mobile, most relentlessly innovative society in world history. By now that dynamism inheres in every aspect of our lives, from the dominant national ethos to the structure of our economic institutions down to the deportment of individuals.

The ideological counterpart to the nation's physical expansion has been its celebration of quantity. What has been valued most in American popular culture is growth, development, size (bigness), and — by extension — change, novelty, innovation, wealth, and power. This tendency was noted a long while ago, especially by foreign travelers, but only recently have historians begun to appreciate the special contribution of Christianity to this quantitative expansionary ethos. The crux here is the aggressive, man-centered attitude toward the environment fostered by Judeo-Christian thought: everything in nature, living or inorganic, exists to serve man. For only man can hope (by joining God) to transcend nature. According to one historian of science, Lynn White (11), the dynamic thrust of Western science and technology derives in large measure from this Christian emphasis, unique among the great world religions, upon the separation of man from nature.

But one need not endorse White's entire argument to recognize that Americans, from the beginning, found in the Bible a divine sanction for their violent assault upon the physical environment. To the Puritans of New England, the New World landscape was Satan's territory, a hideous wilderness inhabited by the unredeemed and fit chiefly for conquest. What moral precept could have served their purpose better than the Lord's injunction to be fruitful and multiply and subdue the earth and exercise dominion over every living creature? Then, too, the millennial cast of evangelical protestantism made even more dramatic the notion that this earth, and everything upon it, is an expendable support system for man's voyage to eternity. Later, as industrialization gained momentum, the emphasis shifted from the idea of nature as the devil's country to the idea of nature as commodity. When the millennial hope was secularized, and salvation was replaced by the goal of economic and social progress, it became possible to quantify the rate of human improvement. In our time this quantifying bent reached its logical end with the enshrinement of the gross national product — one all-encompassing index of the state of the nation itself.

Perhaps the most striking thing about this expansionary ethos, from an ecological viewpoint, has been its capacity to supplant a whole range of commonsense notions about man's relations with nature which are recognized by some preliterate peoples and are implicit in the behavior of certain animal species. These include the ideas that natural resources are exhaustible, that the unchecked growth of a species will eventually lead to its extinction, and that other organisms may have a claim to life worthy of respect.

The Expansionary System

The record of American business, incomparably successful according to quantitative economic measures like the gross national product, also looks quite different when viewed from an ecological perspective. Whereas the environmental ideal I have been discussing affirms the need for each organism to observe limits set by its ecosystem, the whole thrust of industrial capitalism has been in the opposite direction: it has placed the highest premium upon ingenious methods for circumventing those limits. After comparing the treatment that various nations have accorded their respective portions of the earth, Fairfield Osborn said this of the United States (3, p. 175): "The story of our nation in the last century as regards the use of forests, grasslands, wildlife and water sources is the most violent and the most destructive in the long history of civilization." If that estimate is just, a large part of the credit must be given to an economic system unmatched in calling forth man's profit-making energies. By the same token, it is a system that does pitifully little to encourage or reward those constraints necessary for the long-term ecological well-being of society. Consider, for example, the fate of prime agricultural lands on the borders of our burgeoning cities. What happens when a landowner is offered a small fortune by a developer? Who sees to it that housing, factories, highways, and shopping centers are situated on the far more plentiful sites where nothing edible ever will grow? The answer is that no such agencies exist, and the market principle is allowed to rule. Since World War II approximately one-fifth of California's invaluable farm land has been lost in this way. Here, as in many cases of air and water pollution, the dominant motive of our business system—private profit—leads to the violation of ecololgical standards.

Early in the industrial era one might reasonably have expected, as Thorstein Veblen did, that the scientific and technological professions, with their strong bent toward rationality and efficiency, would help to control the ravening economic appetites whetted by America's natural abundance. Veblen assumed that well-trained technicians, engineers, and scientists would be repelled by the wastefulness of the business system. He therefore looked to them for leadership in shaping alternatives to a culture obsessed with "conspicuous consumption." But, so far, that leadership has not appeared. On the contrary, this new technical elite, with it commitment to highly specialized, valuefree research, has enthusiastically placed its skill in the service of business and military enterprise. This is one reason, incidentally, why today's rebellious young are unimpressed by the claim that the higher learning entails a commitment to rationality. They see our best-educated, most "rational" elite serving what strikes them as a higher irrationality. So far from providing a counterforce to the business system, the scientific and technological professions in fact have strengthened the ideology of American corporate capitalism, including its large armaments sector, by bringing it to their high-minded faith in the benign consequences of the most rapidly accelererating rate of technological innovation attainable.

But not only are we collectively committed, as a nation, to the idea of continuing growth; each subordinate unit of the society holds itself to a similar standard of success. Each state, city, village, and neighborhood; each corporation, independent merchant, and voluntary organization; each ethnic group, family, and child — each person — should, ideally speaking, strive for growth. Translated into ecological terms, this popular measure of success — becoming bigger, richer, more powerful — means gaining control over more and more of the available resources. When resources were thought to be inexhaustible, as they were thought to be throughout most of our national history, the release of these unbounded entrepreneurial energies was considered an aspect of individual liberation. And so it was, at least for large segments of the population. But today, when that assumption no longer makes sense, those energies are still being generated. It is as if a minaturized version of the nation's expansionary ethos had been implanted in every citizen — not excluding the technicians and scientists. And when we consider the extremes to which the specialization of function has been carried in the sciences, each expert working his own minuscule sector of the knowledge industry, it is easier to account for the unresponsiveness of the scientific community to the urgent warnings of alarmed ecologists. If most scientists and engineers seem not to be listening, much less acting, it is because these highly skilled men are so busy doing what every good American is supposed to do.

On the other hand, it is not surprising that a clever novelist like Norman Mailer (12), or a popular interpreter of science like Rachel Carson (13), or an imaginative medical researcher like Alan Gregg (14) each found it illuminating in recent years to compare the unchecked growth of American society, with all the resulting disorder, to the haphazard spread of cancer cells in a living organism. There is nothing new, of course, about the analogy between the social order and the human body; the conceit has a long history in literature. Since the early 1960's, however, Mailer has been invoking the more specific idea of America as a carcinogenic environment. Like any good poetic figure, this one has a basis in fact. Not only does it call to mind the radioactive matter we have deposited in the earth and the sea, or the work of such allegedly cancer-producing enterprises as the tobacco and automobile industries, or the effects of some of the new drugs administered by doctors in recent years, but, even more subtly, it reminds us of the parallel between cancer and our expansionary national ethos, which, like a powerful ideological hormone, stimulates the reckless, uncontrolled growth of each cell in the social organism.

In the interests of historical accuracy and comprehensiveness, needless to say, all of these sweeping generalizations would have to be extensively qualified. The record is rich in accounts of determined, troubled Americans who have criticized and actively resisted the nation's expansionary abandon. A large part of our government apparatus was created in order to keep these acquisitive, self-aggrandizing energies within tolerable limits. And of course the full story would acknowledge the obvious benefits, especially the individual freedom and prosperity, many Americans owe to the very dynamism that now threatens our survival. But in this brief compass my aim is to emphasize that conception of man's relation to nature which, so far as we can trace its consequences, issued in the *dominant* forms of national behavior. And that is a largely one-sided story. It is a story, moreover, to which our classic American writers, to their inestimable credit, have borne eloquent witness. If there is a single native institution which has consistently criticized American life from a vantage like that of ecology, it is the institution of letters.

America's Pastoral Literature

A notable fact about imaginative literature in America, when viewed from an ecological perspective, is the number of our most admired works written in obedience to a pastoral impulse (15). By "pastoral impulse" I mean the urge, in the face of society's increasing power and complexity, to retreat in the direction of nature. The most obvious form taken by this withdrawal from the world of established institutions is a movement in space. The writer or narrator describes, or a character enacts, a move away from a relatively sophisticated to a simpler, more "natural" environment. Whether this new setting is an unspoiled wilderness, like Cooper's forests and plains, Melville's remote Pacific, Faulkner's Big Woods, or Hemingway's Africa, or whether it is as tame as Emerson's New England village common, Thoreau's Walden Pond, or Robert Frost's pasture, its significance derives from the plain fact that it is "closer" to nature: it is a landscape that bears fewer marks of human intervention.

This symbolic action, which reenacts the initial transit of Europeans to North America, may be understood in several ways, and no one of them can do it justice. To begin with, there is an undeniable element of escapism about this familiar, perhaps universal desire to get away from the imperatives of a complicated social life. No one has conveyed this feeling with greater economy or simplicity than Robert Frost in the first line of his poem "Directive": "Back out of all this now too much for us." Needless to say, if our literary pastoralism lent expression only to this escapist impulse, we would be compelled to call it self-indulgent, puerile, or regressive.

But fortunately this is not the case. In most American pastorals the movement toward nature also may be understood as a serious criticism, explicit or implied, of the established social order. It calls into question a society dominated by a mechanistic system of value, keyed to perfecting the routine means of existence, yet oblivious to its meaning and purpose. We recall Thoreau's description, early in *Walden*, of the lives of quiet desperation led by his Concord neighbors, or the first pages of Melville's *Moby-Dick*, with Ishmael's account of his moods of suicidal depression as he contemplates the meaningless work required of the inhabitants of Manhattan Island. At one time this critical attitude toward the workaday life was commonly dismissed as aristocratic or elitist. We said that it could speak only for a leisure class for whom deprivation was no problem. But today, in a society with the technological capacity to supply everyone with an adequate standard of living, that objection has lost most of its force. The necessary conditions for giving a decent livelihood to every citizen no longer include harder work, increased productivity, or endless technological innovation. But of course such an egalitarian economic program would entail a more equitable distribution of wealth, and the substitution of economic sufficiency for the goal of an endlessly "rising" standard of living. The mere fact that such possibilities exist explains why our literary pastorals, which blur distinctions between the economic, moral, and esthetic flaws of society, now seem more cogent. In the 19th century, many pastoralists, like today's radical ecologists, saw the system as potentially destructive in its innermost essence. Their dominant figure for industrial society, with its patent confusion about ends and means, was the social machine. Our economy is the kind of system, said Thoreau, where men become the tools of their tools.

Of course, there is nothing particularly American about this pessimistic literary response to industrialism. Since the romantic movement it has been a dominant theme of all Western literature. Most gifted writers have expended a large share of their energy in an effort to discover—or, more precisely, to imagine—alternatives to the way of life that emerged with the industrial revolution. The difference is that in Europe there was a range of other possible lifestyles which had no counterpart in this country. There were enclaves of preindustrial culture (provincial, esthetic, religious, aristocratic) which retained their vitality long after the bourgeois revolution, and there also was a new, revolutionary, urban working class. This difference, along with the presence in America of a vast, rich, unspoiled landscape, helps to explain the exceptionally strong hold of the pastoral motive upon the native imagination. If our writers conceived of life from something like an ecological perspective, it is largely because of their heightened sensitivity to the unspoiled environment, and man's relation to it, as the basis for an alternative to the established social order.

What, then, can we learn about possible alternatives from our pastoral literature? The difficulty here lies in the improbability which surrounds the affirmative content of the pastoral retreat. In the typical American fable the high point of the withdrawal toward nature is an idyllic interlude which gains a large measure of its significance from the sharp contrast with the everyday, "real" world. This is an evanescent moment of peace and contentment when the writer (or narrator, or protagonist) enjoys a sense of integration with the surrounding environment that approaches ecstatic fulfillment. It is often a kind of visionary experience, couched in a language of such intense, extreme, even mystical feeling that it is difficult for many readers (though not significantly, for adherents of today's youth culture) to take it seriously. But it is important to keep in view some of the reasons for this literary extravagence. In a commercial, optimistic, self-satisfied culture, it was not easy for writers to make an alternate mode of experience credible. Their problem was to endow an ideal vision — some would call it utopian — with enough sensual authenticity to carry readers beyond the usual, conventionally accepted limits of commonsense reality. Nevertheless, the pastoral interlude, rightly understood, does have a bearing upon the choices open to a postindustrial society. It must be taken, not as representing a program to be copied, but as a symbolic action which embodies values, attitudes, modes of thought and feeling alternative to those which characterize the dynamic, expansionary life-style of modern America.

The focus of our literary pastoralism, accordingly, is upon a contrast between two environments representing virtually all aspects of man's relation to nature. In place of the aggressive thrust of 19th-century capitalism, the pastoral interlude exemplifies a far more restrained, accommodating kind of behavior. The chief goal is not, as Alexander Hamilton argued it was, to enhance the nation's corporate wealth and power, rather it is the Jeffersonian "pursuit of happiness." In economic terms, then, pastoralism entails a distinction between a commitment to unending growth and the concept of material sufficiency. The aim of the pastoral economy is *enough*— enough production and consumption to insure a decent quality of life. Jefferson's dislike of industrialization was based on this standard; he was bent on the subordination of quantitative to qualitative "standards of living."

From a psychological viewpoint, the pastoral retreat affirmed the possibility of maintaining man's mental equilibrium by renewed emphasis upon his inner needs. The psychic equivalent of the balance of nature (in effect the balance of *human* nature) is a more or less equal capacity to cope with external and internal sources of anxiety. In a less-developed landscape, according to these fables, behavior can be more free, spontaneous, authentic—in a word, more natural. The natural in psychic experience refers to activities of mind which are inborn or somehow primary. Whether we call them intuitive, unconscious, or preconscious, the significant fact is that they do not have to be learned or deliberately acquired. By contrast, then, the expansionary society is figured forth as dangerously imbalanced on the side of those rational faculties conducive to the manipulation of the physical environment. We think of Melville's Ahab, in whom the specialization of function induces a peculiar kind of power-obsessed, if technically competent, mentality. "My means are sane," he says, "my motive and my object mad."

The suspicion of the technical, highly trained intellect comports with the emphasis in our pastoral literature upon those aspects of life that are common to all men. Whereas the industrial society encourages and rewards the habit of mind which analyzes, separates, categorizes, and makes distinctions, the felicity enjoyed during the pastoral interlude is a tacit tribute to the opposite habit. This kind of pleasure derives from the connection-making, analogizing, poetic imagination — one that aspires to a unified conception of reality. At the highest or metaphysical level of abstraction, then, romantic pastoralism is holistic. During the more intense pastoral interludes, an awareness of the entire environment, extending to the outer reaches of the cosmos, affects the perception of each separate thing, idea, event. In place of the technologically efficient but limited concept of nature as a body of discrete manipulatable objects, our pastoral literature presents an organic conception of man's relation to his environment.

A Convergence of Insights

What I am trying to suggest is the striking convergence of the literary and the ecological views of America's dominant institutions. Our literature contains a deep intuition of the gathering environmental crisis and its causes. To be sure, the matter-of-fact idiom of scientific ecology may not be poetic or inspiring. Instead of conveying Wordsworthian impulses from the vernal wood, it reports the rate at which monoxide poisoning is killing the trees. Nevertheless, the findings of ecologists confirm the indictment of the self-aggrandizing way of life that our leading writers have been building up for almost two centuries. In essence it is an indictment of the destructive power-oriented uses to which we put scientific and technological knowledge. The philosophic source of this dangerous behavior is an arrogant conception of man, and above all of human consciousness, as wholly unique — as an entity distinct from, and potentially independent of, the rest of nature.

As for the alternative implied by the pastoral retreat, it also anticipates certain insights of ecology. Throughout this body of imaginative writing, the turn toward nature is represented as a means of gaining access to governing values, meanings, and purposes. In the past, to be sure, many readers found the escapist, sentimental overtones of this motive embarrassing. As a teacher, I can testify that, until recently, many pragmatically inclined students were put off by the obscurely metaphysical, occultish notions surrounding the idea of harmony with nature. It lacked specificity. But now all that is changing. The current environmental crisis has in a sense put a literal, factual, often quantifiable base under this poetic idea. Nature as a transmitter of signals and a dictator of choices now is present to us in the quite literal sense that the imbalance of a ecosystem, when scientifically understood, defines certain precise limits to human behavior. We are told, for example, that if we continue contaminating Lake Michigan at the present rate, the lake will be "dead" in roughly 10 years. Shall we save the lake or continue allowing the cities and industries which pollute it to reduce expenses and increase profits? As such choices become more frequent, man's relations with nature will in effect be seen to set the limits of various economic, social, and political practices. And the concept of harmonious relations between man and the physical environment, instead of seeming to be a vague projection of human wishes, must come to be respected as a necessary, realistic, limiting goal. This convergence of literary and scientific insight reinforces the naturalistic idea that man, to paraphrase Melville, must eventually lower his conceit of attainable felicity, locating it not in power or transcendence but in a prior need to sustain life itself.

Assuming that this sketch of America's dominant institutions as seen from a pastoral-ecological vantage is not grossly inaccurate, what inferences can we draw from it? What bearing does it have upon our current effort to cope with the deterioration of the environment? What special significance does it have for concerned scientists and technologists? I shall draw several conclusions, beginning with a specific recommendation for action by the American Association for the Advancement of Science.

First, then, let me propose that the Association establish a panel of the best qualified scientists, representing as many as possible of the disciplines involved, to serve as a national review board for ecological information. The board would take the responsibility for locating and defining the crucial problems (presumably it would recruit special task forces for specific assignments) and make public recommendations whenever feasible. To be sure, some scientists will be doing a similar job for the government, but, if an informed electorate is to evaluate the government's program, it must have an independent source of knowledge. One probable objection is that scientists often disagree, and feel reluctant to disagree in public. But is this a healthy condition for a democracy? Perhaps the time has come to lift the dangerous veil of omniscience from the world of science and technology. If the experts cannot agree, let them issue minority reports. If our survival is at stake, we should be allowed to know what the problems and the choices are. The point here is not that we laymen look to scientists for *the* answer, or that we expect them to save us. But we do ask for their active involvement in solving problems about which they are the best-informed citizens. Not only should such a topflight panel of scientists be set up on a national basis, but — perhaps more important — similar committees should be set up to help make the best scientific judgment available to the citizens of every state, city, and local community.

But there will also be those who object on the ground that an organization as august as the American Association for the Advancement of Science must not be drawn into politics. The answer, of course, is that American scientists and technologists are now and have always been involved in politics. A profession whose members place their services at the disposal of the government, the military, and the private corporations can hardly claim immunity now. Scientific and technological knowledge unavoidably is used for political purposes. But it also is a national resource. The real question in a democratic society, therefore, is whether that knowledge can be made as available to ordinary voters as it is to those, like the Department of Defense or General Electric, who can most easily buy it. If scientists are worried about becoming partisans, then their best defense is to speak with their own disinterested public voice. To allow the burden of alerting and educating the people to fall upon a few volunteers is a scandal. Scientists, as represented by their professional organizations, have a responsibility to make sure that their skills are used to fulfill as well as to violate the ecological ideal. And who knows? If things get bad enough, the scientific community may take steps to discourage its members from serving the violators.

There is another, perhaps more compelling, reason why scientists and technologists, as an organized professional group, must become more actively involved. It was scientists, after all, who first sounded the alarm. What action we take as a society *and how quickly we take it* depends in large measure upon the credibility of the alarmists. Who is to say, if organized science does not, which alarms we should take seriously? What group has anything like the competence of scientists and technologists to evaluate the evidence? Or, to put it negatively, what group can do more, by mere complacency and inaction, to insure an inadequate response to the environmental crisis? It is a well-known fact that Americans hold the scientific profession in the highest esteem. So long as most scientists go about their business as usual, so long as they seem unperturbed by the urgent appeals of their own colleagues, it is likely that most laymen, including our political representatives, will remain skeptical.

The arguments for the more active involvement of the scientific community in public debate illustrate the all encompassing and essentially political character of the environmental crisis. If the literary-ecological perspective affords an accurate view, we must eventually take into account the deep-seated, institutional causes of our distress. No cosmetic program, no clean-up-the-landscapes activity, no degree of protection for the wilderness, no antipollution laws can be more than the merest beginning. Of course such measures are worthwhile, but in undertaking them we should acknowledge their superficiality. The devestation of the environment is at bottom a result of the kind of society we have built and the kind of people we are. It follows, therefore, that environmentalists should join forces, whenever common aims can be found, with other groups concerned to change basic institutions. To arrest the deterioration of the environment it will be necessary to control many of the same forces which have prevented us from ending the war in Indochina or giving justice to black Americans. In other words, it will be necessary for ecologists to determine where the destructive power of our society lies and how to cope with it. Knowledge of that kind, needless to say, is political. But then it seems obvious, on reflection, that the study of human ecology will be incomplete until it incorporates a sophisticated mode of political analysis.

Meanwhile, it would be folly, given the character of American institutions, to discount the urgency of our situation either on the ground that technology will provide the solutions or on the ground that countermeasures are proposed. We cannot rely on technology because the essential problem is not technological. It inheres in all of the ways in which this dynamic society generates and uses its power. It calls into question the controlling purposes of all the major institutions which actually determine the nation's impact upon the environment: the great business corporations, the military establishment, the universities, the scientific and technological elites, and the exhilarating expansionary ethos by which we all live. Throughout our brief history, a passion for personal and collective aggrandizement has been the American way. One can only guess at the extent to which forebodings of ecological doom have contributed to the revulsion that so many intelligent young people feel these days for the idea of "success" as a kind of limitless ingestion. In any case, most of the talk about the environmental crisis that turns on the word *pollution*, as if we face a cosmic-scale problem of sanitation, is grossly misleading. What confronts us is an extreme imbalance between society's hunger--the rapidly growing sum of human wants--and the limited capacities of the earth.

References and Notes

(1) S.P. Hays, *Conservation and the Gospel of Efficiency* (Harvard Univ. Press, Cambridge, Mass., 1959).

(2) *Man and Nature,* David Lowenthal, Ed. (Harvard Univ. Press, Cambridge, Mass., 1965), p. 43.

(3) F. Osborn, *Our Plundered Planet* (Little, Brown, Boston, 1948).

(4) *New York Times* (19 Nov. 1969).

(5) *Ibid.* (6 Aug. 1969).

(6) *Ibid.* (15 Dec. 1959).

(7) *Ibid.* (5 Dec. 1969).

(8) *Ibid.* (30 Nov. 1969).

(9) *Ibid.* (2 Jan. 1969).

(10) A. de Tocqueville, *Democracy in America,* Phillips Bradley, Ed. (Knopf, New York, new ed. 1946), vol. 1, p. 249.

(11) L. White, Jr. *Science* 155, 1203 (1967).

(12) N. Mailer, *Cannibals and Christians* (Dial, New York, 1966).

(13) R. Carson, *Silent Spring* (Houghton Mifflin, Boston, 1962).

(14) A. Gregg, *Science* 121, 681 (1955).

(15) L. Marx, *The Machine in the Garden: Technology and the Pastoral Ideal in America* (Oxford Univ. Press, New York, 1964).

(16) For comment and criticism I thank my Amherst colleagues L. Brower, B. DeMott, J. Epstein, R. Fink, A. Guttmann, W. Hexter, G. Kateb, R. Snellgrove, W. Taubman, and J.W. Ward; I also thank W. Berthoff, D. Lowenthal, J. Marx, B. McKie, and N. Podhoretz.

THE
RECOMMENDATIONS
OF THE
COMMISSION
ON
POPULATION
GROWTH
AND THE
AMERICAN
FUTURE

INTRODUCTION

The report of the Commission on Population Growth and the American Future is unquestionably the most authoritative statement on the present character of population change and its implications for the nation. Although some people and groups are unable to accept certain of the Commission's recommendations, especially those involving abortion and the provision of contraceptive aid to minors, few have seriously challenged its assessment of the current condition and future course of population developments in the United States. The evidence assembled by the Commission is very impressive. Its conclusions and recommendations are based upon two years of deliberations by twenty-four Commission members representing many diverse constituencies. Their efforts were aided by public hearings and a large number of research papers contributed by a veritable "Who's Who" of American population scientists.

Three chapters from the Commission's report are presented here. Although the full report of the Commission deserves careful reading, these selections reflect the Commission's major concern that the United States check its current rate of population growth and move toward population stabilization — a condition in which births would balance deaths so that, the effects of immigration aside, the size of the nation's population would remain constant. Alan Sweezy discusses the various approaches the United States might take to population stabilization, the likelihood that they might be taken, and the costs entailed.

As the Commission notes, it is time to make choices about future population growth in the United States and such choices involve fundamental questions about the values and goals of our society. It argues that the slowing of demographic growth and eventual population stabilization would provide opportunities to improve the quality of life as well as relieving specific pressures on the economy, society, government, resources, and the environment that are produced by continued increases in the size of our population. In its complete report, the Commission details the specific impact of population growth on each of these areas. The only areas considered here are the related topics of resources and the environment.

As is true with each of the other topics considered, the Commission in terms of resources and environment, could find no compelling argument for continued population growth. Rather, such growth would commit the nation to a "more rapid depletion of domestic and international resources, greater pressures on the environment, greater dependence on continued rapid technological development to solve these problems, and a more contrived and regulated society."

The Commission makes one additional point that can serve us well in the quotation above. Problems are not just demographic or environmental. They are technological and social as well. A failure to check population growth, for example, may require us to address resource problems with new and untried technologies that may be harmful. Further, we may be faced with alterations in life style or even in basic values that may be difficult to accept. The Commission's recommendations are consistent with these concerns and merit careful consideration in their own right. But its specification of the interrelationship between population, the environment (including resources), technology, values, and the social structure is especially worthy of emphasis. It is a theme that has been encountered in previous selections and it is an idea to which we shall next turn in the final section of this volume.

RESOURCES
AND THE
ENVIRONMENT

What are the likely future impacts of population growth on the demand for resources and on the environment in the United States? Here, we have examined the consequences of the population growing according to the 2-child projection and the 3-child projection, and compared the results. For problems such as air pollution, where local concentrations are important, we have examined the implications of population growth in local areas as well as in the nation as a whole.

For several resource and environmental topics, we have extended the analysis beyond the year 2000 to the year 2020; in so doing, we have identified some important effects that do not become particularly noticeable in the shorter period. Beyond the next 50 years, we do not know enough to make quantitative projections. Nonetheless, it is obvious that there are ultimate limits to growth. We live in a finite world. While its limits are unknown because technology keeps changing them, it is clear that the growth of population and the escalation of consumption must ultimately stop. The only questions are when, how, and at what level. The answers to these questions will largely be determined by the course of world population growth, including that of the United States.

Several general conclusions emerge from our research:

1. Population growth is one of the major factors affecting the demand for resources and the deterioration of the environment in the United States. The further we look into the future, the more important population becomes.

2. From an environmental and resource point of view, there are no advantages from further growth of population beyond the level to which our past rapid growth has already committed us. Indeed, we would be considerably better off over the next 30 to 50 years if there were a prompt reduction in our population growth rate. This is especially true with regard to problems of water, agricultural land, and outdoor recreation.

3. While the nation can, if it has to, find ways to solve the problems growth creates, we will not like some of the solutions we will have to adopt. With continued growth, we commit ourselves to a particular set of problems: more rapid depletion of domestic and international resources, greater pressures on the environment, greater dependence on continued rapid technological development to solve these problems, and a

more contrived and regulated society. So long as population growth continues, these problems will grow and will slowly, but irreversibly, force changes in our way of life. And there are further risks: Increasing numbers press us to adopt new technologies before we know what we are doing. The more of us there are, the greater is the temptation to introduce solutions before their side effects are known. With slower population growth leading to a stabilized population, we gain time to devise solutions, resources to implement them, and greater freedom of choice in deciding how we want to live in the future

4. The American future cannot be isolated from what is happening in the rest of the world. There are serious problems right now in the distribution of resources, income, and wealth, among countries. World population growth is going to make these problems worse before they get better. The United States needs to undertake much greater efforts to understand these problems and develop international policies to deal with them.

How Population Affects Resources and the Environment

The pressure that this nation puts on resources and the environment during the next 30 to 50 years will depend on the size of the national population, the size of population in local areas, the amounts and types of goods and services the population consumes, and the ways in which these goods and services are produced, used, and disposed of. All these factors are important. Right now, because of our large population size and high economic productivity, the United States puts more pressure on resources and the environment than any other nation in the world.

We have attempted to separate these factors and estimate the impact of population on resources and the environment using a quantitative model which shows the demand for resources and the pollution levels associated with different rates of economic and population growth. The seriousness of the population-induced effects has then been assessed by evaluating the adequacy of resources to meet these requirements and the environmental impacts of pollution.

In discussing the economy, we indicated that under any set of economic projections, the total volume of goods and services produced in the United States — the gross national product — will be far larger than it is today. It is expected to be at least twice its present size by the year 2000, and in 50 years, with rapid population and economic growth, it could be seven times as large as it is now. Regardless of future population growth, the prospect is that increases in output will cause tremendous increases in demand for resources and impact on the environment.

What happens to population growth will nevertheless make a big difference in the future size of the economy. In the year 2000, the difference in GNP resulting from the different population assumptions could amount to one-fourth of today's GNP. By the year 2020, this difference amounts to more than the total size of today's GNP.

In short, total GNP, which is the principal source of the demand for resources and the production of pollutants, will become much larger than it is now. But if population should grow at the 3-child rate, GNP will grow far more than it will at the 2-child rate.

Minerals

In our research, we examined the demand for 19 major nonfuel minerals: chromium, iron, nickel, potassium, cobalt, vanadium, magnesium, phosphorous, nitrogen, manganese, molybdenum, tungsten, aluminum, copper, lead, zinc, tin, titanium, and sulfur.

Resource consumption will rise more slowly if population grows more slowly. Our estimates indicate that the amount of minerals consumed in the year 2000 would average nine percent lower under the 2-child than under the 3-child population projection. The difference in annual consumption would be 17 percent in the year 2020, and would grow rapidly thereafter.

Population growth exerts an important effect on resource consumption compared with the effect of economic growth. Our research shows that in the year 2000, if GNP per capita were one percent less than projected, the consumption of most minerals would be 0.7 to 1.0 percent less; the consumption of four minerals—cobalt, magnesium, titanium, and sulfur— would be reduced relatively more. In the year 2000, if population were one percent less than projected, minerals consumption would be 0.5 to 0.7 percent less. The population effect, while substantial, is smaller because of an important offsetting effect. As we saw earlier, slower population growth induces higher output per person because of the favorable ratio of labor force to total population. This offsets somewhat the effect that smaller numbers have on the conservation of resources.

While there are clear resource savings from slower population growth, our research supports, with certain qualifications, the view that the United States would have no serious difficulty acquiring the supplies it needs for the next 50 years, even if the population were to grow at the 3-child rate. This is the prospect, even assuming, as we have done, that the resource demands of the rest of the world grow more rapidly than those of the United States, as has been the case in recent years. Although growing demand may pose some problems of adjustment, adequate supplies of all the minerals we studied can be achieved through tolerable price increases. Price increases will equalize supply and demand by stimulating exploration or imports (increased supply) and by stimulating recycling and the use of more plentiful substitutes (reduced demand). The earth's crust still contains immense quantities of lower grade minerals which can be called into production at levels of costs which we could afford to pay, even if the demands of the rest of the world should rise as projected and our population were to grow at the 3-child rate.

This expectation could be altered by several developments. First, prices could fail to anticipate impending shortages; that is, they might not rise long enough in advance to stimulate the changes necessary to avert shortages. Second, mining operations are heavy polluters, and mineral needs could conflict with environmental policy. Finally, and most serious, there are worldwide imbalances in access to resources. While the United States will remain among the "haves," relatively speaking, disparities between world regions may affect international power balances in ways that would involve us.

Energy

Energy makes the difference between poverty and affluence. The reason per capita income in the United States is so high is that the average American worker has at his command more energy, chiefly in the form of electricity, than any other worker in the world. With energy we refine aluminum, make rubber, shape steel, form new synthetic chemical compounds, propel automobiles, and heat our homes.

How much energy we have available depends on the availability of the necessary fuels and on our ability to convert the fuels to energy—the greatest advance in this regard was the development of inexpensive methods of electricity production. The technology of fuels acquisition and the technololgy of energy conversion are both critical. So is purchasing power — the ability to pay for domestic development of fuels or to import them. The original inhabitants of North America occupied a continent rich in energy fuels. But they neither knew how to get the fuels out of the ground nor how to convert them to energy. Some modern countries with advanced means of energy conversion lack their own fuel supplies; they buy them from other countries.

The ability of the United States to meet its future energy needs will be determined chiefly by developments in technology—the technology of conversion and the technology of fuels acquisition. A major question will be whether we can find methods that are environmentally safe. Virtually every stage of energy use—fuel production, delivery, conversion, and consumption—has a significant environmental impact. For example, one third of all coal is produced by strip mining, and the consequence is a scarred landscape and severe runoff into streams and rivers. Oil spills which contaminate the oceans and beaches may result from offshore drilling. Much airborne pollution comes from the use of such relatively dirty fuels as coal and oil. Some scientists are beginning to raise the possibility of thermal pollution resulting from concentrated use of energy in local areas. Nuclear power generation requires the disposal of radioactive atomic wastes. Because of these problems, the development of energy-production capacity could be impaired.

The increase in our energy needs will be immense under any projection, although not as large under the 2-child population projection as under the 3-child projection. The relative difference in energy demands under the different population projections is about the same as for minerals, and it becomes very large after the population with the lower rate of growth stabilizes. Whether population growth will strain fuel supplies, or cause serious environmental damage in the process of acquiring and using the necessary fuels, depends on future developments in technology.

With no major changes in technology, oil and gas supplies could become a problem for the United States by the year 2000—we would be importing more and paying higher prices, and supplies would certainly be a problem for some world regions. These problems could be averted if we found inexpensive means of using such potential sources as oil shale and tar sands, but using these sources is likely to have environmental consequences as serious as those from the strip-mining of coal. If we unlock the secrets of atomic fission, we could have an environmentally clean way of generating electricity, with no fuel supply problem. The energy from converting the deuterium contained in 30 cubic kilometers of seawater would equal that of the earth's original supply of coal and petroleum.

Our review of the energy situation indicates that high priority ought to be given to research and development in clean sources of energy production. The faster population grows, the more urgent such breakthroughs become. We turn now to several areas where population growth dominates other considerations—where we cannot be hopeful about the ability of purchasing power and technical development to avert population problems.

Water

Water requirements already exceed available flow in the southwestern United States. Our research shows that growing population and economic activity will cause the area of water shortage to spread eastward and northward across the country in the decades ahead. Such deficits will spread faster if population growth follows the 3-child projection than if it follows the 2-child projection. This will occur despite large expenditures on water treatment, dams, and reservoirs during the next 50 years. Population growth will be more important than economic growth in causing these growing problems.

Our national abundance of water does not change this picture significantly. If water could be shipped across the country like oil, coal, or manufactured goods, there would be no problems of water shortage. But distances are so long and the amounts of water used so huge, that it would be prohibitively expensive to solve these regional problems by transfers of water from surplus to deficit areas. Nor is there scope for sufficiently large relocation of water users—people and industries—to regions where water is plentiful. An inexpensive method of taking the salt out of seawater could solve the problem, but such technology is not now available. Similarly, artificial control of rain is not advanced enough to be used to any significant extent. While little is known about the extent of groundwater reserves, most experts do not consider the

Figure 1   Regional Water Deficits: Billions of Gallons Per Day

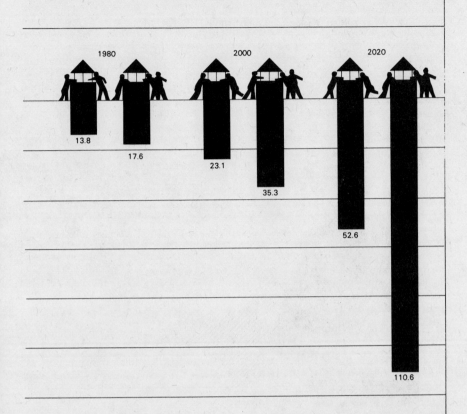

1980 — 13.8 — 17.6
2000 — 23.1 — 35.3
2020 — 52.6 — 110.6

Despite an abundance of water nationally, rapid population growth will cause the extent and severity of regional water deficits to spread more rapidly than they would with slower population growth. This is the case even assuming maximum development of water storage facilities and tertiary treatment of waste water. Chart shows projected effects of growth at 2-child and 3-child rates.

Estimates assume rapid economic growth.

Source: Derived from Ronald G. Ridker, "Future Water Needs and Supplies, with a Note on Land Use" (prepared for the Commission, 1972).

mining of such reserves an adequate alternative.

On the other hand, there is wide scope for reducing use through rationing and the adoption of water conserving technology. Even today, most water is used virtually free of cost or is distributed on a fee basis that provides no incentives for conservation; and free use of water bodies as waste dumping grounds is more the rule than the exception. If the cost of utilizing water for these purposes were raised to more appropriate levels, factories and power plants would install techniques of production that save water instead of wasting it; farmers would modify their irrigation practices or otherwise adjust by changing location or shifting to crops using less water, and households would eventually adjust by reducing lawns and shrubbery.

Sooner or later we will have to deal with water as a scarce resource. The sooner this is done, the fewer water crises will emerge in the years ahead. However, doing this will not be easy technically or politically—most water supplies are run by local governments. And few will like the austerity created by the need to conserve on something as fundamental as water. The rate of national population growth will largely determine how rapidly we must accomplish these changes.

Figure 2   Water Deficit Regions: 3-Child Family

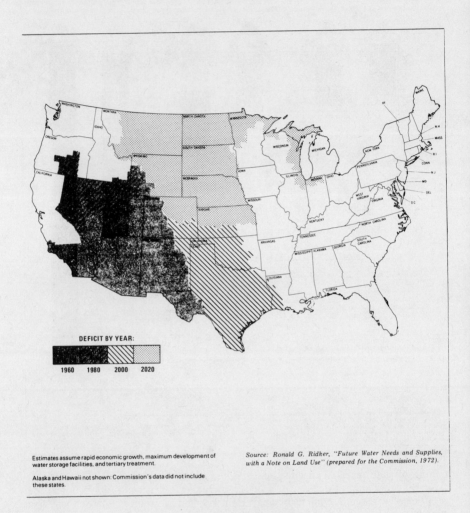

DEFICIT BY YEAR:

1960   1980   2000   2020

Estimates assume rapid economic growth, maximum development of water storage facilities, and tertiary treatment.

Alaska and Hawaii not shown: Commission's data did not include these states.

Source: Ronald G. Ridker, "Future Water Needs and Supplies, with a Note on Land Use" (prepared for the Commission, 1972).

Outdoor Recreation

On a recent holiday weekend, Yosemite National Park had a population of 50,000 people, according to a Park source. Since then, the number of campsites has been reduced and traffic has been restricted in order to reduce noise and pollution. Still, visitors are put on notice that the water in the river is undrinkable. Yellowstone, too has far more applications than can be accommodated in the available campsites. Even so, population densities in the non-wilderness areas of the Park sometimes exceed densities in the suburbs of Dallas.

More and more Americans have the time, the money, and the inclination to enjoy the outdoors. Production of truck campers and camping trailers shot up from 62 thousand in 1961 to over one-half million in 1971. With better roads and easier travel, national parks have in effect become city parks for the residents of nearby metropolitan areas. In the past 10 years, visitors to all national park facilities more than doubled, while the area of the parks increased by only one-fifth. There are many areas to enjoy and more to be developed, but the enjoyment will depend largely on how fast the population grows.

By the year 2000, incomes will nearly double and hours of leisure will rise. More and more people will be inclined to get away and will be able to do so. However, our research on some 24 outdoor recreation activities and the facilities for these activities indicates that population growing at the 3-child rate will exert great pressure on outdoor recreation resources—so great that rather than "getting away" to the outdoors, people will be applying for admission to it.

In the face of rising congestion, many people will substitute organized sports, sightseeing, foreign travel, and artistic and cultural activities, if they so desire. Rising incomes and the increase in man-made facilities will make these alternatives possible. For many, these will be adequate alternatives, but for others they will not.

The prospects for recreation with the 2-child projection are much different for two reasons. First, the population will not be as large as that resulting from the 3-child rate. More important, the percentage of people in the young ages that make especially heavy use of outdoor recreation facilities will be smaller. As a consequence, we estimate that, in the year 2000, the demand for recreational facilities could be as much as 30 percent less under the 2-child than under the 3-child rate of growth.

Either way, recreation will differ from what it is now. The style of life may change with the lower rate of growth as well, shifting from more active to more sedentary pursuits. But in this case it would be voluntary, determined by the individual needs and preferences of an older population, not imposed by the desire to avoid overcrowding.

Agricultural Land and Food Prices

At a time when the federal government pays farmers to hold land out of production, it seems absurd to be looking forward to a scarcity of good agricultural land and rising food prices. Yet these are the prospects indicated by our analysis of what rapid United States population growth implies.

This picture emerges when we combine the requirements for feeding a rapidly growing population with a sound environmental policy which restricts the use of pesticides and chemical fertilizers. There are a number of reasons for believing that the nation will wish to limit application of these chemicals. But to do so will retard improvements in per acre productivity. This means that, to produce a given quantity of food, more acres must be brought into production. It is likely that, with such restrictions, all the high quality land will have been returned to production by the year 2000. Consequently, the task of feeding the more rapidly growing population would force us to bring an additional 50 million acres of relatively low-quality land into production.

This is an expensive undertaking requiring heavy investments in equipment, fertilizer and manpower, for which farmers must be compensated. The result is that 50 years from now the population resulting from the 3-child average could find itself having to pay farm food prices some 40 to 50 percent higher than they would be otherwise. The needs of the population at the lower growth rate could be met with practically no price increase.

The larger population could avoid the price rise by shifting away from consumption of animal livestock towards vegetables and synthetic meats. Perhaps it would shift to a closed system of agriculture — food from factories. One way or another, a solution can be found. The problem for a growing population is to survey the possible solutions and select the ones it dislikes least.

Pollution

As the gross national product goes up, so does the production of pollutants. An irony of economic measurement is that the value of goods and services represented by GNP includes the cost of producing the pollutants as well as expenditures for cleaning up afterward. We may fill our tank with gasoline, but due to engine inefficiency, some portion of that ends up in the atmosphere as air pollution. Such pollutants are not free—we had to pay good money to put them in the air. Yet the cost of putting them there is included in our principal measure of national economic well-being.

If we clean up the pollutants, the cost of the cleanup effort is also added to GNP. But many of the costs, such as poorer health and deteriorated surroundings, are never counted at all. It is an indictment of our ignorance and indifference toward what we do to the environment, that in our national economic accounts we count so few of the "bads," and that even when we do count them, we count them as "goods."

To understand the contribution of population to pollution, we have to distinguish two broad classes of pollutants. The first class includes the major products of combustion—carbon monoxide, carbon dioxide, oxides of nitrogen, oxides of sulfur, hydrocarbons, and particulates— and several measures of water pollution, including biochemical demand for oxygen and suspended and dissolved solids.The pollutants in this group, once produced, endure in the environment for a relatively short time—short enough so that long-term accumulations are not a problem. This group contains the more massive and commonly discussed pollutants, and enough information exists about them so that we can link them to economic activity and population.

The second class of pollutants includes those which endure longer—radiation and pesticides, plus a wide variety of ever-changing chemicals emitted by our high technology industries. Most such chemicals are emitted in small, often highly poisonous amounts. For many of these pollutants, future developments depend more heavily on changes in technology than on changes in population and economic growth. In any case, they are very difficult to link to population and economic growth in a simple and quantitative fashion. For this reason, the results we present here are for the first class of pollutants, although this does not minimize the environmental damage done by the others.

In the next 30 years, most of these pollutants can be eliminated by enforcing treatment standards for pollution emissions. Slower population and economic growth would help; but over this period, by far the biggest reduction in pollution can be achieved by a head-on attack. This is illustrated in Figure 3 for hydrocarbons—a major component of auto exhaust and other combustion. In this example, the treatment standard is the Environmental Protection Agency's 1975 standard for emissions into the air. Even if this standard were not met on schedule, it certainly will be met by the year 2000; indeed, by that time, we are likely to have much tighter standards.

The relationships shown in Figure 3 hold generally for the other pollutants we examined. The reason for the spectacular results from enforcing standards is that we have imposed so little control in the past. The results do not assume any big new technological breakthroughs. It is just that we have only now begun to fight. Many of the required changes could be implemented today. Soap could be used instead of detergent; natural-colored paper could replace heavily bleached paper in many uses; returnable bottles could be used; the horsepower of auto engines could be reduced. It is not difficult to find answers when one begins to look.

Whatever we assume about future treatment policy, pollution emissions in the year 2000 would be less with the 2-child than with the 3-child rate of population growth— from five to 12 percent less, depending on the pollutant. If population were one percent less than projected in the year 2000, pollution emissions would be 0.3 to 0.6 percent less. If GNP per capita were one percent less than projected, emissions would be 0.2 to 0.9 percent less.

Figure   3 Hydrocarbon Emissions

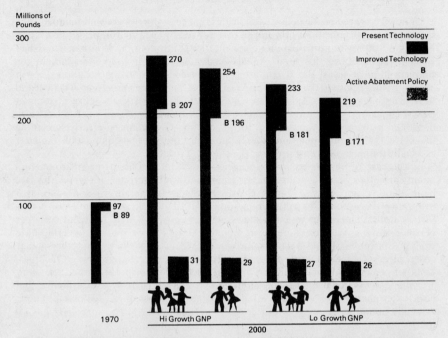

Millions of Pounds

The generation and emission of hydrocarbon pollutants is shown under different assumptions about future population growth, economic growth, changes in technology, and pollution abatement policy.

The bars labeled A, shown for background purposes only, indicate the levels of hydrocarbon wastes that would be generated under present technology: These waste levels would be generated if there were no changes in technology between the 1967-1970 base period and the year 2000.

The bars labeled B show actual emissions of hydrocarbon pollutants in 1970 and expected emissions in the year 2000, assuming no change in pollution abatement policy. The difference between A and B shows the extent to which the introduction of more efficient, less wasteful technology between now and the year 2000 is expected to reduce the generation and emission of pollutants below the levels generated if technology remained unchanged. Such changes in technology are likely to come anyway; they do not depend on public pressure to reduce harmful residuals.

The B bars show that, even with improved technology, pollution levels would be much higher in the year 2000 than they are now. These levels would, however, be somewhat lower if population grew at the 2-child rate rather than the 3-child rate, and if the economy grew at a slower rate rather than a more rapid rate (lo-growth GNP vs. hi-growth GNP).

The bars labeled C show hydrocarbon emissions in the year 2000 assuming an active pollution-abatement policy. The assumed policy is the Environmental Protection Agency's 1975 standard for emissions into the air. The changes in production and waste treatment processes induced by this policy would have a greater effect than would any of the other changes shown—in technology, population growth, or economic growth.

Source: Ronald G. Ridker, "The Economy, Resource Requirements, and Pollution Levels" (prepared for the Commission, 1972).

Once we achieve control over the emissions from each source, pollution will once again rise in response to economic and population growth. We can already see this process at work in rapidly growing parts of the country. At our Los Angeles public hearing, meteorologist James D. Edinger described the successful efforts in Los Angeles to control air pollution from stationary sources —power plants, heavy industry, home heating—and the beginnings of the program to control pollution from motor vehicles. But, he said, in recent years:

... a close race has been run between increasing numbers of sources and decreasing emissions per source. But, as emission levels per source are trimmed lower and lower the effort required to achieve each new increment of improvement gets more and more difficult. The increase in the number of sources, on the other hand, is projected to rise steadily. If the race for acceptable air quality is to be won, the heroic emission control programs, present and anticipated in Los Angeles, must soon be joined by a leveling off, if not a reduction, in the number of sources . . . (1)

Our own research on air pollution indicates that such worries are well founded. The standard for concentrations of nitrogen oxides used by the Environmental Protection Agency is 100 micrograms per cubic meter. In 1970, the air in 36 urban areas had concentrations above this level. An active abatement policy would eliminate the problem in most areas. But if our projections of economic and population growth come anywhere close to the truth, Los Angeles and San Diego in the year 2000 will still have a problem. In Los Angeles, we estimate that even with an active abatement policy, concentrations of nitrogen oxides will still be at least 50 percent above standard, and probably well above that. In this region of the country, clearly something must give, the rate of population growth, the use of the internal combustion engine— especially for personal transport — or the standard itself.

As the case of air quality in Los Angeles illustrates, problems of environmental quality are often worse in metropolitan areas that are larger and in regions that are more densely populated. This is clearly true for air pollution (and associated respiratory disease). noise, traffic congestion, and time spent getting to work. Other factors are less clear. Our research shows that sewage and water treatment costs per person decline as city size increases to about 100,000; above that, engineering data suggest that costs should be the same for conventional facilities, but the actual observed costs appear to rise. If large cities have to change their sewage facilities, costs per person will be much higher. Similarly, solid waste disposal costs either follow a U-shaped curve or increase with city size and density.There is also evidence that large cities change local climate—wind, cloudiness, temperature, and precipitation; we really do not know whether or not such changes are bad. The inner city has all these environmental problems but to a heightened degree.

Yet the underlying cause of poor environmental quality in the larger urban centers may often not be size. Most of our largest centers are the old cities of the north; their problems may arise more from urban forms and transportation systems appropriate to an earlier era, old and uncoordinated facilities, multiple governments, jurisdictions, and the injustices that lead to inadequate financing and high proportions of minority groups and poor in central cities. In new cities as well as old, environmental quality suffers from inadequate pricing of public facilities and common property resources like space and waste disposal media, such as rivers and air. The historical evidence relating environmental quality to metropolitan size may not be applicable to the building of new cities and the refitting of older cities; indeed, many such problems would remain wherever people live.

The total volume of pollutants in the United States responds, as we have seen, to the size of the national economy, which in turn depends heavily on the size of the national population. People consume resources wherever they live. Whether in New York City or a small town in the midwest, people still drive an automobile made of steel using coal mined in West Virginia. In the process, the air in cities is fouled by smoke and the scenery and the streams of West Virginia are spoiled by strip mining. Wherever Americans live, they make huge demands on the nation's and the world's resources and environment.

Risks and Choices

As a nation, we have always faced choice and always will. What matters is the range of choice we have and the urgency with which the need to choose is thrust upon us. The evidence indicates that continued population growth narrows our choices and forces us to choose in haste.

From the standpoint of resources and the environment, the United States can cope with rapid population growth for the next 30 to 50 years. But doing so will become an increasingly unpleasant and risky business—unpleasant because "coping" with growth means adopting solutions we don't like; risky because it means adopting solutions before we understand them. Within the United States, the risks are ecological and social. And, there are risks which involve our relationship with the rest of the world.

We in this country are tampering with the ecosystem in many ways, the consequences of which we do not begin to understand. The crude methods used to estimate the effect of emissions on air quality and the damages and costs of urban pollution illustrate our ignorance all too well. Worse yet is our understanding of the second class of pollutants, bypassed in our analysis precisely because we know so little about them. Because such pollutants endure longer, because they are highly poisonous in small doses, because new pollutants are continually being introduced, and because there are long time lags between emissions and the appearance of damages, we shall not quickly improve our knowledge in this area.

Radioactive wastes are an example. There will be more nuclear power plants if rapid population and economic growth occurs, but nuclear management and technology are changing so fast that there is no stable benchmark from which to estimate the amount of radioactive wastes likely to escape into the environment. We know that, once in the environment, such wastes can travel long distances through space and food chains, and we know the kinds of damage they can cause. But we do not know where they will come to rest, the extent of the damage, or when it will occur. Clearly, we need to know far more about how natural systems function when forced to absorb greater quantities of pollutants.

Beyond pollution, there are profound ecological impacts: (2) the simplification and destabilization of ecosystems associated with modern one-crop agriculture; the reduction in the variety of gene pools in our most important plants; the threat to the sequences of climate changes caused by man's activities and many more.

Population growth is clearly not the sole culprit in ecological damage. To believe that it is, is to confuse how things are done with how many people are doing them. Much of the damage we do results from efforts to satisfy fairly trivial preferences — for unblemished fruit, detergents, rapidly accelerating cars, and bright colored paper products. We can and should cut back on frivolous and extravagant consumption that pollutes. The way things are done can, to a significant degree, be changed regardless of how many people are doing them. But the overall effect is a product of numbers times styles of life taken together. One multiplies the other to produce the total impact.

The real risk lies in the fact that increasing numbers press us to adopt new technologies before we know what we are doing. The more of us there are the greater is the temptation to introduce solutions before their side effects are known. It might be far better environmentally to postpone the introduction of nuclear power plants until the inherently cleaner fusion reactors are developed. When one pesticide or food additive is found to be dangerous to man, it is replaced with another about which we know less. We undertake the expenditure of billions on water treatment, without knowing whether the benefits outweigh the costs of other opportunities foregone. Slower population growth will not eliminate this situation, but it will reduce the urgency, the "crash program" character of much that we do. It will buy time for the development of sensible solutions.

We can cope with population growth for another half century if we have to; the question is whether we want to. We can cope with resource shortages—if we cannot mine a resource, we can import, design around it, find a substitute, or reduce consumption. Where water deficits threaten, we can choose between charging more for its use, transferring people and industry to other parts of the country, and constructing longer and larger canals. If pollution emissions cannot be tolerated, we can change production processes, improve treatment, separate pollutants from their victims, treat the symptoms, or simply produce less of the commodity causing the pollution. Congestion during commuter hours can be handled by restricting the use of private cars, developing mass transit, and staggering work hours. Congestion at recreation sites can be handled by building additional facilities, improving management, encouraging substitutes such as foreign travel, and if necessary, by staggering vacations. Even land shortages for agriculture can be handled, given sufficient lead time, through farming the sea, changing our diet, developing synthetic foods, and so forth.

Such changes pose physical, technical, and managerial challenges that we can probably meet if we must. But in so doing, we shall pay a cost reckoned not in dollars but in our way of life.

Population growth forces upon us slow but irreversible changes in life style. Imbedded in our traditions as to what constitutes the American way of life is freedom from public regulation — virtually free use of water; access to uncongested, unregulated roadways; freedom to do as we please with what we own; freedom from permits, licenses, fees, red tape, and bureaucrats; and freedom to fish, swim, and camp where and when we will. Clearly, we do not live this way now. Maybe we never did. But everything is relative. The population of 2020 may look back with envy on what, from their vantage point, appears to be our relatively unfettered way of life.

Conservation of water resources, restrictions on pollution emissions, limitations on fertilizer and pesticides, preservation of wilderness areas, and protection of animal life threatened by man—all require public regulation. Rules must be set and enforced, complaints heard and adjudicated. Granted, the more we can find means of relying on the price system, the easier will be the bureaucratic task. Indeed, we ought to be experimenting right now with ways of making price incentives induce appropriate use of the environment and resources. At present, most monetary incentives work the wrong way, inducing waste and pollution rather than the opposite.

But even if effluent changes and user fees became universal, they will have to be set administratively; emissions and use will have to be metered, and fees collected. It appears inevitable that a larger portion of our lives will be devoted to filling out forms, arguing with the computer or its representatives, appealing decisions, waiting for our case to be handled, finding ways to evade or to move ahead in line. In many small ways, everyday life will become more contrived.

Many such changes will have to occur no matter which population projection occurs. But the difference, small at first, would grow with time until, a half century from now, the two societies may appear qualitatively different.

Another price we pay for having to cope with continued population growth is the pressure to keep on postponing the solution of social problems. While growth continues, top priority will be given to finding the necessary resources, controlling pollutants, correcting the damages they have done, and building ever larger water canals, highways, and mass transit systems. A large and perhaps growing fraction of our physical and intellectual capital is directly or indirectly, devoted to these tasks— to finding ways to cope with the problems that continued growth generates. From past experience, we can predict with a fair degree of confidence that such priorities will continue to subordinate efforts devoted to resolving fundamental social problems. When something must give because the system is becoming overloaded, it is unlikely to be the building of another dam.

The point is that continued population growth limits our options. In the case of the larger population, with less land per person and more people to accommodate, there are fewer alternatives, less room for diversity, less room for error. To cope with continued growth, technology *must* advance; lifestyles *must* change. Slower population growth offers us the difference between choice and necessity, between prudence and living dangerously.

The research done for the Commission showed that the United States will greatly enlarge its demands on world resources, especially minerals and petroleum, over the decade ahead. We will be requiring substantially larger imports of many minerals, such as chromium, vanadium, cobalt, and nickel, for which domestic supplies are not available or are available only at substantially higher costs.

The demand of other countries for minerals, petroleum, and other resources will certainly also rise sharply over the coming decades. This will result from rapid increases in output per person in other industrialized countries and from the rapid modernization of agriculture and industry in developing countries. The rates of increase in production in other parts of the world are likely to be higher than those of the United States. Their rates of increase in demand for mineral supplies are likely to rise even more sharply, because they are at an earlier stage of the industrialization process and because the composition of their GNP includes proportionately more goods and fewer services than does that of the United States.

Taking into account the huge increases in population which are in prospect, it seems clear that demands for natural resources in other parts of the world will rise more rapidly than demands in the United States; thus, the share of the United States in the use of world resources will steadily decline. For example, projections made for the Commission indicate that over the next 50 years the share of the United States in the world's use of aluminum may decline from 37 percent in 1968 to as low as nine percent by the year 2020. In the same time period, the share of the United States of total world copper requirements may drop from 22 percent to five percent.

While all such figures necessarily reflect uncertain assumptions about production, income, and technology, nevertheless they indicate the extremely important extent to which the United States is inextricably involved in the development and use of resources on a worldwide scale.

Our research also demonstrates that environmental issues will have to be faced increasingly on an international basis over the years ahead. There are already conspicuous cases of environmental damage and risk which cannot be solved on a national basis. The continuing problem of petroleum pollution in the oceans is such a case. Neither the oceans nor the atmosphere can be successfully dealt with if one looks only at the territory within a nation's boundary. And many additional issues of international ecological significance will be increasingly important—such as the effects of enormous increases in world use of pesticides and chemical fertilizers, the environmental impact of multi-national corporations, and many more.

The Commission has been deeply impressed by the unprecedented size and significance of the looming problems of resources and environment on a world scale. We see the need for much greater efforts than are underway now to analyze and understand these problems, and to develop international policies and programs to deal with them. We foresee potentially grave issues of clashing interests among nations and world regions, which could have very serious effects on the United States.

Therefore, we believe strongly that, in its own interest, the United States should work positively and constructively with other countries and international organizations in analyzing and solving problems related to natural resources and the environment in the world. We have made no special study of the detailed policies and programs which the United States should pursue for these purposes. We do now emphatically urge, however, that the nation join vigorously and cooperatively, in solving problems of international trade, assistance to less-developed countries, and other pressing issues which will affect so sharply not only the future well-being of others in the world but the direct prospects for a sensible and respectable future for ourselves. We should not approach such problems in a spirit of charity, or largesse. Our own future depends heavily on the evolution of a sensible international economic order, capable of dealing with natural resources and environmental conditions on a world scale.

Long-Term Strategic Planning

Our consideration of the problems and prospects involved in this country's long-term future convinces us that an important dimension of policy formation is being overlooked. This dimension involves the identification, study, and initiation of actions with respect to future problems that may require lead times of decades rather than years to resolve. There is a need for continuous monitoring and evaluation of the long-term implications of demographic changes, of future resource demands and supplies, of possible pollution overload situations, and of the underlying trends in technology and patterns of social behavior that influence these factors.

Once future problems are identified, there is a need to undertake the necessary research and development and to formulate the policies to resolve them. We need to study our social, political, and economic institutions with a view towards recommending modifications that will reduce the discrepancy between the private and the public interest. Practical procedures for utilizing the effluent charge approach to environmental quality management and for initiating a national system of land-use planning are important cases in point. We need to develop technologies that conserve particularly scare physical and environmental resources. While appropriate effluent charges will encourage private business to move in this direction, government sponsorship of "yardstick" research on industrial technologies is necessary, particularly when our concern is with the problems farther in the future than private business can afford to look.

While parts of these tasks are being performed by isolated agencies, coordination and analytical assessment on a broad level are lacking. Private business firms and most government agencies are of necessity too present-oriented or mission-oriented to serve these functions adequately; nor can they be left to *ad hoc* commissions such as this one. On the other hand, we do feel that some group should be assigned central responsibility for such functions. Such a body would serve as a "lobby for the future" to identify potential population, resource, and environmental problems well in advance of their occurrence; to establish priorities and sponsor technical and social research directed towards their resolution; and where necessary to formulate and recommend policies to that end.

Notes

Nearly all of the source material for this paper came from the resource and environmental research done for the Commission by Resources for the Future, Inc. Their work includes a summary chapter on the resource and environmental consequences of population growth in the United States by Ronald G. Ridker, as well as more detailed supporting work which includes an analysis of pollution, recycling, adequacy of nonfuel minerals, energy, outdoor recreation, agriculture, water supplies, and urban scale.

(1) James G. Edinger, in hearings before the Commission, Los Angeles, California, May 4, 1971.

(2) Paul R. Ehrlich and John P. Holdren, "One-Dimensional Ecology," *Science and Public Affairs*, Spring 1972.

POPULATION
AND
PUBLIC POLICY

In reviewing population trends in the United States and their implications, four things stand out. First, the effects of our past rapid growth are going to be with us for a long time. Second, we have to make a choice about our future growth. Third, the choice involves nothing less than the quality of American life. And, fourth, slower population growth provides opportunities to improve the quality of life, but special efforts are required if the opportunities are to be well used.

A Legacy of Growth

Regardless of what happens to the birthrate from now on, our past growth commits us to substantial additional growth in the future. At a minimum, we will probably add 50 million more Americans by the end of the century, and the figure could easily be much higher than that.

We will be living for a long time with the consequences of the baby boom. Not long ago, that surge of births caused double sessions, school in trailers, and a teacher shortage. Now it is crowding the colleges and swelling the number of people looking for jobs. As these young people grow older, they will enter the ranks of producers as well as consumers, and they will eventually reenter dependency—the dependency of the aged.

We are going to have to plan for this. Swelling numbers of job applicants put an extra burden on full employment policy, if only because failure in this respect now affects so many more people than it did once. This will continue to be true for many years. People think the "baby boom" ended in the 1950's. Not so. That was only when it reached its peak. The last year when births exceed four million was 1964, only eight years ago. (1) In fact, today's eight-year-olds are just as numerous as 18-year-olds. So it is not too late to try to do better by the youngest of the baby-boom babies than we did by the oldest.

The baby boom is not over. The babies have merely grown older. It has become a boom in the teens and twenties. In a few decades, it will be turning into a retirement boom. During the second decade of the next century, 30 million people will turn 65, compared with 15 million who had their 65th birthday in the past 10 years. (2) Will the poverty of the aged be with us then? Census Bureau reports disclose that 25 percent of today's aged are in poverty, compared with eight percent of people in the young working ages of 22 to 45. (3) Thirty years from now, will we do better by the swelling numbers of aged than we do by those we have now? Will we develop alternatives to treating the elderly as castoffs? Not if we don't try. Not if we don't plan for it.

We may be through with the past, but the past is not done with us. Our demographic history shapes the future, even though it does not determine it. It sets forth needs as well as opportunities. It challenges us to get ready. While we cannot predict the future, much of it is foreseeable. For this much, at least, we should be prepared.

The Choice About Future Growth

We have to make a choice about our future growth. As a Commission, we have formed a definite judgment about the choice the nation should make. We have examined the effects that future growth alternatives are likely to have on our economy, society, government, resources, and environment, and we have found no convincing argument for continued national population growth. On the contrary, the plusses seem to be on the side of slowing growth and eventually stopping it altogether. Indeed, there might be no reason to fear a decline in population once we are past the period of growth that is in store.

Neither the health of our economy nor the welfare of individual businesses depend on continued population growth. In fact, the average person will be markedly better off in terms of traditional economic values if population growth slows down than if it resumes the pace of growth experienced in the recent past.

With regard to both resources and the environment, the evidence we have assembled shows that slower growth would conserve energy and mineral resources and would be a significant aid in averting problems in the areas of water supply, agricultural land supply, outdoor recreation resources, and environmental pollution.

Slower population growth can contribute to the nation's ability to solve its problems in these areas by providing an opportunity to devote resources to the quality of life rather than its quantity, and by "buying time" — that is, slowing the pace at which problems accumulate so as to provide opportunity for the development of orderly and democratic solutions.

For government, slower population growth offers potential benefits in the form of reduced pressures on educational and other services, and, for the people, it enhances the potential for improved levels of service in these areas. We find no threat to national security from slower growth. While population growth is not by any means the sole cause of governmental problems, it magnifies them and makes their solution more difficult. Slower growth would lessen the increasing rate of strain on our federal system. To that extent, it would enhance the likelihood of achieving true justice and more ample well-being for all citizens even as it would preserve more individual freedom.

Each one of the impacts of population growth — on the economy, resources, the environment, government, or society at large — indicates the desirability, in the short run, for a slower rate of growth. And, when we consider these together, contemplate the ever-increasing problems involved in the long run, and recognize the long lead time required to arrest growth, we must conclude that continued population growth — beyond that to which we are already committed by the legacy of the baby boom — is definitely not in the interest of promoting the quality of life in the nation.

The Quality of American Life

We are concerned with population trends only as they impede or enhance the realization of those values and goals cherished in, by, and for American society.

What values? Whose goals? As a Commission, we do not set ourselves up as an arbiter of those fundamental questions. Over the decades ahead, the American people themselves will provide the answers, but we have had to judge proposals for action on population-related issues against their contribution to some version of the good life for this society and, for that matter, the world. What we have sought are measures that promise to move demographic trends in the right direction and, at the same time, have favorable direct effects on the quality of life.

We know that problems of quality exist from the variety of indicators that fall short of what is desirable and possible. There are inequalities in the opportunities for life itself evidenced by the high frequency of premature death an the lower life expectancy of the poor. There is a whole range of preventable illness such as the currently high and rising rate of venereal disease. There are a number of congenital deficiencies attributable to inadequate prenatal care and obstetrical services and, in some cases, to genetic origin. Not all such handicaps are preventable, but they occur at rates higher than if childbearing were confined to ages associated with low incidence and if genetic counseling were more widely available.

Innate human potential often has not been fully developed because of the inadequate quality of various educational, social, and environmental factors. Particularly with regard to our ethnic minorities and the female half of the population, there are large numbers of people occupying social roles that do not capitalize on their latent abilities and interest, or elicit a dedicated effort and commitment. There is hunger and malnutrition, particularly damaging to infants and young children, that should not be tolerated in the richest nation the world has ever known. Sensitive observers perceive in our population a certain frustration and alienation that appears to go beyond what is endemic in the human condition; the sources of these feelings should be explored and better understood.

And we can also identify and measure the limiting factors, the inequalities of opportunity, and the environmental hazards that give rise to such limitations in the quality of life—for example, inadequate distribution of and access to health, education, and welfare services, cultural and social constraints on human performance and development associated with race, ethnic origin, sex, and age; barriers to full economic and cultural participation; unequal access to environmental quality; and unequal exposure to environmental hazard.

There are many other problems of quality in American life. Thus, alongside the challenges of population growth and distribution is the challenge of population quality. The goal of all population policy must be to make better the life that is actually lived.

While slower population growth provides opportunities, it does not guarantee that they will be well used. It simply opens up a range of choices we would not have otherwise. Much depends on how wisely the choices are made and how well the opportunities are used. For example, slower population growth would enable us to provide a far better education for children at no increase in total costs. We want the opportunity presented by slower growth to be used this way, but we cannot guarantee that it will be. The wise use of opportunities such as this depends on public and private decisions yet to be made.

Slowing population growth can "buy time" for the solution of many problems, but, without the determined, long-range application of technical and political skills, the opportunity will be lost. For example, our economic and political systems reward the exploitation of virgin resources and impose no costs on polluters. The technology exists for solving many of these problems. But proper application of this technology will require the recognition of public interests, the social inventiveness to discover institutional arrangements for channeling private interests without undue government regulation, and the political courage and skill needed to institute the necessary changes.

Slower population growth offers time in which to accomplish these things. But if all we do with breathing time is breathe, the value of the enterprise is lost.

Population change does not take place in a vacuum. Its consequences are produced through its joint action with technology, wealth, and the institutional structures of society. Hence, a study of the American future, insofar as it is influenced by population change, cannot ignore, indeed it must comment upon, the features of the society that make population growth troublesome or not.

Hence, while we are encouraged by the improvement in average income that will be yielded by slower population growth, we are concerned with the persistence of vast differences in the distribution of income, which has remained fixed now for a quarter of a century.

While we are encouraged by the relief that slower population growth offers in terms of pressure on resources and the environment, we are aware of the inadequacy of the nation's general approach to these problems.

We rely largely on private market forces for conducting the daily business of production and consumption. These work well in general and over the short run to reduce costs, husband resources, increase productivity, and provide a higher material standard of living for the individual. But the market mechanism has been ineffective in allocating the social and environmental costs of production and consumption, primarily because public policies and programs have not provided the proper signals nor required that such cost be borne by production and consumption activities. Nor has the market mechanism been able to provide socially acceptable incomes for people who, by virtue of age, incapacity, or injustice, are poorly equipped to participate in the market system for producing and distributing income.

Our economy's use of the earth's finite resources, and the accompanying pollution or deterioration of the quality of water, air, and natural beauty, has neglected some of the fundamental requirements for acceptable survival. Often the time horizon for both public and private decisions affecting the economy has been too short. It seems clear that market forces alone cannot be relied upon to achieve our social and environmental goals, for reasons that make exchange, though the main organizing principle, inadequate without appropriate institutional and legal underpinnings. (4)

In short, even if we achieve the stabilization of population, our economic, environmental, governmental, and social problems will still be with us unless by will and intelligence we develop policies to deal with the other sources of these problems. The fact that such policies have shown little conspicious success in the past gives rise to the skepticism we have expressed above in our discussion of the relations between government and population growth.

The problem is not so much the impact of population on government as the adequacy of government to respond to the challenge of population and the host of issues that surround it. Long-term planning is necessary to deal with environmental and resource problems, but there are only beginning signs that government is motivated or organized to undertake it. A major commitment is required to bring minorities into the mainstream of American life, but the effort so far is inadequate. It is clear that the "real city" that comprises the metropolis requires a real government to manage its affairs, but the nation is still trying to manage the affairs of complex, interconnected, metropolitan communities with fragmented institutional structures inherited from the 18th century.

Population, then, is clearly not the whole problem. But it is clearly part of the problem, and it is the part given us as the special responsibility of this Commission. How policy in this area should be shaped, depends on how we define the objectives of policy in respect to population.

Policy Goals

Ideally, we wish to develop recommendations worthwhile in themselves, which at the same time, speak to population issues. These recommendations are consistent with American ethical values in that they aim to enhance individual freedom while simultaneously promoting the common good. It is important to reiterate that our policy recommendations embody goals either intrinsically desirable or worthwhile for reasons other than demographic objectives.

Moreover, some of the policies we recommend are irreversible in a democratic society, in the sense that freedoms once introduced cannot be rescinded lightly. This irreversibility characterizes several of the important policies recommended by this Commission. We are not really certain of the demographic impact of some of the changes implied by our recommendations. One or two could conceivably increase the birthrate by indirectly subsidizing the bearing of children. The rest may depress the birthrate below the level of replacement. We are not concerned with this latter contingency because, if sometime in the future the nation wishes to increase its population growth, there are many possible ways to try this; a nation's growth should not depend on the ignorance and misfortune of its citizenry. In any event, it is naive to expect that we can fine-tune such trends.

In the broadest sense, the goals of the population policies we recommend aim at creating social conditions wherein the desired values of individuals, families, and communities can be realized, equalizing social and economic opportunities for women and members of disadvantaged minorities; and enhancing the potential for improving the quality of life.

At the educational level, we wish to increase public awareness and understanding of the implications of population change and simultaneously further our knowledge of the causes and consequences of population change.

In regard to childbearing and child-rearing, the goals of our recommendations are to: 1. maximize information and knowledge about human reproduction and its implication for the family; 2. improve the quality of the setting in which children are raised; 3. neutralize insofar as it is practicable and consistent with other values those legal, social, and institutional pressures that historically have been mainly pronatalist in character, and 4. enable individuals to avoid unwanted childbearing, thereby enhancing their ability to realize their preferences. These particular policies are aimed at facilitating the social, economic, and legal conditions within our society which increase ethical responsibility and the opportunity for unbiased choice in human reproduction and child-bearing. At the same time, by enhancing the individual's opportunity to make a real choice between having few children and having many, between parenthood and childlessness, and between marriage and the single state, these policies together will undoubtedly slow our rate of population growth and accelerate the advent of population stabilization.

In connection with the geographic distribution of population, our objectives are to ease and guide the process of population movement, to facilitate planning for the accommodation of movements, and to increase the freedom of choice in residential locations.

To these ends, therefore, we offer our recommendations in the belief that the American people, collectively and individually, should confront the issues of population growth and reach deliberate informed decisions about the family's and society's size as they affect the achievement of personal and national values.

Notes

(1) U.S. Bureau of the Census, *Current Population Reports,* Series P-23, No. 36, "Fertility Indicators: 1970," 1971.

(2) Estimated from data on population 65 to 74 years old, and survival rates, in U.S. Bureau of the Census, *Current Population Reports,* Series P-25, No. 470, "Projections of the Population of the United States, by Age and Sex: 1970 to 2020," 1971.

(3) U.S. Bureau of the Census, *Current Population Reports,* Series P-60, No. 81, "Characteristics of the Low-Income Population, 1970," 1971.

(4) Joseph J. Spengler, "Declining Population Growth: Economic Effects" (prepared for the Commission, 1972).

POPULATION
STABILIZATION

Soon after the Commission's first meeting in June 1970, it became evident that the question of population stabilization would be a principal issue in its deliberations. A population has stabilized when the number of births has come into balance with the number of deaths, with the result that, the effects of immigration aside, the size of the population remains relatively constant. We recognize that stabilization will only be possible on an average over a period of time, as the annual numbers of births and deaths fluctuate. The Commission further recognizes that to attain a stablized population would take a number of decades, primarily because such a high proportion of our population today is now entering the ages of marriage and reproduction.

As our work proceeded and we received the results of studies comparing the likely effects of continued growth with the effects of stabilization, it became increasingly evident that no substantial benefits would result from continued growth of the nation's population. This is one of the basic conclusions we have drawn from our inquiry. From the accumulated evidence, we further concluded that the stabilization of our population would contribute significantly to the nation's ability to solve its problems. It was evident that moving toward stabilization would provide an opportunity to devote resources to problems and needs relating to the quality of life rather than its quantity. Stabilization would "buy time" by slowing the pace at which growth-related problems accumulated and enhancing opportunities for the orderly and democratic working out of solutions.

The Commission recognizes that the demographic implications of most of our recommended policies concerning childbearing are quite consistent with a goal of population stabilization. In this sense, achievement of population stabilization would be primarily the result of measures aimed at creating conditions in which individuals, regardless of sex, age, or minority status, can exercise genuine free choice. This means that we must strive to eliminate those social barriers, laws, and cultural pressures that interfere with the exercise of free choice and that governmental programs in the future must be sensitized to demographic effects.

Recognizing that our population cannot grow indefinitely, and appreciating the advantages of moving now toward the stabilization of population, the Commission recommends that the nation welcome and plan for a stabilized population.

There remain a number of questions which must be answered as the nation follows a course towards population stabilization. How can stabilization be reached? Is there any particular size at which the population should level off, and when should that occur? What "costs" would be imposed by the various paths to stabilization, and what costs are worth paying?

Criteria for Paths to Stabilization

An important group in our society, composed predominantly of young people, has been much concerned about population growth in recent years. Their concern emerged quite rapidly as the mounting pollution problem received widespread attention, and their goal became "zero population growth." By this, they meant in fact stabilization — bringing births into balance with deaths. To attain their objective, they called for the 2-child family. They recognize, of course, that many people do not marry and that some who do marry either are not able to have or do not want to have children, permitting wide latitude in family size and attainment of the 2-child average.

Some called for zero growth immediately. But this would not be possible without considerable disruption to society. While there are a variety of paths to ultimate stabilization, none of the feasible paths would reach it immediately. Our past rapid growth has given us so many young couples that, even if they merely replaced themselves, the number of births would still rise for several years before leveling off. To produce the number of births consistent with immediate zero growth, they would have to limit their childbearing to an average of only about one child. In a few years, there would be only half as many children as there are now. This would have disruptive effects on the school system and subsequently on the number of persons entering the labor force. Thereafter, a constant total population could be maintained only if this small generation in turn had two children and their grandchildren had nearly three children on the average. And then the process would again have to reverse, so that the overall effort for many years would be that of an accordion-like continuous expansion and contraction. (1)

From considerations such as this, we can begin to develop criteria for paths toward population stabilization. (2) It is highly desirable to avoid another baby boom. Births, which averaged 3.0 million annually in the early 1920's fell to a 2.4 million average in the 1930's, rose to a 4.2 million average in the late 1950's and early 1960's, and fell to 3.6 million in 1971. (3) These boom and bust cycles have caused disruption in elementary and high schools and subsequently in the colleges and in the labor market. And the damage to the long-run career aspirations of the baby-boom generation is only beginning to be felt.

The assimilation of the baby-boom generation has been called "population peristalsis" comparing it to the process in which a python digests a pig. As it moves along the digestive tract, the pig makes a big bulge in the python. While the imagery suggests the appearance of the baby-boom generation as it moves up the age scale and through the phases of the life cycle, there is reason to believe that the python has an easier time with the pig than our nation is having providing training, jobs, and opportunity for the generation of the baby boom.

Thus, we would prefer that the path to stabilization involve a minimum of fluctuations from period to period in the number of births. For the near future, these considerations recommend a course toward population stabilization which would reduce the echo expected from the baby-boom generation as it moves through the childbearing age and bears children of its own.

Our evidence also indicates that it would be preferable for the population to stabilize at a lower rather than a higher level. Our population will continue to grow for decades more before stabilizing, even if those now entering the ages of reproduction merely replace themselves. The population will grow as the very large groups now eight to 25 years of age—the products of the postwar baby boom—grow older and succeed their less numerous predecessors. How much growth there will be depends on the oncoming generations of young parents.

Some moderate changes in patterns of marriage and childbearing are necessary for any move toward stabilization. There are obvious advantages to a path which minimizes the change required and provides a reasonable amount of time for such change to occur.

Population stabilization under modern conditions of mortality means that, on the average, each pair of adults will give birth to two children. This average can be achieved in many ways. For example, it can be achieved by varying combinations of nonmarriage or childlessness coexisting in a population with substantial percentages of couples who have more than two children. On several grounds, it is desirable that stabilization develop in a way which encourages variety and choice rather than uniformity.

We prefer, then, a course toward population stabilization which minimizes fluctuations in the number of births; minimizes further growth of population; minimizes the change required in reproductive habits and provides adequate time for such changes to be adopted; and maximizes variety and choice in life styles, while minimizing pressures for conformity.

An Illustration of an Optimal Path

Our research indicates that there are some paths to stabilization that are clearly preferable. These offer less additional population growth, involve negligible fluctuations in births, provide for a wide range of family sizes within the population, and exact moderate "costs" — that is, changes in marriage and childbearing habits, which are in the same direction as current trends.

A course such as the following satisfies these criteria quite well. (4) (The calculations exclude immigration; the demographic role of immigration is reviewed in Chapter 13 of the Commission's report.)

In this illustration, childbearing would decline to a replacement level in 20 years. This would result if: 1. the proportion of women becoming mothers declined from 88 to 80 percent; 2. the proportion of parents with three or more children declined from 50 to 41 percent; and 3. the proportion of parents with one or two children rose from 50 to 59 percent. Also in this illustration, the average age of mothers when their first child is born would rise by two years, and the average interval between births would rise by less than six months. The results of these changes would be that the United States population would gradually grow until it stabilizes, in approximately 50 years at a level of 278 million (plus the contribution from the net flow of immigrants). Periodic fluctuations in the number of births would be negligible.

The size of the population in the year 2000 will depend both on how fast future births occur as well as on the ultimate number of children people have over a lifetime. Over the next 10 to 15 years especially, we must expect a large number of births from the increasing numbers of potential parents, unless these young people offset the effect of their numbers by waiting somewhat before having their children. Postponement and stretching-out of childbearing, accompanied by a gradual decline in the number of children that people have over a lifetime can effectively reduce the growth we shall otherwise experience.

Beyond this, there are persuasive health and personal reasons for encouraging postponement of childbearing and better spacing of births. Infants of teenage mothers are subject to higher risks of premature birth, infant death, and lifetime physical and mental disability than children of mothers in their twenties. (5) If the 17 percent of all births occurring to teenage mothers were postponed to later ages, we would see a distinct improvement in the survival, health, and ability of these children.

It is obvious that the population cannot be fine-tuned to conform to any specific path. The changes might occur sooner or later than in this illustration. If they took place over 30 years instead of 20 we should expect nine million more people in the ultimate stabilized population — or 287 million rather than 278 million. Or if the average age at childbearing rose only one year instead of two, we would end up with 10 million more people than otherwise.

On the other hand, suppose we drifted toward a replacement level of fertility in 50 years instead of 20, and none of the other factors changed. In that case, the population would stabilize at 330 million. In other words, following this route would result in 50 million more Americans than the one illustrated above.

The Likelihood of Population Stabilization

Many developments — some old and some recent — enhance the likelihood that something close to an optimal path can be realized, especially if the Commission's recommendations bearing on population growth are adopted quickly.

1. The trend of average family size has been downward — from seven or eight children per family in colonial times to less than three children in recent years — interrupted, however, by the baby boom.

2. The birthrate has declined over the past decade and showed an unexpected further decline in 1971.

3. The increasing employment of women, and the movement to expand women's options as to occupational and family roles and life styles, promise to increase alternatives to the conventional role of wife-homemaker-mother.

4. Concern over the effects of population growth has been mounting. Two-thirds of the general public interviewed in the Commission's survey in 1971 felt that the growth of the United States population is a serious problem. Half or more expressed concern over the impact of population growth on the use of natural resources, on air and water pollution, and on social unrest and dissatisfaction (6).

5. Youthful marriage is becoming less common than it was a few years ago. While 20 percent of women now in their thirties married before age 18, only 13 percent of the young women are doing so now. (7) It remains to be seen whether this represents a postponement of marriage or a reversal of the trend toward nearly universal marriage.

6. The family-size preferences of young people now entering the childbearing ages are significantly lower than the preferences reported by their elders at the same stage in life.

7. The technical quality of contraceptives has increased greatly in the past 10 years, although irregular and ineffective use still results in many unplanned and unwanted births.

8. The legalization of abortion in a few states has resulted in major increases in the number of legal abortions. The evidence so far indicates that legalized abortion is being used by many women who would otherwise have had to resort to illegal and unsafe abortions. The magnitude of its effect on the birthrate is not yet clear. (8).

9.. The experience of many other countries indicates the feasibility of sustained replacement levels of reproduction. (9) Within the past half century, Japan, England and Wales, France, Denmark, Norway, West Germany, Hungary, Sweden, and Switzerland have all experienced periods of replacement or near-replacement fertility lasting a decade or more. Additional countries have had shorter periods at or near replacement levels. While much of this experience occurred during the Depression of the 1930's, much of it also occurred since then. Furthermore, during that period, contraceptive technology was primitive compared to what is available today.

On the basis of these facts, the nation might ask, "why worry," and decide to wait and see what happens. Our judgment is that we should not wait. Acting now, we encourage a desirable trend. Acting later, we may find ourselves in a position of trying to reverse an undesirable trend. We should take advantage of the opportunity the moment present rather than wait for what the unknown future holds.

The potential for a repeat of the baby boom is still here. In 1975, there will be six million more people in the prime childbearing ages of 20 to 29 than there were in 1970. By 1985, the figure will have jumped still another five million. Unless we achieve some postponement of childbearing or reduction in average family size, this is going to mean substantial further increases in the number of births. (10).

Furthermore, although we discern many favorable elements in recent trends, there are also unfavorable elements which threaten the achievement of stabilization.

1. For historical reasons which no longer apply, this nation has an ideological addiction to growth.

2. Our social institutions, including many of our laws, often exert a pronatalist effect, even if inadvertent. (11) This includes the images of family life and women's roles projected in television programs; the child-saves-marriage theme in women's magazines; (12) the restrictions on the availability of contraception, sex education, and abortion; and many others.

3. There is an unsatisfactory level of understanding of the role of sex in human life and of the reproductive process and its control.

4. While the white middle-class majority bears the primary numerical responsibility for population growth, it is also true that the failure of our society to bring racial minorities and the poor into the mainstream of American life has impaired their ability to implement small-family goals.

5. If it should happen that in the next few years, our rate of reproduction falls to replacement levels or below, we could experience a strong counterreaction. In the United States in the 1930's, and in several foreign countries, the response to subreplacement fertility has been a cry of anxiety over the national prosperity, security, and virility. Individual countries have found it hard to come to terms with replacement-level fertility rates. (13) About 40 years ago during the Depression, there was great concern about "race suicide" when birthrates fell in Western Europe and in this country. Indeed, an admonition against unwarranted countermeasures was issued in 1938 by the Committee on Population Problems of the National Resources Committee: " . . . there is no occasion for hysteria . . . There is no reason for the hasty adoption of any measures designed to stimulate population growth in this country." (14). Today, several countries approaching stabilization have expressed concerns about possible future labor shortages. The growth ethic seems to be so

imprinted in human consciousness that it takes a deliberate effort of nationality and will to overcome it, but that effort is now desirable.

One purpose of this report and the programs it recommends is to prepare the American people to welcome a replacement level of reproduction and some periods of reproduction below replacement. The nation must face the fact that achieving population stabilization sooner rather than later would require a period of time during which annual fertility was below replacement. During the transition to stabilization, the postponement of childbearing would result in annual fertility rates dropping below replacement, even though, over a lifetime, the childbearing of the parents would reach a replacement level.

In the long-run future, we should understand that a stabilized population means an *average* of zero growth, and there would be times when the size of the population declines. Indeed, zero growth can only be achieved realistically with fluctuations in both directions. We should prepare ourselves not to react with alarm, as some other countries have done recently, when the distant possibility of population decline appears.

Notes

(1) Norman B. Ryder, "A Demographic Optimum Projection for the United States" (prepared for the Commission, 1972). Also Ansley J. Coale, "Alternative Paths to a Stationary Population" (prepared for the Commission, 1972).

(2) Tomas Frejka, "Demographic Paths to a Stationary Population: The U.S. in International Comparison" (prepared for the Commission, 1972); and, "Reflections on the Demographic Conditions Needed to Establish a U.S. Stationary Population Growth," *Population Studies,* November 1968.

(3) U.S. Bureau of the Census, *Current Population Reports,* Series P-23, No. 36, "Fertility Indicators: 1970," 1971.

(4) See Ryder, note 1.

(5) Jane A. Menken, "Teenage Childbearing: Its Medical Aspects and Implications for the United States Population" (prepared for the Commission, 1972).

(6) National Public Opinion Survey conducted for the Commission by the Opinion Research Corporation, 1971.

(7) U.S. Bureau of the Census, *Current Population Reports,* Series P-20. No. 212, "Marital Status and Family Status: March 1970," 1971.

(8) Christopher Tietze, "The Potential Impact of Legal Abortion on Population Growth in the United States" (prepared for the Commission, 1972).

(9) Michael Teitelbaum, "International Experience with Fertility at or near Replacement Level" (prepared for the Commission, 1972).

(10) U.S. Bureau of the Census, *Current Population Reports,* Series P-25, No. 470, "Projections of the Population of the United States, by Age and Sex: 1970 to 2020," 1971,

(11) Judith Blake, "Coercive Pronatalism and Population Policy" (prepared for the Commission, 1972), and other papers cited above in discussion of institutional pressures.

(12) Ellen Peck, in hearings before the Commission, Chicago, Illinois, June 21-22, 1971.

(12) The Population Council, "Japan: Interim Report of the Population Problems Inquiry Council," *Studies in Family Planning,* No. 56, August 1970. See also note 9.

(14) Report of the Committee on Population Problems to the National Resources Committee, *The Problems of a Changing Population,* May 1938.

THE
ECOLOGICAL
VIEW

INTRODUCTION

Whenever we have added commentary to this collection of readings, we have been very sparing in our use of the word "ecology." Although some authors use it as a synonym for "environment," we believe that such usage is too conservative. For us, "ecology" describes a set of interrelationships between the environment and several other important elements: population, technology, social organization, and culture and values.

The principle purpose of this collection is an examination of the contribution that population growth makes to the environmental crisis. However, throughout the volume, we have moved towards a larger, unannounced goal: the examination of the relationship of environment and population in its larger context — one that concerns the organization of society, technological advances, alterations in life styles or values, and many other elements. Most selections have specified some of these factors. As an appropriate conclusion to this collection, we would like, with the aid of Amos H. Hawley's seminal article, "Ecology and Population," to provide a larger framework in which all of the articles can be appreciated.

The first three selections represent an exchange between Garrett Hardin, Beryl Crowe, and Amos H. Hawley. Crowe's article was written to challenge some of Hardin's ideas, while Hawley's contribution is less directed, but as important. Hardin's article, "The Tragedy of the Commons," has become a classic item in the environmentalist's armamentarium, and no collection of readings seems complete without it. It has been reprinted in more than two dozen anthologies, but seldom is it paired with Crowe's direct response to Hardin's ideas. Similarly, Hawley's more recent challenge to the general argument embraced by Hardin and others seems to have attracted little attention.

Hardin raises some challenging issues. His argument that the press of population upon resources is a major problem that has no technical solution is one that has been embraced by many theorists like Malthus who predates Hardin by more than a hundred and fifty years. His description of the problem, as the one provided by Malthus, leads to some drastic prescriptions which may contradict certain values and "freedoms," including the freedom of reproduction. His argument that solutions in population problems, and through them solutions to environmental problems, are not technological is a persuasive one.

But as Crowe and Hawley note, Hardin's approach oversimplifies the conceptualization of the problem (and its possible solutions). It is a replica of the Malthusian model in which population and environment are described and all other variables are held constant. However, these other variables, including man's ability to organize himself in relation to his environment, are not constants. Hawley specifies the situation directly:

> Every population confronts its external world as some form of organization. The critical relation, then, is between an organization and environment. If there are environmental problems, their explanation and their solution must be sought in the way the given organization is constituted. It should be no less evident that adaptation is a collective (that is, organizational) achievement.

From the relatively simple earlier presentations of the relationship of population and environment we have explored several major topics in depth. Readers should, we hope, have gained new perspectives on the contribution of population growth to environmental problems and a sense of where this relationship fits into a larger ecological framework.

However, we want to leave the reader with the notion that this survey is not complete and self-contained. Rather than finish with Hawley's rather definitive statement, we have ended the collection with Keir Nash's excursion into the political, philosophical aspects of population and environmental issues. It is a concern that belongs here, yet it is a beginning rather than an end.

THE
TRAGEDY
OF THE
COMMONS

Garrett Hardin

At the end of a thoughtful article on the future of nuclear war, Wiesner and York (1) concluded that:

> Both sides in the arms race are . . . confronted by the dilemma of steadily increasing military power and steadily decreasing national security. *It is our considered professional judgment that this dilemma has no technical solution.* If the great powers continue to look for solutions in the area of science and technology only, the result will be to worsen the situation.

I would like to focus your attention not on the subject of the article (national security in a nuclear world) but on the kind of conclusion they reached, namely that there is no technical solution to the problem. An implicit and almost universal assumption of discussions published in professional and semipopular scientific journals is that the problem under discussion has a technical solution. A technical solution may be defined as one that requires a change only in the techniques of the natural sciences, little or nothing in the way of change in human values or ideas of morality.

In our day (though not in earlier times) technical solutions are always welcome. Because of previous failures in prophecy, it takes courage to assert that a desired technical solution is not possible. Wiesner and York exhibited this courage; publishing in a science journal, they insisted that the solution to the problem was not to be found in the natural sciences. They cautiously qualified their statement with the phrase, "It is our considered professional judgment . . . " Whether they were right or not is not the concern of the present article. Rather, the concern here is with the important concept of a class of human problems which can be called "no technical solution problems," and, more specifically, with the identification and discussion of one of these.

It is easy to show that the class is not a null class. Recall the game of tick-tack-toe. Consider the problem. "How can I win the game of tick-tack-toe?" It is well known that I cannot, if I assume (in keeping with the conventions of game theory) that my opponent understands the game perfectly. Put another way, there is no "technical solution" to the problem. I can win only by giving a radical meaning to the word "win." I can hit my opponent over the head; or I can drug him; or I can falsify the records. Every way in which I "win" involves, in some sense, an abandonment of the game, as we intuitively understand it. (I can also, of course, openly abandon the game—refuse to play it. This is what most adults do).

The class of "No technical solution problems" has members. My thesis is that the "population problem" as conventionally conceived is a member of this class. How it is conventionally conceived needs some comment. It is fair to say that most people who anguish over the population problem are trying to find a way to avoid the evils of overpopulation without relinquishing any of the privileges they now enjoy. They think that farming the seas or developing new strains of wheat will solve the problem — technologically. I try to show here that the solution they seek cannot be found. The population problem cannot be solved in a technical way, any more than can the problem of winning the game of tick-tack-toe.

What Shall We Maximize?

Population, as Malthus said, naturally tends to grow "geometrically," or as we would now say, exponentially. In a finite world this means that the per capita share of the world's goods must steadily decrease. Is ours a finite world?

A fair defense can be put forward for the view that the world is infinite; or that we do not know that it is now. But, in terms of the practical problems that we must face in the next few generations with the foreseeable technology, it is clear that we will greatly increase human misery if we do not during the immediate future, assume that the world available to the terrestrial human population is finite. "Space" is no escape (2).

A finite world can support only a finite population; therefore, population growth must eventually equal zero. (The case of perpetual wide fluctuations above and below zero is a trival variant that need not be discussed.) When this condition is met, what will be the situation of mankind? Specifically, can Bentham's goal of "the greatest good for the greatest number" be realized?

No—for two reasons, each sufficient by itself. The first is a theoretical one. It is not mathematically possible to maximize for two (or more) variables at the same time. This was clearly stated by von Neumann and Morgenstern (3), but the principle is implicit in the theory of partial differential equations, dating back at least to D'Alembert (1717-1783).

The second reason springs directly from biological facts. To live, any organism must have a source of energy (for example, food). This energy is utilized for two purposes: mere maintenance and work. For man, maintenance of life requires about 1600 kilocalories a day ("maintenance calories"). Anything that he does over and above merely staying alive will be defined as work, and is supported by "work calories" which he takes in. Work calories are used not only for what we call work in common speech; they are also required for all forms of enjoyment, from swimming and automobile racing to playing music and writing poetry. If our goal is to maximize population it is obvious what we must do: We must make the work calories per person approach as close to zero as possible. No gourmet meals, no vacations, no sports, no music, no literature, no art. . .I think that everyone will grant, without argument or proof, that maximizing population does not maximize goods. Bentham's goal is impossible.

In reaching this conclusion I have made the usual assumption that it is the acquisition of energy that is the problem. The appearance of atomic energy has led some to question this assumption. However, given an infinite source of energy, population growth still produces an inescapable problem. The problem of the acquisition of energy is replaced by the problem of its dissipation, as J.H. Fremlin has so wittily shown (4). The arthimetic signs in the analysis are, as it were, reversed; but Bentham's goal is still unobtainable.

The optimum population is, then, less than the maximum. The difficulty of defining the optimum is enormous; so far as I know, no one has seriously tackled this problem. Reaching an acceptable and stable solution will surely require more than one generation of hard analytical work—and much persuasion.

We want the maximum good per person; but what is good? To one person it is wilderness, to another it is ski lodges for thousands. To one it is estuaries to nourish ducks for hunters to shoot; to another it is factory land. Comparing one good with another is, we usually say, impossible because goods are incommensurables. Incommensurables cannot be compared.

Theoretically this may be true; but in real life incommensurables *are* commensurable. Only a criterion of judgment and a system of weighing are needed. In nature the criterion is survival. Is it better for a species to be small and hideable, or large and powerful? Natural selection commensurates the incommensurables. The compromise achieved depends on a natural weighting of the values of the variables.

Man must imitate this process. There is no doubt that in fact he already does, but unconsciously. It is when the hidden decisions are made explicit that the arguments begin. The problem for the years ahead is to work out an acceptable theory of weighting, Synergistic effects, nonlinear variation, and difficulties in discounting the future make the intellectual problem difficult, but not (in principle) insoluble.

Has any cultural group solved this practical problem at the present time, even on an intuitive level? One simple fact proves that none has: there is no prosperous population in the world today that has, and has had for some time, a growth rate of zero. Any people that has intuitively identified its optimum point will soon reach it, after which its growth rate becomes and remains zero.

Of course, a positive growth rate might be taken as evidence that a population is below its optimum. However, by any reasonable standards, the most rapidly growing populations on earth today are (in general) the most miserable. This association (which need not be invariable) casts doubt on the optimistic assumption that the positive growth rate of a population is evidence that it has yet to reach its optimum.

We can make little progress in working toward optimum population size until we explicitly exorcize the spirit of Adam Smith in the field of practical demography. In economic affairs, *The Wealth of Nations* (1776) popularized the "invisible hand," the idea that an individual who "intends only his own gain," is, as it were, "led by an invisible hand to promote. . . .ths public interest" (5). Adam Smith did not assert that this was invariably true, and perhaps neither did any of his followers. But he contributed to a dominant tendency of thought that has ever since interfered with positive action based on rational analysis, namely, the tendency to assume that decisions reached individually will, in fact, be the best decisions for an entire society. If this assumption is correct it justifies the continuance of our present policy of laissez-faire in reproduction. If it is correct we can assume that men will control their individual fecundity so as to produce the optimum population. If the assumption is not correct, we need to reexamine our individual freedoms to see which ones are defensible.

Tragedy of Freedom in a Commons

The rebuttal to the invisible hand in population control is to be found in a scenario first sketched in a little-known pamphlet (6) in 1833 by a mathematical amateur named William Forster Lloyd (1794-1852). We may call it "the tragedy of the commons," using the word "tragedy" as the philosopher Whitehead used it (7): "The essence of dramatic tragedy is not unhappiness. It resides in the solemnity of the remorseless working of things." He then goes on to say, "This inevitableness of destiny can only be illustrated in terms of human life by incidents which in fact involve unhappiness. For it is only by them that the futility of escape can be made evident in the drama."

The tragedy of the commons develops in this way. Picture a pasture open to all. It is to be expected that each herdsman will try to keep as many cattle as possible on the commons. Such an arrangement may work reasonably satisfactorily for centuries because tribal wars, poaching, and disease keep the numbers of both man and beast well below the carrying capacity of the land. Finally, however, comes the day of reckoning, that is, the day when the long-desired goal of social stability becomes a reality. At this point, the inherent logic of the commons remorselessly generates tragedy.

As a rational being, each herdsman seeks to maximize his gain. Explicitly or implicitly, more or less consciously, he asks, "What is the utility *to me* of adding one more animal to my herd?" This utility has one negative and one positive component. 1) The positive component is a function of the increment of one animal. Since the herdsman receives all the proceeds from the sale of the additional animal, the positive utility is nearly plus one. 2) The negative component is a function of the additional overgrazing created by one more animal. Since, however, the effects of overgrazing are shared by all the herdsmen, the negative utility for any particular decision-making herdsman is only a fraction of minus one.

Adding together the component partial utilities, the rational herdsman concludes that the only sensible course for him to pursue is to add another animal to his herd. And another; and another . . . But this is the conclusion reached by each and every rational herdsman sharing a commons. Therein is the tragedy. Each man is locked into a system that compels him to increase his herd without limit—in a world that is limited. Ruin is the destination toward which all men rush, each pursuing his own best interest in a society that believes in the freedom of the commons. Freedom in a commons brings ruin to all.

Some would say that this is a platitude. Would that it were! In a sense, it was learned thousands of years ago, but natural selection favors the forces of psychological denial (8). The individual benefits as an individual from his ability to deny the truth even though society as a whole, of which he is a part, suffers. Education can counteract the natural tendency to do the wrong thing, but the inexorable succession of generations requires that the basis for this knowledge is constantly refreshed.

A simple incident that occurred a few years ago in Leominster, Massachusetts, shows how perishable the knowledge is. During the Christmas shopping season the parking meters downtown were covered with plastic bags that bore tags reading. "Do not open until Christmas. Free parking courtesy of the mayor and city council." In other words, facing the prospect of an increased demand for already scarce space, the city fathers reinstituted the system of the commons. (Cynically, we suspect that they gained more votes than they lost by this retrogressive act.)

In an approximate way. the logic of the commons has been understood for a long time, perhaps since the discovery of agriculture or the invention of private property in real estate. But it is understood mostly only in special cases which are not sufficiently generalized. Even at this late date, cattlemen leasing national land on the western ranges demonstrate no more than an ambivalent understanding, in constantly pressuring federal authorities to increase the head count to the point where overgrazing produces erosion and weed-dominance. Likewise, the oceans of the world continue to suffer from the survival of the philosophy of the commons. Maritime nations still respond automatically to the shibboleth of the "freedom of the seas." Professing to believe in the "inexhaustible resources of the oceans," they bring species after species of fish and whales closer to extinction(9).

The National Parks present another instance of the working out of the tragedy of the commons. At present, they are open to all, without limit. The parks themselves are limited in extent—there is only one Yosemite Valley—whereas population seems to grow without limit. The values that visitors seek in the parks are steadily eroded. Plainly, we must soon cease to treat the parks as commons or they will be of no value to anyone.

What shall we do? We have several options. We might sell them off as private property. We might keep them as public property, but allocate the right to enter them. The allocation might be on the basis of wealth, by the use of an auction system. It might be on the basis of merit, as defined by some agreed-upon standards. It might be by lottery. Or it might be on a first-come, first-served basis, administered to long queues. These, I think, are all the reasonable possibilities. They are all objectionable. But we must choose—or acquiesce in the destruction of the commons that we call our National Parks.

Pollution

In a reverse way, the tragedy of the commons reappears in problems of pollution. Here it is not a question of taking something out of the commons, but of putting something in—sewage, or chemical, radioactive, and heat wastes into water; noxious and dangerous fumes into the air; and distracting and unpleasant advertising signs into the line of sight. The calculations of utility are much the same as before. The rational man finds that his share of the cost of the wastes he discharges into the commons is less than the cost of purifying his wastes before releasing them. Since this is true for everyone, we are locked into a system of "fouling our own nest," so long as we behave only as independent, rational, free-enterprisers.

The tragedy of the commons as a food basket is averted by private property, or something formally like it. But the air and waters surrounding us cannot readily be fenced, and so the tragedy of the commons as a cesspool must be prevented by different means, by coercive laws or taxing devices that make it cheaper for the polluter to treat his pollutants than to discharge them untreated. We have not progressed as far with the solution of this problem as we have with the first. Indeed, our particular concept of private property, which deters us from exhausting the positive resources of the earth, favors pollution. The owner of a factory on the bank of a stream—whose property extends to the middle of the stream—often has difficulty seeing why it is not his natural right to muddy the waters flowing past his door. The law, always behind the times, requires elaborate stitching and fitting to adapt it to this newly perceived aspect of the commons.

The pollution problem is a consequence of population. It did not much matter how a lonely American frontiersman disposed of his waste. "Flowing water purifies itself every 10 miles," my grandfather used to say, and the myth was near enough to the truth when he was a boy, for there were not too many people. But as population became denser, the natural chemical and biological recycling processes became overloaded, calling for a redefinition of property rights.

How To Legislate Temperance?

Analysis of the pollution problem as a function of population density uncovers a not generally recognized principle of morality, namely: *the morality of an act is a function of the state of the system at the time it is performed*(10). Using the commons as a cesspool does not harm the general public under frontier conditions, because there is no public; the same behavior in a metropolis is unbearable. A hundred and fifty years ago a plainsman could kill an American bison, cut out only the tongue for his dinner, and discard the rest of the animal. He was not in any important sense being wasteful. Today, with only a few thousand bison left, we would be appalled at such behavior.

In passing, it is worth noting that the morality of an act cannot be determined from a photograph. One does not know whether a man killing an elephant or setting fire to the grassland is harming others until one knows the total system in which his act appears. "One picture is worth a thousand words," said an ancient Chinese; but it may take 10,000 words to validate it. It is as tempting to ecologists as it is to reformers in general to try to persuade others by way of the photographic shortcut. But the essence of an argument cannot be photographed; it must be presented rationally—in words.

That morality is system-sensitive escaped the attention of most codifiers of ethics in the past. "Thou shalt not . . ." is the form of traditional ethical directives which make no allowance for particular circumstances. The laws of our society follow the pattern of ancient ethics, and therefore are poorly suited to governing a complex, crowded, changeable world. Our epicyclic solution is to augment statutory law with administrative law. Since it is practically impossible to spell out all the conditions under which it is safe to burn trash in the back yard or to run an automobile without smog-control, by law we delegate the details to bureaus, The result is administrative law, which is rightly feared for an ancient reason—*Quis custodiet ipsos custodes?*— Who shall watch the watchers themselves?" John Adams said that we must have "a government of laws and not men." Bureau administrators, trying to evaluate the morality of acts in the total system, are singularly liable to corruption, producing a government by men, not laws.

Prohibition is easy to legislate (although not necessarily to enforce); but how do we legislate temperance? Experience indicates that it can be accomplished best through the mediation of administrative law. We limit possibilities unneccessarily if we suppose that the sentiment of *Quis custodiet* denies us the use of administrative law. We should rather retain the pnrase as a perpetual reminder of fearful dangers we cannot avoid. The great challenge facing us now is to invent the corrective feedbacks that are needed to keep custodians honest. We must find ways to legitimate the needed authority of both the custodians and the corrective feedbacks.

Freedom To Breed Is Intolerable

The tragedy of the commons is involved in population problems in another way. In a world governed solely by the principle of "dog eat dog"—if indeed there ever was such a world—how many children a family had would not be a matter of public concern. Parents who bred ، o exuberantly would leave fewer descendants, not more, because they would be unable to care adequately for their children. David Lack and others have found that such a negative feedback demonstrably controls the fecundity of birds (11). But men are not birds, and have not acted like them for milleniums, at least.

If each human family were dependent only on its own resources; if the children of improvident parents starved to death; if, thus, overbreeding brought its own "punish-ment" to the germ line—*then* there would be no public interest in controlling the breeding of families. But our society is deeply committed to the welfare state (12), and hence is confronted with another aspect of the tragedy of the commons.

In a welfare state, how shall we deal with the family, the religion, the race, or the class (or indeed any distinguishable and cohesive group) that adopts overbreeding as a policy to secure its own aggrandizement (13)? To couple the concept of freedom to breed with the belief that everyone born has an equal right to the commons is to lock the world into a tragic course of action.

Unfortunately this is just the course of action that is being pursued by the United Nations. In late 1967, some 30 nations agreed to the following (14);

> The Universal Declaration of Human Rights describes the family as the natural and fundamental unit of society. It follows that any choice and decision with regard to the size of the family must irrevocably rest with the family itself, and cannot be made by anyone else.

It is painful to have to deny categorically the validity of this right; denying it, one feels as uncomfortable as a resident of Salem, Massachusetts, who denied the reality of witches in the 17th century. At the present time, in liberal quarters, something like a taboo acts to inhibit criticism of the United Nations. There is a feeling that the United Nations is "our last and best hope," that we shouldn't find fault with it; we shouldn't play into the hands of the archconservatives. However, let us not forget what Robert Louis Stevenson said: "The truth that is suppressed by friends is the readiest weapon of the enemy." If we love the truth we must openly deny the validity of the Universal Declaration of Human Rights, even though it is promoted by the United Nations. We should also join with Kingsley Davis (15) in attempting to get Planned Parenthood-World Population to see the error of its ways in embracing the same tragic ideal.

Conscience Is Self-Eliminating

It is a mistake to think that we can control the breeding of mankind in the long run by an appeal to conscience. Charles Galton Darwin made this point when he spoke on the centennial of the publication of his grandfather's great book. The argument is straightforward and Darwinian.

People vary. Confronted with appeals to limit breeding, some people will undoubtedly respond to the plea more than others. Those who have more children will produce a larger fraction of the next generation than those with more susceptible consciences. The difference will be accentuated, generation by generation.

In C.G. Darwin's words: "It may well be that it would take hundreds of generations for the progenitive instinct to develop in this way, but if it should do so, nature would have taken her revenge, and the variety *Homo contracipiens* would become extinct and would be replaced by the variety *Homo progenitivus*"(16).

The argument assumes that conscience or the desire for children (no matter which) is hereditary—but hereditary only in the most general formal sense. The result will be the same whether the attitude is transmitted through germ cells, or exosomatically, to use A.J. Lotka's term. (If one denies the latter possibility as well as the former, then what's the point of education?) The argument has here been stated in the context of the population problem, but it applies equally well to any instance in which society appeals to an individual exploiting a commons to restrain himself for the general good—by means of his conscience. To make such an appeal is to set up a selective system that works toward the elimination of conscience from the race.

Pathogenic Effects of Conscience

The long-term disadvantage of an appeal to conscience should be enough to condemn it; but has serious short-term disadvantages as well. If we ask a man who is exploiting a commons to desist "in the name of conscience," what are we saying to him? What does he hear? — not only at the moment but also in the wee small hours of the night when, half asleep, he remembers not merely the words we used but also the nonverbal communication cues we gave him unaware? Sooner or later, consciously or subconsciously, he senses that he has received two communications, and that they are contradictory: (i) (intended communication) "If you don't do as we ask, we will openly condemn you for not acting like a responsible citizen"; (ii) (the unintended communication) "If you *do* behave as we ask, we will secretly condemn you for a simpleton who can be shamed into standing aside while the rest of us exploit the commons."

Everyman then is caught in what Bateson has called a "double bind." Bateson and his co-workers have made a plausible case for viewing the double bind as an important causative factor in the genesis of schizophrenia (17). The double bind may not always be so damaging, but it always endangers the mental health of anyone to whom it is applied. "A bad conscience," said Nietzsche, "is a kind of illness."

To conjure up a conscience in others is tempting to anyone who wishes to extend his control beyond the legal limits. Leaders at the highest level succumb to this temptation. Has any President during the past generation failed to call on labor unions to moderate voluntarily their demands for higher wages, or to steel companies to honor voluntary guidelines on prices? I can recall none. The rhetoric used on such occasions is designed to produce feelings of guilt in noncooperators.

For centuries it was assumed without proof that guilt was a valuable, perhaps even an indispensable ingredient of the civilized life. Now, in this post-Freudian world, we doubt it.

Paul Goodman speaks from the modern point of view when he says: "No good has ever come from feeling guilty, neither intelligence, policy, nor compassion. The guilty do not pay attention to the object but only to themselves, and not even to their own interests, which might make sense, but to their anxieties"(18).

One does not have to be a professional psychiatrist to see the consequences of anxiety. We in the Western world are just emerging from a dreadful two-centuries-long Dark Ages of Eros that was sustained partly by prohibition laws, but perhaps more effectively by the anxiety-generating mechanisms of education. Alex Comfort has told the story well in *The Anxiety Makers* (19); it is not a pretty one.

Since proof is diffucult, we may even concede that the results of anxiety may sometimes, from certain points of view, be desirable. The larger question we should ask is whether, as a matter of policy, we should ever encourage the use of a technique the tendency (if not the intention) of which is psychologically pathogenic. We hear much talk these days of responsible parenthood; the coupled words are incorporated into the titles of some organizations devoted to birth control. Some people have proposed massive propaganda campaigns to instill responsibility into the nation's (or the world's) breeders. But what is the meaning of the word responsibility in this context? Is it not merely a synonym for the word conscience? When we use the word responsibility in the absence of substantial sanctions are we not trying to browbeat a free man in a commons into acting against his own interests? Responsibility is a verbal counterfeit for a substantial *quid pro quo*. It is an attempt to get something for nothing.

If the word responsibility is used at all, I suggest that it be in the sense Charles Frankel uses it (20). "Responsibility," says this philosopher, "is the product of definite social arrangements." Notice that Frankel calls for social arrangements—not propaganda.

Mutual Coercion Mutually Agreed Upon

The social arrangements that produce responsibility are arrangements that create coercion, of some sort. Consider bank-robbing. The man who takes money from a bank acts as if the bank were a commons. How do we prevent such action? Certainly not by trying to control his behavior solely by a verbal appeal to his sense of responsibility. Rather than rely on propaganda we follow Frankel's lead and insist that a bank is not a commons; we seek the definite social arrangements that will keep it from becoming a commons. That we thereby infringe on the freedom of would-be robbers we neither deny nor regret.

The morality of bank-robbing is particularily easy to understand because we accept complete prohibition of this activity. We are willing to say "Thou shalt not rob banks," without providing for exceptions. But temperance also can be created by coercion. Taxing is a good coercive device. To keep downtown shoppers temperate in their use of parking space we introduce parking meters for short periods, and traffic fines for longer ones. We need not actually forbid a citizen to park as long as he wants to; we need merely make it increasingly expensive for him to do so. Not prohibition, but carefully biased options are what we offer him. A Madison Avenue man might call this persuasion; I prefer the greater candor of the word coercion.

Coercion is a dirty word to most liberals now, but it need not forever be so. As with the four-letter words, its dirtiness can be cleansed away by exposure to the light, by saying it over and over without apology or embarrassment. To many, the word coercion implies arbitrary decisions of distant and irresponsible bureaucrats; but this is not a necessary part of its meaning. The only kind of coercion I recommend is mutual coercion, mutually agreed upon by the majority of the people affected.

To say that we mutually agree to coercion is not to say that we are required to enjoy it, or even to pretend we enjoy it. Who enjoys taxes? We all grumble about them. But we accept compulsory taxes because we recognize that voluntary taxes would favor the conscienceless. We institute and (grumblingly) support taxes and other coercive devices to escape the horror of the commons.

An alternative to the commons need not be perfectly just to be preferable. With real estate and other material goods, the alternative we have chosen is the institution of private property coupled with legal inheritance. Is this system perfectly just? As a genetically trained biologist I deny that it is. It seems to me that, if there are to be differences in individual inheritance, legal possession should be perfectly correlated with biological inheritance—that those who are biologically more fit to be the custodians of property and power should legally inherit more. But genetic recombination continually makes a mockery of the doctrine of "like father, like son" implicit in our laws of legal inheritance. An idiot can inherit millions, and a trust fund can keep his estate intact. We must admit that our legal system of private property plus inheritance is unjust—but we put up with it because we are not convinced, at the moment, that anyone has invented a better system. The alternative of the commons is too horrifying to contemplate. Injustice is preferable to total ruin.

It is one of the peculiarities of the warfare between reform and the status quo that it is thoughtlessly governed by a double standard. Whenever a reform measure is proposed it is often defeated when its opponents triumphantly discover a flaw in it. As Kingley Davis has pointed out (21), worshippers of the status quo sometimes imply that no reform is possible without unanimous agreement, an implication contrary to historical fact. As nearly as I can make out, automatic rejection of proposed reforms is based on one of two unconscious assumptions: (i) that the status quo is perfect; or (ii) that the choice we face is between reform and no action; if the proposed reform is imperfect, we presumably should take no action at all, while we wait for a perfect proposal.

But we can never do nothing. That which we have done for thousands of years is also action. It also produces evils. Once we are aware that the status quo is action, we can then compare its discoverable advantages and disadvantages with the predicted advantages and disadvantages of the proposed reform, discounting as best we can for our lack of experience. On the basis of such a comparison, we can make a rational decision which will not involve the unworkable assumption that only perfect systems are tolerable.

Recognition of Necessity

Perhaps the simplest summary of this analysis of man's population problems is this: the commons, if justifiable at all, is justifable only under conditions of low-population density. As the human population has increased, the commons has had to be abandoned in one aspect after another.

First we abandoned the commons in food gathering, enclosing farm land and restricting pastures and hunting and fishing areas. These restrictions are still not complete throughout the world.

Somewhat later we saw that the commons as a place for waste disposal would also have to be abandoned. Restrictions on the disposal of domestic sewage are widely accepted in the Western world; we are still struggling to close the commons to pollution by automobiles, factories, insecticide sprayers, fertilizing operations, and atomic energy installations.

In a still more embryonic state is our recognition of the evils of the commons in matters of pleasure. There is almost no restriction on the propagation of sound waves in the public medium. The shopping public is assaulted with mindless music, without its consent. Our government is paying out billions of dollars to create supersonic transport which will disturb 50,000 people for every one person who is whisked from coast to coast 3 hours faster. Advertisers muddy the airwaves of radio and television and pollute the view of travelers. We are a long way from outlawing the commons in matters of pleasure. Is this because our Puritan inheritance makes us view pleasure as something of a sin, and pain (that is, the pollution of advertising) as the sign of virtue?

Every new enclosure of the commons involves the infringement of somebody's personal liberty. Infringements made in the distant past are accepted because no contemporary complains of a loss. It is the newly proposed infringements that we vigorously oppose; cries of "rights" and "freedom" fill the air. But what does "freedom" mean? When men mutually agreed to pass laws against robbing, mankind became more free, not less so. Individuals locked into the logic of the commons are free only to bring on universal ruin; once they see the necessity of mutual coercion, they become free to pursue other goals. I believe it was Hegel who said, "Freedom is the recognition of necessity."

The most important aspect of necessity that we must now recognize, is the necessity of abandoning the commons in breeding. No technical solution can rescue us from the misery of overpopulation. Freedom to breed will bring ruin to all. At the moment, to avoid hard decisions many of us are tempted to propagandize for conscience and responsible parenthood. The temptation must be resisted, because an appeal to independently acting consciences selects for the disappearance of all conscience in the long run, and an increase in anxiety in the short.

The only way we can preserve and nurture other and more precious freedoms is by relinquishing the freedom to breed, and that very soon, "Freedom is the recognition of necessity"—and it is the role of education to reveal to all the necessity of abandoning the freedom to breed. Only so, can we put an end to this aspect of the tragedy of the commons.

Notes

(1) J.B. Wiesner and H.F. York, *Sci. Amer.* 211 (No. 4), 27 (1964).

(2) G. Hardin, *J. Hered.* 50, 68 (1959); S. von Hoernor, *Science* 137, 18 (1962).

(3) J. von Neumann and O. Morgenstern, *Theory of Games and Economic Behavior* (Princeton Univ. Press, Princeton, N.J., 1947), p. 11.

(4) J.H. Fremlin, *New Sci.* No. 415 (1964), p. 285.

(5) A. Smith, *The Wealth of Nations* (Modern Library, New York, 1937), p. 423.

(6) W.F. Lloyd, *Two Lectures on the Checks to Population* (Oxford Univ. Press, Oxford, England, 1833), reprinted (in part) in *Population, Evolution, and Birth Control*, G. Hardin, Ed. (Freeman, San Francisco, 1964) p. 37.

(7) A.N. Whitehead, *Science and the Modern World* (Mentor, New York, 1948), p. 17.

(8) G. Hardin, Ed. *Population, Evolution, and Birth Control* (Freeman, San Francisco, 1964), p. 56.

(9) S. McVay, *Sci. Amer.* 216 (No. 8), 13 (1966).

(10) J. Fletcher, *Situation Ethics* (Westminster, Philadelphia, 1966).

(11) D. Lack, *The Natural Regulation of Animal Numbers* (Clarendon Press, Oxford, 1954).

(12) H. Girvetz, *From Wealth to Welfare* (Stanford Univ. Press, Stanford, Calif., 1950).

(13) G. Hardin, *Perspec. Biol. Med.* 6, 366 (1963).

(14) U. Thant, *Int. Planned Parenthood News*, No. 168 (February 1968), p.3.

(15) K. Davis, *Science* 158, 730 (1967).

(16) S. Tax, Ed., *Evolution after Darwin* (Univ. of Chicago Press, Chicago, 1960), vol. 2, p. 469.

(17) G. Bateson, D.D. Jackson, J. Haley, J. Weakland, *Behav. Sci.* 1, 251 (1956).

(18) P. Goodman, *New York Rev. Books* 10(8), 22 (23 May 1968).

(19) A. Comfort, *The Anxiety Makers* (Nelson, London, 1967).

(20) C. Frankel, *The Case for Modern Man* (Harper, New York, 1955), p. 203.

(21) J.D. Roslansky, *Genetics and the Future of Man* (Appleton-Century-Crofts, New York, 1966), p. 177.

THE
TRAGEDY
OF THE
COMMONS
REVISITED

Beryl L. Crowe

There has developed in the contemporary natural sciences a recognition that there is a subset of problems, such as population, atomic war, and environmental corruption, for which there are no techinical solutions (1.?). There is also an increasing recognition among contemporary social scientists that there is a subset of problems, such as population, atomic war, environmental corruption, and the recovery of a livable urban environment, for which there are no current political solutions (3). The thesis of this article is that the common area shared by these two subsets contains most of the critical problems that threaten the very existence of contemporary man.

The importance of this area has not been raised previously because of the very structure of modern society. This society, with its emphasis on differentiation and specialization, has led to the development of two insular scientific communities—the natural and the social — between which there is very little communication and a great deal of envy, suspicion, disdain, and competition for scarce resources. Indeed, these two communities more closely resemble tribes living in close geographic proximity on university campuses than they resemble the "scientific culture" that C.P. Snow placed in contrast to and opposition to the "humanistic culture"(4).

Perhaps the major problems of modern society have, in large part, been allowed to develop and intensify through this structure of insularity and specialization because it serves both psychological and professional functions for both scientific communities. Under such conditions, the natural sciences can recognize that some problems are not technically soluble and relegate them to the nether land of politics, while the social sciences recognize that some problems have no current political solutions and then postpone a search for solutions while they wait for new technologies with which to attack the problem. Both sciences can thus avoid responsibility and protect their respective myths of competence and relevance, while they avoid having to face the awesome and awful possibility that each has independently isolated the same subset of problems and given them different names. Thus, both never have to face the consequences of their respective findings. Meanwhile, due to the specialization and insularity of modern society, man's most critical problems lie in limbo, while the specialists in problem-solving go on to less critical problems for which they can find technical or political solutions.

In this circumstance, one psychologically brave, but professionally foolhardy soul, Garrett Hardin, has dared to cross the tribal boundaries in his article "The Tragedy of the Commons"(1). In it, he gives vivid proof of the insularity of the two scientific tribes in at least two respects: first, his "rediscovery" of the tragedy was in part wasted effort, for the knowledge of this tragedy is so common in the social sciences that it has generated some fairly sophisticated mathematical models (5); second, the recognition of the existence of a subset of problems for which science neither offers nor aspires to offer technical solutions is not likely, under the contemporary conditions of insularity, to gain wide currency in the social sciences. Like Hardin, I will attempt to avoid the psychological and professional benefits of this insularity by tracing some of the political and social implications of his proposed solution to the tragedy of the commons.

The commons is a fundamental social institution that has a history going back through our own colonial experience to a body of English common law which antidates the Roman conquest. That law recognized that in societies there are some environmental objects which have never been, and should never be, exclusively appropriated to any individual or group of individuals. In England the classic example of the commons is the pasturage set aside for public use, and the "tragedy of the commons" to which Hardin refers was a tragedy of overgrazing and lack of care and fertilization which resulted in erosion and underproduction so destructive that there developed in the late 19th century an enclosure movement. Hardin applies this social institution to other environmental objects such as water, atmosphere, and living space.

The cause of this tragedy is exposed by a very simple mathematical model, utilizing the concept of utility drawn from economics. Allowing the utilities to range between a positive value of 1 and a negative value of 1, we may ask, as did the individual English herdsman, what is the utility of me adding one more animal to my herd that grazes on the commons? His answer is that the positive utility is near 1 and the negative utility is only a fraction of minus 1. Adding together the component partial utilities, the herdsman concludes that it is rational for him to add another animal to his herd; then another, and so on. The tragedy to which Hardin refers devolops because the same rational conclusion is reached by each and every herdsman sharing the commons.

In passing the technically insoluble problems over to the political and social realm for solution, Hardin has made three critical assumptions:1. that there exists, or can be developed a "criterion of judgment and a system of weighting . . . " that will "render the incommensurables . . . commensurable . . . " in real life; 2. that, possessing this criterion of judgment, "coercion can be mutually agreed upon," and that the application of coercion to effect a solution to problems will be effective in modern society; and 3. that the administrative system, supported by the criterion of judgment and access to coercion, can and will protect the commons from further desecration.

If all three of these assumptions were correct, the tragedy which Hardin has recognized would dissolve into a rather facile melodrama of setting up administrative agencies. I believe these three assumptions are so questionable in contemporary society that a tragedy remains in the full sense in which Hardin used the term. Under contemporary conditions, the subset of technically insoluble problems is also politically insoluble, and thus we witness a full-blown tragedy wherein "the essence of dramatic tragedy is not unhappiness. It resides in the remorseless working of things.

The remorseless working of things in modern society is the erosion of three social myths which form the basis for Hardin's assumptions, and this erosion is proceeding at such a swift rate that perhaps the myths can neither revitilize nor reformulate in time to prevent the "population bomb" from going off, or before an accelerating "pollution immersion," or perhaps even an "atomic fallout."

Eroding Myth of the Common Value System

Hardin is theoretically correct, from the point of view of the behavioral sciences, in his argument that "in real life incommensurables *are* commensurable." He is moreover, on firm ground in his assertion that to fulfill this condition in real life one needs only "a criterion of judgment and a system of weighting." In real life, however, values are the criteria of judgment, and the system of weighting is dependent upon the ranging of a number of conflicting values in a hierarchy. That such a system of values exists beyond the confines of the nation-state is hardly tenable. At this point in time one is more likely to find such a system of values within the boundaries of the nation-state. Moreover, the nation-state is the only political unit of sufficient dimension to find and enforce political solutions to Hardin's subset of "technically insoluble problems." It is on this political unit that we will fix our attention.

In America there existed until very recently, a set of conditions which perhaps made the solution to Hardin's problem subset possible: we lived with the myth that we were "one people indivisible . . . " This myth postulated that we were the great "melting pot" of the world wherein the diverse cultural ores of Europe were poured into the crucible of the frontier experience to produce a new alloy—an American civilization. This new civilization was presumably united by a common value system that was democratic, equalitarian and existing under universally enforceable rules contained in the Constitution and the Bill of Rights.

In the United States today, however, there is emerging a new set of behavior patterns which suggest that the myth is either dead or dying. Instead of believing and behaving in accordance with the myth, large sectors of the population are developing life-styles and value hierarchies that give contemporary Americans an appearance more closely analogous to the particularistic, primitive forms of "tribal" organizations living in geographic proximity than to that shining new alloy, the American civilization.

With respect to American politics for example, it is increasingly evident tnat the 1960 election was the last election in the United States to be played out according to the rules of pluralistic politics in a two-party system. Certainly 1964 was, even in terms of voting behavior, a contest between the larger tribe that was still committed to the pluralistic model of compromise and accommodation within a winning coalition, and an emerging tribe that is best seen as a millennial revitalization movement directed against mass society—a movement so committed to the revitalization of old values that it would rather lose the election than compromise its values. Under such circumstances former real-life commensurables within the Republican Party suddenly became incommensurable.

In 1968 it was the Democratic Party's turn to suffer the degeneration of commensurables into incommensurables as both the Wallace tribe and the McCarthy tribe refused to play by the old rules of compromise, accommodation, and exchange of interests. Indeed, as one looks back on the 1968 election, there seems to be a common theme in both these camps—a theme of return to more simple and direct participation in decision-making that is only possible in the tribal setting. Yet, despite this similarity, both the Wallaceites and the McCarthyites responded with a value perspective that ruled out compromise and they both demanded a drastic change in the dimension in which politics is played. So firm were the value commitments in both of these tribes that neither (as was the case with the Goldwater forces in 1964) was willing to settle for a modicum of power that could accrue through the processes of compromise with the national party leadership.

Still another dimension of this radical change in behavior is to be seen in the black community where the main trend of the argument seems to be, not in the direction of accommodation, compromise, and integration, but rather in the direction of fragmentation from the larger community, intransigence in the areas where black values and black culture are concerned, and the structuring of a new community of like-minded and like-colored people. But to all appearances even the concept of color is not enough to sustain commensurables in their emerging community as it fragments into religious nationalism, secular nationalism, integrationists, separationists, and so forth. Thus those problems which were commensurable, both interracial and intraracial, in the era of integration became incommensurable in the era of Black Nationalism.

Nor can the growth of commensurable views be seen in the contemporary youth movements. On most of the American campuses today there are at least ten tribes involved in "tribal wars" among themselves and against the "imperialistic" powers of those "over 30." Just to tick them off, without any attempt to be comprehensive, there are the up-tight protectors of the status quo who are looking for middle-class union cards, the revitalization movements of the Young Americans for Freedom, the reformists of pluralism represented by the Young Democrats and the Young Republicans, those committed to New Politics, the Students for a Democratic Society, the Yippies, the Flower Children, the Black Students Union, and the Third World Liberation Front. The critical change in this instance is not the rise of new groups; this is expected within the pluralistic model of politics. What is new are value positions assumed by these groups which lead them to make demands, not as points for bargaining and compromise with the opposition, but rather as points which are "not negotiable." Hence, they consciously set the stage for either confrontation or surrender, but not for rendering incommensurables commensurable.

Moving out of formalized politics and off the campus, we see the remnants of the "hippie" movement which show clear-cut tribal overtones in their commune movements. This movement has, moreover, already fragmented into an urban tribe which can talk of guerilla warfare against the city fathers, while another tribe finds accommodation to urban life untenable without sacrificing its values and therefore moves out to the "Hog Farm," "Morning Star," or "Big Sur." Both hippie tribes have reduced the commensurables with the dominant WASP tribe to the point at which one of the cities on the Monterey Peninsula felt sufficiently threatened to pass a city ordinance against sleeping in trees, and the city of San Francisco passed a law against sitting on sidewalks.

Even among those who still adhere to the pluralistic middle-class American image, we can observe an increasing demand for a change in the dimension of life and politics that has disrupted the elementary social processes: the demand for neighborhood (tribal?) schools, control over redevelopment projects, and autonomy in the setting and payment of rents to slumlords. All of these trends are more suggestive of tribalism than of the growth of the range of commensurables with respect to the commons.

We are, moreover, rediscovering other kinds of tribes in some very odd ways. For example, in the educational process, we have found that one of our first and best empirical measures in terms both of validity and reproducibility—the I.Q. test — is a much better measure of the existence of different linguistic tribes than it is a measure of "native intellect" (6). In the elementary school, the different languages and different values of these diverse tribal children have even rendered the commensurables that obtained in the educational system suddenly incommersurable.

Nor are the empirical contradictions of the common value myth as new as one might suspect. For example, with respect to the urban environment, at least 7 years ago Scott Greer was arguing that the core city was sick and would remain sick until a basic sociological movement took place in our urban environment that would move all the middle classes to the suburbs and surrender the core city to the " . . . segregated, the insulted, and the injured"(7). This argument by Greer came at a time when most of us were still talking about compromise and accommodation of interests, and was based upon a perception that the life styles, values, and needs of these two groups were so disparate that a healthy, creative restructuring of life in the core city could not take place until pluralism had been replaced by what amounted to geographic or territorial tribalism; only when this occurred would urban incommensurables become commensurable.

Looking at a more recent analysis of the sickness of the core city, Wallace F. Smith has argued that the productive model of the city is no longer viable for the purposes of economic analysis (8). Instead, he develops a model of the city as a site for leisure consumption, and then seems to suggest that the nature of this model is such that the city cannot regain its health because it cannot make decisions, and that it cannot make decisions because the leisure demands are value-based and, hence, do not admit of compromise and accommodation; consequently there is no way of deciding among these various value-oriented demands that are being made on the core city.

In looking for the cause of the erosion of the myth of a common value system, it seems to me that so long as our perceptions and knowledge of other groups were formed largely through the written media of communication, the American myth that we were a giant melting pot of equalitarians could be sustained. In such a perceptual field it is tenable, if not obvious, that men are motivated by interests. Interests can always be compromised and accommodated without undermining our very being by sacrificing values. Under the impact of the electronic media, however, this psychological distance has broken down and we now discover that these people with whom we could formerly compromise on interests are not, after all, really motivated by interests but by values. Their behavior in our very living room betrays a set of values, moreover, that are incompatable with our own, and consequently the compromises that we make are not those of contract but of culture. While the former are acceptable, any form of compromise on the latter is not a form of rational behavior but is rather a clear case of either apostasy or heresy. Thus, we have arrived not at an age of accommodation but one of confrontation. In such an age "incommensurables" remain "incommensurable" in real life.

Erosion of the Myth of the Monopoly of Coercive Force

In the past, those who no longer subscribed to the values of the dominant culture were held in check by the myth that the state possessed a monopoly on coercive force. This myth has undergone continued erosion since the end of World War II owing to the success of the strategy of guerrilla warfare, as first revealed to the French in Indochina, and later conclusively demonstrated in Algeria. Suffering as we do from what Senator Fulbright has called "the arrogance of power," we have been extremely slow to learn the lesson in Vietnam, although we now realize that war is political and cannot be won by military means. It is apparent that the myth of the monopoly of coercive force as it was first qualified in the civil rights conflict in the South, then in our urban ghettos, next on the streets of Chicago, and now on our college campuses has lost its hold over the minds of Americans. The technology of guerrilla warfare has made it evident that, while the state can win battles, it cannot win wars of values. Coercive force which is centered in the modern state cannot be sustained in the face of the active resistance of some 10 percent of its population unless the state is willing to embark on a deliberate policy of genocide directed against the value dissident groups. The factor that sustained the myth of coercive force in the past was the acceptance of a common value system. Whether the latter exists is questionable in the modern nation-state. But, even if most members of the nation-state remain united around a common value system which makes incommensurables for the majority commensurable, that majority is incapable of enforcing its decisions upon the minority in the face of the diminished coercive power of the governing body of the nation-state.

Erosion of the Myth of Administrators of the Commons

Hardin's thesis that the administrative arm of the state is capable of legislating temperance accords with current administrative theory in political science and touches on one of the concerns of that body of theory when he suggests that the ". . .great challenge facing us now is to invent the corrective feedbacks that are needed to keep the custodians honest."

Our best empirical answers to the questions—*Quis custodiet ipsos custodes?*— "Who shall watch the watchers themselves?"— have shown fairly conclusively (9) that the decisions, orders, hearings, and press releases of the custodians of the commons, such as the Federal Communications Commission, the Interstate Commerce Commission, the Federal Trade Commission, and even the Bureau of Internal Revenue, give the large but unorganized groups in American society symbolic satisfaction and assurances. Yet, the actual day-to-day decisions and operations of these administrative agencies contribute, foster, aid, and indeed legitimate the special claims of small but highly organized groups to differential access to tangible resources which are extracted from the commons. This has been so well documented in the social sciences that the best answer to the question of who watches over the custodians of the commons is the regulated interests that make incursions on the commons.

Indeed, the process has been so widely commented upon that one writer has postulated a common life cycle for all of the attempts to develop regulatory policies (10). This life cycle is launched by an outcry so widespread and demanding that it generates enough political force to bring about the establishment of a regulatory agency to insure the equitable, just, and rational distribution of the advantages among all holders of interest in the commons. This phase is followed by the symbolic reassurance of the offended as the agency goes into operation, developing a period of political quiescence among the great majority of those who hold a general but unorganized interest in the commons. Once this political quiescence has developed, the highly organized and specifically interested groups who wish to make incursions into the commons bring sufficient pressure to bear through other political processes to convert the agency to the protection and furthering of their interests. In the last phase even stalling of the regulating agency is accomplished by drawing the agency administrators from the ranks of the regulated.

Thus, it would seem that, even with the existence of a common value system accompanied by a viable myth of the monopoly of coercive force, the prospects are very dim for saving the commons from differential exploitation or spoliation by the administrative devices in which Hardin places his hope. This being the case, the natural sciences may absolve themselves of responsibility for meeting the environmental challenges of the contemporary world by relegating those problems for which there are no technical solutions to the political or social realm. This action will, however, make little contribution to the solution of the problem.

Are the Critical Problems of Modern Society Insoluble?

Earlier in this article I agreed that perhaps until very recently, there existed a set of conditions, which made the solution to Hardin's problem subset possible; now I suggest that the concession is questionable. There is evidence of structural as well as value problems which make comprehensive solutions impossible and these conditions have been present for some time.

For example, Aaron Wildavsky, in a comprehensive study of the budgetary process, has found that in the absence of a calculus for resolving "intrapersonal comparison of utilities," the governmental budgetary process proceeds by a calculus that is sequential and incremental rather than comprehensive. This being the case ". . .if one looks at politics as a process by which the government mobilizes resources to meet pressing problems" (11) the budget is the focus of these problem responses and the responses to problems in contemporary America are not the sort of comprehensive responses required to bring order to a disordered environment. Another example of the operation of this type of rationality is the American involvement in Vietnam; for, what is the policy of escalation but the policy of sequential incrementalism given a new Madison Avenue euphemism? The question facing us all is the question of whether incremental rationality is sufficient to deal with 20th-century problems.

The operational requirements of modern institutions make incremental rationality the only viable form of decision-making, but this only raises the prior question of whether there are solutions to any of the major problems raised in modern society. It may well be that the emerging forms of tribal behavior noted in this article are the last hope of reducing political and social institutions to a level where incommensurables become commensurable in terms of value *and* in terms of comprehensive responses to problems. After all, in the history of man on earth, we might well assume that the departure from the tribal experience is a short-run deviant experiment that failed. As we stand "on the eve of destruction," it may well be that the return to face-to-face life in the small community unmediated by the electronic media is a very functional response in terms of the perpetuation of the species.

There is, I believe, a significant sense in which the human environment is directly in conflict with the source of man's ascendancy among the other species of the earth. Man's evolutionary position hinges, not on specialization, but rather on generalized adaptability. Modern social and political institutions, however, hinge on specialized, sequential, incremental decision-making and not on generalized adaptability. This being the case, life in the nation-state will continue to require a singleness of purpose for success but in a very critical sense this singleness of purpose becomes a straitjacket that makes generalized adaptation impossible. Nowhere is this conflict more evident than in our urban centers where there has been a decline in the livability of the total environment that is almost directly proportionate to the rise of special purpose districts. Nowhere is this conflict between institutional singleness of purpose and the human dimension of the modern environment more evident than in the recent warning of S. Goran Lofroth, chairman of a committee studying pesticides for the Swedish National Research Council, that many breast-fed children ingest from their mother's milk "more than the recommended daily intake of DDT" (12) and should perhaps be switched to cow's milk because cows secrete only 2 to 10 percent of the DDT they ingest.

Science and the Saving of the Commons

It would seem that, despite the nearly remorseless working of things, science has some interim contributions to make to the alleviation of those problems of the commons which Hardin has pointed out.

These contributions can come at two levels: 1. Science can concentrate more of its attention on the development of technological responses which at once alleviate those problems and reward those people who no longer desecrate the commons. This approach would seem more likely to be successful than the " . . . fundamental extension in morality . . . " by administrative law; the engagement of interest seems to be a more reliable and consistent motivator of advantage-seeking groups than does administrative wrist-slapping or constituency pressure from the general public. 2. Science can perhaps, by using the widely proposed environmental monitoring systems, use them in such a way as to sustain a high level of "symbolic disassurance" among the holders of generalized interests in the commons—thus sustaining their political interest to a point where they would provide a constituency for the administrator other than those bent on denuding the commons. This latter approach would seem to be a first step toward the " . . . invention of the corrective feedbacks that are needed to keep custodians honest." This would require a major change in the behavior of science, however, for it could no longer rest content with development of the technology of monitoring and with turning the technology over to some new agency. Past administrative experience suggests that the use of technology to sustain a high level of "dis-assurance" among the general population would also require science to take up the role and the responsibility for maintaining, controlling, and disseminating the information.

Neither of these contributions to maintaining a habitable environment will be made by science unless there is a significant break in the insularity of the two scientific tribes. For, if science must, in its own insularity, embark on the independent discovery of "the tragedy of the commons," along with the parameters that produce the tragedy, it may be too slow a process to save us from the total destruction of the planet. Just as important, however, science will, by pursuing such a course, divert its attention from the production of technical tools, information, and solutions which will contribute to the political and social solutions for the problems of the commons.

Because I remain very suspicious of the success of either demands or pleas for fundamental extensions in morality, I would suggest that such a conscious turning by both the social and the natural sciences is, at this time, in their immediate self-interest. As Michael Polanyi has pointed out, ". . .encircled today between the crude utilitarianism of the philistine and the ideological utilitarianism of the modern revolutionary movement, the love of pure science may falter and die" (13). The sciences, both social and natural, can function only in a very special intellectual environment that is neither universal or unchanging, and that environment is in jeopardy. The questions of humanistic relevance raised by the students at M.I.T., Stanford Research Institute, Berkeley, and wherever the headlines may carry us tomorrow, pose serious threats to the maintenance of that intellectual environment. However ill-founded *some* of the questions raised by the new generation may be, it behooves us to be ready with at least some collective, tentative answers — if only to maintain an environment in which both sciences will be allowed and fostered. This will not be accomplished so long as the social sciences continue to defer the most critical problems that face mankind to future technical advances, while the natural sciences continue to defer those same problems which are about to overwhelm all mankind to false expectations in the political realm.

Notes

(1) G. Hardin, *Science* 162, 1243 (1968).

(2) J.B. Wiesner and H.F. York, *Sci. Amer.* 211 (No. 4), 27 (1964).

(3) C. Woodbury, *Amer. J. Public Health* 45, 1 (1955); S. Marquis, *Amer. Behav. Sci.* 11, 11 (1968); W.H. Ferry, *Center Mag.* 2, 2 (1969).

(4) C.P. Snow, *The Two Cultures and the Scientific Revolution* (Cambridge Univ. Press, New York, 1959).

(5) M. Olson, Jr., *The Logic of Collective Action* (Harvard Univ. Press, Cambridge,

Mass., 1965).

(6) G.A. Harrison *et al., Human Biology* (Oxford Univ. Press, New York, 1964), p. 292; W.W. Charters, Jr. in *School Children in the Urban Slum* (Free Press, New York, 1967).

(7) S. Greer, *Governing the Metropolis* (Wiley, New York, 1962), p. 148.

(8) W.F. Smith, "The Class Struggle and the Disquieted City," a paper presented at the 1969 annual meeting of the Western Economic Association, Oregon State University, Corvallis.

(9) M. Bernstein, *Regulating Business by Independent Commissions* (Princeton Univ. Press, Princeton, N.J., 1955); E.P. Herring, *Public Administration and the Public Interest* (McGraw-Hill, New York, 1936); E.M. Redford, *Administration of National Economic Control* (Macmillan, New York, 1952).

(10) M. Edelman, *The Symbolic Uses of Politics* (Univ. of Illinois Press, Urbana, 1964).

(11) A. Wildavsky, *The Politics of the Budgetary Process* (Little Brown, Boston, Mass., 1964).

(12) Corvallis *Gazette-Times*, 6 May 1969, p. 6.

(13) M. Polanyi, *Personal Knowledge* (Harper & Row, New York, 1964), p. 182.

ECOLOGY
AND
POPULATION

Amos H. Hawley

Man's occupance of the earth is everywhere under attack by environmentalists and conservationists. Man is harassed for using nature's resources, for building dams, for exterminating bothersome species, for disposing of his refuse, for using the waters, for cultivating the topsoil, for employing insecticides, and for just being present. One gets the impression from this cacophony that nature has been contrived for all species of life except man. Even the ecologists, who should know better belabor man with an environmental rhetoric that fails to acknowledge the many parallels between the behaviors of populations of lower and higher forms of life. It is possible that such statements as "man is a shocking biological innovation," "man is a conflict with nature," "population growth causes a disproportionate negative impact on environment," and "urbanization is a cancerous growth" may serve a useful purpose in the campaign to bring about a more sensible use of resources and environment. But since these colorful statements are put forth in the name of ecology and in the interest of solving the population problem, there is reason to enquire into their accuracy. What in other words, is ecology, and what is its contribution to population study?

Ecology as commonly defined, is the study of the relation of organism to environment. Inasmuch as organism and environment make up all of nature, ecology would seem to be the study of the relation of everything to everything else. An undertaking of that scope is manifestly far too ambitious to be very productive within specifiable intervals of time. Some sort of limitation of the subject, arbitrary though it may be, is essential if anything is to be accomplished during a scholar's lifetime. The holistic approach, moreover, when held too rigidly, leads to a disappearance of variables; every property tends to be seen as an aspect of another property. On this score, too, expediency must be consulted. Despite these inherent difficulties, an approach that attempts to deal directly with complex wholes is a useful complement to the usual analytical treatment of actual events.

The scaling down of ecology to manageable proportions proceeds along either of two lines. One is represented in studies of relations between given species and particular environmental features. Problems of the effects of variations in light on the reproduction of a plant species, of the relation of vegetative cover to the nesting habits of ground-testing birds, and of the effects of a parasite on its host are illustrative. A second kind of limitation is what might be called a systems approach, as exemplified in attempts to analyze the interactions among a set of species in the process of adapting to their environment. Studies of this type represent the ecological point of view most fully, although they are not the most common.

The clearest illustration of the systems approach in ecology is found in the uses of the ecosystem concept. This has been set forth succinctly in a recent paper by Eugene Odum who says that an ecosystem ''. . . is considered to be made up of all of the organisms in a given area (that is, "community") interacting with the physical environment so that a flow of energy leads to characteristic trophic structure and material cycles within the system" (1). The community-environment interaction as thus described takes the form of a developmental process known as succession. In that process, each association of species (that is, community) alters the chemical and sometimes the physical characteristics of a unit of territory through its occupance of the area, thereby preparing the way for its displacement by succeeding association of species, and so on. After two, three, or more such stages, the process culminates in a climax stage, which comprises an association of species that can maintain itself indefinitely in the area. The climax stage is described by Odum as one in which the "maximum biomass (or high information content) and symbiotic function between organisms are maintained per unit of available energy flow" (1). In short, succession is directional, developmental, and predictable: it is the ontogenetic counterpart of biological evolution (3).

As a theory, the concept of the ecosystem is attractive. It is simple in design, it appears to identify and describe a unitary phenomenon, it indicates how structure might be a predictable outcome of change, and it suggests the possibility of forecasting the population size of a mature biotic community. Its virtues, however, are also its limitations. For example, viewing the environment as a specific unit of territory seems inadequate. It is hard to believe that the organisms in adjacent territory are without effect on events in the area marked off as environment. Nor is any information given concerning the species displaced in the course of succession. Furthermore, the equilibrium attained in the climax phase of succession is allowed to stand without qualification: perhaps the balance of numbers in the several species and the balance of the entire community with energy resources in the environment should be regarded as a process rather than as a stable state. The tendency of animals to multiply to the maximum carrying capacity of their habitats has not been clearly established in reports on their territorial habits. However, every abstract formulation neglects or obscures a great amount of information in the interest of parsimony: presumably, important substantive issues are taken up as the occasion arises.

The more pertinent question of the moment is, What relevance does the ecologist's concept of the ecosystem have for mankind? On this point there seems to be no small amount of inconsistency. Many environmentalists who profess an ecological point of view are inclined to exclude man from eco-systems. Although they may acknowledge that all of life is interrelated, they nevertheless look upon the human species as a sort of apocalyptic force thrust upon nature from some anti-nature. Their ambivalence is whimsical, to say the least. While man is being buffeted with criticism for his misuses of the environment, there is silence on the activities of the beavers that cut more trees than they need, on the animals that trod out pathways which become channels of erosion, and on various polluting effects of animal behavior. Evidently there is a beneficent homeostasis that operates to correct the depredations caused by lower forms of life, but not those of man. It is also strange than many species can disappear through excessive inbreeding or some other error in animal judgment without bringing on ecological catastrophe, yet the threatened elimination of the bald eagle or the jaguar is a disaster of major proportions. Eutrophication, that word with the curiously inverted connotation, turns out to be no more than an esthetic tragedy, unless nature doesn't really set as high a value on green plants as we have been led to believe. This confusion of personal preferences, esthetic predilections, and moral judgments with scientific principles can hardly be of service to ecology.

Professional ecologists, on the other hand, show a much greater willingness to include man in ecosystems whenever it is appropriate to do so. They often err in another direction. That is, they tend to treat man simply as a species, as an aggregate of homogeneous individuals rather than as a highly differentiated and organized population. This viewpoint may result from the biological perspective that dominates most ecological work. The great strides that have been made in adapting demographic techniques to plant and animal population studies have not been matched by an awakening to the effects of social and economic structure on the man-environment relationship.

Of central importance in appraising the applicability of the ecosystem concept to human society is the design of the concept itself. It will have been noted, no doubt, that it is almost as exact replica of the Malthusian model. There is the notion of a specific unit of territory with fixed resources, an irresistable tendency for organisms to multiply to the maximum carrying capacity of the resources, the emergence of an equilibrium of numbers with resources at a subsistence level, and, finally, an implicit assumption, by virtue of the subject matter, that all other possible variables are constant. Both the ecosystem in Odum's hands, and the Malthusian theory are analytical constructs.

There is nothing wrong, of course, with an analytical model, as long as its use is confined to the purposes for which it was constructed. That, unfortunately, has not been the experience with either the ecological or the Malthusian form of the ecosystem concept. The all-important limiting assumption of a fixed state of the art has lulled many people into either forgetting that the state of the art is a variable of consequence or believing that the variable has been neutralized to the point where environment is the determining factor in population growth. Hence the model has been freely employed both as a description of actual situations and as a diagnosis of societal problems.

The Malthusian conceptualization of the man-environment relationship is widely favored, especially by biologists and others who have had little or no exposure to models of thinking in the social sciences. Garrett Hardin, for example, thinks of human population in a simple-minded analogy with grazing animals in a fenced pasture (4). He measures current population trends against "foreseeable technology," by which he means an unchanging technology. His is a view that has been informed by neither a historic perspective nor a competent assessment of the existing informational and institutional resources for change. The Malthusian model also supplies the major intellectual underpinning for a great deal of contemporary family planning ideology. Wherever it is assumed, by action if not by explicit statement, that population is the only factor which can be expected to vary, or which can be manipulated, one finds an iteration of the classical view. Popular scientific literature is full of oversimplified explanations of pollution, of malnutrition, of poverty, and of psychological tensions in cities.

Constructions other than Odum's can be put on the term "ecosystem." Odum's is a system with boundaries determined by the physical limits of a settled population, a definition that may be appropriate for plants, but not for animals. The more general use of the term is in reference to systems with boundaries delineated by the outer reaches of functional relationships — that is, by the circulations of energy producing matter rather than by place of occupance (5). On this basis, ecosystems vary greatly in scope and in composition (6). The more diversified the food habits and other activities of an association of species, the more far-reaching and intricate its ecosystem. In this sense, the human ecosystem exceeds that of any other class of organism. It is further complicated by the fact that human beings enter into energy cycles not as a simple aggregate, but in a highly differentiated way. For these reasons, the role of mankind in an ecosystem should be examined separately and in detail before comparisons with other communities are carried beyond the analogical stage.

It is at this point that a human ecology, as distinct from bioecology, makes its appearance. The extension of the ecological point of view to the study of *Homo sapiens* carries with it two assumptions, both of which are implicit in the concept of the ecosystem. First, adaptation to environment is an imperative and omnipresent concern for every class of living thing. Second, adapation in all but a few physiological respects is a collective phenomenon; it is achieved not by individuals acting independently, but by combining their special abilities in an organization that operates as a unit of a higher order. The assumed transferability of methods and concepts from lower to higher forms of life is based mainly on the greater degrees of similarity among populations (which are the units of ecological study) than among individuals. Differences between levels of life appear, of course, in the applications of the assumptions.

The first assumption, that environmental adaptation is necessary, needs no exposition, although the pervasiveness of its implications in human affairs is not universally appreciated. There is some room for uncertainity, however, in what constitutes environment and in what the nature of the adaptive relationship is. In discussing these points, I retrace some of the ground covered by Ansley Coale (7). My purpose in doing so is to explore the application of ecology to population study; it is not to try to improve upon his statement.

It should be noted that the term "environment" has no fixed denotation. It is a generic concept for whatever is external to and potentially influential upon a unit under study. The environment of a population is different from that of an individual and from that of a set of populations. Thus the act of defining refers one back to the thing environed. That thing, from the standpoint of ecology, is a population which is organized or in the process of organization. The clarity of the environmental definition can be no greater than that of the environed unit.

A great deal of what is external to any entity is often overlooked in considerations of environment. The usual practice is to restrict the term to those externalities that are close by and directly experienced. While that may be expedient in some situations, the restriction is clearly arbitrary. Numerous repercussions from distant events are felt in any given locality. Still, the fact of the matter is that the content and the boundaries of environment are affected by the accessibility of the unit or by its facility for movement. Environment, in other words, includes as much of what is external as can be reached in any given interval of time. Obviously, then, both location and the transportation and communication facilities possessed by a community or society are determinants of their environment.

Where the means of movement are crude and costly, where production techniques are primitive, and where marketing facilities are nonexistent, a community lives in a narrowly circumscribed area and in intimate association with its biophysical environment. The model of the closed ecosystem is very nearly approximated under such conditions. Even so, population is regulated by the personnel requirements of the community which may remain fairly constant over long periods of time. Instances of this kind, once rather commonplace, are vanishing from the human scene (8).

The disappearance of easily recognized ecosystems has followed the accumulation of human culture and the expansion of organization. I need not linger over the character of the expansion process. Dudley Duncan's "Social organization and the ecosystem"(9) leaves little to be said. It is enough to repeat here that in the long sweep of Western history the scale of territorial organization has advanced from the small, village-centered system delineated by a pedestrian ambit to the vast, urban-dominated, interregional domain knit together by various mechanical means of transportation and communication. The spreading territorial division of labor has arrayed population centers and their respective tributary areas in functional hierarchies, while extending commercial and cultural influences outward in many directions. There are now numerous large, diffuse, and multicentered urban systems that overlie and interpenetrate one another at many points. Many of the events in the West of the last two or three centuries are being repeated in the developing nations, albeit in an uneven and faltering fashion. The prospect is that the urban systems now being formed in the developing nations will ultimately fall into appropriate functional positions in the world's urban hierarchy.

Organizational expansion has produced a number of large-scale changes in the human population's relation to its environment. First, the local environment (that which is encompassed in the daily and weekly circulations of a resident population) has been converted from a source of substance to so much space within which nonextractive uses are arranged. In that setting, adaptation has become largely a housekeeping task. As the importance of the local environment has receded before the widening scope of the extra-local environment, land uses in the former have been regulated increasingly by events in the latter. There are other notable consequences of the enlargement of the environment. For example, each localized population now draws its food and other materials from such a wide area that an accurate description of its effective environment poses an almost insurmountable measurement problem. That problem is further complicated by frequent shifts and substitutions of resource use brought about by technological changes. A related effect of expansion concerns the extent to which the physical and biotic environment is mediated through other organized populations (10). The thickening web of exchange relations that has spread across the world has created a social environment between each local population and the physical environment. Much of the latter has been so effectively screened from view that it has been easy for people to acquire an attitude of indifference and neglect toward their physical world. A third effect of expansion is that the environments, both physical and social, of all human groups have become increasingly alike. Virtually everyone in the Western world can now remain at a given place and still have access to all of the world's products and all of the information available in repositories, wherever located. Environmental standardization in this sense will soon become worldwide.

It may be that this merging of societies and consequent sharing of a single environment will, as it progresses, result in some loss of adaptability and some risk to survival. Formerly, when human settlement consisted of many somewhat isolated communities or societies, catastrophe could strike one or more without affecting others. Had there been radical shifts in environmental conditions, some societies might have succumbed, while others could have successfully adapted to the change. Adaptive innovations acquired thereby would then be available for diffusion to other localized societies. Diffusion, the accumulation of innovations, expansion, absorption of people in enlarging societies, and further expansion have taken us far from the early state of adaptive anarchy. With the approach of an embracive social system, there might be no more than one chance at adapting to drastic environmental shifts and no more than one chance to survive a major upheaval.

What I have been saying in a roundabout way is that there is no direct relation between population and environment. Every population confronts its external world as some form of organization. The critical relation, then, is between an organization and environment. If there are environmental problems, their explanation and their solution must be sought in the way the given organization is constituted. It should be no less evident that adaptation is a collective (that is, organizational) achievement.

If it is true that adaptation is necessarily accomplished through organization, the fact has profound implications for the importance of the individual in the determination of societal events. His contribution to the adaptive process, it logically follows, is confined largely to his performance of a more or less specialized function in a division of labor. There are certain functions, of course, that place some individuals at the confluxes of information flows. Those few individuals have opportunities, assuming other conditions are favorable, for contributing to adaptation through invention and discovery. But in general, most of the options open to individuals consist of using or not using, or making choices among, the goods, services, vocations, and avocations generated by the same division of labor in which they are themselves involved. How those amenities are used is also determined by the structure of the system.

This seems to fly in the face of common sense. Everyone knows, from long experience as an initiator of action, that it is the individual who wills things to be done and it is the aggregate of willing that produces social phenomena. People act alike in a given situation so goes the reasoning, because they have common values, a term that probably is translatable as common motives. But to the ecologically minded student, that proposition merely begs the question, for it leaves unanswered the question of how commonality of values or motives come into being. It would seem that in the degree to which behavior is similar, the explanation of that behavior cannot be found in psychological variables — it must be sought in the processes involved in the operation of the social system. Individuals may expound at length on the reasons for their having a given number of children, for migrating from one place to another, or for engaging in any other kind of activity, but only a few are perceptive enough to recognize that the degrees of freedom in their decision-making are fixed in the structure of society.

Thus the belief that birthrates remain high in developing countries because people are not motivated to reduce their fertility seems to confuse a fact with its explanation. It fails to take account of the very strong probability that fertility behavior is so enmeshed in a web of institutionalized relationships and practices that it cannot be isolated for separate treatment. Even though death rates may have fallen substantially in areas undergoing modernization, birthrates tend to remain high because for most of the population the family is still the primary producing unit, the network of kinship obligations is unaltered, production continues to be labor intensive, and no substitute for the family as a source of old-age security has emerged. As long as the structural features of an agrarian society persist, it seems unlikely that contraceptive distribution programs can do more than reduce the frequency of pregnancies to what is needed to maintain a given number of surviving children per couple. The dependence of changes in vital rates on changes in the social structure has been recognized, notably by Ronald Freedman (11), but it has had relatively little acceptance in either research or policy spheres to date.

It is entirely consistent with this line of reasoning to infer that population problems are essentially problems of adjusting the size and characteristics of population to the personnel requirements of a social system. This may be clear enough where simple societies are concerned, but the adjustment becomes much more involved in the case of complex societies. I shall pursue one aspect of the relation of population to society, if only for illustrative purposes.

Consider the population requirements in an expanding system. The demographic transition model will serve as a useful vehicle in examining those requirements. In that context, I start with the assumption that, prior to the onset of cumulative population growth, rates of birth and death are high and in an unstable equilibrium and that the balancing of vital rates is a function of an equilibrium between population and organization. In other words, birthrates tend to adjust to mortality and thereby to maintain the number and kinds of people needed to staff an organization.

That being the case, any significant change in the manpower needs of an organization upsets the vital equilibrium. If that change is in the direction of permanent increases in productivity and in the amount of product, birthrates and death rates will move downward (death rates declining more rapidly), eventually reaching a new equilibrium at a lower rate. To reason from the transition model would lead one to believe that the new birth-death equilibrium implies a new population-organization equilibrium. If that inference were correct, the nature of the new population-organization equilibrium would be quite different from the one that is assumed to have existed before. In the developed countries, while birthrates and death rates are approximating equivalence, organizational complexity and technological accumulation continue to increase exponentially. Clearly this is an outcome that Malthus did not anticipate. It is doubtful, moreover, that it has any parallel among lower forms of life.

An explanation of the detachment of birth-death equilibrium from population-organization equilibrium is probably to be found in the operation of one or more substitution principles. Perhaps one of these substitutions involves reckoning in terms of man-years rather than in terms of number of individuals. If each live birth yields an average of 68 years of life instead of 30 years, then obviously a given aggregate number of man-years of life can be realized from fewer than half the number of births. Of equal, if not greater, importance is the substitution of capital equipment for people. In other words, it appears that in the process of technological change a point is reached at which productivity becomes independent of the size of the labor force. This may be why Simon Kuznets found negligible correlations between population growth and economic growth in the histories of developed countries (12). Gains in the efficiency of tools and productive organization feed off· accumulated information and consequently displace increasing numbers of workers. In the United States, for example, the ratio of capital to labor has been rising at about 1.25 percent per year for the past century (13). It is this circumstance which lies behind the shift of industrial predominance in the economy from primary to secondary to tertiary sectors. As far as population size is concerned, it appears that a social system has an asymptotic property that is fixed by the manpower requirements of the technology in use.

But what are the manpower requirements of an industrialized society? It does appear that they are considerably higher than those of an agrarian society. A point of uncertainty in this connection has to do with what should serve as a basis for comparison. It may be observed that industrialization supports many more people in a given amount of space than did the preceding agrarian economy. Now, if more people are necessary in societies that are advancing to higher levels of productivity, then the lagging decline of the birthrate in the demographic transition was also necessary. Only thus could the increased numbers of people required to fill the growing diversity of roles be obtained; people can be born anywhere, of course, and move to the region undergoing change. Does this mean that the experience of the West must be repeated in the developing nations? Will industrialization necessitate substantial increases in the populations of India, mainland China, and other crowded parts of the world? Perhaps not. Recent population growth in those areas, out of phase though it might have been, might already have produced enough people to man a highly complex economic and social order.

The transformation to an industrialized society appears to call for a rather intricate demographic involution. Unfortunately, it has not been possible to demonstrate some of the aspects of the reallocation of manpower very satisfactorily. It is more than probable that, as industrialization advances, the proportion of the population comprising the labor force declines. But the measurement problems are such that official statistics give us only the numbers that occupy conventionally recognized positions in the economy. The data normally exclude housewives, children who perform useful chores around farm and house, and old people engaged in light tasks. Longitudinal studies on the proportion of a population in the labor force are confounded by transfers of workers from unpaid to paid employment. A standardized enumeration of all people who participate in economies, were that feasible, would probably show relatively more people doing productive work in agrarian than in industrialized societies.

A decline in the relative size of the labor force does not, however, contradict the need for large numbers of people in an industrially advanced society. While such a society needs comparatively few workers, it needs relatively more consumers. In an agrarian society, everybody, excluding only the very young child and the infirm adult, is both a producer and a consumer, although not in the same degrees. In the industrial society, on the other hand, a large body of specialized consumers, whose economic contribution to the system is that of consumption, emerges. That includes virtually everyone under 17 years of age, a substantial and increasing proportion of those aged 17 to 22, and most people over 65. It might be argued that the product consumed by persons under 22 years of age is also an investment, but all consumption might be so regarded. The specialized consumer role, viewed as parasitic in some quarters, is vital to a highly productive economy. Unless this role is diligently cultivated, all of the goods and services produced will not be taken off the market, the scale of industry could not then be maintained, and the advantages of mass production will have been curtailed.

Several contingencies will affect the consumer function now and in the future. One of these concerns the reliance of industrial economies on foreign populations for some of the consumption needed to sustain them at efficient levels of production. The dumping of surplus products in foreign markets, ordinary trade relations, and foreign aid have served that end. But it may not be possible to depend on foreign populations to the same extent in the future as in the past. As the economies of developing nations mature to the point where they can supply their own populations with full ranges of consumer goods, their assistance in maintaining the economies of the developed nations will decline.

A possible second contingency is a decline in the ratio of children to adults. This might be thought to reduce dependency and thus contract the market for consumer durables and numerous services to households. As already suggested, however, that effect is being offset by increases in the ratio of nonworkers to workers. An estimate prepared by Juanita Krebs and Joseph Spengler indicates that, if productivity continues along the trend it has followed since the turn of the century (that is, increasing at about 2.5 percent per year), the increment in the years from 1965 to 1985 would represent an increase in per capita income of 82 percent. Or, if per capita income could be held constant and the labor forces reduced instead, some 45 percent of it, or around 28 million workers, would be converted to consumers (14).

A third contingency that could significantly affect the consuming power of a population is governmental action aimed at substantially improving the standard of living of the disadvantaged mem ers of the society. In the United States, the approximately 13 percent of the households that are regarded as below the poverty ceiling, or the 27 percent of households with incomes below $5,000 in 1970, offer a considerable opportunity for expanding consumption. There are numerous other ways to dispose of the excess productive capacity of the economy, such as rebuilding the urban settlement structure, cleaning up the environment, or engaging in bigger wars. To the extent that these latter alternatives are resorted to, consumption becomes independent of population size.

Enough has been said to indicate that population is not regulated by the physical and biotic environment. Although the environment may be finite, organizational determinants will come into force long before the environment itself operates as a restraint on population. The population problem is a problem of adjusting numbers and their characteristics to the demographic requirements of a particular society. If the line of reasoning followed here is correct, at some time in the course of technological and economic development population size becomes a neutral factor in the amounts and kinds of uses of natural resources to be expected. The power for technical and organizational innovation implicit in the already accumulated fund of knowledge is inestimable, and it is constantly being enlarged. The exploitation of the potentialities of that reservoir, carried on by a relatively small and perhaps declining number of specialists, means a steadily rising level of productivity and a persistent problem of how to sustain it.

I should like, in conclusion, to return briefly to the question of the contribution of ecology to population study. In a word, the contribution is the formulation of the population-environment problem in organizational terms; adaptation is necessarily an organizational process. The bioecologist might ignore this approach from time to time without getting into serious difficulty, and the social scientist may set it aside for certain analytical purposes. But neither will gain a very full understanding of population change and structure apart from the organizational context in which they occur. Thus human ecology, although it may start with an interest in the similarities among all life forms, converges upon and becomes identified with social science. It becomes, however, a synthetic social science; that is, the nature of the ecological problem is of such breadth that it cannot be adequately treated from the standpoint of sociology, economics, political science, or any other similar abstraction. Human ecology constitutes a different abstraction, one that pertains to the interrelations among institutions rather than to a single class of institutional behavior. As a synthetic social science, human ecology seems well suited to population study, for population belongs to no one discipline.

Notes

(1) E. Odum. *Science* 164, 262 (1969).

(2) A simpler definition is offered by Lee R. Dice: "An ecologic community together with its habitat constitutes an ecosystem" (*National Communities,* Univ. of Michigan Press, Ann Arbor, 1952), p. 21.

(3) See also W.C. Allee, A. Engerson, O. Park, T. Park, K.P. Schmidt, *Principles of Animal Ecology* (Saunders, Philadelphia, 1955), pp. 695-729; R. Buchsbaum and M. Buchsbaum, *Basic Ecology* (Boxwood, Pittsburgh, 1957), pp. 98-127; and R. Margalef, *Perspectives in Ecological Theory* (Univ. of Chicago Press, Chicago, 1968), pp. 26-50.

(4) G. Hardin, *Science* 162, 1243 (1968).

(5) See M. Bates, in *Resources and Man* (Freeman, San Francisco, 1969), pp. 21-30.

(6) Impressive advances in the measurement of the energy converted, lost, and transmitted at each stage of the cycling process are being made in the new science of energetics, as described by H. T. Odum, *Environment, Power and Society* (Wiley-Interscience, New York, (1971); *Sci. Amer.* 224, 224 (Sept. 1971).

(7) A. Coale, *Science* 170, 132 (1970).

(8) I. Taeuber in *Man's Place in the Island Ecosystems.* F. R. Fosberg, ed. (Univ. of Hawaii Press, Honolulu, 1961), pp. 226-262, analyzes how absorption into expanding societies affects the age and sex composition of populations in formerly isolated social systems.

(9) O. D. Duncan, *Handbook for Modern Sociology,* R. E. L. Faris, ed. (Rand McNally, Chicago, 1964), pp. 36-82.

(10) K. Boulding describes the human ecosystem as the "totality of human organizations" in *The Organizational Revolution* (Quadrangle, Chicago, 1952), p. xxii, and O. D. Duncan notes that the cycling of information is a unique feature of the human ecosystem (9, pp. 40-42).

(11) R. Freedman, *Pop. Index* 31, 417 (1965).

(12) S. S. Kuznets, *Proc. Amer. Philos. Soc.* 111, 170 (1967).

(13) M. Abramowitz, *Amer. Econ. Rev.* 46, 8 (1965).

(14) J. Krebs and J. Spengler, in *Technology and the American Economy* (Report of the National Commission on Technology, Automation, and Economic Progress, Government Printing Office, Washington, D.C., 1966), vol. 2, pp. 359-360.

GOING
BEYOND
JOHN LOCKE?

A.E. Keir Nash

Not long ago Robert S. McNamara argued cogently that the present facts of the world's population explosion are distressing enough to "jolt one into action." (1) If current rates of population growth are maintained, by the year 2000, a mere six years will add an increment equal to the entire expansion in the world's population-size from the formation of the Roman Empire to the middle of the nineteenth century. A person born in the 1970's and living a normal American life expectancy would witness a world of 15 billion people. "In six and a half centuries from now — the same insignificant period of time separating us from the poet Dante—there would be one human being standing on every square foot of land on earth: a fantasy of horror that even the Inferno could not match." (2)

It is extremely doubtful that man's increasing capacity to use the planet's land and ocean resources can forever keep pace with population growth. If neither voluntary nor governmental effort curbs population growth, the day will likely come when natural or unnatural forces will impose an unpleasant solution — whether through famine, disease, pollution, nuclear holocaust, homosexuality or cannibalism. (3)

To be sure, different patterns of population dispersion both in this country and throughout the world, and different patterns of resource consumption and cycling, could for a time decrease the already plenteous pockets of ecologic strain. Nonetheless, the planet's "carrying capacity" is finite, even if it is not yet practically enumerable. Ultimately, one comes up against the laws of thermodynamics. (4) And, well short of such physical limits, one may come up against the boundaries of psychologic tolerance for crowding, urbanization and separation from the natural environment. (5)

The tact that the United States, as a developed economy, has not had to contend with the typical vicious spiral of underdeveloped countries — wherein national indices of economic growth are seriously dilated by annual increments of population—does not justify a lack of concern for population problems. During the past decade population imploding into the American "center city" has contributed to several hundred violent challenges to the government's "monopoly of legitimate force."(6) In turn, these riots have engendered abundant conservative political reactions from other, less-crowded, more affluent living areas. Similarly, environmental pollution and transportation congestion indicate that well short of the upper limits described by thermodynamics, population growth and distribution present severe problems to a polity attempting to govern a "developed economy." (7)

A governmental practice of abstaining from systematic intervention in the course of population growth, whether the outgrowth of a reasoned decision or of inaction, constitutes a political result as freighted with consequences as a decision to intervene systematically. Moreover, as Daniel Moynihan has argued recently, (8) nonintervention is frequently an illusion. In reality, intervention is often present in the unintended form of a helter-skelter of side effects flowing from explicit governmental programs in other areas. Thus, building a freeway from the center of a city to a suburb may ostensibly be just one part of a transportation policy. Yet it actually exerts pressures upon the "natural flow" of intra-urban migration. In this sense, the side effects of other policies produce a "hidden population policy." (9) Thus, the conclusion is inescapable that excessive population growth constitutes a political and not merely a technical problem. One resulting analytic question is, consequently: what sort of a future response by America is likely? It is the aim of this essay to analyze the major characteristics of the American political system that argur less than a speedy and adequate response.

Four Barriers in the American Political System

An era is sometimes best delineated by the contours of its leading social and economic strains. In such an era the prospects for a society depend substantially upon a dual capacity: 1 for timely perception of such strains as problems requiring political action; and 2. for solving these problems by means of "normal" political channels. Otherwise, the society runs the risk of disaster. At least, its government must be able to temporize with the problem and leave it to the next generation.

It can hardly be doubted that the phenomenon of nuclear power has posed an overriding political problem for mid-twentieth century America. That an equally important political problem of the late twentieth century will be the population explosion scarely warrants greater doubt. American politics of the mid-twentieth century accomplished the necessary minimum of deferring the nuclear issue. However, for several reasons political scientists may be less optimistic with respect to the capacity of the American polity in confronting the population explosion. To begin with, by comparison the nuclear problem had one great "advantage" — its obviousness. By comparison, population has been a quiet issue. Furthermore, it is arguable that in at least four ways the American economic, political and ideological structures were far better adapted to grappling with the nuclear issue.

The first — and least serious — structural barrier to adequate grappling is economic. Restrictive population growth has at least an apparent short-run disadvantage to American business. Unlike nuclear deterrence, if successful, it provides fewer, not more, consumers. As an interest-group pushing for massive government financial aid, G.D. Searle Co. and its competitors in the contraceptive market are hardly a match for defense-related industries.

Second — and more significant — even before Hiroshima, at least a few powerful members of the military, political and scientific elites were cognizant of the problematic nature of "the bomb."

Third, except for the strand of isolationism, which is notably weakened, nothing in the tapestry of American politics hindered the acceptance of the nuclear issue as a political problem. Rather, it sprang directly out of a long-standing problem — national security. The cold war underlined its crucial character to both politicians and public. In contrast, perception of population growth as a political problem is not built into the normal decision-making patterns of American politics. To be sure, the United States has not wholly lacked national political leaders concerned about population issues—particularly former Senators Gruening of Alaska and Clark of Pennsylvania, Senator Joseph Tydings of Maryland, Senator Robert Packwood of Oregon and former Secretary of Defense McNamara. Nonetheless, and despite the Congressional creation in March, 1970, of a National Commission on Population Growth and the American Future, (10) one could hardly describe American political attitudes as yet characterized by a pervasive sense of overwhelming urgency about it. (11) Despite their efforts the two former Senators became "former" by acts of the electorate not two years after Tydings rightly singled them out as "pioneers." (12) Similarly hinting at resistances in American politics to ready problem-perception, not until Robert S. McNamara left the Defense Department and moved to the World Bank did he find an adequate powerbase from which to attack the problem wholeheartedly.

It is hard to believe that any of these structural barriers will prove insurmountable in the future. In marked contrast, a fourth structural disincentive may be serious enough to warrant extended examination. Achieving a comprehensive population policy threatens to be gravely complicated by American political ideology. (13) On its face, the notion of nonvoluntary methods of control seems "un-American." Moreover, at least for significant groups in the American population, even the idea of voluntary birth control cuts against the attitudinal grain.

The American Legacy of John Locke

The policy of any country selects social and economic strains for political debate and corrective legislation in a nonrandom discriminatory fashion. It is likely to be more susceptible to certain types of social or economic stress than to others. On the many factors that may determine the speed with which such a stress or strain is picked up in the political arena and transferred into a problem of governance, probably the most important is the ideologic spectrum of that arena. That is, social or economic strains that can be intellectually "diagnosed" and "prescribed for" within the prevailing ideologic spectrum are more likely to get a "quick hearing." Those that fall outside it find difficulty getting onto the political stage at all.

To say this is to focus upon a different and earlier part of the political process than that to which American political scientists generally point when praising the American political system. The usual focus fixes upon the advantages in problem-solving capacity accruing from agreement upon fundamental ideals and basic procedures. This — so the prevailing wisdom declares — accounts for the past success of the American two-party system: it has produced relatively quick solutions because it has functioned as a "brokerage house" of competing interests rather than as the battleground of fundamentally conflicting world views. (14) Thus—so the argument process' essential ideological unity has allowed far more expeditious solving of political problems than has characterized most European political systems since the French Revolution of 1789 unleashed grand ideologic conflicts upon the European continent.

This argument may well be correct so far as it goes. But it is very partial because it overlooks the point just made. It overlooks the question of the breadth of ideologic spectrum and its relation to whether a problem is, or is not, speedily recognized. It focuses, thus, upon the later problem-solving stage rather than upon the earlier, initial question of problem-perception. Yet, it is this that may be most important in respect to the population problem. It is possible, in other words, that the difficulty posed to the government of America by population growth is precisely that it raises an issue that lies outside the normal political spectrum. Let us examine this.

As Louis Hartz has so cogently urged, it is probably the thorough-going yet essentially unconscious commitment of the United States, since the revolution of 1776, to the classic liberalism of John Locke that has historically most distinguished American political life from the politics of other industrialized nations. (15) This is by no means to deny that American political conflicts have been "vital" and "real" since the armies of George III departed American shores. It is merely to note that the ideologic differences between major political factions contending in the American political arena have been narrow of scope when compared with the wide spectrum of major European political movements since 1789. Rather than presenting a vast array of political values from those of monarchists and aristocrats on the feudal Right to those of socialists and communists on the political left, American politics has been restricted to the placid liberal meadows in the center of the European political landscape. If one leaves aside the few possible exceptions comprised by some early New England Federalists and a few apologists for slavery in the South, the United States has actually not seen genuine conservative politicians. Thus, American advocates of the inherited rights of aristocracies and of absolute monarchs have been chiefly conspicuous by their absence. So too, at least until the decade of the 1960's (and on this score the issue is still very much in doubt), genuine socialism has been either absent or powerless upon the American political scene.

What has passed for American conservatism — whether that of the nineteenth-century pro-business Whigs or that of contemporary Goldwaterites — has not in any fundamental sense been an American counterpart of European conservatism. Rather the American conservative has duplicated the political values of the right wing of European liberalism — a right wing still very much in the European center. American conservatives have strikingly avoided embracing the major sociopolitical postulates of European conservatism: belief in the inherent inequality of men; conviction that men are naturally more prone to irrationality than to rationality; and in consequence, insistence upon their inability to govern themselves without wide-reaching governmental limitations upon the individual's pursuit of property and liberty. Quite the contrary, American conservatism has advocated almost exactly the opposite tenets; the natural right of the individual, whether laborer or capitalist, to work out his own economic and social destiny in the absence of, or at most in the minimal presence of, political constraints. In short, the American conservative has virtually reproduced the rationalist view of human nature and the belief in economic laissez-faire that has characterized the great philosophic descendants of John Locke in Europe — Adam Smith, Jeremy Bentham and James Mill. So too, at the popular level, American conservatism has advocated the "platform" of "haut bourgeois" liberal political movements of Europe.

With respect to the economic realm, the leading characteristic of the liberal left of the United States has, similarly, not been advocating the chief political solution of socialism for curing the ills of mankind — abolishing private property. Quite the contrary, again, from the time of the trust-busting Progressives under Teddy Roosevelt through FDR's New Deal to the present, its two principal economic thrusts have been different not merely in degree but in kind. One has been a tendency to seek economic solutions by "regulating against" concentrations of business power to swing the country back to a golden Jeffersonian era in the past composed of small rural and industrial enterprises. The other has been to build compensations into capitalism — either by tempering the natural "Smithian" swings of boom-and-bust cycles through very modest use of Keynesian techniques of political control over the economy, or by encouraging the wider distribution and hence enjoyment of still-very-private property rights—by means of unemployment compensation, progressive income taxation and trade unionism — the very *bete noir* of true Marxian socialism.

The net of all this is a most curious paradox of comparative political ideologies. The economic solutions proposed by the Democratic left, which have been most bitterly assailed by the American right as "creeping socialism," are precisely those that European Marxists-Leninists have most sweepingly denounced on precisely the grounds that by ameliorating rather than exacerbating the "internal contradictions of capitalism" they would delay the coming of the Communist revolution.

To say this, however, is to say more than to point up a curiosity of ideological history. It is to suggest that America's very concensus on basic political beliefs may have precisely the opposite effect upon the perception and solution of population problems from that which it has generally had in American political history. Far from expediting resolution within the two-party system, that consensus may cause the American polity to display less rather than greater solving ability than in European counterparts.

Why might this be? Should it come to pass, it would be because "dealing with" population seems to entail extensive governmental control over individual autonomy. Further, if the typical European political style has been to engage in endless debates about the merits of a particular governmental control, the typical American political style has been to react emotionally and "axiomatically" (16) against any such idea. The European ideologic spectrum has been able to encompass a political proposition entailing governmental control with far less alarm at the initial point than the narrower American spectrum. Thus, ideologic reflexes in the United States may engender a perceptual barrier to problem-solving of population growth.

Simply to note the probable existence of such an ideologic barrier is not to describe its height. In attempting that, it is initially necessary to venture into the admittedly precarious domain of speculation about the "logical inevitability" of conflict between various population control measures and Lockean norms of American individualism. Hence, it may be useful to attempt a categorization of the many population proposals that have been advanced according to their apparent conflicts both with the political values emanating from that Lockean norm and with the facts of contemporary American relations between the individual and the political system. Such a categorization discloses four types of proposals. (17)

The first category comprises those proposals that would simply heighten the possibilities for self-determination by the individual mother or by the married couple. Thus, this category would include all proposals of a noncompulsory, essentially informational sort: problems for disseminating as broadly as possible arguments for, and methods of, fertility control and family planning, regardless of whether the actual disseminating agent be an individual physican, a marriage counselor, a private educator or an employee of some branch of the government. Furthermore, it would include proposals for liberalizing laws on induced abortions — inasmuch as whatever else they may bode, they share in company with proposals for disseminating information the goal of increasing the capacity of the individual to make an autonomous decision. (18) The one attempts to increase access to information; the other urges a greater range of choice based upon information so gained.

The second category includes all proposals (19) for adopting courses on population growth, family planning and the like as a regular part of the curriculum in public schools. It could, of course, be urged that this category is simply a subdivision of the first group of proposals for improved dissemination of information. However, the two differ in one important respect. The first type offers the information to a willing hearer. He presumably can "turn it off" at will. By contrast, the second legislates "sitting through."

The third category of population measures would involve the government in creating inducements to voluntary restrictions upon childbearing. The large number of proposals of this sort may be subdivided into two kinds. One consists of positive incentive payments for limiting births, (20) for spacing children through periods of nonpregnancy or nonbirth (21) and for voluntary sterilization. (22) The other consists of negative incentives that would be built into the income tax structure—for example, taking away exemptions for exceeding N children (23) or levying fees on births above the Nth. (24)

Last, the fourth set of proposals would create involuntary controls. (25) These include: "marketable licenses to have children," (26) temporary sterilization of all females (27) or males or permanent sterilization after N births; (28) required abortion of illegitimate (29) or post-Nth pregnancies; and finally, general fertility agents (30) placed in, for example, the public water supply with counteracting agents distributed as the government sees fit to individuals who have demonstrated their emotional and economic capacity for parenthood.

Estimating the Clash Between Proposals and Ideology

The four categories of population control proposals are, clearly, ordered with respect to the degree of their potential conflict with American norms of the autonomous political person. From the standpoints of both likely ease of acceptance by the American people and the extent of change in the structure of American political values that they entail, the "best" solution to population problems is that which "does the job" by relying as heavily as possible upon the lower-numbered types. But here, time may well constitute the essence of freedom. Failure to act as the problem builds may require greater reliance upon more restrictive governmental measures. A "package" of lower numbered techniques adequate today might not be adequate in a generation. Therefore, it is important to face population problems before measures highly restrictive of freedoms become necessary. In turn, consequently, it is important that timely consideration be given to potential attitudinal hostilities to these types of proposals.

With respect to the first category, it is doubtful that a commonly raised difficulty — Roman Catholic aversion to birth control — will prove a potent long-term political force. If the reaction of the Catholic laity in the United States to Pope Paul's Encyclical reaffirming the traditional Roman abhorrence of interfering with "natural processes" be any guide, it is difficult to believe that the Encyclical will greatly affect lay behavior, despite any conflicts in attitude that it may presently impose on the Catholic population. (31)

If, indeed, one is to be concerned about resistances that may manifest themselves among particular groups within the American population, in all probability one's concern is best directed elsewhere—to two other varieties of resistance that until not long ago were largely unperceived.

The first pertains to lower-status group views as to the optimal size of family. In 1969, Judith Blake argued provocatively that an unpleasant fact remains after due allowances are made for religious beliefs. (32)In her view all the statistics point away from the "accepted wisdom" of family planners that lower-income group mothers have too many children just because they are ignorant of contraceptive techniques. Rather, since 1952, a gap in attitudes has appeared between high and low socioeconomic status groups about the optimal family size. Among upper-status non-Catholic women the "ideal" number of children has fluctuated closely around a median of 3.1 Among lower-status non-Catholic women the "ideal number" has hovered much closer to four. (33) That difference casts a shadow over assumptions that mere governmental provision of information about contraceptives will suffice.

Judith Blake's "gloomy view" engendered a substantial scholarly dispute as to its merits. (34) Moreover, a year later Larry Bumpass and Charles F. Westoff reported a set of empirical findings very different in thrust. (35) Their research indicated that almost one-fifth of recent births in the American population were "unwanted," and that, if anything, the percentage of such births was greater among lower economic and educational groups and among ethnic minorities. In their view, ignorance about, and the unavailability of contraceptive techniques among "lower-status groups"—rather than desires for larger families—accounted for such groups' higher rates of fertility. If so, then voluntary measures could be expected to go a considerable way toward minimizing population growth.

Be the respective merits of the varying viewpoints about present desires concerning family size as they may, it is more difficult to be sanguine about the future import of a different, ideologically based resistance in ethnic-minority sectors to family planning schemes. This resistance is most clearly manifested in the militants' charge that such schemes directed at the poor are — given the coincidence of minority racial status and poverty — sugar-coated genocide pills. (36) The crux of the problem here has, of course, nothing to do with the charge's abstract merits or demerits as an interpretation of family planners' motives. Rather it turns on the real existence and on both the present and future extent of such attitudes among minority groups. On balance, it is difficult to believe that hostility based upon racial-ideologic foundations will disappear, or even lessen, in the face of marginal standards of living. On the contrary, the increasing amount of racially based violence in American politics during recent years suggests, if anything, a short-run strengthening of such hostile attitudes.

In consequence, substantially changing American population growth rates may well require the prior satisfaction of at least three economic and political conditions: 1. elevating the living standards of the "forgotten fourth" to a degree such that the norm of a small family would have even a vague possibility of being universally accepted as the "ideal." 2. restructuring abortion laws so that couples have freedom of choice with respect to carrying pregnancies to term; and 3. large-scale adoption of the second type of proposal-building courses on population into the public educational curriculum.

It lies beyond the scope of this article to prognosticate about fulfillment of the first condition. However, judgments may be rendered with respect to second and third. In the absence of a really violent pendular swing toward Right or Left during the 1970s in American politics, it seems plausible to anticipate a scattering of reactions against "sex education" in state legislatures (37) overcome by a stronger long-term movement toward both more permissive laws on abortion and incorporating population courses into school educational programs.

Essentially, there are four reasons for so anticipating. One: resistance to reform of abortion laws, (38) is chiefly based upon a combination of legislative inertia and neofundamentalist (39) fears that so doing would increase "sexual promiscuity." Such fears, compounded perhaps by a residue of Victorianism in respect to discussing the birds and the bees, underlie recent movements to prevent or to repeal sex education courses in public schools. It is doubtful that such motivations for resistance can long maintain a decisive strength in the face of the greater political truth of the relation between poverty, large families and urban unrest, and in the face of the inability of such statutory restrictions to alter sexual behavior among the post-Kinsey generation, to prevent the gaining of such knowledge in "extracurricular ways" or to prevent illegitimate pregnancies.

Two: neofundamentalist laws against abortion clash with yet another fundamental tenet of American political 'beliefs — the virtue of individual self-determination. Consequently, an inner contradiction exists in the value-structures of many persons opposed to liberalizing abortion laws and sex education. Such inner contradiction does not maximize long-run strength.

Three: it is not clear that such antipathies to "sex-education" would necessarily carry over to curricular innovations entitled "population problems." (40)

Four: as the college students of today become the opinion-setters of tomorrow, and as their generation swells the voting ranks, it is probable that more permissive attitudes will dominate. Thus, samples of university students in two states with recently liberalized abortion laws suggest strongly that the present liberal legal position requiring a physician's therapeutic judgment rather than merely a couple's decision, will not be thought very liberal in ten years time. Despite California's 1967 reform, 92.6 per cent of a sample of University of California students wanted further liberalization. (41) Indeed, asked to judge the desirability of legal reform in ten different areas, they felt abortion-law reform most important — even more so than legal reform with respect to marijuana. In a similar vein, a sample of second-year medical students at the University of North Carolina displayed a heavy commitment to voluntarism. (42) None of the medical students opposed family planning, but only nine believed that family planning information and education would prove adequate to solve problems of American population expansion. Over 90 per cent of the medical students favored abortion when carrying to term would threaten the mother's emotional or physical health. Importantly, these students would not require any showing of potential danger to life itself. All students in this sample proceeded beyond present North Carolina statutory allowances for abortion in the event of *rubella* — with its known linkage to birth defects — during the "first trimester." All would permit abortion on a showing that *any parental condition* posed a substantially greater than normal chance of a defective child. Last, 90 per cent of these students would legalize abortion without interposing a "physician's veto" if both husband and wife jointly desired one. In sum, these samples suggest among the younger generation a strong commitment to principals of voluntarism. And too, they suggest similar support for public school curricular innovation.

By comparison with the first two categories of proposals, the third-governmental establishment of positive or negative incentives to limiting child births — raises issues of a much more serious, yet potentially soluble, political nature. In the long-run the chief question is probably not, will general attitudes shift to favoring such incentives, but when? The survey of medical students disclosed an interesting split in opinion on this issue. Considerably greater support was given to the indirect "negative" incentives than to direct governmental payments. Thus, of the 43 students, 12 favored incentive payments for voluntary sterilization, over one-third *reversing* tax exemptions for exceeding a certain number of children determined by statue, and over half favored *limiting* the maximum number of tax exemptions.

Possibly the opinion survey tapped a difference in attitudinal reflexes peculiar to members of a profession among whom the less obvious reward of a "tax-write-off" collides less blatantly with laissez-faire ideologic premises about self-help than does direct dispersal of tax-payers' funds by the government. On a sensible economic basis, however, such a distinction is difficult to defend. Nothing procedurally novel exists in the relation between government and individual entailed by reversing tax exemptions. Just so, nothing is really new about direct incentive payments. In both instances, the government simply reverses a former policy of rewarding citizens for "furthering the national interest" by having more children, and promotes another "national interest" by rewarding restraint. Whichever way the tax exemptions run, or whether there be more or fewer child welfare payments, the government is carrying out a policy by inducement. The present structure of tax exemptions in child welfare payments may constitute a less conscious population policy, but it is still a population policy. That it is hidden does not make it absent. Further, no genuine economic difference exists between direct and indirect "rewards" with respect to possible "threats" to the American Democratic ethos. The only logically viable distinction is in the much more restrictive terms of "who is affected." Tax exemptions for not having children are more — if not very — likely to take hold on certain middle-income brackets than upon upper-income families who could not care less or upon those whose incomes are so low that they do not pay taxes anyhow. Reversing, that is reducing, tax exemptions for having more children might, particularly if *ex post facto*, affect matters all right, but they might well be unconstitutional. And, they might simply affect the welfare rather than the number of children. In the absence of a general national minimal standard of affluence and in the absence of pervasive adoption of the small family norm, direct payments may be required if this third category of proposals is to be sufficiently effective to avoid ultimate future recourse to the fourth type of proposal. And, the sharp conflict of such "compulsory general legislation" with American liberal individualism is clear.

A Debatable Conclusion

If the foregoing analysis of the potential clash between population proposals and American norms of freedom is substantially correct, only the fourth category of proposal offers a logically tenable showing of "inevitable conflict." The first three types are, by contrast, logically consonant with American norms of individualism and consistent with fiscal inducement policies typical of compensated capitalism since the New Deal.

To say that, however, is not to "solve" the political problem. What Oliver Wendell Holmes once suggested characterized the law — that its life lay not in logic but in experience — may be paraphrased here. The life of American politics has by no means worked out along the logical Madisonian lines of "wise representatives debating rationally the public interest" and making law upon the conclusions thus reached. (43) This is not the place to work out the extended implications for solving the population problem of that shift from "rational search for the national interest" to the contemporary era's difficult "mix" of great genteel "countervailing powers" (44) playing brokerage-politics and of lower-status ethnic and generational minorities engaging in an increasingly violent politics of "going for broke." It must suffice here to enumerate the reasons for doubting that such a "mix" favors speedy consensus on proper population policies.

To put the matter in a comparative light, the relative success of a handful of other industrialized countries in achieving a population growth rate much under one per cent does not necessarily bode a similar American success. Two countries come to mind here. Japan in the postwar era and France between 1880 and 1940. At least three crucial differences in the political cultures of these countries warrant caution. So too, does one difference in their international political positions.

First, both French and Japanese ideologies historically have been far less inclined than America's Lockean Liberalism to suspicion of a societal effort purporting to be at once "coordinated" and "voluntary."

Second, an additional cultural characteristic, though not strictly "political," may be important enough to merit brief mention: psychological attitudes relating masculinity to the male's capacity to produce male offspring. The existing "survey research" is insufficient to support a "confident statistical judgment" as to the likely strength of such attitudes. Nonetheless, if literature in any way represents the salient concerns of the society from which it springs, (45) it is worth noting that concern for "masculinity" has been a running major theme of American literature whereas it has not been one in European literature. (46) Oddly enough, in this respect the United States may warrant comparison not so much with industrialized Northern European countries as with the underdeveloped nations of Latin America where, in company with motivations to assure "old age security," *machismo* has hindered many a family planning scheme. It would be foolhardy to predict "insolubility" for this reason, but it would be remiss not to note it as an attitude requiring possible future reckoning.

Third, neither Japan nor France had large racial minorities that could argue from long and persistent discrimination that birth-control constituted a "threat of genocide."

Fourth, the very fact of American desires for "free world leadership" may present an additional political problem. (47) It is not inconceivable that American advice to underdeveloped countries to impose population controls may provoke the reaction, "But what of yourselves?" The point here is related to the burden of past suspicion engendered by the widely unpopular combination of private American enterprises abroad and Marshall Plan, Point Four aid and so forth. It is, to abuse Shakespeare, a "Polonian" problem. Forced to be a lender because of the dulled edge of world husbandry, the United States — if it is not to suffer the slings and arrows of ungrateful friendship — may be called upon to "set an example." In this sense, the external ambitions of America's international policy may impose internal strains, which would not weigh upon "middle-powers" such as France or Japan.

The foregoing analysis may seem to paint a rather gloomy picture of the American political system's likely capacity for timely action in respect to population growth. Surely, it would be fair to pose the question: might not the conclusion differ if one looked in more detail at the most "progressive" part of the political structure? Might not such a part undertake the task of "leadership" in treating the problem? It is easy enough to identify that part — the federal judicial system, and particularly the post-1937 Supreme Court. Yet, whatever one may say of the Court's "task-solving" leadership in general, it offers little ground for reaching a more optimistic conclusion in specific. How so?

If any gross generalization can be safely made about the American political system since the New Deal, it is surely that the Supreme Court has been the major governmental architect of sociopolitical change. One has, in substantiating this, merely to recite the cases of Brown vs. Board of Education, (48) Baker vs. Carr, (49) and Miranda vs. Arizona. (50) Now quite possibly — with the replacement of Earl Warren by Warren Earl Burger — the Court may jettison that role of chief governmental agent of change. However, one aspect, and the crucially relevant aspect here, is not likely to alter. Underlying the Warren Court's running debate between judicial libertarians and judicial conservatives has remained a common political premise that civil rights cases have presented essentially a conflict between rights of individuals. At no point during even the thickest of the skirmishes between those two judicial "giants" of the past third of a century, Hugo Black and Felix Frankfurter, was there a denial of the Lockean consensus on the primacy of individualism.(51)

Nowhere is this underlying unity of ideology more apparent than in the decision family planners have most applauded — Griswold vs. Connecticut, (52) overturning that state's antibirth-control statute. In one sense, at least, Griswold deserves to rank among the most unusual civil rights decisions in the Court's history. But that sense is not one which in the longer view of things should give much comfort to population planners anticipating Supreme Court leadership. That reason was, of course the extraordinary split of judges compared with "normal" Warren Court cleavages. The seven-man majority included both the Court's most ardent libertarian, William O. Douglas, and its most august conservative, John Marshall Harlan. The two-man minority — no less oddly — was composed of Hugo Black and Potter Stewart, both of whom in recent years have generally played the role of "swing men" at the Court's center. What that suggested was further underlined by the number and quality of the opinions handed down. The nine Justices produced no less than five opinions, holding the law, respectively: silly but constitutional,(53) violative of the hardly ever before used Ninth Amendment; (54) contradictory to the Fourteenth Amendment's "concept of ordered liberty;"(55) and finally in violation of a right older than the Bill of Rights, American political parties and the school system — the right to privacy in marriage. (56) Doubtless the Justices caught the sense of post-Kinsey American society as to what should be done; but equally certain, they were not at all sure how to do it.

Surely, indeed, deeper scrutiny of Griswold brings into sharp question any inkling that it portended a day of open hunting for population control advocates. One common and unsaid premise lay at the base of the five apparently disparate opinions just as it has lain beneath the surface of the integration, reapportionment and criminal procedure decisions: a continuing assumption of the vital reality of the Lockean consensus. Each majority opinion had a distinctly Lockean undertone. In short, precious little constitutional fodder may be found for those who might hope that Griswold argued judicial leadership into the post-Lockean world of mandatory legislation concerning population control. The "community values" balanced in Griswold, as elsewhere, were quintessentially the values of a community consisting of autonomous individuals. Griswold did not even begin to reckon seriously with the Rousseauan view of community that individuals could be "forced to be free." Quite the opposite. Thus, the leadership of Griswold, besides displaying uncertainly of specific reasoning, was also very short of direction. It stopped, in effect, at the first half of the first category of proposal types — the right to information and to "tools" if wanted. Nothing in Griswold boded recognition of procreation as part of a greater population problem. The essence of Griswold was that the government may not, by interference with a right to privacy, compel the individual not to know. That was where it seemed to stop. And that stopping-hint was surely born out by the refusal of the Warren Court in its final, numbered days to hear a challenge to New Jersey's abortion law.(57) Nothing in judicial sensibilities, in short, gives much inkling of "going beyond Locke." To conclude, if the Supreme Court, even in the era of its balmiest libertarianism from 1962 to 1969, was not to suggest a way through a political-ideologic log-jam, what reason is there to expect imminent "breakthrough" by other "less-progressive" substructures of the political system?

Notes

(1) McNamara, R. S., Address to the University of Notre Dame, May 1, 1969, p. 4.
(2) *Ibid.*
(3) See Hauser, P.M., On Non-Family Planning Methods of Population Control. Paper prepared for the International Conference on Family Planning, at Dacca, Pakistan, January 28-February 4, 1969, p. 1. Needless to say, like Hauser, I am not advocating the latter three despite the quickness of solution offered by the first, the low birth rate attendant upon the second or the admirable symmetry of the third whereby food supply increases as population diminishes.
(4) Fremlin, J. H., How Many People Can the World Support?, *New Scientist*, No. 415, 285-287, 1964.
(5) See, e.g., Hare N., Black Ecology, *The Black Scholar*, pp. 1-8, April, 1970: and Udall, M.K., Standing Room Only on Spaceship Earth, *Arizona Magazine*, July 27, 1969.
(6) The reference is to Max Weber's definition of the State as that entity possessing a monopoly of legitimate force.
(7) Note that I do not use the term "developed polity." The circumlocution is deliberate. For the reasons, see Nash, A. B. K., Pollution, Population, and the Cowboy Economy: Anomalies in the Developmentalist Paradigm and Samuel Huntington, *Journal of Comparative Administration*, 2, 109-128, May, 1970.
(8) Moynihan, D., Policy vs. Program in the '70's, *The Public Interest*, No. 20, 90-100, Summer, 1970.
(9) *Ibid.*, p. 93.
(10) P. L. 91-223, 91st Congress, Second Session.
(11) Opinion polls seem to vary on this question, apparently largely depending upon how much is "fed" to the interviewee and upon how serious is "serious." Contrast Kantner, J. F., American Attitudes on Population Policy: Recent Trends, *Studies in Family Planning*, No. 12, 1-7, May, 1968; with the preliminary findings of National Analysts, Inc., Planned Parenthood Study, April, 1970. On balance, it seems fairest to say that Americans may be willing to respond vaguely that a problem exists, but perceive it as lying outside the United States. And certainly, there is no substantial evidence that it motivates the voter.
(12) See his statement in the *Congressional Record*, February 28, 1966. See also Hearing on S. 2993, U.S. Senate Subcommittee on Employment, Manpower, and Poverty, 89th Congress, Second Session, p. 31. See also T. R. B., "Ex-Sen. Ernest Gruening (D-Alaska) had the guts to hold public hearings on birth control, sitting alone, day after day, when most of his colleagues fought shy of the delicate subject. " T. R. B., Population: an Infected Planet's Biggest Problem, *Los Angeles Times*, July 30, 1969, Part II, p. 9.
(13) Note that throughout this essay I am not using "ideology" as necessarily opposed to "pragmatism" *a la*, e.g., Carl Friedrich. Rather, following Clifford Geertz, by "ideology" I mean: "a cognitive and moral map of reality in terms of which an individual inescapably perceives and orders phenomena external to him." See Geertz,

C., Ideology as a Cultural System, in Apter, D. E. (Editor), *Ideology and Discontent*, New York, The Free Press, 1964, p. 62. Nor need the ordering necessarily be self-conscious.

(14) Lowell, A. L., *Public Opinion and Popular Government*, New York, Longmans, Green and Co., 1913, pp. 57-67.

(15) Hartz, L., *The Liberal Tradition in America*, New York, Harcourt, Brace, and Co., 1955.

(16) May, E. R., The Nature of Foreign Policy: the Calculated versus the Axiomatic, *Daedalus*, 653-667, Fall, 1962.

(17) For a most useful and more detailed overview of population proposals divided on a different "descriptive" basis into eight types, see Berelson, B., Beyond Family Planning, Studies in Family Planning, No. 38, Population Council, February, 1969.

(18) Davis, K., Population Policy: Will Current Programs Suceed?, *Science*, 158, 730-739, November 10, 1967; Ehrlich, P. R., *The Population Bomb*, New York, Ballantine Books, Inc., 1968, p. 139.

(19) Visaria, P., Population Assumptions and Policy, *Economic Weekly*, p. 1343, August 8, 1964. Wayland, S., Family Planning and the School Curriculum, in Berelson, B., *et al*, (Editors), Family Planning and Population Programs, Chicago, University of Chicago Press, 1966, pp. 353-62; Davis, supra note 18.

(20) Enke, S., Government Bonuses for Smaller Families, *Population Review*, 4, 47-54, 1960; Cowles, R.B., The Non-Baby Bonus, originally published in Brower, D. (Editor), *The Meaning of Wilderness to Science*, San Francisco Sierra Club, 1960, reprinted in Hardin, G. (Editor), *Population, Evolution, and Birth Control*, San Francisco, W. H. Freeman and Co., 1969, pp. 339-340.

(21) Enke, S., The Gains to India from Population Control, *The Review of Economics and Statistics*, 179-180, May, 1960. Leasure, J. W., Some Economic Benefits of Birth Prevention, *Milbank Memorial Fund Quarterly*, 45, 417-425, 1967.

(22) Approaches to the Human Fertility Problem," prepared by the Carolina Population Center for the United Nations Advisory Committee on the Application of Science and Technology to Development, October, 1968, p. 68; Samuel T. J., The Strengthening of the Motivation for Family Limitation in India, *The Journal of Family Welfare*, 13, 11-12, 1966; Sripati Chandrasekhar, Indian Minister of Health, reported in *New York Times*, July 19, 1967, p. 41; Davis, supra note 18.

(23) Titmuss and Abel-Smith, *Social Policies and Population Growth in Mauritius*, London, Methuen, 1960, pp. 130-131; Davis, supra note 18; Ehrlich, supra note 18; Samuel, supra note 22.

(24) Samuel, supra note 22.

(25) Hardin, G., The Tragedy of the Commons, *Science*, 162, 1247, December 13, 1968.

(26) Boulding, K. E., *The Meaning of the Twentieth Century: The Great Transition*, New York, Harper & Row, 1964, pp. 135-136.

(27) Shockley, W. B., in lecture at McMaster University, Hamilton, Ontario, reported in *New York Post*, December 12, 1967.

(28) Chandrasekhar, supra note 22.

(29) Davis, supra note 18.

(30) Ketchel, M. M., Fertility Control Agents as a Possible Solution to the World Population Problem, *Perspectives in Biology and Medicine*, 11, 687-703, Summer, 1968.

(31) For an amplification of the reasons for this conclusion, see Nash, E. M. and Nash, A. E. K., Sociocultural Attitudes Affecting Practice in Physicians, in Calderone, M. S. (Editor), *Manual of Family Planning and Contraceptive Practice*, second edition, Baltimore, The Williams & Wilkins Co., 1970, pp. 209-221. This speculation, of course, does not apply to Latin America.

(32) Blake, J., Population Policy for Americans: Is the Government Being Mislead?, *Science*, 164, 522, May 2, 1969.

(33) Clearly, of course, upper-strata desires if carried into execution would not "level off" the population rate. Nonetheless, the difference in degree manifested is sufficient to warrant attention, particularly in light of the lower-strata "ideologic justification" next described.

(34) See e.g., Harkavy, O., Jaffe, F.S. and Wishik, Samuel, Family Planning and Public Policy: Who is Misleading Whom?, *Science*, 165, 367-373, July 1969.

(35) Bumpass, L. and Westoff, C. F., The "Perfect Contraceptive" Population, *Science*, 169, 1177-1182, September, 1970.

(36) Thus, Mexican-American union "organizer" Corkey Gonzales of Denver, Colorado, addressing the University of California, Santa Barbara, on "Moratorium Day," October 15, 1969. It is not clear yet how strong a force this is likely to become. See Kantner, J. F. and Zelnik, M., Exploratory Studies of Negro Family Formation: Common Conceptions about Birth Control. *Studies in Family Planning*. No. 47, 10-13, 1969. Kantner and Zelnik discovered that Negro women whom they interviewed either had not heard of the genocide charge or did not take it very seriously. At present the charge appears to come primarily from Negro males. This might, of course, change. In this connection, see Beryl Crowe's interesting speculations about the "rebirth of tribalism" in Crowe, B., The Tragedy of the Commons Revisited, *Science*, 166, 1103-1107, November 28, 1969.

(37) Thus, on July 31, 1969, the California Assembly approved by 55-15 a bill that effectually isolates sex education from other sources in the public school curricula. The bill gives parents a veto over sex education classes for their children and provides that the teaching credential "of any school official or teacher can be revoked if he fails to make course material available to parents. . .or keeps a child in a sex education course against his parents' written objections." *Santa Barbara News-Press*, July 31, 1969, Section A, p. 7. Unheeded by the Assembly went Assemblyman Carlos Bee's objection that this might open a Pandora's box: "He warned that parents might then want to examine material for history, English, math and other courses — a job now left to local school boards." *Ibid*.

(38) For a short-run "defeat" see the 17-16 rejection of a bill in the Michigan Legislature despite an impassioned plea by a woman legislator, Mrs. N. Lorraine Beebe, who admitted to having had a therapeutic abortion illegally done two decades ago in a vain effort to persuade her male colleagues. *Santa Barbara News-Press*, June 13, 1969, Section A, p. 6.

(39) It is a probable reflection on the religious plane of Louis Hartz's political fragment thesis that in the United States "fundamentalism" and "religious orthodoxy" tend to be equated. See, e.g., Eaton, C.O., *Freedom of Thought in the Old South*. Durham, Duke University Press, 1940. In the classical European Christian tradition, what could be historically less "orthodox" than the "fundamentalist revivalisms" of Anabaptism, Methodism and so forth? The relevance of the point here, of course, is that the equation tends to strengthen the political hand of the neofundamentalist point of view in resisting "reform."

(40) Arguably, "Sex Education" is, from the standpoint of political tactics, an unfortunate nomenclature whatever its substantive virtues. The findings of Kantner and Zelnik, supra note 36, suggest another difficulty of nomenclature in the field of population control. Many lower-status Negroes they interviewed took the middle-class euphemism "family planning" to mean either: deciding about the desirability of marriage; or studying family financial budgets.

(41) Random sample of 200 University of California, Santa Barbara male students on "Attitudes and Behavior toward Law," undertaken by A. E. Keir Nash and Peter M. Hall (Department of Sociology, York University, Toronto), Spring, 1968.

(42) Undertaken by A. E. Keir Nash and Ethel M. Nash, April, 1969.

(43) See *The Federalist Papers*, particularly Number 10, for Madison's confidence that a federal legislative forum would prevent the factional bargaining detrimental to the public interest, which he found characteristic of the State Legislatures under the

1776 Articles of Confederation. For a brilliant analysis of dominant concepts of "good representation" — and particularly of the shift from "debating wise men" of late eighteenth century political theory to the "rubber-stamp'" delegate of the people's will characteristic of Jacksonian democracy, see Beer, S., *British Politics in the Collectivist Age*, New York, Alfred A. Knopf, 1966.

(44) See Galbraith, J.K., *American Capitalism*, Boston, Little, Brown & Co., 1952, p. 118.

(45) See Auerbach, E., *Mimesis*, Princeton, Princeton University Press, 1953.

(46) Where, for example, is the European equivalent of William Faulkner's *Absalom, Absalom!* — or of Hemingway's writing in general? See along these lines, Steiner, G., The Americanness of American Literature, *The Listener*, 1959, and Fiedler, L., *An End to Innocence*, Boston, Beacon Press, 1955.

(47) See Ehrlich, P., Paying the Piper, *New Scientist*, 36, 652-655, 1967.

(48) 347 U. S. 483, 74 S. Ct. 686, 98 L.Ed. 873 (1954).

(49) 369 U. S. 186, 82 S.Ct. 691, 7 L.Ed. 2d 663 (1962).

(50) 384 U.S. 436, 86 S. Ct. 1602, 16 L.Ed. 2d 694 (1966).

(51) The opposition between Black and Frankfurter has sometimes been presented as a conflict between, respectively, "atomistic individualism" and a modern "group theory" of American politics. See, e.g., Thomas, H. S., *Felix Frankfurter*, Baltimore, The Johns Hopkins Press, 1960, particularly, ch. IV, "Group Conflict in Modern Society," 69-95. But this interpretation of Frankfurter does not address itself to the crucial point here. The Frankfurtian "groups" and ideas of "social unity" are still essentially Lockean. The individual is still primary: he does not as in Rousseau achieve his identity primarily as a member of a social unity; rather he voluntarily belongs to any number of political groups for "reasons of political precedure" — to have his individual wants met.

(52) 381 U. S. 479, 85 S.Ct. 1678, 14 L.Ed. 2d 510 (1965).

(53) Stewart and Black, JJ.

(54) Goldberg, Brennan, JJ., and Warren, C. J.

(55) Harlan, J.

(56) Douglas, J.

(57) Moretti vs. New Jersey, 21 L.Ed. 2d 363 (1969), *certiorari denied*. Compare also a recent decision of perhaps the most liberal State Supreme Court — California's — striking down a lower court conviction of a doctor for violating an 1850 State abortion statute shortly before it was superseded in 1967. In State vs. Belous the California Court "took the position. . .that the decision of whether or not to bear a child is one of the civil rights of the woman concerned. . ." By contrast, the State prosecutor vainly argued "that the State had an 'interest' in the life of the embryo." *Los Angeles Times*, September 25, 1969, Part IV, p. 1.

INDEX